Measure for Measure

Texts and Contexts

WILLIAM SHAKESPEARE

Measure for Measure

Texts and Contexts

———————————— ✜ ————————————

Edited by

IVO KAMPS

KAREN RABER

University of Mississippi

Bedford / *St. Martin's*   BOSTON ◆ NEW YORK

For Bedford/St. Martin's

Editorial Assistant: Sarah Whitesel
Assistant Editor, Publishing Services: Maria Burwell
Production Supervisor: Jennifer Wetzel
Senior Marketing Manager: Jenna Bookin Barry
Project Management: Stratford Publishing Services, Inc.
Cover Design: Donna Lee Dennison
Cover Art: The Betrothed Couple by Lucas van Leyden; *The Last Judgment* by Cristoforo de
   Predis © Archivo Iconografico, S.A./CORBIS
Composition: Stratford Publishing Services, Inc.
Printing and Binding: LSC Communications

President: Joan E. Feinberg
Editorial Director: Denise B. Wydra
Editor in Chief: Karen S. Henry
Director of Marketing: Karen Melton Soeltz
Director of Editing, Design, and Production: Marcia Cohen
Manager, Publishing Services: Emily Berleth

Library of Congress Control Number: 2003116352

For information, write: Bedford/St. Martin's, 75 Arlington Street, Boston, MA 02116
(617-399-4000)

ISBN-10: 0-312-39506-X
ISBN-13: 978-0-312-39506-3

*Acknowledgments and copyrights are continued at the back of the book on pages 363–64, which
constitute an extension of the copyright page.*

Published and distributed outside North America by

PALGRAVE MACMILLAN
Houndmills, Basingstoke, Hampshire RG21 2XS and London
Companies and representatives throughout the world.

ISBN: 1-4039-3237-9

A catalogue record for this book is available from the British Library.

About the Series

><

Shakespeare wrote his plays in a culture unlike, though related to, the culture of the emerging twenty-first century. The Bedford Shakespeare Series resituates Shakespeare within the sometimes alien context of the sixteenth and seventeenth centuries while inviting students to explore ways in which Shakespeare, as text and as cultural icon, continues to be part of contemporary life. Each volume frames a Shakespearean play with a wide range of written and visual material from the early modern period, such as homilies, polemical literature, emblem books, facsimiles of early modern documents, maps, woodcut prints, court records, other plays, medical tracts, ballads, chronicle histories, and travel narratives. Selected to reveal the many ways in which Shakespeare's plays were connected to the events, discourses, and social structures of his time, these documents and illustrations also show the contradictions and the social divisions in Shakespeare's culture and in the plays he wrote. Engaging critical introductions and headnotes to the primary materials help students identify some of the issues they can explore by reading these texts with and against one another, setting up a two-way traffic between the Shakespearean text and the social world these documents help to construct.

Jean E. Howard
Columbia University
Series Editor

About This Volume

————————————— ⋊⋉ —————————————

Not since New Criticism has a critical movement made its way into under-graduate classrooms as effectively as New Historicism, launched by the publication of Stephen Greenblatt's *Renaissance Self-Fashioning* (1980). This can be explained in part by the fact that many of today's university and col-lege professors, the editors of this volume included, were educated in the 1980s and 1990s, and owe much of their critical orientation to the writings of Greenblatt, Louis Montrose, Fredric Jameson, Louis Althusser, Terry Eagle-ton, Raymond Williams, and Michel Foucault. But more crucial is that New Historicism, together with certain strains in feminist criticism and cultural materialist criticism, has demonstrated to us all just how exciting and re-warding it can be to return a literary text to the culture and historical con-ditions of its production and reception. Not only has this led to a "return to history" in the literature classroom in the sense that we discuss history again, it has also renewed interest in examining the historical archive itself, that is, the texts that early modern men and women produced.

The academic publishing industry is responding to this new emphasis on historical context not merely in its monographs or essay collections (written by and large for scholars) but also in the textbooks it publishes. The Bedford Shakespeare Series is a case in point. If typical editions of Shakespeare published throughout most of the twentieth century focused primarily on Shakespeare's text (perhaps with historical introductions and summaries of Shakespeare's sources included), we now see a move toward placing Shakespeare's text side-by-side with documents that present us with slices of early modern life. The big advantage of the Bedford editions for students is that they rely less on knowledge digested by scholars and more on what students themselves can glean from the words of Shakespeare's contemporaries. Whether Shakespeare actually read these documents is of course relevant to the question of where he got his information, but it is not a focus of our edition. Rather, we are concerned with the complex matrix of more elusive cultural influences that formed the climate in which Shakespeare wrote his plays. When we consider the style of rule of *Measure for Measure*'s Duke, for instance, we offer excerpts from the writings of James I not because we think that Shakespeare read those writings (though he may have) and borrowed James's ideas, but because James's writings and Shakespeare's play are both part of an early seventeenth-century discourse on governance. Hence, we offer a variety of voices heard in the debate on governance: Machiavelli, Sir Walter Raleigh, Ben Jonson, George Buchanan, Thomas Middleton, and others. By the same token, *Measure for Measure* is clearly a play concerned with issues of sex and marriage. But it would be a mistake to assume that only one point of view would emerge from contemporary debates about these subjects, or even that Shakespeare himself would have held a single consistent position on them. In order to suggest the wide variety of opinions and attitudes toward sex and marriage — and the ubiquity of public argument about both topics — we set against the official and legal documents of the *Book of Common Prayer* and Henry Swinburne's *Treatise of Spousals* some actual cases of adultery and fornication prosecuted in court, as well as a sample of a more lenient comic view of prostitution from one of Shakespeare's fellow dramatists, John Marston.

Our thinking in putting together this contextual edition of *Measure for Measure* has therefore been twofold. We always aim to present students with a range of views on topics relevant to the play. Not only does this reflect the heterogeneous nature of early modern society, it should also foster debate among students and illuminate various aspects of *Measure for Measure*. In framing issues raised by the play, we have often presented readers with problems that do not appear to have easy solutions, and with questions that may have no final answers, in order to stimulate further creative thought. But although we consider the encouragement of student debate as the *raison d'être* of this edition, the editors do not wish to pretend that we come to this labor without some fairly strong notions of what is at stake in the documents and how they might relate to Shakespeare's play. We have, therefore, at times used the primary documents to interpret aspects of the play and stake the occasional critical claim. When we lean in one interpretive direction or another, however, we do so not to close down debate, but to add our voice to it. We therefore expect readers to test our views against their own readings of both the play and the primary documents. Our hope is that this volume will not only help readers discover how to develop a critical claim and incorporate primary works as "proof texts," but will also encourage them to keep those claims open to revision in light of an ever-broadening understanding of Shakespeare's intellectual and material milieu. While we believe the primary documents we have included outline a number of crucial areas the play invites us to consider, no volume of this kind can be comprehensive, and so we hope that our work inspires the reader to further research, while providing her or him with a model of how to continue.

As is the case with the other editions in this series, we have, in order to make the reading experience more pleasant, silently modernized spelling and punctuation in the documents included here, but we have also limited our editorial intervention to preserve their early modern flavor and added explanatory notes when necessary.

ACKNOWLEDGMENTS

At the University of Mississippi, we would like to thank Alice Clark (Vice Chancellor for Research), Glen Hopkins (Dean of Liberal Arts), Carolyn Staton (Provost), Robert Hawes (Chair of the Department of History), and Joe Urgo (Chair of the Department of English) for their help in acquiring the Early English Books Online database for the library. Having so many of the printed texts of early modern England at our fingertips on our office computers has made putting together this edition of *Measure for Measure* immeasurably easier.

We are grateful to Gregory Heyworth (for his Latin expertise), John Jowett, Marc Showalter (for his biblical expertise), Gary Taylor (for helpful suggestions and showing us a couple of his essays in manuscript), Michael Landon (for his legal expertise), and Joe Ward (for answering many historical questions). We thank the University of Maastricht Library in the Netherlands, The Folger Shakespeare Library, the Huntington Library, Martha Swan and her Interlibrary Loan staff in the John D. William Library at The University of Mississippi, for all their help securing permissions, information, and images for this project.

Thanks to Jean Howard and Karen Henry for infinite patience and support. Thanks also to Emily Berleth and Linda DeMasi, for their expertise in managing the production of this edition, and to Kate Cohen for careful copyediting. We are also grateful to the reviewers who helped us shape this edition: William Carroll, Karen Cunningham, Frances Dolan, Elizabeth Hanson, Theodore Leinwand, and Susanne Wofford.

Ivo Kamps
Karen Raber

Contents

———————— ✣ ————————

Illustrations

————————————— ✷ —————————————

Measure for Measure

Texts and Contexts

Introduction

————————————— ✂ —————————————

Measure for Measure is one of William Shakespeare's most challenging plays because it does not easily conform to the familiar patterns of the Elizabethan comedic and tragic genres, and because it unflinchingly addresses the "darker" side of the human condition: rampant sexuality, deception, injustice, and death. Those who are beguiled by the play revel in the complex tapestry of moral, judicial, and governance issues woven into its fabric; those who dislike it are disturbed by Shakespeare's apparent refusal neatly and satisfactorily to wrap up those same issues by the end of the fifth act. John Dryden deemed *Measure for Measure* part of a group of Shakespeare's plays "which were either grounded on impossibilities, or at least, so meanly written, that the Comedy neither caus'd your mirth, nor the serious part your concernment" (qtd. in Vickers, *Shakespeare* 145). In 1662, playwright William D'Avenant tried to "fix" *Measure for Measure* by conflating it with the more light-hearted Shakespearean comedy *Much Ado about Nothing*. The resulting play is something of a "bad dream" (Vickers 6) that seeks to suppress much of the "unpleasantness" commonly associated with it. Concurring with Dryden, the poet and critic Samuel Taylor Coleridge in 1827 called *Measure for Measure* "a hateful work" (Coleridge 250) in which the comic parts are "disgusting" and the tragic parts "horrible" (249). More recently, E. M. W. Tillyard dubbed the play "radically schizophrenic" and maintained that it belongs to a small group of Shakespeare's dramas termed "problem plays" not because it deals with "interesting problems" but because the play itself "*is*" a problem (Tillyard 2).

In large part, the negative judgments of these and subsequent commentators have been predicated on an intense dissatisfaction with the play's ending, which vexingly complicates the familiar resolution of a number of Shakespeare's romantic comedies. Coleridge, for instance, is baffled and appalled by Angelo's marriage to Mariana and the subsequent overturning of his death sentence. The marriage, Coleridge insists, degrades Mariana and women in general, while sparing Angelo's life is a gross injustice because we doubt that he has "*morally*" repented of his "cruelty," "lust and damnable baseness" (249–50). We, however, strongly agree with Graham Bradshaw, who rejects the notion that *Measure for Measure* is somehow fundamentally flawed. Bradshaw asks, "Might the play's own final verdict or verdicts be problematic by design — both more ironically unsettling, and more challenging in its implications for our own attempts to *think* about law and morality, than those piecemeal judgments which the Duke so confidently offers as examples of an ideal and exemplary justice?" (165). We think that the answer to Bradshaw's question is an emphatic "yes," and that *Measure for Measure* is not a problem *as* a play but a play full of "interesting problems."

The difficulty that Dryden and Coleridge have with *Measure for Measure* stems from their desire to have the play conform to conventional ideas of poetic justice and the conventions of romantic comedy. Shakespeare's play defies their expectations. They are not alone, of course. When Shakespeare's fellow actors, John Heminges and Henry Condell, guided the publication of the first collected edition of Shakespeare's plays in 1623, they placed *Measure for Measure* among the comedies and unknowingly laid the foundation for much critical dissatisfaction. Giving voice to this dissatisfaction, some critics have recategorized *Measure for Measure* as a "dark comedy" or as a "problem play" (terms now routinely attached to *Measure for Measure*), suggesting that it does not belong with romantic comedies such as *A Midsummer Night's Dream*, *As You Like It*, *Much Ado about Nothing*, and *Twelfth Night*. Like these romantic comedies, *Measure for Measure* does have a genuine love story — the story of Claudio and Juliet — but this tale is hardly at the emotional or thematic center of the drama. What is more, when we think of Shakespearean comedy, we generally think of stories in which multiple sets of lovers overcome certain trials and obstacles and get married in the end, assuring a measure of personal happiness and proper social (and biological) reproduction. This movement "from confusion to order, from ignorance to understanding, from law to liberty, from unhappiness to satisfaction, from separation to union, from barrenness to fertility, from singleness to marriage" (McDonald 81), together with a movement from the city to the forest (or other "green zone"), constitute the typical pattern of Shakespearean comedy.[1] But in *Measure for Measure* we miss the movement to Arden's forest, Portia's Belmont, or Athens' wood. And the marriages that we see at the end of *Measure for Measure* lack romantic authenticity. Angelo has been tricked into sleeping with Mariana, and we can only assume that he marries her because the Duke forces him to. Lucio is ordered to marry a prostitute he got pregnant, a punishment that he apparently considers the equivalent of a death sentence. The Duke himself proposes to Isabella, but the text gives no indication how she responds to this unexpected offer. Nowhere in the play does Isabella suggest that she wants to be anything other than a celibate nun, and the Duke, who boasts that he is not particularly interested in women (3.2.99–100), never courts her or in any other way conveys to anyone (including the audience) that he is falling in love with her. It is of course true that Shakespeare's more typical romantic comedies also present us with "problem" endings when it comes to tying their characters into the social fabric. The fact that the Demetrius-Helena union in *A Midsummer Night's Dream* is possible only because of a magical potion that radically alters Demetrius's affections (which are centered on Hermia for most of the play) indicates that individual desire and freedom of choice must be sacrificed to enable biological and social reproduction. Likewise, the exclusions of Olivia's suitor Sir Andrew Aguecheek, her steward Malvolio, and the sea captain Antonio from *Twelfth Night's* concluding harmony suggests that there is no place in mainstream society for silly, effeminate knights, puritanical men with dreams of upward social mobility, or for apparent homosexuals. We could say similar things about *Much Ado about Nothing*, *The Merchant of Venice*, and other comedies, but still it seems that in *Measure for Measure* Shakespeare decided to go further, to take the romance out of the comedy. Duke Vincentio's manipulations of Vienna's citizens are more evocative of the *realpolitik* of the history plays than they are of the desire-driven world of Shakespeare's other comedies. We can discern more feeling in Henry V's opportunistic yet witty wooing of Katherine of France (who is his "capitol demand") than in the Duke's stupefying "Give me your hand and say you will be mine" (5.1.491). Perhaps this failure of romance is why *Measure for Measure* is Shakespeare's last comedy before he turns exclusively to the composition of tragedies between 1604 and 1610.[2] It is therefore

---

[1] Other kinds of comedy were of course written during the early modern period. Ben Jonson's satirical comedies (which do not end in marriage) are examples.

reasonable to consider whether Shakespeare in *Measure for Measure* is gesturing toward the standard comedic resolution while emphatically withholding it. Picking up on the eccentricity of the Duke's marriage proposal, productions of *Measure for Measure* have in recent years staged the play's final moments to reflect Shakespeare's refusal of the comedic resolution. John Barton's 1970 production with the Royal Shakespeare Company, for instance, ends with Isabella alone on stage clearly in a state of torment and puzzlement. One may even wish to imagine Isabella spitting contemptuously in the Duke's face. A widespread respect for and fear of authority would make it extremely unlikely for a Jacobean commoner to confront a noble in this manner; nor is there any explicit support for it in the language or stage directions of the play. A daringly insubordinate gesture like this, however, does make explicit the scorn that is almost certainly implied in Isabella's pointed silence, and thus presents an enticing possibility to audience members who feel that the callously controlling Duke has done nothing to deserve the girl.

To be sure, the play's dark tone also differs from most of Shakespeare's other comedies. *Measure for Measure*'s Vincentio, "duke of dark corners," disguises himself to spy on his people while his tyrannical substitute attempts to coerce a Catholic novice named Isabella into having sex with him to save the life of her brother, Claudio, who is under sentence of death for getting his betrothed pregnant. In prison, Claudio desperately pleads with his sister to sleep with Angelo and save his life, but Isabella refuses, apparently valuing her chastity and salvation over her brother's neck. Claudio's anguished meditation on death reminds us more of Hamlet's "To be or not to be" soliloquy than of anything in Shakespeare's comedies:

> Ay, but to die, and go we know not where,
> To lie in cold obstruction and to rot,
> This sensible warm motion to become
> A kneaded clod, and the delighted spirit
> To bathe in fiery floods, or to reside
> In thrilling region of thick-ribbed ice;
> To be imprisoned in the viewless winds
> And blown with restless violence round about
> The pendent world; or to be worse than worst
> Of those that lawless and incertain thought

---

[2] Between 1605 and 1610, Shakespeare wrote *King Lear* (c. 1605), *Macbeth* (c. 1606), *Timon of Athens* (c. 1605–08), *Antony and Cleopatra* (1606–07), *Coriolanus* (c. 1608), and *Cymbeline* (c. 1608–10), which was grouped with the tragedies in the First Folio.

Imagine howling — 'tis too horrible!
The weariest and most loathed worldly life
That age, ache, penury, and imprisonment
Can lay on nature is a paradise
To what we fear of death.   (3.1.119–33)

Hamlet's and Claudio's situations are of course different — one is contemplating suicide while the other is facing a death sentence — but both apprehensively peek into the abyss and decide that a life of pain and agony is preferable over "the dread of something after death, / The undiscover'd country from whose bourn / No traveler returns" (*Hamlet* 3.1.79–80).

And what about Juliet's pregnancy by Claudio? The rakish Lucio refers to the sexual encounter as a "game of tick-tack," a minor indiscretion, but Claudio himself at first views his "offence" far more seriously and compares his sexual desires to those of "rats that ravin down their proper bane" and die (1.2.106–07). Angelo of course sentences Claudio to death for the infraction. English society frowned on childbirth out of wedlock in part because such infants often became a financial charge to the community, but to fault Claudio for this crime one must presume that he and Juliet aren't legally married. Whether or not the "true contract" to which Claudio refers constitutes a legal marriage would, in fact, have been a serious issue for Shakespeare's audiences. We will address this matter in some detail in the section "Sex, Marriage, and Society," so let it suffice here to say that many in Shakespeare's day believed that the exchange of vows constituted a legally binding marriage. When, in John Webster's *The Duchess of Malfi* (1612), the duchess secretly marries her steward, Antonio, she says to him, "I have heard lawyers say, a contract in a chamber, / *Per verba de presenti* [by words about the present], is absolute marriage" (1.2.391–92). Her wording makes it clear that she is confident of her actions, but also that she is basing her opinion on hearsay. She further suggests that a church ceremony "must but echo" (1.2.406) her exchange of vows with Antonio, and that the "Church [cannot] force more" (1.2.401).[3] Moreover, in Shakespeare's *Much Ado about Nothing*, the issue also arises, and is dealt with somewhat differently. Thinking that his bride-to-be has cheated on him the night before the wedding, Claudio

---

[3] The situation is somewhat complicated by the fact that *The Duchess of Malfi* is set in Italy, a Catholic state. In 1563, the Catholic Church first required that a priest be present "for a valid and binding marriage" (Stone 30), but this is of course after the English Reformation, and although the established Church of England tried to intensify its control over the marriage ceremony, "the civil lawyers who ran the courts continued to recognize the spousals before witnesses" (Stone 30).

publicly denounces her at the start of the ceremony. The bride's father, Leonato, addresses Claudio, and this exchange ensues:

> LEONATO: Dear my lord, if you, in your own proofs,
> Have vanquish'd the resistance of her youth,
> And made defeat of her virginity —
> CLAUDIO: I know what you would say: if I have known her,
> You will say she did embrace me as a husband,
> And so extenuate the 'forehand sin.   (4.1.44–49)

The paranoid and self-absorbed Claudio is of course wrong about his fiancée's supposed infidelity, but his ability to anticipate Leonato's statement suggests that a promise before witnesses to marry in the future *(per verba de futuro)* was widely believed to "extenuate" the "defeat" of a woman's virginity (see Stone 31). Indeed, Isabella's immediate response to her brother's transgression is, "O, let him marry her" (1.4.49). But if the problem simply goes away in *Much Ado about Nothing* (because the accused bride is proven innocent), it does not in *Measure for Measure*, not until the very end of the play, when the returned Duke simply elects to ignore Vienna's statute against fornication.

And this is hardly the only instance in the play in which sexual appetite runs foul of the law. *Measure for Measure* features a brothel keeper, Mistress Overdone, and her pimp, Pompey, who find themselves victims of the zealous Angelo, who is closing Vienna's brothels to regulate sexuality in the city. When arrested and brought before Angelo and Escalus, the audacious Pompey argues that unless city officials mean "to geld and splay all the youth" it will be impossible to suppress unregulated sexuality (2.1.191–92). This very insight appears to be at odds fundamentally with the comedic genre, which relies on marriage for its resolution, for the proper regulation of sexuality, and for the satisfactory reproduction of class differences. Then there is Mariana, a woman who gladly accepts the role of sexual substitute for Isabella so she can trick Angelo into consummating a broken-off betrothal. Note that the bed-trick in *Measure for Measure* is of a more serious nature than the bed-trick in Shakespeare's *All's Well That Ends Well*. In the latter play, Helena prevents her husband, Bertram, from having an extramarital affair by substituting herself for a woman with whom Bertram hopes to have an illicit sexual encounter. There are complicating factors surrounding this bed-trick as well, but at least the sex involves two characters who are legally married. Angelo and Mariana are not.

In short, we spend too much time in prisons and brothels, and thinking about corruption, injustice, coercive sex, sex for money, and death to feel truly uplifted by the Duke's return to power in Vienna at the end of the play.

We are not exactly sure what to think of his double dealings and clever manipulations of his subjects. Is he a divine-right ruler who, like a god, sees and knows all, or is he a scheming hypocrite who evades his ducal responsibilities and spies on his people to entrap them? And what should we make of Isabella's doctrinal fetishization of her chastity, which she values over her brother's life? Is this Catholic novice too cold or is she right to refuse to jeopardize her immortal soul? How would she appear to a Protestant audience in a nation that had long ago closed the nunneries? And what are we to make of Isabella's extraordinary speech in which she tells Angelo, "Th' impression of keen whips I'd wear as rubies, / And strip myself to death, as to a bed / That longing have been sick for, ere I'd yield / My body up to shame" [that is, to Angelo's lust] (2.4.101–04)? Is she in pursuit of sensual martyrdom (Black 81) or (inadvertently?) evoking "a gleam in the eye of the most depraved marquis in the audience, to say nothing of a saint-turned-sensualist like Angelo"? (Hawkins 89). Moreover, is Lucio a contemptible rogue and slanderer or a savvy observer of Vienna society? Is Pompey a despicable pimp or an astute voice on questions of human sexuality? Is getting Juliet with child such a crime that Claudio must die or would marrying Juliet be a satisfactory alternative? And how should we feel about the enforced marriage between Angelo and Mariana? These and other questions have vexed audiences and readers over the years. But far from suggesting that Measure for Measure's interpretative difficulties render it an "aesthetic failure" (to borrow a phrase T. S. Eliot applied to Hamlet) or a "problem" (as Tillyard thought), we maintain that these are the very questions that animate the play and arrest the attention of readers and playgoers alike.

If readers and playgoers have found it difficult to adopt Measure for Measure as a favorite, this may well be because the play is more palpably and problematically steeped in early modern history than most of Shakespeare's others. All the plays are, of course, products of a historical moment, but most of Measure for Measure's interpretive cruxes seem directly linked to evolving events, controversies, and genuine uncertainties around the time of its making. The early modern documents we place side by side with Shakespeare's play in this edition are not meant to solve old critical problems. Rather, they are printed here to show, for instance, that when Shakespeare wrote his play about a duke who is trying to reassert his authority over his subjects by having Angelo strictly enforce the city's sex laws, England had just crowned a new king who was trying to define his authority over his new subjects at a time when the city of London was "pulling down" the houses of ill repute in the so-called liberties (a suburban area outside the city walls and "outside of London's effective domain" [Mullaney 21; see also Stuart Royal Proclamation in this volume, p. 281; Marcus 175ff]). By suggesting a relationship between *Measure for Measure* and its historical context we are not, however, implying that the play should be read topically, as if it were an allegory in which Vienna is really London and Duke Vincentio is King James I, and so on. What we are suggesting is that the play and the documents in this volume share the same cultural fabric, and that early modern English culture was just as eclectic and paradoxical in its views on topics such as marriage, justice, religion, prostitution, and sex as is Shakespeare's magnificent play.

Like other editions in Bedford's "Texts and Contexts" series, our edition of *Measure for Measure* takes a non-conventional approach to the issue of the play's "sources." Traditionally, editions of Shakespeare plays have a separate section or appendix that reproduces those texts that Shakespeare may have consulted and or cannibalized while writing a particular drama. In his massive *Narrative and Dramatic Sources of Shakespeare*, Geoffrey Bullough reprints no fewer than six likely sources for *Measure for Measure*, and refers to a number of other texts that may have influenced Shakespeare, or that may have influenced the texts that influenced Shakespeare. The study of sources can of course be highly instructive because it can tell us where Shakespeare got an idea or plot line or even a theme. From reading the sources we learn, for instance, that the story of the corrupt magistrate, the so-called bed-trick, and the figure of the disguised duke are not original to Shakespeare. Perhaps even more important, reading texts that Shakespeare read while writing *Measure for Measure* may give us a glimpse of the playwright's mind in action, by showing us not only what Shakespeare borrowed but also what changes he made to his source materials. But there are also significant problems with the whole notion of "source" insofar as it attempts to identify a text of origin that lies "behind" the dramatic text. It suggests, erroneously, that we have to go back to that "original" text and consider its meaning if we want to understand the play it may have influenced. This places the play in a very narrow universe of influence, and creates the illusion that the play is primarily a product of the author's creative reworking of a finite and identifiable number of source texts: the sources are the rough materials out of which the author fashioned the play.[4] Aside from the fact that the sources almost never help us figure out what something in the play means or what its significance is, a preoccupation with them encourages us to ignore the wide range of other texts and ideas circulating in Shakespeare's England

---

[4] In some cases, this approach is of course more helpful than in others. The study of narrative histories by Holinshed, Hall, Grafton, and others is a virtual necessity if we read Shakespeare's history plays in the context of English history.

that are far more important to the play than the textual origin of a plot line, device, or character.

Let us consider for a moment the story of the cruel and corrupt magistrate. Most scholars agree that a tale from G. B. Giraldi Cinthio's *Gli Hecatommithi* (1565) probably influenced the Angelo-Isabella plot line in *Measure for Measure*. In Cinthio, a young man named Vico forcibly has sex with a young woman he desires (but to whom he is not betrothed). When this fact comes to the attention of Juriste, the governor of Innsbruck, he immediately has Vico arrested and, according to the law, condemns him to die for his crime. Vico's sister, Epitia, is greatly dismayed by her brother's actions but even more aggrieved by his imminent death. She goes to Juriste and argues that her brother committed "adultery through the force of love and not in order to wrong a lady's husband," and therefore "deserve[s] a less severe punishment" (Lever 156). Juriste, like Shakespeare's Angelo, suddenly finds his passion inflamed by the young woman, and tells her that he will spare Vico's life if she has sex with him. He also says that he *may* marry her afterward. Epitia refuses on grounds it puts her "honor in danger" (Lever 158), and she demands a guarantee of marriage. But Juriste declines to give her any assurance, and Epitia visits her brother in prison to discuss the matter. Vico convinces her to accept Juriste's offer, and Epitia promises her brother that she will "give herself to Juriste, should he agree to save Vico's life and support her hope of marriage" (Lever 159). Juriste, however, proves deceitful and cruel: after having sex with Epitia, he orders Vico's execution and sends his dead body to Epitia's house, "the head placed at the feet" (Lever 160). Epitia first contemplates killing Juriste but decides instead to launch a complaint against Innsbruck's governor with Emperor Maximian. The emperor believes Epitia's story, and his judgment against Juriste consists of two parts: he has to marry "the forced lady" as compensation for the rape (Lever 163), and he must lose his head for having executed Vico after promising Epitia that he would spare her brother's life. At this point, Epitia shows her "natural kindness" and successfully pleads for her husband's life (Lever 164).

Now what can we make of this story's relevance to *Measure for Measure*? There are some obvious similarities between Cinthio's text and Shakespeare's. Both give us a story of sexual blackmail made possible because a brother is under sentence of death. But the differences between the stories are far more numerous than the similarities. Shakespeare sets his play in Vienna, not in Innsbruck (which may be of considerable importance); Isabella is about to become a nun whereas Epitia is not; Juriste hints at a possible marriage with Epitia whereas Angelo never raises the subject with Isabella; Epitia actually sleeps with Juriste but Isabella does not sleep with

Angelo (Shakespeare puts Mariana in her place); Juriste actually has Vico executed, whereas Claudio's life is saved by the Duke; on Maximian's command, Juriste marries Epitia, whereas Isabella is offered marriage by the Duke (who is the "equivalent" of Emperor Maximian). What is the significance of these differences? We could speculate that Shakespeare did not think that feelings of love for a woman partly justified raping her (as Epitia appears to think). He might also have thought that a marriage should perhaps not result from a desire to save one's brother's life. Maybe he even thought that a woman should not be forced to marry the man who executed her brother in order to save her honor. We can make many more guesses, as long as we recognize that Shakespeare's choices in *Measure for Measure* were influenced more deeply by his own cultural context than they were by Cinthio's tale. Or, to put it differently, Shakespeare did not write *Measure for Measure* for an audience steeped in Italian stories, and he certainly would not want his audience's understanding of his play to depend on their knowledge of tales and plays that had not even been translated into English.

Sources as such, therefore, while often instructive, almost never yield us clear and definitive answers to difficult questions. Looking beyond the play for textual antecedents and allusions, however, does often offer us instructive perspectives and does give us a sense of the range of possible meanings. The play's title, *Measure for Measure*, is a case in point. About to sentence Angelo to death in act 5, scene 1, Duke Vincentio declaims:

> The very mercy of the law cries out
> Most audible, even from his proper tongue,
> "An Angelo for a Claudio, death for death!"
> Haste still pays haste, and leisure answers leisure;
> Like doth quit like, and *measure still for measure*.
> (403–07; emphasis added)

The Duke here echoes both an Old Testament notion of justice — "an eye for an eye" — and a New Testament interpretation from the sermon on the Mount: "Judge not that ye be not judged. For with the judgment you pronounce you will be judged, and the measure you give will be the measure you get" (Matthew 7:1–3). There is, then, a clear set of biblical allusions grounding the play, and so the Bible might itself reasonably figure as a source text. But we ask, as we did in the case of the Italian source, what does the biblical source explain and how?

Pronouncing judgments is, of course, one of the functions that defines the legal and political authority of a prince, and in judging Angelo the Duke restores that part of his own authority he temporarily ceded, while turning the letter of the law against the character who seemed most wedded to lit-

FIGURE 1 *Scene of an execution. from Raphael Holinshed.* The First Volume of the Chronicles of England, The History of Scotland *(London 1577).*

eral legal interpretations. Because Angelo could find no mercy for Claudio, and because he has committed essentially the same crime Claudio did, he merits the full measure of punishment he applied to Claudio: "We do condemn thee to the very block / Where Claudio stooped to death, and with like haste" (5.1.410–11).

If we believe that Duke Vincentio functions as a representative of divine justice in the play, then the apparent balance he achieves by so sentencing Angelo neatly redresses the excesses that have marked Angelo's surrogacy (see Fig. 1). But if we understand that the purpose of laws against fornication are primarily to ensure legal marriages and legitimate reproduction, then cutting off Angelo's head seems as monumental a waste and as contrary to the spirit of the fornication laws as the execution of Claudio would have been in the first place.[5] Nor is Claudio in fact dead. Nor does the Duke's echo of Matthew support his action here — "judge *not*" it tells us. "Why seest thou the mote that is in your brother's eye, and perceivest not the beam that is in thine own eye?" asks Jesus in his sermon, directing the

---

[5] That Shakespeare is sensitive to this issue is clear in, for instance, *A Midsummer Night's Dream,* when Theseus overrules the right of Hermia's father, Egeus, to dispose of his daughter as he sees fit. By overruling Egeus, Theseus can achieve two marriages within the aristocratic class. If he supported Egeus's right, there would be only one.

FIGURE 2 *Panorama/View of London by C. L. Visscher (1616).*

judging gaze inward, away from its usual judicial and political objects. The biblical passage suggests that he who judges must be free of the flaw he condemns before his judgment can be anything but hypocrisy. We should remember that Lucio describes the Duke as one "who has some feeling for the sport" of fornication, and that the Duke blames himself for having been an erring "fond father" in permitting Vienna to run wild for so long. In fact, the Duke's speech and sentence on Angelo is just another piece of clever stage-management: by threatening Angelo with death, the Duke gives Isabella and Mariana a chance to plead forcefully for his life. The knees that Isabella refused to bend for her brother in act 2 must here become supple in defense of the man she probably hates most in the world. The extent of Isabella's commitment to mercy is tested, while the Duke's own merciful and brilliant manipulations are revealed when he produces the living Claudio.

There are, however, other contexts for the play's title, more mundane than its biblical origins, but no less important to the play's investigation of political and legal authority. Alan Powers has pointed out that James I issued a proclamation for the "reformation of abuses in Measures" on June 1, 1603, and another on July 5 of the same year. The king was officially responsible for ensuring that weights and measures used in shops and markets were calibrated correctly to prevent shortchanging. Kingly authority was the only guarantee of balance and value in even such ordinary daily events as visiting the butcher, the apothecary, or the grocer. Not only did the king's hand intervene in the process of measuring but his image on the coins traded in markets and shops reminded their owners that without him, currency had no fixed exchange rate. In effect, the scales of commerce and the scales of justice are intimately related. Perhaps Pompey's presence in the

prison as apprentice executioner speaks to this idea — the bawd who traded in women's "maidenheads," or who sold virgins, now serves justice by taking heads for the king.

Balance, judicial and commercial, relies on a system of equivalencies — "an Angelo for a Claudio" or two pence for a bushel — that must be policed regularly against "abuses." Without a quasi-divine and somewhat arbitrary rule maker, that system falls apart. In what sense, after all, is an Angelo the equivalent of a Claudio? Only in the sense that the Duke has made him so through the bed-trick, which similarly reduces Isabella and Mariana to substitutable equals. Whatever passion Angelo felt for Isabella's unique qualities is reduced in the act of sex to a general lust easily satisfied by any woman's body; his crime thus repeats the logic of brothels, where customers may purchase sex, translating the value of a woman into coinage. A seventeenth-century engraving of a brothel from Crispijn de Passe's *Le Mirroir des Plus Belles Dames* (Fig. 18, p. 260) illustrates a young gallant selecting his lady of the evening from a series of portraits on the wall, laying out his coins (which have value because they are stamped with the king's image) on the table below. In this fashion, the logic of equivalencies, the measured *balance* that is ensured by the monarch, migrates into the world not merely of commerce, but even of prostitution.

"Measure for measure," then, does not only refer the playgoer to a divine biblical principle of mercy and self-examination, or to a legal system that owes its authority to the prince who writes and enforces the law. It also works against the apparent distinctions the play seems to make between good and bad, licit and illicit, legitimate and illegitimate. The Duke's purely arbitrary decisions at the play's beginning and end, if read against such a meaning for "measuring," present not so much a problem the play must resolve as the condition of rule itself.

FIGURE 3 *Vienna, from Georg Braun,* Civitates Orbis Terrarum.

In the sections that follow, we have therefore handled the source materials with an eye to foregrounding certain issues integral to our four general chapters, "Governance," "Marriage, Sex, and Society," "The Underworld," and "Religion and Geography." Instead of a linear set of relationships, we offer documents that locate the text in a network of intersecting discourses about rulership, religion, sex, and misbehavior. We have included an excerpt from Thomas Middleton's *The Phoenix* (1603–04) in our "Governance" section, for instance, not merely because it has a disguised ruler in it who may have been a "source" for Shakespeare's duke, but because Middleton's portrayal of a prince in disguise appears altogether sympathetic and sheds potential light on how early Jacobean audiences may have received Duke Vincentio, who has often been vilified by critics. Other documents in that section could contribute to a reading of Vincentio as a tyrant; still others support an understanding of his character as an absolute, but divinely sanctioned leader. Our discussion of "Marriage, Sex, and Society" incorporates contemporary reflections on fornication as sinful and damnable, but also offers documents on spousals (betrothal) and marriage that shed light on how Claudio and Juliet's situation might have struck the play's audience as all too common and understandable. Religion in the play is no less multivalent, since Angelo's "puritanical" attitudes are contrasted with an appar-

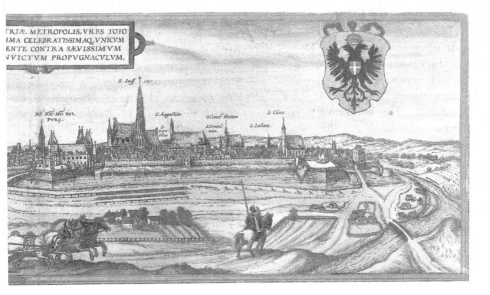

ently Catholic Duke's merciful judgment — all in a play for a Protestant audience. Further, without understanding the problem of the play's geographical location it is impossible to begin to untangle what these religious distinctions mean, and so "Religion and Geography" clarifies the possible arguments for setting the play in Vienna or seeing "Vienna" as "London" with another name — and offers arguments about entirely different settings that might have been attached to different versions of the play. "The Underworld" includes diatribes like Thomas Dekker's against the sins of the suburbs, that area of London where both the brothels and the theaters might be found, and where one might have gone to find Mistress Overdone's house of ill repute. But it also includes a defense (albeit a bit tongue-in-cheek) of the prostitute's profession. We offer both historical and imaginative accounts of London's prisons, to illustrate how audiences might have thought about, or even recognized, the dark, terrifying surroundings the Duke, Claudio, Isabella, and others come to inhabit for a time.

The documents collected here, in short, prompt us to consider that the "problems" in the play would have resonated in early Jacobean London, and that Londoners would not have all agreed what the proper solution to those "problems" would have been. We have therefore tried to frame questions in a way that encourages debate, not simply by gathering pro and con positions on every issue, but by trying to reflect the range of viewpoints available to

Shakespeare and his audiences. There is no doubt that it can be exciting to debate issues such as Claudio and Juliet's betrothal, Isabella's ethics, Angelo's duplicity, and the Duke's maneuverings from a purely twenty-first century point of view, but it can also be deeply satisfying and energizing to search beyond our own values and ideological horizons and get a feel for the many things *Measure for Measure* might have meant to Shakespeare's early audiences. This edition of the play in context is dedicated to helping students do both.

PART ONE

WILLIAM SHAKESPEARE

Measure for Measure

Edited by David Bevington

Measure for Measure

><-

[DRAMATIS PERSONAE

VINCENTIO, *the Duke*
ANGELO, *the deputy*
ESCALUS, *an ancient lord*
CLAUDIO, *a young gentleman*
LUCIO, *a fantastic*
Two other like GENTLEMEN
PROVOST
THOMAS, ⎫ *two friars*
PETER, ⎭
[A JUSTICE]
[VARRIUS, *a friend of the Duke*]

ELBOW, *a simple constable*
FROTH, *a foolish gentleman*
CLOWN [POMPEY, *a servant to Mistress Overdone*]
ABHORSON, *an executioner*
BARNARDINE, *a dissolute prisoner*

ISABELLA, *sister to Claudio*
MARIANA, *betrothed to Angelo*
JULIET, *beloved of Claudio*
FRANCISCA, *a nun*
MISTRESS OVERDONE, *a bawd*

[A SERVANT *of Angelo*
BOY *singer*
A MESSENGER *from Angelo*

Lords, Officers, Citizens, Servants, and other Attendants]

SCENE: *Vienna*]

ACT I, SCENE I°

Enter Duke, Escalus, lords, [and attendants].

DUKE: Escalus.

ESCALUS: My lord.

DUKE:

Of government the properties to unfold°
Would seem in me t' affect speech and discourse,°
Since I am put to know° that your own science°   5
Exceeds, in that,° the lists° of all advice
My strength° can give you. Then no more remains
But that to your sufficiency . . . . .
. . . . as your worth is able,°
And let them work. The nature of our people,   10
Our city's institutions, and the terms°
For common justice, you're as pregnant in
As art° and practice hath enrichèd any
That we remember. There is our commission,   *[giving a paper]*
From which we would not have you warp.° — Call hither,   15
I say, bid come before us Angelo.   *[Exit one.]*
What figure of us think you he will bear?°
For you must know, we have with special soul°
Elected° him our absence to supply,°
Lent him our terror,° dressed him with our love,   20
And given his deputation° all the organs°
Of our own power. What think you of it?

ESCALUS:

If any in Vienna be of worth
To undergo° such ample grace and honor,
It is Lord Angelo.

Enter Angelo.

ACT I, SCENE I. Location: Vienna. The court of Duke Vincentio. **3. Of . . . unfold:** to explain the qualities needed in governing well. **4. seem . . . discourse:** i.e., make me seem enamored of the sound of my own voice. **5. put to know:** obliged to admit. **science:** knowledge. **6. that:** i.e., properties of government (line 3). **lists:** limits. **7. strength:** power of mind. **8–9. But . . . able:** (The passage appears in the Folio as a single line. Several attempts at emendation have been made, but the most plausible explanation is that something has been deleted or inadvertently omitted.) **11. terms:** terms of court; or, modes of procedure. **13. art:** learning, theory. **15. warp:** deviate. **17. What . . . bear:** i.e., how do you think he will do as my substitute? **18. special soul:** all the powers of the mind; whole heart. **19. Elected:** chosen. **supply:** fill, make up for. **20. terror:** power to inspire awe and fear. **21. his deputation:** him as deputy. **organs:** instruments. **24. undergo:** bear the weight of.

DUKE: Look where he comes.   25

ANGELO:
  Always obedient to Your Grace's will,
  I come to know your pleasure.

DUKE: Angelo,
  There is a kind of character° in thy life
  That to th' observer doth thy history
  Fully unfold. Thyself and thy belongings°   30
  Are not thine own so proper° as to waste
  Thyself upon thy virtues, they on thee.°
  Heaven doth with us as we with torches° do,
  Not light them for themselves; for if our virtues
  Did not go forth of us,° 'twere all alike°   35
  As if we had them not. Spirits° are not finely touched°
  But to fine issues,° nor Nature never lends
  The smallest scruple° of her excellence
  But, like a thrifty goddess, she determines°
  Herself° the glory° of a creditor,   40
  Both thanks and use.° But I do bend° my speech
  To one that can my part in him advertise.°
  Hold, therefore, Angelo:
  In our remove° be thou at full° ourself.°
  Mortality° and mercy in Vienna   45
  Live in thy tongue and heart. Old Escalus,
  Though first in question,° is thy secondary.
  Take thy commission.   [*He gives a paper.*]

ANGELO: Now, good my lord,
  Let there be some more test made of my mettle°
  Before so noble and so great a figure   50
  Be stamped upon it.

---

28. **character:** writing.   30. **belongings:** attributes, endowments.   31. **proper:** exclusively.
31–32. **as to . . . thee:** that you can expend all your efforts on your own talents or use them
solely for your own advantage.   33. **torches:** (Compare Jesus' command that we not hide
our light under a bushel, Matthew 5:14–16.)   35. **forth of us:** out of us and into the world.
'twere all alike: it would be exactly the same.   36. **Spirits:** souls.   **finely touched:** excel-
lently endowed and tested.   37. **fine issues:** noble purposes.   38. **scruple:** bit. (Literally,
a small weight.)   39. **determines:** assumes.   40. **Herself:** for herself.   **glory:** privileges.
41. **use:** interest.   **bend:** direct.   42. **that . . . advertise:** who can instruct that part of me now
vested in him, i.e., who knows already what I have to say.   44. **remove:** absence.   **at full:** in
every respect.   **ourself:** i.e., myself. (The royal plural.)   45. **Mortality:** the full rigor of the
law, the death sentence.   47. **first in question:** senior and first appointed.   49. **mettle:** substance, quality (with play on "metal," a common variant spelling, continued in the coining
imagery of lines 50–51).

DUKE: No more evasion.
We have with a leavened° and preparèd choice
Proceeded to you; therefore take your honors.
Our haste from hence is of so quick condition
That it prefers itself° and leaves unquestioned°
Matters of needful value. We shall write to you,   55
As time and our concernings° shall importune,°
How it goes with us, and do look to know°
What doth befall you here. So, fare you well.
To th' hopeful° execution do I leave you   60
Of your commissions.
ANGELO: Yet give leave,° my lord,
That we may bring you something° on the way.
DUKE: My haste may not admit° it;
Nor need you, on mine honor, have to do°
With any scruple.° Your scope is as mine own,   65
So to enforce or qualify the laws
As to your soul seems good. Give me your hand.
I'll privily away.° I love the people
But do not like to stage me° to their eyes;
Though it do well,° I do not relish well   70
Their loud applause and "aves"° vehement,
Nor do I think the man of safe° discretion
That does affect° it. Once more, fare you well.
ANGELO:
The heavens give safety to your purposes!
ESCALUS:
Lead° forth and bring you back in happiness!   75
DUKE: I thank you. Fare you well.   *Exit.*
ESCALUS:
I shall desire you, sir, to give me leave
To have free° speech with you; and it concerns me

---

52. **leavened:** i.e., carefully considered (just as yeast is given time to leaven dough).   54–55. **Our . . . itself:** the cause for my hasty departure is so urgent (*quick*) that it takes precedence over all other matters.   55. **unquestioned:** not yet considered.   57. **concernings:** affairs.   **importune:** urge.   58. **look to know:** expect to be informed.   60. **hopeful:** exciting hopes of success. **execution:** carrying out.   61. **leave:** permission.   62. **bring you something:** accompany you for a short distance.   63. **admit:** permit.   64. **have to do:** have concern.   65. **scruple:** misgiving.   68. **I'll privily away:** I'll go away secretly.   69. **stage me:** make a show of myself. 70. **do well:** i.e., serves a political purpose.   71. **aves:** hails of acclamation.   72. **safe:** sound. 73. **affect:** desire, court.   75. **Lead:** may they conduct you.   78. **free:** frank.

To look into the bottom of my place.°
A power I have, but of what strength and nature   80
I am not yet instructed.

ANGELO:
'Tis so with me. Let us withdraw together,
And we may soon our satisfaction have
Touching that point.

ESCALUS: I'll wait upon your honor.   *Exeunt.*

ACT I, SCENE 2°

Enter Lucio and two other Gentlemen.

LUCIO: If the Duke with the other dukes come not to composition° with
the King of Hungary, why then all the dukes fall upon° the King.

FIRST GENTLEMAN: Heaven grant us its peace, but not the King of
Hungary's!

SECOND GENTLEMAN: Amen.   5

LUCIO: Thou conclud'st like the sanctimonious pirate that went to sea
with the Ten Commandments but scraped one out of the table.°

SECOND GENTLEMAN: "Thou shalt not steal"?

LUCIO: Ay, that he razed.°

FIRST GENTLEMAN: Why, 'twas a commandment to command the captain   10
and all the rest from their function; they put forth° to steal. There's not a
soldier of us all that, in the thanksgiving° before meat,° do relish the petition well that prays for peace.

SECOND GENTLEMAN: I never heard any soldier dislike it.

LUCIO: I believe thee, for I think thou never wast where grace was said.   15

SECOND GENTLEMAN: No? A dozen times at least.

FIRST GENTLEMAN: What, in meter?

LUCIO: In any proportion° or in any language.

FIRST GENTLEMAN: I think, or in any religion.

LUCIO: Ay, why not? Grace is grace,° despite of all controversy, as, for   20
example, thou thyself art a wicked villain, despite of all grace.

---

79. the bottom of my place: the extent of my commission.   ACT I, SCENE 2. Location: A
public place.   1. composition: agreement.   2. fall upon: attack.   7. table: tablet.   9. razed:
scraped out. (The word may also suggest *rased,* "erased.")   11. put forth: set out to sea.
12. thanksgiving: prayer of thanksgiving, grace.   meat: the meal.   18. proportion: form.
20. Grace is grace: (Refers to the Catholic-Protestant *controversy,* line 20, as to whether
humanity can be saved by works or by grace alone; with punning on *grace* as "thanks for a meal,"
line 15, and "gracefulness" or "becomingness," line 21.)

FIRST GENTLEMAN: Well, there went but a pair of shears between us.°
LUCIO: I grant; as there may between the lists and the velvet. Thou art the list.°
FIRST GENTLEMAN: And thou the velvet. Thou art good velvet; thou'rt a   25
three-piled° piece, I warrant thee. I had as lief° be a list of an English
kersey° as be piled,° as thou art piled, for a French velvet. Do I speak
feelingly° now?
LUCIO: I think thou dost, and indeed with most painful feeling of thy
speech. I will, out of thine own confession, learn to begin thy health° but,   30
whilst I live, forget to drink after thee.°
FIRST GENTLEMAN: I think I have done myself wrong,° have I not?
SECOND GENTLEMAN: Yes, that thou hast, whether thou art tainted° or free.

Enter bawd [Mistress Overdone].

LUCIO: Behold, behold, where Madam Mitigation° comes! I have pur-
chased as many diseases under her roof as come to —   35
SECOND GENTLEMAN: To what, I pray?
LUCIO: Judge.°
SECOND GENTLEMAN: To three thousand dolors° a year.
FIRST GENTLEMAN: Ay, and more.
LUCIO: A French crown° more.   40
FIRST GENTLEMAN: Thou art always figuring° diseases in me, but thou art
full of error. I am sound.°

---

22. there . . . between us: i.e., we're cut from the same cloth.   23–24. as . . . list: (Lucio jokes
that the shears might also cut between, i.e., distinguish between, the mere *lists* or selvages,
edges of a woven fabric, and the *velvet* betokening a true gentleman. Lucio wittily asserts himself to be a true gentleman; the other, not.)   26. three-piled: having a threefold pile or nap
(the best grade of velvet).   as lief: as soon, rather.   27. kersey: a coarse woolen fabric. (The
First Gentleman turns the joke on Lucio by saying he would rather be a plain, homespun
Englishman than a Frenchified velvet gentleman in decay and threadbare. *Velvet* suggests prostitutes and venereal disease, as in the following notes.)   be piled: (1) have a cloth nap (2) suffer
from hemorrhoids (3) be pilled or peeled, i.e., hairless, bald, as a result of mercury treatment for
venereal disease (known as the "French disease"; see *French velvet* in the same line and *French
crown*, line 40).   28. feelingly: to the purpose, so as to hit home. (But Lucio's reply quibbles
on "painfully," meaning the Gentleman's mouth is affected by the French disease; hence,
Lucio will not drink from the same cup after him.)   30. begin thy health: begin drinking
to your health.   31. forget . . . thee: take care not to drink from your cup.   32. done myself
wrong: i.e., asked for that.   33. tainted: infected.   34. Mitigation: (So called because her
function is to relieve desire.)   37. Judge: guess.   38. dolors: (quibbling on *dollars;* spelled
Dollours in the Folio.)   40. French crown: (1) gold coin (2) bald head incurred through
syphilis, the "French disease."   41. figuring: (1) imagining (2) reckoning (recalling the mone-
tary puns of lines 38 and 40).   42. sound: (1) healthy (2) resounding (because of hollow bones
caused by syphilis).

LUCIO: Nay, not, as one would say, healthy, but so sound as things that are hollow. Thy bones are hollow; impiety° has made a feast of thee.

FIRST GENTLEMAN: [to Mistress Overdone] How now, which of your hips has 45 the most profound sciatica?°

MISTRESS OVERDONE: Well, well; there's one yonder arrested and carried to prison was worth five thousand of you all.

SECOND GENTLEMAN: Who's that, I pray thee?

MISTRESS OVERDONE: Marry,° sir, that's Claudio, Signor Claudio. 50

FIRST GENTLEMAN: Claudio to prison? 'Tis not so.

MISTRESS OVERDONE: Nay, but I know 'tis so. I saw him arrested, saw him carried away; and, which° is more, within these three days his head to be chopped off.

LUCIO: But, after° all this fooling, I would not have it so. Art thou sure of 55 this?

MISTRESS OVERDONE: I am too sure of it; and it is for getting Madam Julietta with child.

LUCIO: Believe me, this may be. He promised to meet me two hours since, and he was ever° precise in promise-keeping. 60

SECOND GENTLEMAN: Besides, you know, it draws something near to° the speech we had to such a purpose.°

FIRST GENTLEMAN: But most of all agreeing with the proclamation.

LUCIO: Away! Let's go learn the truth of it.

Exit [Lucio with the Gentlemen].

MISTRESS OVERDONE: Thus, what with the war, what with the sweat,° 65 what with the gallows, and what with poverty, I am custom-shrunk.°

Enter Clown [Pompey].

How now, what's the news with you?

POMPEY: Yonder man is carried to prison.

MISTRESS OVERDONE: Well, what has he done?°

POMPEY: A woman. 70

MISTRESS OVERDONE: But what's his offense?

POMPEY: Groping for trouts in a peculiar° river.

---

44. impiety: wickedness. 46. sciatica: a disease affecting the sciatic nerve in the hip and thigh, thought to be a symptom of syphilis. 50. Marry: i.e., by the Virgin Mary. 53. which: what. 55. after: notwithstanding. 60. ever: always. 61. draws . . . near to: approaches, sounds somewhat like. 62. to . . . purpose: on that topic. 65. sweat: sweating sickness; a form of the plague. 66. custom-shrunk: having fewer customers. 69. done: (Pompey quibbles in line 70 on a sexual sense of the word, present also in Mistress Overdone's name.) 72. peculiar: privately owned (with bawdy suggestion).

MISTRESS OVERDONE: What? Is there a maid with child by him?

POMPEY: No, but there's a woman with maid° by him. You have not heard
of the proclamation, have you? 75

MISTRESS OVERDONE: What proclamation, man?

POMPEY: All houses° in the suburbs° of Vienna must be plucked down.

MISTRESS OVERDONE: And what shall become of those in the city?

POMPEY: They shall stand for seed.° They had gone down too, but that a
wise burgher° put in for them.° 80

MISTRESS OVERDONE: But shall all our houses of resort in the suburbs be
pulled down?

POMPEY: To the ground, mistress.

MISTRESS OVERDONE: Why, here's a change indeed in the commonwealth!
What shall become of me? 85

POMPEY: Come, fear not you. Good counselors° lack no clients. Though
you change your place, you need not change your trade; I'll be your
tapster° still. Courage! There will be pity taken on you. You that have
worn your eyes almost out° in the service, you will be considered.

MISTRESS OVERDONE: What's to do here, Thomas Tapster? Let's withdraw. 90

POMPEY: Here comes Signor Claudio, led by the Provost° to prison; and
there's Madam Juliet. *Exeunt.*

Enter Provost, Claudio, Juliet, Officers; Lucio and two Gentleman [follow].

CLAUDIO: [*to the Provost*]
Fellow, why dost thou show me thus to the world?
Bear me to prison, where I am committed.

PROVOST:
I do it not in evil disposition 95
But from Lord Angelo by special charge.

CLAUDIO:
Thus can the demigod Authority
Make us pay down for our offense, by weight,
The words of heaven. On whom it will, it will;

---

74. **woman with maid:** (Pompey playfully corrects Mistress Overdone's use of the word *maid*,
joking that a pregnant woman cannot be a virgin [*maid*] though the child she carries is one.)
77. **houses:** i.e., brothels. **suburbs:** (Location of the brothels in Shakespeare's London, as
in other walled cities.) 79. **for seed:** to preserve the species (with ribald pun). 80. **burgher:**
citizen. **put . . . them:** interceded on their behalf, offered to acquire them. 86. **counselors:**
counseling lawyers. 88. **tapster:** one who draws beer in an alehouse. 89. **worn . . . out:** i.e.,
worked so hard (perhaps with an ironic reference to the traditional image of the blind Cupid).
91. **Provost:** officer charged with apprehension, custody, and punishment of offenders.

On whom it will not, so;° yet still 'tis just.   100

LUCIO:
Why, now now, Claudio? Whence comes this restraint?

CLAUDIO:
From too much liberty, my Lucio, liberty.
As surfeit° is the father of much fast,°
So every scope,° by the immoderate use,
Turns to restraint. Our natures do pursue,   105
Like rats that ravin down their proper bane,°
A thirsty evil, and when we drink we die.

LUCIO: If I could speak so wisely under an arrest, I would send for certain of my creditors.° And yet, to say the truth, I had as lief° have the
foppery° of freedom as the morality of imprisonment. What's thy of-   110
fense, Claudio?

CLAUDIO:
What but to speak of would offend again.

LUCIO:
What, is 't murder?

CLAUDIO: No.

LUCIO: Lechery?

CLAUDIO:
Call it so.

PROVOST: Away, sir, you must go.

CLAUDIO:
One word, good friend. — Lucio, a word with you.   115

LUCIO:
A hundred, if they'll do you any good.
Is lechery so looked after?°

CLAUDIO:
Thus stands it with me: upon a true contract°
I got possession of Julietta's bed.
You know the lady; she is fast my wife,°   120

98–100. **pay ... so:** pay the full penalty for our offense called for in the Bible (Romans 9:18):
"Therefore hath he [God] mercy on whom he will have mercy, and whom he will he
hardeneth." 103. **surfeit:** excess. **fast:** abstinence. 104. **scope:** freedom. 106. **ravin ...
bane:** greedily devour what is poisonous to them. 109. **creditors:** (who would arrest me
for debt.) **lief:** willingly. 110. **foppery:** folly. 117. **looked after:** kept under observation.
118. **a true contract:** i.e., one made in the presence of witnesses, though without a religious ceremony. (Such a precontract was binding but, in the eyes of the Church, did not confer the right
of sexual consummation before the nuptials.) 120. **fast my wife:** i.e., firmly bound by precontract.

Save that we do the denunciation° lack
Of outward order.° This we came not to,
Only for propagation° of a dower
Remaining in the coffer of her friends,°
From whom we thought it meet to hide our love   125
Till time had made them for us.° But it chances
The stealth of our most mutual entertainment
With character too gross° is writ on Juliet.

LUCIO:
With child, perhaps?

CLAUDIO: Unhappily, even so.
And the new deputy now for the Duke —   130
Whether it be the fault and glimpse of newness,°
Or whether that the body public be
A horse whereon the governor doth ride,
Who, newly in the seat, that it may know
He can command, lets it straight° feel the spur;   135
Whether the tyranny be in his place,°
Or in his eminence° that fills it up,
I stagger in° — but this new governor
Awakes me° all the enrollèd° penalties
Which have, like unscoured armor, hung by the wall   140
So long that nineteen zodiacs° have gone round
And none of them been worn; and for a name°
Now puts the drowsy and neglected act
Freshly on me. 'Tis surely for a name.

LUCIO: I warrant it is, and thy head stands so tickle° on thy shoulders that   145
a milkmaid, if she be in love, may sigh it off. Send after the Duke and
appeal to him.

CLAUDIO:
I have done so, but he's not to be found.
I prithee, Lucio, do me this kind of service:
This day my sister should the cloister° enter   150

---

121. **denunciation:** formal declaration.   122. **outward order:** public ceremony.   123. **propagation:** increase, begetting.   124. **friends:** relatives.   126. **made . . . us:** disposed them in our favor.   128. **character too gross:** writing too evident.   131. **the fault . . . newness:** the faulty flashiness of novelty.   135. **straight:** at once.   136. **in his place:** inherent in the office. 137. **his eminence:** the eminence of him.   138. **I stagger in:** I am uncertain.   139. **Awakes me:** i.e., awakes, activates. (*Me* is used colloquially.)   **enrollèd:** written on a roll or deed. 141. **zodiacs:** i.e., years.   142. **for a name:** for reputation's sake.   145. **tickle:** uncertain, unstable.   150. **cloister:** i.e., convent.

And there receive her approbation.°
Acquaint her with the danger of my state;
Implore her, in my voice, that she make friends
To° the strict deputy; bid herself assay° him.
I have great hope in that, for in her youth   155
There is a prone° and speechless dialect°
Such as move men; besides, she hath prosperous art°
When she will play with reason and discourse,
And well she can persuade.

LUCIO: I pray she may, as well for the encouragement of the like,° which   160
else° would stand under grievous imposition,° as for the enjoying of
thy life, who I would be sorry should be thus foolishly lost at a game
of tick-tack.° I'll to her.

CLAUDIO: I thank you, good friend Lucio.

LUCIO: Within two hours.   165

CLAUDIO: Come, officer, away!   *Exeunt.*

ACT I, SCENE 3°

Enter Duke and Friar Thomas.

DUKE:
    No, holy Father, throw away that thought;
    Believe not that the dribbling° dart of love
    Can pierce a complete° bosom. Why I desire thee
    To give me secret harbor° hath a purpose
    More grave and wrinkled° than the aims and ends   5
    Of burning youth.

FRIAR THOMAS: May Your Grace speak of it?

DUKE:
    My holy sir, none better knows than you
    How I have ever loved the life removed°
    And held in idle price° to haunt assemblies
    Where youth and cost° witless bravery keeps.°   10

---

151. **approbation:** novitiate, period of probation.   154. **To:** with.   **assay:** try, test.   156. **prone:** eager, apt, supplicating.   **dialect:** language.   157. **prosperous art:** skill or ability to gain favorable results.   160. **the like:** i.e., similar offenders.   161. **else:** otherwise.   **imposition:** accusation.   163. **tick-tack:** a form of backgammon in which pegs were fitted into holes (here applied bawdily).   ACT I, SCENE 3. **Location:** A friary.   2. **dribbling:** falling short or wide of the mark.   3. **complete:** perfect, whole, strong.   4. **harbor:** shelter.   5. **wrinkled:** i.e., mature.   8. **removed:** retired.   9. **in idle price:** as little worth. *Idle* means "unprofitable."   10. **cost:** costly expenditure.   **witless . . . keeps:** maintain a foolish display.

I have delivered to Lord Angelo,
A man of stricture° and firm abstinence,
My absolute power and place here in Vienna,
And he supposes me traveled to Poland;
For so I have strewed it in the common ear,   15
And so it is received. Now, pious sir,
You will demand of me why I do this.

FRIAR THOMAS: Gladly, my lord.

DUKE:
We have strict statutes and most biting laws,
The needful bits and curbs to headstrong steeds,°   20
Which for this fourteen° years we have let slip,
Even like an o'ergrown° lion in a cave
That goes not out to prey. Now, as fond° fathers,
Having bound up the threatening twigs of birch
Only to stick it in their children's sight   25
For terror, not to use, in time the rod
Becomes more mocked than feared, so our decrees,
Dead to infliction,° to themselves are dead;
And liberty° plucks justice by the nose,
The baby beats the nurse, and quite athwart°   30
Goes all decorum.°

FRIAR THOMAS: It rested in Your Grace°
To unloose this tied-up justice when you pleased;
And it in you more dreadful would have seemed
Than in Lord Angelo.

DUKE: I do fear, too dreadful.
Sith° 'twas my fault to give the people scope,   35
'Twould be my tyranny to strike and gall° them
For what I bid them do; for we bid this be done°
When evil deeds have their permissive pass°
And not the punishment. Therefore indeed, my father,
I have on Angelo imposed the office,°   40

---

12. **stricture:** strictness.   20. **steeds:** (The Folio reading, *weeds*, is possible in the sense of "lawless and uncontrolled impulses.")   21. **fourteen:** (Claudio mentions nineteen years at 1.2.141; possibly the compositor confused *xiv* and *xix*.)   22. **o'ergrown:** too old and large.   23. **fond:** doting.   28. **Dead to infliction:** dead in that they are not executed.   29. **liberty:** license.   30. **athwart:** wrongly, awry.   31. **decorum:** social order.   **rested . . . Grace:** lay in your ducal authority, was incumbent on you.   35. **Sith:** since.   36. **gall:** chafe, injure.   37. **we . . . done:** i.e., we virtually order a crime to be committed.   38. **pass:** sanction.   40. **office:** duty.

Who may in th' ambush° of my name° strike home,°
And yet my nature° never in the fight
To do in slander.° And to behold his sway°
I will, as 'twere a brother of your order,
Visit both prince and people. Therefore, I prithee,   45
Supply me with the habit, and instruct me
How I may formally° in person bear°
Like a true friar. More reasons for this action
At our more° leisure shall I render you.
Only this one: Lord Angelo is precise,°   50
Stands at a guard with envy,° scarce confesses
That his blood flows or that his appetite
Is more to bread than stone.° Hence shall we see,
If power change purpose, what our seemers be.   *Exeunt.*

ACT I, SCENE 4°

Enter Isabella and Francisca, a nun.

ISABELLA:
    And have you nuns no farther privileges?
FRANCISCA: Are not these large enough?
ISABELLA:
    Yes, truly. I speak not as desiring more,
    But rather wishing a more strict restraint
    Upon the sisterhood, the votarists of Saint Clare.°   5
LUCIO: (*within*)
    Ho! Peace be in this place!
ISABELLA: Who's that which calls?
FRANCISCA:
    It is a man's voice. Gentle Isabella,
    Turn you the key, and know his business of him.
    You may, I may not; you are yet unsworn.°

41. in th' ambush: under cover.   name: i.e., ducal authority.   home: to the heart of the matter.   42. nature: i.e., personal identity (as distinguished from official capacity).   43. do in
slander: act so as to invite slander (for being too repressive).   sway: rule.   47. formally: in
outward appearance.   bear: bear myself.   49. more: greater.   50. precise: strict, puritanical.
51. at . . . envy: in a defensive posture against malicious gossip.   52–53. his appetite . . . stone:
he craves bread any more than stone, i.e., has normal human appetites.   ACT I, SCENE 4.
Location: A convent.   5. votarists of Saint Clare: An order founded in 1212 by Saint Francis
of Assisi and Saint Clare; its members were enjoined to a life of poverty, service, and contempla-
tion.   9. you . . . unsworn: i.e., you have not yet taken your formal vows to enter the convent.

When you have vowed, you must not speak with men   10
But in the presence of the prioress;
Then if you speak you must not show your face,
Or if you show your face you must not speak.
He calls again. I pray you, answer him.   [*Exit.*]

ISABELLA:
Peace and prosperity! Who is 't that calls?   15

[*She opens the door. Enter Lucio.*]

LUCIO:
Hail, virgin, if you be, as those cheek roses°
Proclaim you are no less. Can you so stead° me
As° bring me to the sight of Isabella,
A novice of this place, and the fair sister
To her unhappy° brother Claudio?   20

ISABELLA:
Why "her unhappy brother"? Let me ask,
The rather for° I now must make you know
I am that Isabella, and his sister.

LUCIO:
Gentle and fair, your brother kindly greets you.
Not to be weary° with you, he's in prison.   25

ISABELLA: Woe me! For what?

LUCIO:
For that which, if myself might be his judge,
He should receive his punishment in thanks:
He hath got his friend with child.

ISABELLA:
Sir, make me not your story.°

LUCIO: 'Tis true.   30
I would not — though 'tis my familiar° sin
With maids to seem the lapwing,° and to jest,
Tongue far from heart — play with all virgins so.
I hold you as a thing enskied° and sainted
By your renouncement, an immortal spirit   35

16. **cheek roses:** i.e., blushes. 17. **stead:** help. 18. **As:** as to. 20. **unhappy:** unfortunate.
22. **The rather for:** the more so because. 25. **weary:** wearisome. 30. **story:** subject for
mirth. 31. **familiar:** customary. 32. **lapwing:** peewit or plover. (The lapwing runs away
from its nest in order to draw away enemies from its young, much as Lucio throws up smoke-
screens in his seductive talk with young women.) 34. **enskied:** placed in heaven.

And to be talked with in sincerity
As with a saint.
ISABELLA:
You do blaspheme the good in mocking me.°
LUCIO:
Do not believe it.° Fewness and truth,° 'tis thus:
Your brother and his lover have embraced.   40
As those that feed grow full, as blossoming time
That from the seedness the bare fallow brings
To teeming foison,° even so her plenteous womb
Expresseth his full tilth° and husbandry.°
ISABELLA:
Someone with child by him? My cousin Juliet?   45
LUCIO: Is she your cousin?
ISABELLA:
Adoptedly, as schoolmaids change° their names
By vain though apt° affection.
LUCIO: She it is.
ISABELLA:
O, let him marry her.
LUCIO: This is the point.
The Duke is very strangely gone from hence;   50
Bore many gentlemen, myself being one,
In hand and hope of action;° but we do learn,
By those that know the very nerves of state,
His givings-out° were of an infinite distance
From his true-meant design. Upon° his place,   55
And with full line° of his authority,
Governs Lord Angelo, a man whose blood
Is very snow broth;° one who never feels
The wanton stings and motions° of the sense,°
But doth rebate° and blunt his° natural edge°   60

38. You . . . me: you blaspheme goodness itself when you mockingly praise me, unworthy as I am, for saintliness. 39. it: i.e., that I am mocking. Fewness and truth: in few words and truly. 41–43. as . . . foison: as the blossoming season brings the bare untilled land from a state of being sown to abundant harvest (?) (The grammatical construction is unclear.) 44. tilth: tillage. husbandry: (1) tillage (2) duties of a husband and sexual partner. 47. change: exchange. 48. vain though apt: girlish though natural and suitable. 51–52. Bore . . . action: i.e., he misleadingly kept us in expectation of some military action. 54. givings-out: public statements. 55. Upon: in, on the strength of. 56. line: extent. 58. snow broth: melted snow (i.e., ice water). 59. motions: promptings. the sense: sexual passion. 60. rebate: dull, abate. his: its. edge: sharpness of desire.

With profits of the mind, study, and fast.
He — to give fear to use and liberty,°
Which have for long run by the hideous law
As mice by lions — hath picked out an act,
Under whose heavy sense° your brother's life   65
Falls into forfeit. He arrests him on it
And follows close the rigor of the statute
To make him an example. All hope is gone,
Unless you have the grace by your fair prayer
To soften Angelo. And that's my pith of business°   70
Twixt you and your poor brother.
ISABELLA: Doth he so
  Seek his life?
LUCIO: He's censured° him already,
  And, as I hear, the Provost hath a warrant
  For 's execution.
ISABELLA: Alas, what poor
  Ability's in me to do him good?   75
LUCIO: Assay° the power you have.
ISABELLA:
  My power? Alas, I doubt.
LUCIO: Our doubts are traitors,
  And makes° us lose the good we oft might win,
  By fearing to attempt. Go to Lord Angelo,
  And let him learn to know, when maidens sue   80
  Men give like gods, but when they weep and kneel,
  All their petitions° are as freely theirs
  As they themselves would owe them.°
ISABELLA: I'll see what I can do.
LUCIO: But speedily.   85
ISABELLA:
  I will about it straight,
  No longer staying but° to give the Mother°
  Notice of my affair. I humbly thank you.
  Commend me to my brother. Soon at night°
  I'll send him certain word of my success.°   90

---

62. **use and liberty:** habitual licentiousness.   65. **heavy sense:** severe interpretation.   70. **my pith of business:** the essence of my business.   72. **censured:** sentenced.   76. **Assay:** try.   78. **makes:** i.e., make.   82. **their petitions:** i.e., the things the maidens ask for.   83. **As . . . them:** as they themselves would wish to have them.   87. **but:** than.   **Mother:** Mother Superior, prioress.   89. **Soon at night:** early tonight.   90. **my success:** how I have succeeded.

LUCIO:
  I take my leave of you.
ISABELLA: Good sir, adieu.   *Exeunt [separately]*.

ACT 2, SCENE 1°

Enter Angelo, Escalus, and servants, [a] Justice.

ANGELO:
  We must not make a scarecrow of the law,
  Setting it up to fear° the birds of prey,
  And let it keep one shape till custom make it
  Their perch and not their terror.
ESCALUS: Ay, but yet
  Let us be keen° and rather cut a little   5
  Than fall° and bruise° to death. Alas, this gentleman
  Whom I would save had a most noble father!
  Let but your honor know,°
  Whom I believe to be most strait° in virtue,
  That, in the working of your own affections,°   10
  Had time cohered with place, or place with wishing,
  Or that the resolute acting of your blood°
  Could have attained th' effect° of your own purpose,
  Whether you had° not sometime° in your life
  Erred in this point which now you censure him,°   15
  And pulled the law upon you.
ANGELO:
  'Tis one thing to be tempted, Escalus,
  Another thing to fall. I not deny
  The jury, passing on the prisoner's life,
  May in the sworn twelve have a thief or two   20
  Guiltier than him they try. What's open made to justice,
  That justice seizes. What knows the laws
  That thieves do pass on thieves?° 'Tis very pregnant,°
  The jewel that we find, we stoop and take 't

ACT 2, SCENE 1. **Location:** A court of justice.   2. **fear:** frighten.   5. **keen:** sharp.   6. **fall:** let fall heavily.   **bruise:** i.e., crush.   8. **know:** consider.   9. **strait:** strict.   10. **affections:** desires.   12. **blood:** passion.   13. **effect:** realization.   14. **had:** would have.   **sometime:** on some occasion.   15. **censure him:** sentence him for.   22–23. **What . . . on thieves:** i.e., what cognizance can the laws take of the possibility that thieves may pass sentence upon thieves. 23. **pregnant:** clear.

Because we see it; but what we do not see   25
We tread upon and never think of it.
You may not so extenuate his offense
For° I have had such faults; but rather tell me,
When I that censure him do so offend,
Let mine own judgment pattern out° my death   30
And nothing come in partial.° Sir, he must die.

Enter Provost.

ESCALUS:
Be it as your wisdom will.
ANGELO: Where is the Provost?
PROVOST:
Here, if it like° your honor.
ANGELO: See that Claudio
Be executed by nine tomorrow morning.
Bring him his confessor; let him be prepared.   35
For that's the utmost° of his pilgrimage.°   [*Exit Provost.*]
ESCALUS:
Well, heaven forgive him, and forgive us all!
Some rise by sin, and some by virtue fall;
Some run from breaks of ice and answer none,°
And some condemnèd for a fault alone.°   40

Enter Elbow, Froth, Clown [Pompey], officers.

ELBOW: Come, bring them away.° If these be good people in a common-
weal that do nothing but use their abuses in common houses,° I know no
law. Bring them away.
ANGELO: How now, sir, what's your name? And what's the matter?
ELBOW: If it please your honor, I am the poor Duke's° constable, and my 45
name is Elbow. I do lean upon° justice, sir, and do bring in here before
your good honor two notorious benefactors.

---

28. For: because. 30. judgment pattern out: sentence (imposed in this and similar cases),
serve as a model for. 31. nothing . . . partial: let no partiality be allowed. 33. like: please.
36. utmost: furthest point. pilgrimage: i.e., life. 39. Some . . . none: i.e., some run away
from imminent danger, not staying to answer for their sins (?) (A famous crux; the Folio reads
brakes of ice.) 40. a fault alone: one single infraction. 41. away: onward. 42. use . . .
houses: practice their vices in bawdy houses. 45. poor Duke's: i.e., Duke's poor. 46. lean
upon: rely on, appeal to (with an unintended comic reference to the idea of leaning on one's
elbow).

ANGELO: Benefactors? Well, what benefactors are they? Are they not malefactors?

ELBOW: If it please your honor, I know not well what they are; but precise° 50 villains they are, that I am sure of, and void of all profanation° in the world that good Christians ought to have.

ESCALUS: [*to Angelo*] This comes off well. Here's a wise officer.

ANGELO: Go to.° What quality° are they of? — Elbow is your name? Why dost thou not speak, Elbow? 55

POMPEY: He cannot, sir; he's out at elbow.°

ANGELO: What are you, sir?

ELBOW: He, sir? A tapster, sir, parcel-bawd,° one that serves a bad woman, whose house, sir, was, as they say, plucked down in the suburbs; and now she professes a hothouse,° which I think is a very ill house too. 60

ESCALUS: How know you that?

ELBOW: My wife, sir, whom I detest° before heaven and your honor —

ESCALUS: How? Thy wife?

ELBOW: Ay, sir; whom I thank heaven is an honest woman —

ESCALUS: Dost thou detest her therefore? 65

ELBOW: I say, sir, I will detest myself also, as well as she, that this house, if it be not a bawd's house, it is pity of her life,° for it is a naughty° house.

ESCALUS: How dost thou know that, Constable?

ELBOW: Marry, sir, by my wife, who, if she had been a woman cardinally° given,° might have been accused in fornication, adultery, and all unclean- 70 liness there.

ESCALUS: By the woman's means?

ELBOW: Ay, sir, by Mistress Overdone's means; but as she spit in his° face, so she defied him.

POMPEY: Sir, if it please your honor, this is not so. 75

ELBOW: Prove it before these varlets here, thou honorable° man, prove it.

ESCALUS: [*to Angelo*] Do you hear how he misplaces?

---

50. **precise:** complete (or perhaps a blunder for "precious" — a word that unintentionally recalls the description of Angelo as *precise,* i.e., strict or puritanical, at 1.3.50). 51. **pro-fanation:** (A blunder for "profession," or a word meaning "irreverence" where Elbow intends "reverence." Elbow already has used several seeming malapropisms, including *lean upon, bene-factors,* and *precise.*) 54. **Go to:** an expression of impatience or reproof. **quality:** occupation. 56. **out at elbow:** (1) impoverished, threadbare, hence without any ideas (2) missing his cue, i.e., silent (or *out*) after being called by his name. 58. **parcel-bawd:** part-time bawd (and part-time tapster). 60. **professes a hothouse:** professes to run a bathhouse. 62. **detest:** (For "protest.") 67. **pity of her life:** a great pity. **naughty:** wicked. 69. **cardinally:** (For "car-nally.") 70. **given:** inclined. 73. **his:** i.e., Pompey's, who was carrying out Mistress Over-done's wishes and was therefore her *means.* 76. **varlets ... honorable:** (Elbow reverses or *misplaces* these epithets.)

POMPEY: Sir, she came in great with child, and longing, saving your honor's reverence,° for stewed prunes.° Sir, we had but two in the house, which at that very distant° time stood, as it were, in a fruit dish, a dish of some 80 threepence. Your honors have seen such dishes; they are not China dishes, but very good dishes —

ESCALUS: Go to, go to. No matter for the dish, sir.

POMPEY: No, indeed, sir, not of a pin;° you are therein in the right. But to the point. As I say, this Mistress Elbow, being, as I say, with child, and 85 being great-bellied, and longing, as I said, for prunes; and having but two in the dish, as I said, Master Froth here, this very man, having eaten the rest, as I said, and, as I say, paying for them very honestly — for, as you know, Master Froth, I could not give you threepence again.°

FROTH: No, indeed. 90

POMPEY: Very well. You being then, if you be remembered, cracking the stones° of the foresaid prunes —

FROTH: Ay, so I did indeed.

POMPEY: Why, very well; I telling you then, if you be remembered, that such a one and such a one were past cure of the thing you wot of,° unless 95 they kept very good diet, as I told you —

FROTH: All this is true.

POMPEY: Why, very well, then —

ESCALUS: Come, you are a tedious fool. To the purpose. What was done to Elbow's wife, that he hath cause to complain of? Come me° to what was 100 done to her.

POMPEY: Sir, your honor cannot come to that yet.

ESCALUS: No, sir, nor I mean it not.

POMPEY: Sir, but you shall come to it, by your honor's leave. And, I beseech you, look into Master Froth here, sir, a man of fourscore pound a 105 year,° whose father died at Hallowmas. — Was 't not at Hallowmas,° Master Froth?

FROTH: All-hallond eve.°

POMPEY: Why, very well. I hope here be truths. He, sir, sitting, as I say, in

---

78–79. **saving . . . reverence:** i.e., begging your pardon for what I'm about to say. 79. **stewed prunes:** (Commonly served in houses of prostitution, or *stews*, and therefore suggesting prostitutes. The bawdy double entendre continues in *stood, dish, pin, point, cracking the stones,* etc.) 80. **distant:** (Blunder for "instant"?) 84. **a pin:** i.e., an insignificant trifle. 89. **again:** back. 92. **stones:** pits. (With suggestion also of "testicles.") 95. **the thing . . . of:** you know what I mean (i.e., venereal disease). 100. **Come me:** i.e., come. (*Me* is used colloquially. Pompey makes a vulgar joke on the words *come* and *done;* see note at line 119.) 105–06. **of . . . year:** i.e., well off. 106. **Hallowmas:** All Saints' Day, November 1. 108. **All-hallond eve:** Halloween, October 31.

a lower chair,° sir — 'twas in the Bunch of Grapes,° where indeed you   110
have a delight to sit, have you not?

FROTH: I have so, because it is an open° room and good for winter.

POMPEY: Why, very well, then. I hope here be truths.

ANGELO:
This will last out a night in Russia,
When nights are longest there. I'll take my leave   115
And leave you to the hearing of the cause,°
Hoping you'll find good cause to whip them all.

ESCALUS:
I think no less.° Good morrow to your lordship.   *Exit* [*Angelo*].
Now, sir, come on. What was done° to Elbow's wife, once more?

POMPEY: Once, sir? There was nothing done to her once.   120

ELBOW: I beseech you, sir, ask him what this man did to my wife.

POMPEY: I beseech your honor, ask me.

ESCALUS: Well, sir, what did this gentleman to her?

POMPEY: I beseech you, sir, look in this gentleman's face. Good Master
Froth, look upon his honor; 'tis for a good purpose. Doth your honor   125
mark° his face?

ESCALUS: Ay, sir, very well.

POMPEY: Nay, I beseech you, mark it well.

ESCALUS: Well, I do so.

POMPEY: Doth your honor see any harm in his face?   130

ESCALUS: Why, no.

POMPEY: I'll be supposed° upon a book,° his face is the worst thing about
him. Good, then; if his face be the worst thing about him, how could
Master Froth do the Constable's wife any harm? I would know that of
your honor.   135

ESCALUS: He's in the right, Constable. What say you to it?

ELBOW: First, an it like° you, the house is a respected° house; next, this is a
respected fellow; and his mistress is a respected woman.

POMPEY: By this hand, sir, his wife is a more respected person than any of
us all.   140

ELBOW: Varlet, thou liest! Thou liest, wicked varlet! The time is yet to
come that she was ever respected with man, woman, or child.

---

110. **a lower chair:** i.e., an easy chair (?)   **Bunch of Grapes:** (It was not uncommon to designate
particular rooms in inns by such names.)   112. **open:** public.   116. **cause:** case. (With a play
on *cause,* "reason," in the next line. See also the play on *leave* in 115–16.)   118. **I . . . less:** I
think so, too.   119. **done:** (Pompey, in his answer, uses *done* in a sexual sense.)   126. **mark:**
observe.   132. **supposed:** (A malapropism for "deposed," i.e., sworn.)   **book:** i.e., Bible.
137. **an it like:** if it please.   **respected:** (For "suspected.")

POMPEY: Sir, she was respected with him before he married with her.

ESCALUS: Which is the wiser here, Justice or Iniquity?° — Is this true?

ELBOW: O thou caitiff!° O thou varlet! O thou wicked Hannibal!° I re- 145
spected with her before I was married to her? — If ever I was respected
with her, or she with me, let not your worship think me the poor Duke's
officer. — Prove this, thou wicked Hannibal, or I'll have mine action of
battery° on thee.

ESCALUS: If he took° you a box o'° th' ear, you might have your action of 150
slander too.

ELBOW: Marry, I thank your good worship for it. What is 't your worship's
pleasure I shall do with this wicked caitiff?

ESCALUS: Truly, officer, because he hath some offenses in him that thou
wouldst discover° if thou couldst, let him continue in his courses° till 155
thou know'st what they are.

ELBOW: Marry, I thank your worship for it. — Thou seest, thou wicked
varlet, now, what's come upon thee: thou art to continue now, thou varlet,
thou art to continue.°

ESCALUS: [to Froth] Where were you born, friend? 160

FROTH: Here in Vienna, sir.

ESCALUS: Are you of° fourscore pounds a year?

FROTH: Yes, an 't please you, sir.

ESCALUS: So. [To Pompey.] What trade are you of, sir?

POMPEY: A tapster, a poor widow's tapster. 165

ESCALUS: Your mistress' name?

POMPEY: Mistress Overdone.

ESCALUS: Hath she had any more than one husband?

POMPEY: Nine, sir. Overdone by the last.°

ESCALUS: Nine? — Come hither to me, Master Froth. Master Froth, I 170
would not have you acquainted with tapsters. They will draw° you, Master Froth, and you will hang them.° Get you gone, and let me hear no
more of you.

---

144. **Justice or Iniquity:** (Personified characters in a morality play.) 145. **caitiff:** knave,
villain. **Hannibal:** (A blunder for "cannibal," perhaps also suggested by the fact that Hannibal and Pompey were both famous generals in the classical world.) 149. **battery:** (An error
for "slander," as Escalus amusedly points out.) 150. **took:** gave. **o':** on. 155. **discover:**
(1) detect (2) reveal. **courses:** courses of action. 159. **continue:** (Elbow may confuse the
word with its opposite.) 162. **of:** possessed of. 169. **Overdone . . . last:** (1) her name, Overdone, was given her by her last husband (2) she has been worn out (*overdone*) by the last one.
171. **draw:** (1) cheat, take in (2) empty, deplete (with a pun on the tapster's trade of drawing
liquor from a barrel, and on Froth's name) (3) disembowel, or drag to execution. 172. **will
hang them:** will be the cause of their hanging.

FROTH: I thank your worship. For mine own part, I never come into any
room in a taphouse° but I am drawn in.°   175
ESCALUS: Well, no more of it, Master Froth. Farewell. [*Exit Froth.*] Come
you hither to me, Master Tapster. What's your name, Master Tapster?
POMPEY: Pompey.
ESCALUS: What else?
POMPEY: Bum, sir.   180
ESCALUS: Troth, and your bum is the greatest thing about you, so that in
the beastliest sense you are Pompey the Great. Pompey, you are partly a
bawd, Pompey, howsoever you color° it in being a tapster, are you not?
Come, tell me true. It shall be the better for you.
POMPEY: Truly, sir, I am a poor fellow that would live.   185
ESCALUS: How would you live,° Pompey? By being a bawd? What do you
think of the trade, Pompey? Is it a lawful trade?
POMPEY: If the law would allow it, sir.
ESCALUS: But the law will not allow it, Pompey; nor it shall not be allowed
in Vienna.   190
POMPEY: Does your worship mean to geld and splay° all the youth of the
city?
ESCALUS: No, Pompey.
POMPEY: Truly, sir, in my poor opinion, they will to 't then. If your worship
will take order° for the drabs° and the knaves, you need not to fear the   195
bawds.
ESCALUS: There is pretty orders beginning, I can tell you. It is but heading°
and hanging.
POMPEY: If you head and hang all that offend that way but for ten year
together,° you'll be glad to give out a commission° for more heads. If this 200
law hold° in Vienna ten year, I'll rent the fairest house in it after° threepence a bay.° If you live to see this come to pass, say Pompey told you so.
ESCALUS: Thank you, good Pompey. And, in requital of° your prophey,
hark you: I advise you let me not find you before me again upon any complaint whatsoever; no, not for dwelling where you do. If I do, Pompey, I   205
shall beat you to your tent and prove a shrewd° Caesar° to you; in plain

---

175. taphouse: alehouse. drawn in: enticed. (Still another meaning of *draw*, line 171.)
183. color: disguise. 186. live: make a living. 191. splay: spay. 195. take order: take
measures. drabs: prostitutes. 197. but heading: neither more nor less than beheading.
199–200. year together: years at a stretch. 200. commission: order. 201. hold: remain
in force. after: at the rate of. 202. bay: division of a house included under one gable.
203. requital of: return for. 206. shrewd: harsh, severe. Caesar: (Escalus refers to Julius
Caesar's defeat of Pompey at Pharsalia in 48 B.C.E.)

dealing, Pompey, I shall have you whipped. So for this time, Pompey, fare
you well.

POMPEY: I thank your worship for your good counsel. [*Aside.*] But I shall
follow it as the flesh and fortune shall better determine.   210
Whip me? No, no, let carman° whip his jade.°
The valiant heart's not whipped out of his trade.   *Exit.*

ESCALUS: Come hither to me, Master Elbow; come hither, Master Constable. How long have you been in this place of constable?

ELBOW: Seven year and a half, sir.   215

ESCALUS: I thought, by your readiness° in the office, you had continued in
it some time. You say, seven years together?

ELBOW: And a half, sir.

ESCALUS: Alas, it hath been great pains to you. They do you wrong to put
you so oft upon 't. Are there not men in your ward sufficient° to serve it?   220

ELBOW: Faith, sir, few of any wit in such matters. As they are chosen, they
are glad to choose me for them.° I do it for some piece of money and go
through with all.°

ESCALUS: Look° you bring me in the names of some six or seven, the most
sufficient of your parish.   225

ELBOW: To your worship's house, sir?

ESCALUS: To my house. Fare you well.   [*Exit Elbow.*]
What's o'clock, think you?

JUSTICE: Eleven, sir.

ESCALUS: I pray you home to dinner° with me.   230

JUSTICE: I humbly thank you.

ESCALUS:
It grieves me for the death of Claudio;
But there's no remedy.

JUSTICE:
Lord Angelo is severe.

ESCALUS: It is but needful.
Mercy is not itself, that oft looks so;°   235
Pardon is still° the nurse of second woe.
But yet — poor Claudio! There is no remedy.
Come, sir.   *Exeunt.*

---

211. **carman:** one who drives a cart.   **jade:** broken-down horse.   216. **readiness:** proficiency,
alacrity.   220. **sufficient:** able.   222. **for them:** i.e., to take their place.   222–23. **go . . . all:**
i.e., perform my duties thoroughly.   224. **Look:** see to it that.   230. **dinner:** (Dinner was
customarily eaten just before midday.)   235. **Mercy . . . so:** i.e., what seems merciful may not
really be so (since it may encourage crime and hence lead to more punishment).   236. **still:**
always.

ACT 2, SCENE 2°

Enter Provost [and a] Servant.

SERVANT:
  He's hearing of a cause;° he will come straight.°
  I'll tell him of you.
PROVOST: Pray you, do. [*Exit Servant.*] I'll know
  His pleasure; maybe he will relent. Alas,
  He° hath but as offended° in a dream!
  All sects,° all ages° smack° of this vice — and he   5
  To die for 't!

Enter Angelo.

ANGELO: Now, what's the matter, Provost?
PROVOST:
  Is it your will Claudio shall die tomorrow?
ANGELO:
  Did not I tell thee yea? Hadst thou not order?
  Why dost thou ask again?
PROVOST: Lest I might be too rash.   10
  Under your good correction,° I have seen
  When, after execution, judgment hath
  Repented o'er his doom.°
ANGELO: Go to; let that be mine.°
  Do you your office, or give up your place,   15
  And you shall well be spared.°
PROVOST: I crave your honor's pardon.
  What shall be done, sir, with the groaning° Juliet?
  She's very near her hour.°
ANGELO: Dispose of her
  To some more fitter place, and that with speed.   20

[*Enter a Servant.*]

SERVANT:
  Here is the sister of the man condemned

ACT 2, SCENE 2. Location: Adjacent to the court of justice, perhaps at Angelo's official residence. 1. **hearing . . . cause:** listening to a case. **straight:** immediately. 4. **He:** i.e., Claudio. **but as offended:** offended only as if. 5. **sects:** classes of people, ranks. **ages:** i.e., ages of history or of life. **smack:** partake. 11. **Under . . . correction:** i.e., allow me to say. 13. **doom:** sentence. 14. **mine:** my business. 16. **well be spared:** easily be done without. 18. **groaning:** (With labor pains.) 19. **hour:** time of delivery.

Desires° access to you.

ANGELO: Hath he a sister?

PROVOST:

Ay, my good lord, a very virtuous maid,
And to be shortly of a sisterhood,
If not already.

ANGELO: Well, let her be admitted.   [*Exit Servant.*]   25
See you the fornicatress be removed.
Let her have needful but not lavish means.
There shall be order for 't.

Enter Lucio and Isabella.

PROVOST: Save° your honor!

ANGELO: [*to Provost*]
Stay a little while. [*To Isabella.*] You're welcome. What's your will?

ISABELLA:

I am a woeful suitor to your honor,   30
Please but your honor hear me.°

ANGELO: Well, what's your suit?

ISABELLA:

There is a vice that most I do abhor,
And most desire should meet the blow of justice,
For which I would not plead, but that I must;
For which I must not plead, but that I am   35
At war twixt will and will not.

ANGELO: Well, the matter?

ISABELLA:

I have a brother is condemned to die.
I do beseech you, let it be his fault,°
And not my brother.

PROVOST: [*aside*]   Heaven give thee moving graces!

ANGELO:

Condemn the fault, and not the actor of it?   40
Why, every fault's condemned ere it be done.
Mine were the very cipher of a function,
To fine the faults whose fine° stands in record°
And let go by the actor.

---

22. **Desires:** who desires.   28. **Save:** may God save.   31. **Please . . . me:** if only it will please you to hear me.   38. **let . . . fault:** i.e., let the fault die, be condemned.   43. **fine . . . fine:** punish . . . penalty.   **in record:** in the statutes.

ISABELLA: O just but severe law!   45
I had a brother, then. Heaven keep your honor!
LUCIO: [*aside to Isabella*]
Give 't not o'er so.° To him again, entreat him!
Kneel down before him; hang upon his gown.
You are too cold. If you should need a pin,°
You could not with more tame a tongue desire it.   50
To him, I say!
ISABELLA: [*to Angelo*]
Must he needs die?
ANGELO: Maiden, no remedy.
ISABELLA:
Yes, I do think that you might pardon him,
And neither heaven nor man grieve at the mercy.
ANGELO:
I will not do 't.
ISABELLA: But can you, if you would?   55
ANGELO:
Look what° I will not, that I cannot do.
ISABELLA:
But might you do 't, and do the world no wrong,
If so your heart were touched with that remorse°
As mine is to him?
ANGELO: He's sentenced. 'Tis too late.   60
LUCIO [*aside to Isabella*]   You are too cold.
ISABELLA:
Too late? Why, no; I that do speak a word
May call it back again. Well, believe this:
No ceremony that to great ones 'longs,°
Not the king's crown, nor the deputed sword,°   65
The marshal's truncheon,° nor the judge's robe,
Become them with one half so good a grace
As mercy does.
If he had been as you, and you as he,
You would have slipped like him; but he, like you,°   70
Would not have been so stern.

---

47. Give 't . . . so: don't give up so soon.   49. need a pin: i.e., ask for the smallest trifle.
56. Look what: whatever.   58. remorse: pity.   64. 'longs: is fitting, belongs.   65. deputed
sword: sword of justice entrusted to the ruler.   66. truncheon: staff borne by military officers.
70. like you: in your situation.

ANGELO: Pray you, begone.

ISABELLA:
   I would to heaven I had your potency,
   And you were Isabel! Should it then be thus?
   No, I would tell° what 'twere to be a judge
   And what a prisoner.

LUCIO: [aside to Isabella]   Ay, touch him; there's the vein.°   75

ANGELO:
   Your brother is a forfeit° of the law,
   And you but waste your words.

ISABELLA: Alas, alas!
   Why, all the souls that were were forfeit once,
   And He that might the vantage best have took
   Found out the remedy.° How would you be,   80
   If He, which is the top of judgment,° should
   But judge you as you are? O, think on that,
   And mercy then will breathe within your lips,
   Like man new-made.°

ANGELO: Be you content, fair maid.
   It is the law, not I, condemn your brother.   85
   Were he my kinsman, brother, or my son,
   It should be thus with him. He must die tomorrow.

ISABELLA:
   Tomorrow! O, that's sudden! Spare him, spare him!
   He's not prepared for death. Even for our kitchens
   We kill the fowl of season.° Shall we serve heaven   90
   With less respect than we do minister
   To our gross selves? Good, good my lord, bethink you:
   Who is it that hath died for this offense?
   There's many have committed it.

LUCIO: [aside to Isabella]   Ay, well said.

ANGELO:
   The law hath not been dead, though it hath slept.   95
   Those many had not dared to do that evil
   If the first that did th' edict infringe

---

74. **tell:** make known.   75. **there's the vein:** i.e., that's the right approach. (*Vein* means "lode to be profitably mined," or perhaps "vein for bloodletting.")   76. **a forfeit:** one who must incur the penalty.   78–80. **Why . . . remedy:** (A reference to God's redemption of sinful humanity when He would have been justified in destroying humankind.)   81. **top of judgment:** supreme judge.   84. **new-made:** i.e., created new by salvation, born again.   90. **of season:** that is in season and properly mature.

Had answered for his deed. Now 'tis awake,
Takes note of what is done, and like a prophet
Looks in a glass° that shows what future evils,   100
Either now, or by remissness new-conceived°
And so in progress° to be hatched and born,
Are now to have no successive degrees,°
But ere they live,° to end.

ISABELLA: Yet show some pity.

ANGELO:
I show it most of all when I show justice;   105
For then I pity those I do not know,
Which a dismissed° offense would after gall,°
And do him right that, answering° one foul wrong,
Lives not to act another. Be satisfied;
Your brother dies tomorrow. Be content.   110

ISABELLA:
So you must be the first that gives this sentence,
And he that suffers. O, it is excellent
To have a giant's strength, but it is tyrannous
To use it like a giant.

LUCIO: [aside to Isabella]   That's well said.

ISABELLA: Could great men thunder   115
As Jove himself does, Jove would never be quiet,°
For every pelting,° petty officer
Would use his heaven for thunder,
Nothing but thunder! Merciful Heaven,
Thou rather with thy sharp and sulfurous bolt°   120
Splits the unwedgeable° and gnarlèd oak
Than the soft myrtle; but man, proud man,
Dressed in a little brief authority,
Most ignorant of what he's most assured,
His glassy° essence,° like an angry ape°   125

---

100. **glass:** magic crystal.   101. **Either . . . new-conceived:** i.e., both evils already hatched
and those that would be encouraged by continued laxity of enforcement.   102. **in progress:** in
the course of time.   103. **successive degrees:** successors or future stages. (Future evils are to be
aborted before they are born and propagate.)   104. **ere they live:** i.e., before they can be committed.   107. **dismissed:** forgiven.   **gall:** irritate, injure.   108. **do . . . answering:** do justice
to that person who, by paying the penalty for.   116. **be quiet:** have any quiet.   117. **pelting:** paltry.   120. **bolt:** thunderbolt.   121. **unwedgeable:** unable to be split.   124–25. **of
what . . . essence:** i.e., of his own spiritual essence, his natural infirmity and need for God's
grace, something his faith should make him certain of.   125. **glassy:** i.e., reflected from God
but also fragile and illusory, like the image in a mirror.   **angry ape:** i.e., ludicrous buffoon.

Plays such fantastic tricks before high heaven
As makes the angels weep; who, with our spleens,°
Would all themselves laugh mortal.°

LUCIO: [*aside to Isabella*]
O, to him, to him, wench! He will relent.
He's coming,° I perceive 't.

PROVOST: [*aside*]   Pray heaven she win him!   130

ISABELLA:
We cannot weigh our brother with ourself.°
Great men may jest with saints; 'tis wit in them,
But in the less,° foul profanation.

LUCIO: [*aside to Isabella*]
Thou'rt i' the right, girl. More o' that.

ISABELLA:
That in the captain's but a choleric word°   135
Which in the soldier is flat blasphemy.°

LUCIO: [*aside to Isabella*]   Art advised° o' that? More on 't.°

ANGELO:
Why do you put these sayings upon me?°

ISABELLA:
Because authority, though it err like others,
Hath yet a kind of medicine in itself   140
That skins the vice o' the top.° Go to your bosom;
Knock there, and ask your heart what it doth know
That's like my brother's fault. If it confess
A natural guiltiness such as is his,
Let it not sound a thought upon your tongue   145
Against my brother's life.

ANGELO: [*aside*]   She speaks, and 'tis such sense
That my sense° breeds with it. — Fare you well.   [*He starts to go.*]

---

127. **with our spleens:** i.e., if they laughed at folly as we do. (The spleen was thought to be the seat of laughter.)   128. **themselves laugh mortal:** laugh themselves out of immortality (by indulging in uncharitable laughter).   130. **coming:** coming around.   131. **cannot . . . ourself:** cannot judge our fellow men by the same standards we blindly use in judging ourselves.   133. **in the less:** in ordinary persons (it is).   135. **That . . . word:** i.e., we treat the abusive language a commanding officer uses in anger merely as an outburst; we are indulgent toward the feelings of *great men.* (As in lines 131–33, Isabella's point seems to be that our judgments are biased by our inordinate regard for authority.)   136. **blasphemy:** defamation.   137. **advised:** informed, aware.   **on 't:** of it.   138. **put . . . me:** apply these sayings to me.   141. **skins . . . top:** covers over the sore with skin, leaving it unhealed. (The *medicine* of line 140 is thus only a palliative.)   147–48. **sense . . . sense:** import . . . sensuality.

ISABELLA: Gentle my lord,° turn back.

ANGELO:
I will bethink me.° Come again tomorrow.   150

ISABELLA:
Hark how I'll bribe you. Good my lord, turn back.

ANGELO: How? Bribe me?

ISABELLA:
Ay, with such gifts that° heaven shall share with you.

LUCIO: [aside to Isabella]   You had marred all else.°

ISABELLA:
Not with fond° sicles° of the tested° gold,   155
Or stones whose rate° are either rich or poor
As fancy values them, but with true prayers
That shall be up at heaven and enter there
Ere sunrise — prayers from preservèd° souls,
From fasting maids whose minds are dedicate°   160
To nothing temporal.

ANGELO: Well, come to me tomorrow.

LUCIO: [aside to Isabella]   Go to, 'tis well. Away!

ISABELLA:
Heaven keep your honor safe!

ANGELO [aside]   Amen!
For I am that way going to temptation,
Where prayers cross.°

ISABELLA: At what hour tomorrow   165
Shall I attend your lordship?

ANGELO: At any time 'fore noon.

ISABELLA: Save° your honor!   [Exeunt Isabella, Lucio, and Provost.]

ANGELO: From thee, even from thy virtue!
What's this, what's this? Is this her fault or mine?   170
The tempter or the tempted, who sins most, ha?
Not she, nor doth she tempt; but it is I
That, lying by the violet in the sun,
Do, as the carrion° does, not as the flower,

---

149. **Gentle my lord:** my noble lord.   150. **bethink me:** consider.   153. **that:** as.   154. **else:** otherwise.   155. **fond:** i.e., foolishly valued.   **sicles:** shekels (Hebrew coins).   **tested:** purest, tested by the touchstone.   156. **rate:** values.   159. **preservèd:** protected (from the world).   160. **dedicate:** dedicated.   165. **cross:** are at cross purposes.   168. **Save:** may God save.   174. **carrion:** decaying flesh.

Corrupt with virtuous season.° Can it be   175
That modesty° may more betray our sense°
Than woman's lightness?° Having waste ground enough,
Shall we desire to raze the sanctuary
And pitch our evils there?° O, fie, fie, fie!
What dost thou, or what art thou, Angelo?   180
Dost thou desire her foully for those things
That make her good? O, let her brother live!
Thieves for their robbery have authority
When judges steal themselves. What, do I love her,
That I desire to hear her speak again   185
And feast upon her eyes? What is 't I dream on?
O cunning enemy° that, to catch a saint,
With saints dost bait thy hook! Most dangerous
Is that temptation that doth goad us on
To sin in loving virtue. Never could the strumpet,   190
With all her double vigor — art and nature° —
Once stir my temper;° but this virtuous maid
Subdues me quite. Ever till now,
When men were fond,° I smiled and wondered how.   *Exit.*

ACT 2, SCENE 3°

Enter, [meeting,] Duke [disguised as a friar] and Provost.

DUKE:
Hail to you, Provost — so I think you are.
PROVOST:
I am the Provost. What's your will, good Friar?
DUKE:
Bound by my charity and my blest order,
I come to visit the afflicted spirits
Here in the prison. Do me the common right°   5

---

175. **Corrupt . . . season:** i.e., putrefy while all else flourishes. (The warmth of flowering time causes the violet, Isabella, to blossom but causes the carrion lying beside it, Angelo, to rot.)   176. **modesty:** virtue, chastity.   **sense:** sensual nature.   177. **lightness:** immodesty, lust.   179. **pitch our evils there:** i.e., erect a privy, not on *waste ground* (line 177), but on sanctified ground. (*Evils* also has the more common meaning of "wickedness.")   187. **enemy:** i.e., Satan.   191. **double . . . nature:** twofold power (of alluring men) through artifice and a sensuous nature.   192. **temper:** mental balance, temperament.   194. **fond:** foolishly in love.   ACT 2, SCENE 3. **Location:** A prison.   5. **common right:** i.e., right of all clerics.

To let me see them and to make me know
The nature of their crimes, that I may minister
To them accordingly.

PROVOST:
I would do more than that, if more were needful.

Enter Juliet.

Look, here comes one: a gentlewoman of mine,   10
Who, falling in the flaws° of her own youth,
Hath blistered her report.° She is with child,
And he that got° it, sentenced — a young man
More fit to do another such offense
Than die for this.   15

DUKE:
When must he die?

PROVOST: As I do think, tomorrow.
[*To Juliet.*] I have provided° for you. Stay awhile,
And you shall be conducted.°

DUKE:
Repent you, fair one, of the sin you carry?

JULIET:
I do, and bear the shame most patiently.   20

DUKE:
I'll teach you how you shall arraign° your conscience,
And try° your penitence, if it be sound
Or hollowly° put on.

JULIET: I'll gladly learn.

DUKE: Love you the man that wronged you?   25

JULIET:
Yes, as I love the woman that wronged him.

DUKE:
So then it seems your most offenseful act
Was mutually committed?

JULIET: Mutually.

DUKE:
Then was your sin of heavier kind than his.

---

11. **flaws:** sudden gusts (of passion).   12. **blistered her report:** marred her reputation.   13. **got:** begot.   17. **provided:** provided a place to stay.   18. **conducted:** taken there.   21. **arraign:** accuse.   22. **try:** test.   23. **hollowly:** falsely.

JULIET:
    I do confess it and repent it, Father.   30
DUKE:
    'Tis meet so,° daughter. But lest you do repent
    As that° the sin hath brought you to this shame,
    Which sorrow is always toward ourselves,° not heaven,
    Showing we would not spare heaven° as° we love it,
    But as we stand in fear —   35
JULIET:
    I do repent me as it is an evil,
    And take the shame with joy.
DUKE: There rest.°
    Your partner, as I hear, must die tomorrow,
    And I am going with instruction to him.
    Grace go with you. *Benedicite!*°   *Exit.* 40
JULIET:
    Must die tomorrow? O injurious law,
    That respites° me a life whose very comfort
    Is still a dying horror!°
PROVOST: 'Tis pity of° him.   *Exeunt.*

Act 2, Scene 4°

Enter Angelo.

ANGELO:
    When I would pray and think, I think and pray
    To several° subjects. Heaven hath my empty words,
    Whilst my invention,° hearing not my tongue,
    Anchors on Isabel; Heaven in my mouth,
    As if I did but only chew His° name,   5
    And in my heart the strong and swelling evil
    Of my conception.° The state,° whereon I studied,

---

31. 'Tis meet so: it is fitting that you do so. 32. As that: because. 33. toward ourselves: i.e., narrowly self-concerned rather than loving virtue for its own sake. 34. spare heaven: i.e., spare heaven the sorrow felt there for unconfessed sins; or, forbear to offend heaven. as: because. (Also in lines 35 and 36.) 37. There rest: hold fast to that truth. 40. *Benedicite:* blessings on you. 42. respites: prolongs, does not forfeit. (Juliet laments that her life is spared through Angelo's cruel kindness while Claudio's is not.) 42–43. whose . . . horror: whose greatest comfort will always be a deadly horror. 43. pity of: a pity about. ACT 2, SCENE 4. Location: Angelo's official residence. 2. several: separate. 3. invention: imagination. 5. His: i.e., Heaven's, God's. 7. conception: thought. The state: statecraft.

Is like a good thing, being often read,
Grown sere° and tedious. Yes, my gravity,
Wherein — let no man hear me — I take pride, 10
Could I with boot change for an idle plume,
Which the air beats for vain.° O place,° O form,°
How often dost thou with thy case,° thy habit,°
Wrench awe from fools and tie the wiser souls
To thy false seeming!° Blood, thou art blood.° 15
Let's write° "good angel"° on the devil's horn,
'Tis not the devil's crest.°

Enter Servant.

How now? Who's there?

SERVANT:
One Isabel, a sister, desires access to you.

ANGELO:
Teach° her the way. [*Exit Servant.*] O heavens!
Why does my blood thus muster to° my heart, 20
Making both it unable° for itself
And dispossessing all my other parts
Of necessary fitness?
So play° the foolish throngs with one that swoons,
Come all to help him, and so stop the air 25
By which he should revive; and even so
The general subject° to a well-wished° king
Quit their own part° and in obsequious fondness
Crowd to his presence, where their untaught° love
Must needs° appear offense.

Enter Isabella.

9. **sere:** withered, dry, old.   **11–12. Could . . . vain:** I could profitably exchange for a frivolous feather, one that the air beats in reproof of its vanity.   **12. place:** official position, rank.   **form:** dignity of office, ceremony.   **13. case:** mere outward appearance.   **habit:** garb. **14–15. Wrench . . . seeming:** intimidate ordinary foolish men and allure even the wise to the seeming virtue of authority.   **15. Blood . . . blood:** i.e., passions are inherent in human nature, under all these outward appearances.   **16. Let's write:** i.e., if we were to write.   **good angel:** (with a play on Angelo's name).   **17. 'Tis . . . crest:** that still would not make it a true sign of the devil's identity (i.e., it would not make the devil an angel merely to write "good angel" on his horn). The *crest* is an identifying emblem worn on the helmet or coat of arms. **19. Teach:** show.   **20. muster to:** assemble like soldiers in.   **21. unable:** ineffectual.   **24. play:** act.   **27. general subject:** i.e., commoners, subjects.   **well-wished:** attended by good wishes. **28. Quit . . . part:** abandon their proper function and (politely distant) place.   **29. untaught:** ignorant, unmannerly.   **30. Must needs:** will necessarily.

ANGELO: How now, fair maid?   30

ISABELLA: I am come to know your pleasure.

ANGELO:

That you might know it° would much better please me
Than to demand° what 'tis. Your brother cannot live.

ISABELLA:

Even so.° Heaven keep your honor!   [*She turns to leave.*]

ANGELO:

Yet may he live awhile; and, it may be,   35
As long as you or I. Yet he must die.

ISABELLA: Under your sentence?

ANGELO: Yea.

ISABELLA:

When, I beseech you? That in his reprieve,
Longer or shorter, he may be so fitted°   40
That his soul sicken not.

ANGELO:

Ha? Fie, these filthy vices! It were as good
To pardon him that hath from nature stolen
A man already made, as to remit
Their saucy sweetness that do coin heaven's image   45
In stamps that are forbid.° 'Tis all as easy
Falsely to take away a life true made
As to put metal° in restrainèd° means
To make a false one.

ISABELLA:

'Tis set down so in heaven, but not in earth.°   50

ANGELO:

Say you so? Then I shall pose° you quickly:
Which had you rather, that the most just law
Now took your brother's life, or, to redeem him,
Give up your body to such sweet uncleanness

---

32. **know it:** i.e., know my pleasure, my desire. (Angelo is thinking of his desire for Isabella; *know* suggests "have carnal knowledge.")   33. **Than to demand:** than for you to ask.   34. **Even so:** i.e., so be it.   40. **fitted:** prepared.   42–46. **It were . . . forbid:** one might as well pardon the murderer of a man already alive as pardon the wanton pleasures of those persons who produce illegitimate offspring, like counterfeit coiners. (*Heaven's image* is humankind, made in God's likeness; Genesis 1:27.)   48. **metal:** (with a play on *mettle,* a variant spelling, and as it is spelled in the Folio; i.e., substance).   **restrainèd:** prohibited, illicit.   50. **'Tis . . . earth:** i.e., equating murder and bastardizing accords with divine law but not with human law, according to which murder is more heinous.   51. **pose:** nonplus with a question.

As she that he hath stained?
ISABELLA: Sir, believe this,   55
I had rather give° my body than my soul.
ANGELO:
I talk not of your soul. Our compelled sins
Stand more for number than for account.°
ISABELLA: How say you?
ANGELO:
Nay, I'll not warrant that,° for I can speak
Against the thing I say. Answer to this: 60
I, now the voice of the recorded law,
Pronounce a sentence on your brother's life;
Might there not be a charity in sin
To save this brother's life?
ISABELLA: Please you° to do 't,
I'll take° it as a peril to my soul;   65
It is no sin at all, but charity.
ANGELO:
Pleased° you to do 't at peril of your soul
Were equal poise° of sin and charity.
ISABELLA:
That I do beg his life, if it be sin,
Heaven let me bear it! You granting of my suit,   70
If that be sin, I'll make it my morn prayer
To have it added to the faults of mine,
And nothing of your answer.°
ANGELO: Nay, but hear me.
Your sense pursues not mine. Either you are ignorant
Or seem so craftily; and that's not good.   75
ISABELLA:
Let me be ignorant, and in nothing good,
But graciously° to know I am no better.
ANGELO:
Thus wisdom wishes to appear most bright

56. **give:** i.e., give to death or punishment. (Isabella doesn't understand the drift of the question.)   57–58. **Our . . . account:** our sins committed under compulsion are recorded but not charged to our spiritual account.   59. **I'll . . . that:** i.e., I'm not necessarily endorsing the view I just expressed.   64. **Please you:** if you please.   65. **take:** accept.   67. **Pleased:** if it pleased.   68. **Were equal poise:** there would be equal balance.   73. **of your answer:** to which you will have to answer.   77. **graciously:** through divine grace.

When it doth tax itself,° as these° black masks
Proclaim an enshield° beauty ten times louder   80
Than beauty could, displayed. But mark me.
To be receivèd plain,° I'll speak more gross:°
Your brother is to die.
ISABELLA: So.
ANGELO:
And his offense is so, as it appears,   85
Accountant° to the law upon that pain.°
ISABELLA: True.
ANGELO:
Admit° no other way to save his life —
As I subscribe not that, nor any other,
But in the loss of question° — that you, his sister,   90
Finding yourself desired of° such a person
Whose credit with the judge, or own great place,
Could fetch your brother from the manacles
Of the all-binding law; and that there were
No earthly means to save him, but that either   95
You must lay down the treasures of your body
To this supposed,° or else to let him° suffer.
What would you do?
ISABELLA:
As much for my poor brother as myself:
That is, were I under the terms° of death,   100
Th' impression of keen whips I'd wear as rubies,
And strip myself to death as to a bed
That longing have been sick for,° ere I'd yield
My body up to shame.
ANGELO:
Then must your brother die.   105
ISABELLA:
And 'twere the cheaper way.

---

79. **tax itself:** accuse itself (of ignorance).   **these:** (Generically referring to any.)   80. **en-shield:** enshielded, protected from view behind the black masks.   82. **receivèd plain:** plainly understood.   **gross:** openly.   86. **Accountant:** accountable.   **pain:** penalty.   88. **Admit:** suppose.   89–90. **As . . . question:** since I will admit no alternative possibility in our discussion. (*Loss of question* means "forfeiting the terms of our debate.")   91. **of:** by.   97. **supposed:** hypothetical person.   **him:** i.e., Claudio.   100. **terms:** sentence.   103. **That . . . for:** i.e., that I have been sick with longing for. (Isabella's images are of love, death, and flagellation.)

Better it were a brother died at once°
Than that a sister, by redeeming him,
Should die forever.

ANGELO:
Were not you then as cruel as the sentence   110
That you have slandered so?

ISABELLA:
Ignomy° in ransom and free pardon
Are of two houses.° Lawful mercy
Is nothing° kin to foul redemption.

ANGELO:
You seemed of late to make the law a tyrant,   115
And rather proved° the sliding of your brother
A merriment than a vice.

ISABELLA:
O, pardon me, my lord. It oft falls out,
To have what we would have, we speak not what we mean.
I something° do excuse the thing I hate   120
For his advantage that I dearly love.

ANGELO:
We are all frail.

ISABELLA: Else let my brother die,
If not a fedary° but only he
Owe and succeed thy weakness.°

ANGELO: Nay, women are frail too.   125

ISABELLA:
Ay, as the glasses° where they view themselves,
Which are as easy broke as they make forms.°
Women? Help, Heaven! Men their creation mar
In profiting by them.° Nay, call us ten times frail,
For we are soft as our complexions° are,   130
And credulous to false prints.°

---

107. **died at once:** should die once for all, rather than *die forever* (line 109) in the death of the soul through sin. 112. **Ignomy:** ignominy. 113. **of two houses:** i.e., unrelated. 114. **nothing:** not at all. 116. **proved:** argued. 120. **something:** to some extent. 123. **fedary:** confederate, companion who is equally guilty. 124. **Owe . . . weakness:** possess and inherit the weakness you speak of, or the weakness to which all men as a class are prone. (Isabella argues that Claudio should die only if he is the only man who is frail.) 126. **glasses:** mirrors. 127. **forms:** (1) images (2) copies of themselves, i.e., children. 128–29. **Men . . . them:** men mar their creation in God's likeness by taking advantage of women. 130. **complexions:** constitutions, appearance. 131. **credulous . . . prints:** susceptible to false impressions. (The metaphor is from the stamping of metal.)

ANGELO: I think it well.
And from this testimony of° your own sex —
Since I suppose we° are made to be no stronger
Than° faults may shake our frames — let me be bold.
I do arrest your words.° Be that you are,   135
That° is, a woman; if you be more, you're none.°
If you be one, as you are well expressed°
By all external warrants, show it now
By putting on the destined livery.°

ISABELLA:
I have no tongue° but one. Gentle my lord,   140
Let me entreat you speak the former° language.

ANGELO: Plainly conceive, I love you.

ISABELLA: My brother did love Juliet,
And you tell me that he shall die for 't.

ANGELO:
He shall not, Isabel, if you give me love.   145

ISABELLA:
I know your virtue hath a license in 't,
Which seems a little fouler than it is
To pluck on others.°

ANGELO: Believe me, on mine honor,
My words express my purpose.

ISABELLA:
Ha! Little honor to be much believed,   150
And most pernicious purpose! Seeming, seeming!
I will proclaim thee, Angelo, look for 't!
Sign me a present° pardon for my brother,
Or with an outstretched throat I'll tell the world aloud
What man thou art.

ANGELO: Who will believe thee, Isabel?   155
My unsoiled name, th' austereness of my life,
My vouch° against you, and my place i' the state

---

132. **of:** about.   133. **we:** i.e., men and women.   134. **Than:** than that.   135. **arrest your words:** take what you have said and hold you to it.   136. **That:** what.   **if . . . none:** i.e., if you claim to be perfect, you are no longer a woman as we have defined that term.   137. **expressed:** shown to be.   139. **putting . . . livery:** i.e., assuming the characteristic frailty that all women possess.   140. **tongue:** language.   141. **former:** i.e., customary.   146–48. **your . . . others:** i.e., you, although virtuous, are pretending foul purposes in order to mislead (*pluck on*) me.   153. **present:** immediate.   157. **vouch:** testimony.

Will so your accusation overweigh
That you shall stifle in your own report
And smell of calumny.° I have begun,   160
And now I give my sensual race° the rein.
Fit thy consent to my sharp appetite;
Lay by° all nicety° and prolixious° blushes
That banish what they sue for.° Redeem thy brother
By yielding up thy body to my will,   165
Or else he must not only die the death,°
But thy unkindness shall his death draw out
To ling'ring sufferance.° Answer me tomorrow,
Or, by the affection° that now guides me most,
I'll prove a tyrant to him. As for you,   170
Say what you can, my false o'erweighs your true.   *Exit.*

ISABELLA:
To whom should I complain? Did I tell° this,
Who would believe me? O perilous mouths,
That bear in them one and the selfsame tongue,
Either of condemnation or approof,°   175
Bidding the law make curtsy to their will,
Hooking° both right and wrong to th' appetite,
To follow as it draws!° I'll to my brother.
Though he hath fall'n by prompture° of the blood,
Yet hath he in him such a mind of honor   180
That, had he twenty heads to tender down°
On twenty bloody blocks, he'd yield them up
Before his sister should her body stoop
To such abhorred pollution.
Then, Isabel, live chaste, and, brother, die;   185
More than our brother is our chastity.
I'll tell him yet of Angelo's request,
And fit his mind to death, for his soul's rest.   *Exit.*

---

160. **calumny:** slander.   161. **race:** natural or inherited disposition (with a probable quibble on "horse race").   163. **by:** aside. **nicety:** coyness, reserve. **prolixious:** time-wasting.   164. **banish . . . for:** (1) i.e., seem to repulse the sensual pleasure you must really want, or (2) banish all hope of saving Claudio.   166. **die the death:** be put to death.   168. **sufferance:** torture.   169. **affection:** passion.   172. **Did I tell:** if I told.   175. **approof:** approval, sanction.   177. **Hooking:** attaching.   178. **as it draws:** wherever it drags.   179. **prompture:** prompting, suggestion.   181. **tender down:** lay down in payment.

ACT 3, SCENE 1°

Enter Duke [disguised as before], Claudio, and Provost.

DUKE:
So then you hope of pardon from Lord Angelo?
CLAUDIO:
The miserable have no other medicine
But only hope.
I have hope to live and am prepared to die.
DUKE:
Be absolute for death. Either death or life   5
Shall thereby be the sweeter. Reason thus with life:
If I do lose thee, I do lose a thing
That none but fools would keep. A breath thou art,
Servile to all the skyey influences°
That dost this habitation° where thou keep'st°   10
Hourly afflict. Merely,° thou art death's fool,
For him thou labor'st by thy flight to shun,
And yet runn'st toward him still.° Thou art not noble,
For all th' accommodations° that thou bear'st
Are nursed by baseness.° Thou'rt by no means valiant,   15
For thou dost fear the soft and tender fork°
Of a poor worm.° Thy best of rest is sleep,
And that thou oft provok'st,° yet grossly fear'st
Thy death, which is no more. Thou art not thyself,
For thou exists on many a thousand grains   20
That issue out of dust. Happy thou art not,
For what thou hast not, still thou striv'st to get,
And what thou hast, forget'st. Thou art not certain,°
For thy complexion° shifts to strange effects,°
After° the moon. If thou art rich, thou'rt poor,   25
For, like an ass whose back with ingots bows,
Thou bear'st thy heavy riches but a journey,
And death unloads thee. Friend hast thou none,

ACT 3, SCENE 1. Location: The prison. 9. **skyey influences:** influence of the stars. 10. **this habitation:** i.e., the earth (and the body as well). **keep'st:** dwell. 11. **Merely:** utterly, only. 13. **still:** always. 14. **accommodations:** conveniences, civilized comforts. 15. **nursed by baseness:** nurtured by ignoble means. 16. **fork:** forked tongue. 17. **worm:** (1) snake (2) grave worm. 18. **thou oft provok'st:** you often invoke, summon. 23. **certain:** steadfast. 24. **complexion:** constitution. **strange effects:** new appearances, manifestations. 25. **After:** in obedience to, under the influence of.

For thine own bowels° which do call thee sire,
The mere° effusion of thy proper° loins,   30
Do curse the gout, serpigo,° and the rheum°
For ending thee no sooner. Thou hast nor youth° nor age,
But as it were an after-dinner's° sleep
Dreaming on both, for all thy blessèd youth
Becomes as agèd° and doth beg the alms   35
Of palsied eld;° and, when thou art old and rich,
Thou hast neither heat,° affection,° limb, nor beauty
To make thy riches pleasant. What's yet in this
That bears the name of life? Yet in this life
Lie hid more thousand deaths; yet death we fear,   40
That makes these odds all even.°
CLAUDIO: I humbly thank you.
To sue° to live, I find I seek to die,
And, seeking death, find life. Let it come on.

Enter Isabella.

ISABELLA:
What, ho! Peace here; grace and good company!°
PROVOST:
Who's there? Come in. The wish deserves a welcome.   45
                                        [*He goes to greet her.*]
DUKE: [*to Claudio*]
Dear sir, ere long I'll visit you again.
CLAUDIO: Most holy sir, I thank you.
ISABELLA:
My business is a word or two with Claudio.
PROVOST:
And very welcome. — Look, signor, here's your sister.
DUKE: [*aside to the Provost*]   Provost, a word with you.   50
PROVOST: As many as you please.
DUKE:
Bring me to hear them speak, where I may be
Concealed.   [*The Duke and the Provost withdraw.*]

---

29. **bowels:** i.e., offspring. 30. **mere:** very. **proper:** own. 31. **serpigo:** a skin eruption.
rheum: catarrh. 32. **nor youth:** neither youth. 33. **after-dinner's:** i.e., afternoon's. 35. **as
agèd:** like old age, having to depend on it. (Youth is penniless and dependent on the aged,
whereas the old lack the physical capacity of youth.) 36. **eld:** old age. 37. **heat:** vigor.
affection: passion. 41. **makes . . . even:** makes all equal. 42. **To sue:** suing. 44. **grace . . .**
company: may God's grace and the companionship of the angels be yours.

CLAUDIO: Now, sister, what's the comfort?
ISABELLA: Why,
    As all comforts are: most good, most good indeed.
    Lord Angelo, having affairs to heaven,   55
    Intends you for his swift ambassador,
    Where you shall be an everlasting leiger.°
    Therefore your best appointment° make with speed;
    Tomorrow you set on.°
CLAUDIO: Is there no remedy?
ISABELLA:
    None but such remedy as, to save a head,   60
    To cleave a heart in twain.
CLAUDIO: But is there any?
ISABELLA:
    Yes, brother, you may live.
    There is a devilish mercy in the judge,
    If you'll implore it, that will free your life   65
    But fetter you till death.
CLAUDIO: Perpetual durance?°
ISABELLA:
    Ay, just;° perpetual durance, a restraint,
    Though all the world's vastidity you had,
    To a determined scope.°
CLAUDIO: But in what nature?
ISABELLA:
    In such a one as, you consenting to 't,   70
    Would bark° your honor from that trunk you bear
    And leave you naked.
CLAUDIO: Let me know the point.
ISABELLA:
    O, I do fear° thee, Claudio, and I quake
    Lest thou a feverous° life shouldst entertain,°
    And six or seven winters more respect°   75
    Than a perpetual honor. Dar'st thou die?
    The sense of death is most in apprehension,°

---

57. **leiger:** resident ambassador.   58. **appointment:** preparation.   59. **set on:** set forward.
66. **durance:** imprisonment.   67. **just:** just so.   67–69. **a restraint . . . scope:** a confinement
to fixed limits or bounds (i.e., to certain damnation and perpetual remorse for the sinful bargain
you had struck), even if you had the entire vastness of the world to wander in.   71. **bark:** strip
off (as one strips bark from a tree *trunk*).   73. **fear:** fear for.   74. **feverous:** feverish.   **entertain:** maintain, desire.   75. **respect:** value.   77. **apprehension:** anticipation.

And the poor beetle that we tread upon
In corporal sufferance finds a pang as great
As when a giant dies.   80

CLAUDIO:
Why give you me this shame?
Think you I can a resolution° fetch°
From flowery tenderness?° If I must die,
I will encounter darkness as a bride
And hug it in mine arms.   85

ISABELLA:
There spake my brother! There my father's grave
Did utter forth a voice. Yes, thou must die.
Thou art too noble to conserve a life
In base appliances.° This outward-sainted° deputy,
Whose settled visage° and deliberate word   90
Nips youth i' the head,° and follies doth enew°
As falcon doth the fowl, is yet a devil;
His filth within being cast,° he would appear
A pond as deep as hell.

CLAUDIO: The prenzie° Angelo?

ISABELLA:
O, 'tis the cunning livery of hell,   95
The damned'st body to invest and cover
In prenzie guards!° Dost thou think,° Claudio:
If I would yield him my virginity,
Thou mightst be freed!

CLAUDIO: O heavens, it cannot be.

ISABELLA:
Yes, he would give 't thee,° from° this rank offense,   100
So to offend him still.° This night's the time
That I should do what I abhor to name,
Or else thou diest tomorrow.

---

82. **resolution:** fixity of purpose. **fetch:** derive. 83. **flowery tenderness:** i.e., comforting figures of speech. 89. **In base appliances:** by means of ignoble devices, remedies. **outward-sainted:** outwardly holy. 90. **settled visage:** composed features. 91. **Nips . . . head:** i.e., strikes at the head, like a falcon swooping upon its prey. **enew:** drive prey down into the water or into covert. 93. **cast:** vomited; cleared out; reckoned up (?). 94, 97. **prenzie:** (A word unknown elsewhere, perhaps meaning "princely" or "precise.") 95–97. **'tis . . . guards:** it is the cunning disguise of the devil to clothe and conceal the wickedest man imaginable in decorously proper trimmings. 97. **Dost thou think:** i.e., would you believe. 100. **give 't thee:** i.e., grant you license. **from:** in return for, as a result of. 101. **So . . . still:** i.e., to continue with your fornication.

CLAUDIO: Thou shalt not do 't.

ISABELLA: O, were it but my life,   105
I'd throw it down for your deliverance
As frankly° as a pin.

CLAUDIO: Thanks, dear Isabel.

ISABELLA:
Be ready, Claudio, for your death tomorrow.

CLAUDIO:
Yes. Has he affections° in him,
That thus can make him bite the law by the nose°   110
When he would force° it? Sure it is no sin,
Or of the deadly seven it is the least.

ISABELLA: Which is the least?

CLAUDIO:
If it were damnable, he being so wise,
Why would he for the momentary trick°   115
Be perdurably fined?° O Isabel!

ISABELLA:
What says my brother?

CLAUDIO: Death is a fearful thing.

ISABELLA: And shamèd life a hateful.

CLAUDIO:
Ay, but to die, and go we know not where,
To lie in cold obstruction° and to rot,   120
This sensible° warm motion° to become
A kneaded clod,° and the delighted spirit°
To bathe in fiery floods, or to reside
In thrilling° region of thick-ribbèd ice;
To be imprisoned in the viewless° winds   125
And blown with restless violence round about
The pendent° world; or to be worse than worst
Of those that lawless and incertain thought°
Imagine howling — 'tis too horrible!

---

107. frankly: freely. 109. affections: passions. 110. bite . . . nose: i.e., flout the law. 111. force: enforce. (Claudio wonders that lust can drive Angelo to make a mockery of the law even while seeking to enforce it.) 115. trick: trifle. 116. perdurably fined: everlastingly punished. 120. obstruction: cessation of vital functions. 121. sensible: endowed with feeling. motion: organism. 122. kneaded clod: shapeless lump of earth. delighted spirit: spirit attended with delight; or, beloved spirit. 124. thrilling: piercingly cold. 125. viewless: invisible. 127. pendent: hanging in space. (A Ptolemaic concept.) 128. lawless . . . thought: i.e., wild conjecture.

The weariest and most loathèd worldly life 130
That age, ache, penury,° and imprisonment
Can lay on nature is a paradise
To° what we fear of death.
ISABELLA: Alas, alas!
CLAUDIO: Sweet sister, let me live. 135
What sin you do to save a brother's life,
Nature dispenses with° the deed so far
That it becomes a virtue.
ISABELLA: O you beast!
O faithless coward! O dishonest° wretch!
Wilt thou be made a man out of my vice? 140
Is 't not a kind of incest, to take life
From thine own sister's shame? What should I think?
Heaven shield° my mother played my father fair!
For such a warpèd slip of wilderness°
Ne'er issued from his blood. Take my defiance, 145
Die, perish! Might but° my bending down
Reprieve thee from thy fate, it should proceed.
I'll pray a thousand prayers for thy death,
No word to save thee.
CLAUDIO:
Nay, hear me, Isabel.
ISABELLA: O, fie, fie, fie! 150
Thy sin's not accidental,° but a trade.°
Mercy to thee would prove itself a bawd;°
'Tis best that thou diest quickly.
CLAUDIO: O, hear me, Isabella!

[*The Duke comes forward.*]

DUKE:
Vouchsafe° a word, young sister, but one word. 155
ISABELLA: What is your will?
DUKE: Might you dispense with your leisure, I would by and by have some
speech with you. The satisfaction I would require° is likewise your own
benefit.

---

131. **penury:** extreme poverty.   133. **To:** compared to.   137. **dispenses with:** grants a dispensa-
tion for, excuses.   139. **dishonest:** dishonorable.   143. **shield:** forfend, forbid.   144. **warpèd
. . . wilderness:** perverse, licentious scion, one that reverts to the original wild stock.   146. **but:**
merely.   151. **accidental:** casual.   **trade:** established habit.   152. **prove . . . bawd:** i.e., provide opportunity for sexual license.   155. **Vouchsafe:** allow.   158. **require:** ask.

ISABELLA: I have no superfluous leisure — my stay must be stolen out of   160
other affairs — but I will attend° you awhile.   [*She walks apart.*]
DUKE: Son, I have overheard what hath passed between you and your sister. Angelo had never the purpose to corrupt her; only he hath° made an
assay° of her virtue to practice his judgment with the disposition of
natures.° She, having the truth of honor in her, hath made him that   165
gracious° denial which he is most glad to receive. I am confessor to
Angelo, and I know this to be true; therefore prepare yourself to death.
Do not satisfy your resolution with hopes that are fallible. Tomorrow you
must die. Go to your knees and make ready.
CLAUDIO: Let me ask my sister pardon. I am so out of love with life that I   170
will sue to be rid of it.
DUKE: Hold you there.° Farewell. [*Claudio retires.*] Provost, a word with you.

[*The Provost comes forward.*]

PROVOST: What's your will, Father?
DUKE: That now you are come, you will be gone. Leave me awhile with
the maid. My mind promises with my habit° no loss shall touch her by   175
my company.
PROVOST: In good time.°   *Exit [Provost with Claudio].*

[*Isabella comes forward.*]

DUKE: The hand that hath made you fair hath made you good. The goodness that is cheap in beauty makes beauty brief in goodness;° but grace,
being the soul of your complexion,° shall keep the body of it ever fair.   180
The assault that Angelo hath made to you, fortune hath conveyed to my
understanding; and, but that° frailty hath examples° for his falling, I
should wonder at Angelo. How will you do to content this substitute°
and to save your brother?
ISABELLA: I am now going to resolve him.° I had rather my brother die by   185
the law than my son should be unlawfully born. But, O, how much is the
good Duke deceived in Angelo! If ever he return and I can speak to him,
I will open my lips in vain, or discover his government.°

---

161. attend: await; listen to.   163. only he hath: he has only.   164. assay: test.   164–65. to
practice . . . natures: to test his ability to judge and control people's characters.   166. gracious: virtuous.   172. Hold you there: hold fast to that resolution.   175. with my habit: as
well as my priestly garb (that).   177. In good time: i.e., very well.   178–79. The goodness . . .
in goodness: i.e., the physical graces that come easily with beauty make beauty soon cease to be
morally good.   180. complexion: character and appearance.   182. but that: were it not that.
examples: precedents.   183. this substitute: i.e., the deputy, Angelo.   185. resolve him: set
his mind at rest.   188. discover his government: i.e., expose Angelo's misconduct.

DUKE: That shall not be much amiss. Yet, as the matter now stands, he will avoid° your accusation; he made° trial of you only. Therefore fasten your   190
ear on my advisings. To the love I have in doing good a remedy presents itself. I do make myself believe that you may most uprighteously do a poor wronged lady a merited benefit, redeem your brother from the angry law, do no stain to your own gracious person, and much please the absent Duke, if peradventure he shall ever return to have hearing of this   195
business.

ISABELLA: Let me hear you speak farther. I have spirit° to do anything that appears not foul in the truth° of my spirit.°

DUKE: Virtue is bold, and goodness never fearful.° Have you not heard speak of Mariana, the sister of Frederick, the great soldier who miscar-   200
ried at sea?

ISABELLA: I have heard of the lady, and good words went with her name.

DUKE: She should this Angelo have married,° was° affianced to her by oath, and the nuptial appointed; between which time of the contract and limit of the solemnity,° her brother Frederick was wrecked at sea, having in   205
that perished vessel the dowry of his sister. But mark how heavily this befell to the poor gentlewoman. There she lost a noble and renowned brother, in his love toward her ever most kind and natural; with him, the portion and sinew° of her fortune, her marriage dowry; with both, her combinate husband,° this well-seeming Angelo.   210

ISABELLA: Can this be so? Did Angelo so leave her?

DUKE: Left her in her tears, and dried not one of them with his comfort; swallowed his vows whole, pretending° in her° discoveries of dishonor; in few,° bestowed her on her own lamentation,° which she yet wears° for his sake; and he, a marble to° her tears, is washed with them but relents not.   215

ISABELLA: What a merit were it in death to take this poor maid from the world! What corruption in this life, that it will let this man live! But how out of this can she avail?°

DUKE: It is a rupture that you may easily heal, and the cure of it not only saves your brother but keeps you from dishonor in doing it.   220

ISABELLA: Show me how, good Father.

---

190. **avoid:** evade, refute.   **he made:** i.e., he will say that he made.   197. **spirit:** courage.
198. **truth:** righteousness.   **spirit:** soul.   199. **fearful:** afraid.   203. **She . . . married:** Angelo was supposed to have married her.   **was:** i.e., he was.   204–05. **limit . . . solemnity:** date set for the ceremony.   209. **sinew:** i.e., mainstay.   210. **combinate husband:** i.e., betrothed.
213. **pretending:** falsely alleging.   **in her:** i.e., to have found in her.   214. **in few:** in short.
bestowed . . . lamentation: left her to her grief (with quibble on *bestowed*, meaning "gave in marriage").   **wears:** i.e., carries in her heart.   215. **a marble to:** i.e., unmoved by.   218. **avail:** benefit.

DUKE: This forenamed maid hath yet in her the continuance of her first affection; his unjust unkindness, that in all reason should have quenched her love, hath, like an impediment in the current, made it more violent and unruly. Go you to Angelo; answer his requiring with a plausible obedience; agree with his demands to the point.° Only refer yourself to this advantage:° first, that your stay with him may not be long, that the time may have all shadow° and silence in it, and the place answer to convenience. This being granted in course — and now follows all — we shall advise this wronged maid to stead up your appointment,° go in your place. If the encounter acknowledge itself hereafter,° it may compel him to her recompense. And here, by this, is your brother saved, your honor untainted, the poor Mariana advantaged, and the corrupt deputy scaled.° The maid will I frame° and make fit for his attempt. If you think well to carry this as you may, the doubleness of the benefit defends the deceit from reproof. What think you of it?   225   230   235

ISABELLA: The image of it gives me content already, and I trust it will grow to a most prosperous perfection.

DUKE: It lies much in your holding up.° Haste you speedily to Angelo. If for this night he entreat you to his bed, give him promise of satisfaction. I will presently to Saint Luke's; there, at the moated grange,° resides this dejected Mariana. At that place call upon me; and dispatch° with Angelo, that it may be quickly.   240

ISABELLA: I thank you for this comfort. Fare you well, good Father.

Exit. [The Duke remains.]

Act 3, Scene 2°

Enter [to the Duke] Elbow, Clown [Pompey, and] officers.

ELBOW: Nay, if there be no remedy for it but that you will needs buy and sell men and women like beasts, we shall have all the world drink brown and white bastard.°

DUKE: O heavens, what stuff is here?

---

226. **to the point:** precisely.   226–27. **refer . . . advantage:** obtain these conditions.   228. **shadow:** darkness, secrecy.   230. **stead . . . appointment:** go in your stead.   231. **If the . . . hereafter:** i.e., if she should become pregnant.   233. **scaled:** weighed (and found wanting). 234. **frame:** prepare.   239. **holding up:** ability to carry it off.   241. **moated grange:** country house surrounded by a ditch.   242. **dispatch:** settle, conclude (business).   ACT 3, SCENE 2. **Location:** Scene continues. The Duke remains onstage.   3. **bastard:** sweet Spanish wine. (Used quibblingly.)

POMPEY: 'Twas never merry world since, of two usuries,° the merriest was   5
    put down, and the worser allowed by order of law a furred gown° to keep
    him warm, and furred with fox on lambskins too, to signify that craft,
    being richer than innocency, stands for the facing.°
ELBOW: Come your way, sir. — Bless you, good Father Friar.
DUKE: And you, good Brother Father.° What offense hath this man made   10
    you, sir?
ELBOW: Marry, sir, he hath offended the law; and, sir, we take him to be a
    thief too, sir, for we have found upon him, sir, a strange picklock,° which
    we have sent to the deputy.
DUKE: [*to Pompey*]
    Fie, sirrah, a bawd, a wicked bawd!   15
    The evil that thou causest to be done,
    That is thy means to live. Do thou but think
    What 'tis to cram a maw° or clothe a back
    From such a filthy vice; say to thyself,
    From their abominable and beastly touches°   20
    I drink, I eat, array myself, and live.
    Canst thou believe thy living is a life,
    So stinkingly depending?° Go mend, go mend.
POMPEY: Indeed, it does stink in some sort, sir. But yet, sir, I would
    prove° —   25
DUKE:
    Nay, if the devil have given thee proofs for° sin,
    Thou wilt prove° his. — Take him to prison, officer.
    Correction and instruction must both work
    Ere this rude beast will profit.
ELBOW: He must° before the deputy,° sir; he has given his warning. The   30
    deputy cannot abide a whoremaster. If he be a whoremonger and comes
    before him, he were as good go a mile on his errand.°

---

5. **two usuries:** i.e., moneylending (the *worser*) and procuring for fornication (the *merriest*), both of which yield increase.   6. **furred gown:** (Characteristic attire of usurers.)   8. **stands . . . facing:** represents the outer covering. (Fox symbolizes *craft* or craftiness, lambskin, *innocency*.)   10. **Brother Father:** (The Duke's retort to Elbow's *Father Friar,* i.e., Father Brother.)   13. **strange picklock:** (referring to a chastity belt).   18. **cram a maw:** fill a stomach.   20. **touches:** sexual encounters.   23. **depending:** supported.   25. **prove:** i.e., argue, demonstrate.   26. **proofs for:** arguments in defense of.   27. **prove:** turn out to be.   30. **must:** must go.   **deputy:** i.e., Angelo (though Escalus gave Pompey the warning).   32. **he . . . errand:** i.e., he will have a hard road to travel.

DUKE:
That° we were all, as some would seem to be,
From our faults, as faults from seeming, free!°

Enter Lucio.

ELBOW: His neck will come to your waist — a cord,° sir.   35

POMPEY: I spy comfort, I cry bail. Here's a gentleman and a friend of mine.

LUCIO: How now, noble Pompey? What, at the wheels of Caesar?° Art thou led in triumph? What, is there none of Pygmalion's images,° newly made woman, to be had now, for putting the hand in the pocket and 40 extracting it clutched?° What reply, ha? What sayst thou to this tune, matter, and method? Is 't not drowned i' the last rain,° ha? What sayst thou, trot?° Is the world as it was, man? Which is the way? Is it sad, and few words?° Or how? The trick° of it?

DUKE: Still thus, and thus; still worse!   45

LUCIO: How doth my dear morsel, thy mistress? Procures she still, ha?

POMPEY: Troth, sir, she hath eaten up all her beef,° and she is herself in the tub.°

LUCIO: Why, 'tis good. It is the right of it, it must be so. Ever your fresh whore and your powdered bawd;° an unshunned° consequence, it must be 50 so. Art going to prison, Pompey?

POMPEY: Yes, faith, sir.

LUCIO: Why, 'tis not amiss, Pompey. Farewell. Go, say I sent thee thither. For debt, Pompey? Or how?

ELBOW: For being a bawd, for being a bawd.   55

LUCIO: Well, then, imprison him. If imprisonment be the due of a bawd, why, 'tis his right. Bawd is he doubtless, and of antiquity° too; bawd-born.°

---

33. That: would that.   **34. From . . . free:** i.e., free from faults, and our faults free from dissembling.   **35. His . . . cord:** i.e., he is likely to hang by a cord like that around your waist. (The Duke is habited like a friar.)   **38. Caesar:** (who defeated Pompey at Pharsalia and led his sons in triumph after defeating them at Munda).   **39. Pygmalion's images:** i.e., prostitutes, so called because they were "painted" with cosmetics like a painted statue. (Pygmalion was a sculptor, according to legend, whose female statue came to life "newly made.")   **41. clutched:** i.e., with money in it (but also with sexual suggestion).   **41–42. What sayst . . . rain:** i.e., what do you say now to this latest turn of events? Are our prospects a little dampened?   **43. trot:** old bawd.   **43–44. Which . . . words?:** i.e., what is the latest fashion? Is melancholy now in vogue? (A wry comment on Pompey's silence.)   **44. trick:** fashion.   **47. eaten . . . beef:** i.e., run through all her prostitutes.   **47–48. in the tub:** being treated for venereal disease by the sweating-tub treatment (much as beef was salted down in a tub to preserve it).   **49–50. Ever . . . bawd:** i.e., it always happens that young whores turn into old bawds, "powdered" like beef in a tub and caked with cosmetics.   **50. unshunned:** unshunnable, unavoidable.   **57. antiquity:** long continuance.   **bawd-born:** a born bawd and born of a bawd.

Farewell, good Pompey. Commend me to the prison, Pompey. You will
turn good husband° now, Pompey; you will keep the house.°

POMPEY: I hope, sir, your good worship will be my bail. 60

LUCIO: No, indeed, will I not, Pompey; it is not the wear.° I will pray,
Pompey, to increase your bondage. If you take it not patiently, why, your
mettle is the more.° Adieu, trusty Pompey. — Bless you, Friar.

DUKE: And you.

LUCIO: Does Bridget paint° still, Pompey, ha? 65

ELBOW: [to Pompey] Come your ways,° sir, come.

POMPEY: [to Lucio] You will not bail me, then, sir?

LUCIO: Then,° Pompey, nor now. — What news abroad, Friar? What news?

ELBOW: Come your ways, sir, come.

LUCIO: Go to kennel, Pompey, go. [Exeunt Elbow, Pompey, and Officers.] What 70
news, Friar, of the Duke?

DUKE: I know none. Can you tell me of any?

LUCIO: Some say he is with the Emperor of Russia; other some,° he is in
Rome. But where is he, think you?

DUKE: I know not where; but wheresoever, I wish him well. 75

LUCIO: It was a mad fantastical trick of him to steal° from the state and
usurp the beggary° he was never born to. Lord Angelo dukes it well in his
absence; he puts transgression to 't.°

DUKE: He does well in 't.

LUCIO: A little more lenity to lechery would do no harm in him. Some- 80
thing° too crabbed° that way, Friar.

DUKE: It is too general a vice, and severity must cure it.

LUCIO: Yes, in good sooth, the vice is of a great kindred;° it is well allied.
But it is impossible to extirp° it quite, Friar, till eating and drinking be
put down. They say this Angelo was not made by man and woman after° 85
this downright° way of creation. Is it true, think you?

DUKE: How should he be made, then?

LUCIO: Some report a sea maid° spawned him; some, that he was begot
between two stockfishes.° But it is certain that when he makes water his

---

59. **good husband:** thrifty manager. **keep the house:** stay indoors (with pun on the pimp's
function as doorkeeper). 61. **wear:** fashion. 62–63. **your . . . more:** (1) your spirit is revealed
all the more (2) your shackles will be made heavier (playing on *mettle/metal*). 65. **paint:** use
cosmetics. 66. **Come your ways:** come along. 68. **Then:** neither then. 73. **other some:**
some others. 76. **steal:** steal away. 77. **beggary:** i.e., status of a wanderer or traveler (with
unconscious ironic appropriateness; Lucio clearly does not see through the Duke's disguise as a
mendicant friar). 78. **puts . . . to 't:** puts lawbreaking under severe restraint. 80–81. **Something:** somewhat. 81. **crabbed:** harsh. 83. **kindred:** i.e., family, numerous and well connected.
84. **extirp:** eradicate. 85. **after:** in accordance with. 86. **downright:** straightforward, usual.
88. **sea maid:** mermaid. 89. **stockfishes:** dried codfish.

urine is congealed ice; that I know to be true. And he is a motion un- 90
generative;° that's infallible.

DUKE: You are pleasant,° sir, and speak apace.°

LUCIO: Why, what a ruthless thing is this in him, for the rebellion of a
codpiece° to take away the life of a man! Would the Duke that is absent
have done this? Ere he would have hanged a man for the getting a hun- 95
dred bastards, he would have paid for the nursing a thousand. He had
some feeling of the sport; he knew the service,° and that instructed him
to mercy.

DUKE: I never heard the absent Duke much detected° for women. He was
not inclined that way. 100

LUCIO: O, sir, you are deceived.

DUKE: 'Tis not possible.

LUCIO: Who, not the Duke? Yes, your beggar of fifty; and his use° was to
put a ducat in her clack-dish.° The Duke had crotchets in him. He would
be drunk too, that let me inform you. 105

DUKE: You do him wrong, surely.

LUCIO: Sir, I was an inward of his. A shy fellow was the Duke, and I believe I know the cause of his withdrawing.

DUKE: What, I prithee, might be the cause?

LUCIO: No, pardon. 'Tis a secret must be locked within the teeth and the 110
lips. But this I can let you understand: the greater file of the subject held
the Duke to be wise.

DUKE: Wise? Why, no question but he was.

LUCIO: A very superficial, ignorant, unweighing° fellow.

DUKE: Either this is envy° in you, folly, or mistaking. The very stream of 115
his life and the business he hath helmed° must, upon a warranted need,°
give him a better proclamation.° Let him be but testimonied in his own
bringings-forth,° and he shall appear to the envious° a scholar, a states-
man, and a soldier. Therefore you speak unskillfully;° or, if your knowledge be more, it is much darkened in your malice. 120

LUCIO: Sir, I know him, and I love him.

90–91. **motion ungenerative:** masculine puppet, without sexual potency.   92. **pleasant:** jocose.
apace: fast and idly.   94. **codpiece:** An appendage to the front of close-fitting hose or breeches
worn by men, often ornamented and indelicately conspicuous; hence, slang for "penis."
97. **the service:** i.e., prostitution.   99. **detected:** accused.   103. **use:** custom.   104. **clack-
dish:** beggar's wooden dish with a lid, which was "clacked" to attract attention; probably
used metaphorically here for the female pudenda.   114. **unweighing:** injudicious.   115. **envy:**
malice.   116. **helmed:** steered.   **upon . . . need:** if a warrant were needed.   117. **give . . .**
proclamation: proclaim him better (than you assert).   117–18. **in . . . bringings-forth:** by
his own public actions.   118. **to the envious:** even to the malicious.   119. **unskillfully:** in
ignorance.

DUKE: Love talks with better knowledge, and knowledge with dearer love.

LUCIO: Come, sir, I know what I know.

DUKE: I can hardly believe that, since you know not what you speak. But if ever the Duke return, as your prayers are he may, let me desire you to make your answer before him. If it be honest you have spoke, you have courage to maintain it. I am bound to call upon you; and, I pray you, your name?   125

LUCIO: Sir, my name is Lucio, well known to the Duke.

DUKE: He shall know you better, sir, if I may live to report you.   130

LUCIO: I fear you not.

DUKE: O, you hope the Duke will return no more, or you imagine me too unhurtful an opposite.° But indeed I can do you little harm; you'll forswear this° again.°

LUCIO: I'll be hanged first. Thou art deceived in me, Friar. But no more of this. Canst thou tell if Claudio die tomorrow or no?   135

DUKE: Why should he die, sir?

LUCIO: Why? For filling a bottle with a tundish.° I would the Duke we talk of were returned again. This ungenitured agent° will unpeople the province with continency. Sparrows° must not build in his house eaves, because they are lecherous. The Duke yet would have dark deeds darkly° answered; he would never bring them to light. Would he were returned! Marry, this Claudio is condemned for untrussing.° Farewell, good Friar. I prithee, pray for me. The Duke, I say to thee again, would eat mutton on Fridays.° He's now past it,° yet, and I say to thee, he would mouth° with a beggar, though she smelt brown bread° and garlic. Say that I said so. Farewell.   *Exit.*   140 145

DUKE:
No might nor greatness in mortality°
Can censure scape;° back-wounding calumny°
The whitest virtue strikes. What king so° strong   150
Can° tie the gall up in the slanderous tongue?
But who comes here?

132–33. **too . . . opposite:** too harmless an adversary.   133–34. **forswear this:** deny under oath what you've said.   134. **again:** another time.   138. **tundish:** funnel (here representing the penis).   139. **ungenitured agent:** sexless deputy.   140. **Sparrows:** (Proverbially lecherous birds.)   141. **darkly:** secretly.   143. **untrussing:** undressing. (Specifically, untying the points used to fasten hose to doublet.)   144–45. **eat . . . Fridays:** i.e., frequent loose women in flagrant disregard of the law. (Literally, violate religious observance by eating meat on fast days.)   145. **past it:** beyond the age for it.   **mouth:** kiss.   146. **smelt brown bread:** smelled of coarse bran bread.   148. **mortality:** humankind; human life.   149. **scape:** escape.   **back-wounding calumny:** back-biting slander.   150. **so:** be he never so.   151. **Can:** i.e., that he can.

Enter Escalus, Provost, and [officers with] bawd [Mistress Overdone].

ESCALUS: Go, away with her to prison.

MISTRESS OVERDONE: Good my lord, be good to me. Your honor is accounted a merciful man. Good my lord. 155

ESCALUS: Double and treble admonition, and still forfeit in the same kind!°
This would make mercy° swear and play the tyrant.

PROVOST: A bawd of eleven years' continuance, may it please your honor.

MISTRESS OVERDONE: My lord, this is one Lucio's information° against
me. Mistress Kate Keepdown was with child by him in the Duke's time; 160
he promised her marriage. His child is a year and a quarter old, come
Philip and Jacob.° I have kept it myself; and see how he goes about° to
abuse me!

ESCALUS: That fellow is a fellow of much license. Let him be called before
us. Away with her to prison! Go to, no more words. [*Exeunt Officers with* 165
Mistress Overdone.] Provost, my brother° Angelo will not be altered; Claudio must die tomorrow. Let him be furnished with divines° and have all
charitable preparation. If my brother wrought by my pity,° it should not
be so with him.

PROVOST: So please you, this friar hath been with him, and advised him 170
for th' entertainment° of death.

ESCALUS: Good even, good Father.

DUKE: Bliss and goodness on you!

ESCALUS: Of whence are you?

DUKE:
Not of this country, though my chance is now 175
To use° it for my time.° I am a brother
Of gracious order, late come from the See°
In special business from His Holiness.

ESCALUS: What news abroad i' the world?

DUKE: None but that there is so great a fever on goodness that the dis- 180
solution of it must cure it. Novelty is only in request,° and, as it is, as

---

156. forfeit . . . kind: guilty of the same offense.   157. mercy: i.e., even mercy.   159. information: accusation.   162. Philip and Jacob: the Feast of Saint Philip and Saint James
(*Jacobus* in Latin), May 1.   goes about: busies himself.   166. brother: i.e., fellow officer of
state.   167. divines: clergymen.   168. wrought . . . pity: acted in accord with my impulses of
pity.   171. entertainment: reception, acceptance.   176. use: dwell in.   time: present occasion.   177. the See: Rome.   180–81. the dissolution . . . cure it: i.e., only by dying can goodness be rid of the disease.   181. is only in request: is the only thing people seek.

dangerous to be aged in any kind of course as it is virtuous to be constant
in any undertaking.° There is scarce truth enough alive to make societies
secure, but security enough to make fellowships accursed.° Much upon
this riddle° runs the wisdom of the world. This news is old enough, yet it   185
is every day's news. I pray you, sir, of what disposition was the Duke?

ESCALUS: One that, above all other strifes,° contended especially to know
himself.

DUKE: What pleasure was he given to?

ESCALUS: Rather rejoicing to see another merry than merry at anything   190
which professed° to make him rejoice — a gentleman of all temperance.
But leave we him to his events,° with a prayer they may prove prosperous,
and let me desire to know how you find Claudio prepared. I am made to
understand that you have lent him visitation.°

DUKE: He professes to have received no sinister measure° from his judge   195
but most willingly humbles himself to the determination of justice; yet
had he framed to himself,° by the instruction of his frailty,° many deceiv-
ing promises of life, which I, by my good leisure, have discredited to him,
and now is he resolved to die.

ESCALUS: You have paid the heavens your function, and the prisoner the   200
very debt of your calling.° I have labored for the poor gentleman to the
extremest shore of my modesty,° but my brother justice have I found so
severe that he hath forced me to tell him he is indeed Justice.

DUKE: If his own life answer the straitness° of his proceeding, it shall
become him well; wherein if he chance to fail, he hath sentenced himself.   205

ESCALUS: I am going to visit the prisoner. Fare you well.

DUKE: Peace be with you!   [*Exeunt Escalus and Provost.*]
He who the sword of heaven will bear
Should be as holy as severe;

182–83. **as it . . . undertaking:** as things currently stand, (it is) as dangerous to be constant in
any undertaking as it is virtuous to be thus constant.   183–84. **There . . . accursed:** i.e., there
is hardly enough integrity and trust extant to bind men in sincere affection, but binding contractual obligations enough to make ordinary transactions intolerable. (The Duke thus puns
on *security* [1] a sense of trust [2] financial pledge required to borrow money, and on *fellowship* [1] friendship [2] corporations formed for trading ventures.)   184–85. **upon this riddle:** in
this riddling fashion.   187. **strifes:** endeavors.   191. **professed:** attempted.   192. **his events:**
the outcome of his affairs.   194. **lent him visitation:** paid him a visit.   195. **sinister measure:**
unfair treatment meted out to him.   197. **framed to himself:** formulated in his mind.   **by . . .
frailty:** at the prompting of his natural human weakness.   200–01. **the prisoner . . . calling:**
what your calling as a friar obliges you to give the prisoner, i.e., the comforts of spiritual counsel.   202. **shore . . . modesty:** limit of propriety.   204. **straitness:** strictness.

Pattern in himself to know,° 210
Grace to stand, and virtue go;°
More nor less to others paying
Than by self-offenses weighing.°
Shame to him whose cruel striking
Kills for faults of his own liking! 215
Twice treble shame on Angelo,
To weed my vice and let his grow!°
O, what may man within him hide,
Though angel on the outward side!
How may likeness made in crimes, 220
Making practice on the times,
To draw with idle spiders' strings
Most ponderous and substantial things!°
Craft against vice I must apply.
With Angelo tonight shall lie 225
His old betrothèd but despisèd;
So disguise shall, by the disguisèd,
Pay with falsehood false exacting
And perform an old contracting.° *Exit.*

ACT 4, SCENE 1°

Enter Mariana, and Boy singing.

Song.

BOY:

Take, O, take those lips away,
That so sweetly were forsworn,
And those eyes, the break of day,
Lights that do mislead the morn;°

---

210. **Pattern . . . know:** to find an example or *pattern* in himself by which to conduct himself or judge others. 211. **Grace . . . go:** (to find in himself) grace to keep himself upright and virtue to guide himself in the straight path. 212–13. **More . . . weighing:** inflicting no more and no less punishment on others than conscience teaches him after weighing his own offenses. 217. **my vice . . . grow:** i.e., vice in everyone else. 220–23. **How . . . things:** (Seemingly a corrupt passage, perhaps missing two lines. The meaning may be: how can false seeming, composed of guilt within, practicing deception on the world, draw away in time with the web of legal deception the very substance of social order?) 227–29. **So . . . contracting:** so shall disguise, by means of a disguised person, pay back with illusion (Mariana's disguise) the false exaction (of Angelo), and thus fulfill an old contract. **ACT 4, SCENE 1. Location:** The moated grange at Saint Luke's. 4. **Lights . . . morn:** i.e., eyes that mislead the morn into thinking the sun has risen.

But my kisses bring again,° bring again,   5
Seals° of love, but sealed in vain, sealed in vain.

Enter Duke [disguised as before].

MARIANA:
Break off thy song, and haste thee quick away.
Here comes a man of comfort, whose advice
Hath often stilled my brawling° discontent.   *[Exit Boy.]*
I cry you mercy,° sir, and well could wish   10
You had not found me here so musical.
Let me excuse me, and believe me so,
My mirth it much displeased, but pleased my woe.°

DUKE:
'Tis good; though music oft hath such a charm
To make bad good,° and good provoke to harm.   15
I pray you, tell me, hath anybody inquired for me here today? Much
upon° this time have I promised here to meet.

MARIANA: You have not been inquired after. I have sat here all day.

Enter Isabella.

DUKE: I do constantly° believe you. The time is come even now. I shall
crave your forbearance a little.° Maybe I will call upon you anon,° for   20
some advantage to yourself.

MARIANA: I am always bound to you.   *Exit.*

DUKE: Very well met, and welcome.
What is the news from this good deputy?

ISABELLA:
He hath a garden circummured° with brick,   25
Whose western side is with a vineyard backed;
And to that vineyard is a planchèd° gate,
That makes his° opening with this bigger key.   *[She shows keys.]*
This other doth command a little door

---

5. **again:** back.   6. **Seals:** confirmations, pledges.   9. **brawling:** clamorous.   10. **cry you mercy:** beg your pardon.   13. **My . . . woe:** i.e., it suited not a merry but a melancholy mood.   15. **bad good:** i.e., bad seem good, attractive. (The Duke, echoing Renaissance conceptions of the psychological effects of music, warns that music may soothe melancholy at times but may also produce unvirtuous effects on the mind.)   16–17. **Much upon:** pretty nearly about.   19. **constantly:** confidently.   20. **crave . . . little:** i.e., ask you to withdraw briefly. **anon:** presently.   25. **circummured:** walled about.   27. **planchèd:** made of boards, planks.   28. **his:** its.

Which from the vineyard to the garden leads;   30
There have I made my promise, upon° the
Heavy middle of the night, to call upon him.

DUKE:
But shall you on your knowledge find this way?

ISABELLA:
I have ta'en a due and wary note upon 't.
With whispering and most guilty diligence,   35
In action all of precept,° he did show me
The way twice o'er.

DUKE: Are there no other tokens
Between you 'greed concerning her observance?°

ISABELLA:
No, none, but only a repair° i' the dark,
And that I have possessed° him my most stay°   40
Can be but brief; for I have made him know
I have a servant comes with me along,
That stays upon° me, whose persuasion° is
I come about my brother.

DUKE: 'Tis well borne up.°
I have not yet made known to Mariana   45
A word of this. — What, ho, within! Come forth!

Enter Mariana.

I pray you, be acquainted with this maid;
She comes to do you good.

ISABELLA: I do desire the like.

DUKE:
Do you persuade yourself that I respect you?°

MARIANA:
Good Friar, I know you do, and have found it.°   50

DUKE:
Take then this your companion by the hand,
Who hath a story ready for your ear.

---

31. **upon:** during, at. 36. **In action . . . precept:** i.e., teaching by demonstration. 38. **her observance:** what she is supposed to do. 39. **repair:** act of going or coming to a place. 40. **possessed:** informed. **my most stay:** my stay at the longest. 43. **stays upon:** waits for. **persuasion:** belief. 44. **borne up:** sustained, carried out. 49. **respect you:** are concerned for your welfare. 50. **found it:** i.e., found it to be true.

I shall attend your leisure. But make haste;
The vaporous night approaches.

MARIANA: Will't please you walk aside?   *Exit [with Isabella].*   55

DUKE:
O place and greatness! Millions of false eyes
Are stuck° upon thee. Volumes of report
Run with these false and most contrarious quests
Upon thy doings;° thousand escapes° of wit
Make thee the father of their idle dream°   60
And rack° thee in their fancies.

Enter Mariana and Isabella.

                              Welcome. How agreed?

ISABELLA:
She'll take the enterprise upon her, Father,
If you advise it.

DUKE: It is not° my consent,
But my entreaty too.

ISABELLA: Little have you to say°
When you depart from him but, soft and low,   65
"Remember now my brother."

MARIANA: Fear me not.°

DUKE:
Nor, gentle daughter, fear you not at all.
He is your husband on a precontract;°
To bring you thus together, 'tis no sin,
Sith that° the justice of your title to him   70
Doth flourish° the deceit. Come, let us go.
Our corn's to reap, for yet our tithe's° to sow.°   *Exeunt.*

---

57. **stuck:** fastened.   57–59. **Volumes . . . doings:** innumerable rumors follow a false scent
and hunt counter in pursuing your activities.   59. **escapes:** sallies.   60. **Make . . . dream:**
credit you with being the source of their fantasies.   61. **rack:** stretch as on the rack, distort.
63. **not:** not only.   64. **Little . . . say:** say little.   66. **Fear me not:** i.e., don't worry about my
carrying out my part.   68. **precontract:** legally binding agreement entered into before any
church ceremony. (Compare Claudio's and Juliet's *true contract* at 1.2.118.)   70. **Sith that:**
since.   71. **flourish:** adorn, make fair.   72. **Our corn's . . . sow:** we must first sow grain before
we can expect to reap a harvest; i.e., we must get started.   **tithes:** grain sown for tithe dues; or,
an error for "tilth."

ACT 4, SCENE 2°

Enter Provost and Clown [Pompey].

PROVOST: Come hither, sirrah. Can you cut off a man's head?

POMPEY: If the man be a bachelor, sir, I can; but if he be a married man, he's his wife's head,° and I can never cut off a woman's head.°

PROVOST: Come, sir, leave me your snatches,° and yield me a direct answer. Tomorrow morning are to die Claudio and Barnardine. Here is in our   5
prison a common° executioner, who in his office lacks a helper. If you will take it on you to assist him, it shall redeem you from your gyves;° if not, you shall have your full time of imprisonment and your deliverance with an unpitied whipping, for you have been a notorious bawd.

POMPEY: Sir, I have been an unlawful bawd time out of mind, but yet I will   10
be content to be a lawful hangman. I would be glad to receive some instruction from my fellow partner.

PROVOST: What, ho, Abhorson! Where's Abhorson, there?

Enter Abhorson.

ABHORSON: Do you call, sir?

PROVOST: Sirrah, here's a fellow will help you tomorrow in your execution.   15
If you think it meet, compound° with him by the year, and let him abide here with you; if not, use him for the present and dismiss him. He cannot plead his estimation° with you; he hath been a bawd.

ABHORSON: A bawd, sir? Fie upon him! He will discredit our mystery.°

PROVOST: Go to, sir, you weigh equally; a feather will turn the scale. *Exit.*   20

POMPEY: Pray, sir, by your good favor — for surely, sir, a good favor° you have, but that you have a hanging look° — do you call, sir, your occupation a mystery?

ABHORSON: Ay, sir, a mystery.

POMPEY: Painting,° sir, I have heard say, is a mystery, and your whores, sir,   25
being members of my occupation, using painting, do prove my occupation a mystery. But what mystery there should be in hanging, if I should be hanged, I cannot imagine.

ABHORSON: Sir, it is a mystery.

ACT 4, SCENE 2. Location: The prison.   3. **wife's head:** (Compare Ephesians 5:23: "The husband is the head of the wife."). **head:** i.e., maidenhead.   4. **leave . . . snatches:** leave off your quips.   6. **common:** public.   7. **gyves:** fetters, shackles.   16. **compound:** make an agreement.   18. **plead his estimation:** claim any respect on account of his reputation.   19. **mystery:** craft, occupation.   21. **favor . . . favor:** leave . . . face.   22. **hanging look:** (1) downcast look (2) look of a hangman.   25. **Painting:** (1) painting of pictures (2) applying cosmetics.

POMPEY: Proof?   30

ABHORSON: Every true man's apparel fits your thief. If it be too little for
your thief, your true man thinks it big enough;° if it be too big for your
thief, your thief thinks it little enough.° So every true man's apparel fits
your thief.

Enter Provost.

PROVOST: Are you agreed?   35

POMPEY: Sir, I will serve him, for I do find your hangman is a more penitent trade than your bawd: he doth oftener ask forgiveness.°

PROVOST: You, sirrah, provide your block and your ax tomorrow four
o'clock.

ABHORSON: Come on, bawd. I will instruct thee in my trade. Follow!   40

POMPEY: I do desire to learn, sir; and I hope, if you have occasion to use
me for your own turn,° you shall find me yare.° For truly, sir, for your
kindness I owe you a good turn.

PROVOST:
Call hither Barnardine and Claudio.   *Exit [Pompey, with Abhorson].*
Th' one has my pity; not a jot the other,   45
Being a murderer, though he were my brother.

Enter Claudio.

Look, here's the warrant, Claudio, for thy death.
'Tis now dead midnight, and by eight tomorrow
Thou must be made immortal.° Where's Barnardine?

CLAUDIO:
As fast° locked up in sleep as guiltless labor°   50
When it lies starkly° in the traveler's bones.°
He will not wake.

PROVOST: Who can do good on him?

31–33. **Every . . . enough:** (Just as Pompey argues that whores belong to a skilled craft because
they are like painters, Abhorson implies that hangmen are skilled craftsmen because they are
like thieves, who, in turn, are like tailors; both thieves and tailors "fit" honest men's apparel,
by stealing or adjusting it. Hangmen, in turn, are like thieves because they receive the garments
of the men they execute.)   32. **big enough:** i.e., enough of a loss.   33. **little enough:** little
enough for his efforts.   37. **he doth . . . forgiveness:** (The executioner perfunctorily asked
forgiveness of those whose lives he was about to take.)   42. **for . . . turn:** (1) as a pimp to provide for your sexual needs (2) as your hangman when it is your turn to be hanged or "turned
off" the ladder.   **yare:** ready, alacritous.   49. **made immortal:** i.e., executed.   50. **fast:** firmly,
soundly.   **guiltless labor:** (A personification of the well-earned weariness that tires the innocent laborer.)   51. **starkly:** stiffly.   **traveler's bones:** bones of one who travails or labors.

Well, go, prepare yourself. [*Knocking within.*] But hark, what noise?
Heaven give your spirits comfort! [*Exit Claudio.*] By and by. —
I hope it is some pardon or reprieve   55
For the most gentle Claudio.

Enter Duke [disguised as before].

                              Welcome, Father.
DUKE:
   The best and wholesom'st spirits of the night
   Envelop you, good Provost! Who called here of late?
PROVOST: None since the curfew rung.
DUKE:
   Not Isabel?
PROVOST: No.
DUKE: They will, then, ere 't be long.   60
PROVOST: What comfort is for Claudio?
DUKE:
   There's some in hope.
PROVOST: It is a bitter deputy.
DUKE:
   Not so, not so. His life is paralleled
   Even with° the stroke and line° of his great justice.
   He doth with holy abstinence subdue   65
   That in himself which he spurs on° his power
   To qualify° in others. Were he mealed° with that
   Which he corrects, then were he tyrannous;
   But this being so, he's just. [*Knocking within.*] Now are they come.
                                  [*The Provost goes to the door.*]
   This is a gentle provost; seldom when°   70
   The steelèd° jailer is the friend of men.   [*Knocking within.*]
   How now? What noise? That spirit's possessed with haste
   That wounds th' unsisting° postern° with these strokes.
PROVOST: [*speaking at the door*]
   There he must stay until the officer
   Arise to let him in. He is called up.   [*He returns to the Duke.*]   75

63–64. **is paralleled . . . with:** runs parallel and in exact conformity with.   64. **stroke and line:** rigorous and exact course.   66. **spurs on:** encourages, urges.   67. **qualify:** mitigate. **mealed:** spotted, stained.   70. **seldom when:** i.e., it is seldom that.   71. **steelèd:** hardened. 73. **unsisting:** unassisting, unresting, or unresisting (?).   **postern:** small door.

DUKE:

Have you no countermand for Claudio yet,
But he must die tomorrow?

PROVOST: None, sir, none.

DUKE:

As near the dawning, Provost, as it is,
You shall hear more ere morning.

PROVOST: Happily°

You something know, yet I believe there comes   80
No countermand. No such example° have we;
Besides, upon the very siege° of justice
Lord Angelo hath to the public ear
Professed the contrary.

Enter a Messenger.

This is his lordship's man.

DUKE:

And here comes Claudio's pardon.   85

MESSENGER: [*giving a paper*] My lord hath sent you this note, and by me
this further charge, that you swerve not from the smallest article of it,
neither in time, matter, or other circumstance. Good morrow; for, as I
take it, it is almost day.

PROVOST: I shall obey him.   [*Exit Messenger.*]   90

DUKE: [*aside*]

This is his pardon, purchased by such sin
For which the pardoner himself is in.°
Hence hath offense his quick celerity,
When it is borne in high authority.°
When vice makes mercy, mercy's so extended   95
That for the fault's love° is th' offender friended.° —
Now, sir, what news?

PROVOST: I told you. Lord Angelo, belike° thinking me remiss in mine office, awakens me with this unwonted putting-on° — methinks strangely,
for he hath not used it before.   100

DUKE: Pray you, let's hear.

---

79. **Happily:** haply, perhaps.   81. **example:** precedent.   82. **siege:** seat.   92. **in:** engaged.
93–94. **Hence . . . authority:** i.e., any offense of which the person in authority is himself guilty
will spread quickly. (*His* means "its own.")   96. **the fault's love:** love of the fault.   **friended:**
befriended, countenanced.   98. **belike:** perchance.   99. **unwonted putting-on:** unaccus-
tomed urging.

PROVOST: [*reads*] *the letter* "Whatsoever you may hear to the contrary, let Claudio be executed by four of the clock, and in the afternoon Barnardine. For my better satisfaction,° let me have Claudio's head sent me by five. Let this be duly performed, with a thought that more depends on it than we must yet deliver.° Thus fail not to do your office, as you will answer it at your peril." 105

What say you to this, sir?

DUKE: What is that Barnardine who is to be executed in th' afternoon?

PROVOST: A Bohemian born, but here° nursed up and bred; one that is a prisoner nine years old.° 110

DUKE: How came it that the absent Duke had not either delivered him to his liberty or executed him? I have heard it was ever his manner to do so.

PROVOST: His friends still wrought reprieves for him; and indeed his fact,° till now in the government of Lord Angelo, came not to an undoubtful proof. 115

DUKE: It is now apparent?

PROVOST: Most manifest, and not denied by himself.

DUKE: Hath he borne himself penitently in prison? How seems he to be touched?° 120

PROVOST: A man that apprehends death no more dreadfully but° as a drunken sleep — careless, reckless, and fearless of what's past, present, or to come; insensible of mortality, and desperately mortal.°

DUKE: He wants advice.°

PROVOST: He will hear none. He hath evermore° had the liberty of the prison;° give him leave to escape hence, he would not. Drunk many times a day, if not many days entirely drunk. We have very oft awaked him, as if to carry him to execution, and showed him a seeming warrant for it; it hath not moved him at all. 125

DUKE: More of him anon. There is written in your brow, Provost, honesty and constancy; if I read it not truly, my ancient skill beguiles me, but, in the boldness of my cunning, I will lay myself in hazard.° Claudio, whom here you have warrant to execute, is no greater forfeit to the law than Angelo who hath sentenced him. To make you understand this 130

---

104. **better satisfaction:** greater assurance. 106. **deliver:** make known. 110. **here:** i.e., in Vienna. 111. **a prisoner . . . old:** nine years a prisoner. 114. **fact:** crime. 120. **touched:** affected. 121. **no more dreadfully but:** with no more dread than. 123. **insensible . . . mortal:** incapable of comprehending the meaning of death, and without hope of immortality or of escaping execution. 124. **wants advice:** needs spiritual counsel. 125. **evermore:** constantly. 125–26. **the liberty . . . prison:** freedom to go anywhere within the prison. 132. **in the . . . hazard:** confident in my knowledge (of human character), I will put myself at risk.

in a manifested effect,° I crave but four days' respite, for the which you   135
are to do me both a present° and a dangerous courtesy.
PROVOST: Pray, sir, in what?
DUKE: In the delaying death.
PROVOST: Alack, how may I do it, having the hour limited,° and an express
command, under penalty, to deliver his head in the view of Angelo? I   140
may make my case as Claudio's, to cross this in the smallest.
DUKE: By the vow of mine order I warrant you, if my instructions may be
your guide. Let this Barnardine be this morning executed, and his head
borne to Angelo.
PROVOST: Angelo hath seen them both and will discover the favor.°   145
DUKE: O, death's a great disguiser, and you may add to it. Shave the head,
and tie° the beard, and say it was the desire of the penitent to be so bared
before his death. You know the course is common. If anything fall to°
you upon this more than thanks and good fortune, by the saint whom I
profess,° I will plead against it with my life.   150
PROVOST: Pardon me, good Father, it is against my oath.
DUKE: Were you sworn to the Duke or to the deputy?
PROVOST: To him, and to his substitutes.
DUKE: You will think you have made no offense if the Duke avouch° the
justice of your dealing?   155
PROVOST: But what likelihood is in that?
DUKE: Not a resemblance,° but a certainty. Yet since I see you fearful, that
neither my coat, integrity, nor persuasion can with ease attempt° you, I
will go further than I meant, to pluck all fears out of you. Look you, sir,
here is the hand and seal of the Duke. [*He shows a letter.*] You know the   160
character,° I doubt not, and the signet is not strange° to you.
PROVOST: I know them both.
DUKE: The contents of this is the return of the Duke. You shall anon over-
read it at your pleasure, where you shall find within these two days he will
be here. This is a thing that Angelo knows not, for he this very day   165
receives letters of strange tenor, perchance of the Duke's death, perchance entering° into some monastery, but by chance nothing of what is
writ.° Look, th' unfolding star° calls up the shepherd. Put not yourself

---

135. in . . . effect: by means of concrete proof.   136. present: immediate.   139. limited:
fixed, set.   145. discover the favor: recognize the face.   147. tie: trim, or tie in preparation
for beheading (?).   148. fall to: befall.   150. profess: acknowledge.   154. avouch: confirm.
157. resemblance: seeming.   158. attempt: win, tempt.   161. character: handwriting.   strange:
unknown.   167. entering: of his entering.   168. writ: i.e., written here.   168. unfolding
star: i.e., morning star, Venus, which bids the shepherd lead his sheep from the fold.

into amazement how these things should be; all difficulties are but easy
when they are known. Call your executioner, and off with Barnardine's   170
head. I will give him a present shrift° and advise him for a better place.
Yet° you are amazed, but this shall absolutely resolve you.° Come away; it
is almost clear dawn.   *Exit [with Provost].*

ACT 4, SCENE 3°

Enter Clown [Pompey].

POMPEY: I am as well° acquainted here as I was in our house of profession.
One would think it were Mistress Overdone's own house, for here be
many of her old customers. First, here's young Master Rash;° he's in for
a commodity of brown paper and old ginger,° nine-score and seventeen
pounds, of which he made five marks, ready money. Marry, then ginger   5
was not much in request, for the old women° were all dead. Then is there
here one Master Caper,° at the suit of Master Three-pile° the mercer,° for
some four suits° of peach-colored satin, which now peaches him° a beggar. Then have we here young Dizzy,° and young Master Deep-vow,° and
Master Copper-spur,° and Master Starve-lackey° the rapier and dagger   10
man, and young Drop-heir° that killed lusty° Pudding,° and Master
Forthlight° the tilter,° and brave° Master Shoe-tie° the great traveler, and
wild Half-can° that stabbed Pots,° and I think forty more, all great doers
in our trade, and are now "for the Lord's sake."°

---

171. **present shrift:** immediate absolution for sins (after confession).   172. **Yet:** still.   **re-**
solve you: dispel your uncertainties.   ACT 4, SCENE 3. **Location:** The prison.   1. **well:**
widely.   3. **Rash:** (All the names mentioned by POMPEY apparently glance at contemporary
social affectations and defects. *Rash* means "reckless.")   4. **a commodity . . . ginger:** (To circumvent the laws against excessive rates of interest, moneylenders often advanced cheap commodities to gullible borrowers in lieu of cash at a high rate of interest. Master Rash, having
agreed to a valuation of one hundred ninety-seven pounds for such merchandise, has been able
to resell it for five marks, each worth about two-thirds of a pound, and has been thrown
into prison for debt.)   6. **old women:** (Proverbially fond of ginger.)   7. **Caper:** (To *caper* was
to dance or leap gracefully.)   **Three-pile:** the thickest nap and most expensive grade of velvet.
mercer: cloth merchant.   8. **suits:** (with a play on *suit,* line 7).   **peaches him:** denounces him
as (with a play on *peach*).   9. **Dizzy:** i.e., giddy, foolish?   **Deep-vow:** One who swears
earnestly and often.   10. **Copper-spur:** (Copper was often used fraudulently to simulate
gold.)   **Starve-lackey:** (Spendthrift gallants often virtually starved their pages.)   11. **Drop-**
heir: (Perhaps referring to those who disinherited or preyed on unsuspecting heirs; or else
Drop-hair, losing hair from syphilis.)   **lusty:** vigorous.   **Pudding:** i.e., sausage.   12. **Forth-**
light: (Unexplained; perhaps an error for *Forthright,* referring to a style of tilting.)   **tilter:**
jouster.   **brave:** showy, splendidly dressed.   **Shoe-tie:** (Evidently a nickname for travelers and
others who affected the foreign fashion of elaborate rosettes on the tie of the shoe.)   13. **Half-**
can: i.e., a small drinking tankard.   **Pots:** i.e., ale pots.   14. **for . . . sake:** (The cry of prisoners from jail grates to passersby to give them food or alms.)

Enter Abhorson.

ABHORSON: Sirrah, bring Barnardine hither.   15

POMPEY: Master Barnardine! You must rise and be hanged,° Master Barnardine!

ABHORSON: What, ho, Barnardine!

BARNARDINE: [*within*]   A pox o' your throats! Who makes that noise there?
What are you?   20

POMPEY: Your friends, sir, the hangman. You must be so good, sir, to rise
and be put to death.

BARNARDINE: [*within*]   Away, you rogue, away! I am sleepy.

ABHORSON: Tell him he must awake, and that quickly, too.

POMPEY: Pray, Master Barnardine, awake till you are executed, and sleep   25
afterwards.

ABHORSON: Go in to him, and fetch him out.

POMPEY: He is coming, sir, he is coming. I hear his straw rustle.

Enter Barnardine.

ABHORSON: Is the ax upon the block, sirrah?

POMPEY: Very ready, sir.   30

BARNARDINE: How now, Abhorson? What's the news with you?

ABHORSON: Truly, sir, I would desire you to clap into° your prayers; for,
look you, the warrant's come.

BARNARDINE: You rogue, I have been drinking all night. I am not fitted
for 't.   35

POMPEY: O, the better, sir, for he that drinks all night and is hanged
betimes° in the morning may sleep the sounder all the next day.

Enter Duke [disguised as before].

ABHORSON: Look you, sir, here comes your ghostly° father. Do we jest
now, think you?

DUKE: Sir, induced by my charity, and hearing how hastily you are to   40
depart, I am come to advise you, comfort you, and pray with you.

BARNARDINE: Friar, not I. I have been drinking hard all night, and I
will have more time to prepare me, or they shall beat out my brains with
billets.° I will not consent to die this day, that's certain.

---

16. **be hanged:** (with a play on the imprecation; compare "go to the devil"). 32. **clap into:** quickly begin. 37. **betimes:** early. 38. **ghostly:** spiritual. 44. **billets:** cudgels, blocks of wood.

DUKE:
O, sir, you must, and therefore I beseech you   45
Look forward on the journey you shall go.
BARNARDINE: I swear I will not die today for any man's persuasion.
DUKE: But hear you —
BARNARDINE: Not a word. If you have anything to say to me, come to my
ward,° for thence will not I today.   *Exit.*   50

Enter Provost.

DUKE:
Unfit to live or die. O gravel° heart!
After him, fellows. Bring him to the block.   [*Exeunt Abhorson and Pompey.*]
PROVOST:
Now, sir, how do you find the prisoner?
DUKE:
A creature unprepared, unmeet° for death;
And to transport him° in the mind he is°   55
Were damnable.
PROVOST: Here in the prison, Father,
There died this morning of a cruel fever
One Ragozine, a most notorious pirate,
A man of Claudio's years, his beard and head
Just of his color. What if we do omit°   60
This reprobate till he were well inclined,
And satisfy the deputy with the visage
Of Ragozine, more like to Claudio?
DUKE:
O, 'tis an accident that heaven provides!
Dispatch it presently;° the hour draws on   65
Prefixed° by Angelo. See this be done,
And sent according to command, whiles I
Persuade this rude° wretch willingly to die.
PROVOST:
This shall be done, good Father, presently.
But Barnardine must die this afternoon.   70
And how shall we continue° Claudio,

---

50. ward: cell.   51. gravel: stony.   54. unmeet: unready, unfit.   55. transport him: i.e., send
him to his doom.   he is: he is in.   60. omit: ignore, overlook.   65. presently: immediately
(as also in line 69).   66. Prefixed: appointed beforehand, stipulated.   68. rude: uncivilized.
71. continue: preserve.

To save me from the danger that might come
If he were known alive?

DUKE: Let this be done:
Put them in secret holds,° both Barnardine and Claudio.
Ere twice the sun hath made his journal° greeting   75
To yond° generation, you shall find
Your safety manifested.

PROVOST: I am your free dependent.°

DUKE:
Quick, dispatch, and send the head to Angelo.   *Exit [Provost].*
Now will I write letters to Varrius° —   80
The Provost, he shall bear them — whose contents
Shall witness to him I am near at home,
And that, by great injunctions,° I am bound
To enter publicly. Him I'll desire
To meet me at the consecrated fount°   85
A league° below the city; and from thence,
By cold gradation and well-balanced form,°
We shall proceed with Angelo.

Enter Provost [with Ragozine's head].

PROVOST:
Here is the head. I'll carry it myself.

DUKE:
Convenient° is it. Make a swift return,   90
For I would commune° with you of such things
That want° no ear but yours.

PROVOST: I'll make all speed.   *Exit.*

ISABELLA: [*within*]:   Peace, ho, be here!

DUKE:
The tongue of Isabel. She's come to know
If yet her brother's pardon be come hither.   95

---

74. **holds:** cells, dungeons.   75. **journal:** daily.   76. **yond:** i.e., beyond these walls, outside the perpetually dark prison (?). Sometimes it is emended to *th' under,* the people of the Antipodes, on the opposite side of the earth, or, people under the sun, the human race.   78. **free dependent:** willing servant.   80. **to Varrius:** (The Folio reads to *Angelo,* but see line 86 below and 4.5.12–14; evidently, the Duke's plan is to meet Varrius "a league below the city" and then proceed to the rendezvous with Angelo.)   83. **by great injunctions:** by powerful precedent or for compelling reasons.   85. **fount:** spring.   86. **league:** (A measure of varying length but usually about three miles.)   87. **cold . . . form:** i.e., moving deliberately and with proper observance of all formalities.   90. **Convenient:** timely, fitting.   91. **commune:** converse.   92. **want:** require.

But I will keep her ignorant of her good,
To make her heavenly comforts of° despair
When it is least expected.

Enter Isabella.

ISABELLA: Ho, by your leave!
DUKE:
Good morning to you, fair and gracious daughter.
ISABELLA:
The better, given me by so holy a man.   100
Hath yet the deputy sent my brother's pardon?
DUKE:
He hath released him, Isabel, from the world.
His head is off and sent to Angelo.
ISABELLA:
Nay, but it is not so!
DUKE: It is no other.
Show your wisdom, daughter, in your close patience.°   105
ISABELLA:
O, I will to him and pluck out his eyes!
DUKE:
You shall not be admitted to his sight.
ISABELLA:
Unhappy Claudio! Wretched Isabel!
Injurious world! Most damnèd Angelo!
DUKE:
This nor hurts° him nor profits you a jot.   110
Forbear it therefore; give your cause to heaven.
Mark what I say, which you shall find
By° every syllable a faithful verity.
The Duke comes home tomorrow. Nay, dry your eyes,
One of our convent, and his confessor,   115
Gives me this instance.° Already he hath carried
Notice to Escalus and Angelo,
Who do prepare to meet him at the gates,
There to give up their pow'r. If you can, pace° your wisdom
In that good path that I would wish it go,   120

---

97. **of:** from, transformed out of. 105. **close patience:** silent enduring. 110. **nor hurts:** neither hurts. 113. **By:** with respect to. 116. **instance:** proof. 119. **pace:** teach to move in response to your will, as with a horse.

And you shall have your bosom° on this wretch,
Grace of° the Duke, revenges to° your heart,
And general honor.

ISABELLA: I am directed by you.

DUKE:
This letter, then, to Friar Peter give.   [*He gives her a letter.*]
'Tis that° he sent me of° the Duke's return.   125
Say, by this token, I desire his company
At Mariana's house tonight. Her cause and yours
I'll perfect° him withal,° and he shall bring you
Before the Duke, and to the head° of Angelo
Accuse him home and home.° For my poor self,   130
I am combinèd° by a sacred vow,
And shall be absent. Wend° you with this letter.
Command these fretting° waters from your eyes
With a light heart. Trust not my holy order
If I pervert your course. Who's here?   135

Enter Lucio.

LUCIO: Good even. Friar, where's the Provost?
DUKE: Not within, sir.
LUCIO: O pretty Isabella, I am pale at mine heart° to see thine eyes so red.
Thou must be patient. I am fain° to dine and sup with water and bran; I
dare not for my head° fill my belly; one fruitful° meal would set me to 't.°   140
But they say the Duke will be here tomorrow. By my troth, Isabel, I loved
thy brother. If the old fantastical Duke of dark corners had been at home,
he had lived.   [*Exit Isabella.*]
DUKE: Sir, the Duke is marvelous° little beholding° to your reports; but the
best is, he lives not in them.°   145
LUCIO: Friar, thou knowest not the Duke so well as I do. He's a better
woodman° than thou tak'st him for.
DUKE: Well, you'll answer this one day. Fare ye well.   [*He starts to go.*]

---

121. **bosom:** desire.   122. **Grace of:** manifestation of favor from.   **to:** in accord with.
125. **that:** that which.   **of:** concerning.   128. **perfect:** acquaint completely.   **withal:** with.
129. **head:** i.e., face.   130. **home and home:** thoroughly.   131. **combinèd:** bound.   132. **Wend:**
go.   133. **fretting:** corroding.   138. **pale . . . heart:** i.e., pale from sighing, since sighs cost
the heart loss of blood.   139. **fain:** compelled (as also in line 155).   140. **for my head:**
i.e., on my life.   **fruitful:** abundant.   **set me to 't:** i.e., awaken my lust and thus place me in
danger of Angelo's edict.   144. **marvelous:** marvelously.   **beholding:** beholden.   145. **he
. . . them:** i.e., he is not accurately described by them.   147. **woodman:** i.e., hunter (of
women).

LUCIO: Nay, tarry, I'll go along with thee. I can tell thee pretty tales of the Duke. 150

DUKE: You have told me too many of him already, sir, if they be true; if not true, none were enough.

LUCIO: I was once before him for getting a wench with child.

DUKE: Did you such a thing?

LUCIO: Yes, marry, did I, but I was fain to forswear it. They would else have 155 married me to the rotten medlar.°

DUKE: Sir, your company is fairer than honest. Rest you well.

LUCIO: By my troth, I'll go with thee to the lane's end. If bawdy talk offend you, we'll have very little of it. Nay, Friar, I am a kind of burr; I shall stick. *Exeunt.* 160

ACT 4, SCENE 4°

Enter Angelo and Escalus, [reading letters].

ESCALUS: Every letter he hath writ hath disvouched° other.

ANGELO: In most uneven and distracted manner. His actions show much like to madness. Pray heaven his wisdom be not tainted!° And why meet him at the gates and redeliver our authorities there?

ESCALUS: I guess not.° 5

ANGELO: And why should we proclaim it in an hour° before his entering, that if any crave redress of injustice, they should exhibit° their petitions in the street?

ESCALUS: He shows his reason for that: to have a dispatch° of complaints, and to deliver us from devices° hereafter, which shall then have no power 10 to stand against us.

ANGELO: Well, I beseech you, let it be proclaimed. Betimes° i' the morn I'll call you at your house. Give notice to such men of sort° and suit° as are to meet him.

ESCALUS: I shall, sir. Fare you well. 15

ANGELO: Good night. *Exit [Escalus].*
This deed unshapes me quite, makes me unpregnant°
And dull to all proceedings. A deflowered maid,
And by an eminent body° that enforced

---

156. **medlar:** A fruit that was eaten after it had begun to rot; here, signifying a prostitute.   ACT 4, SCENE 4. Location: In Vienna.   1. **disvouched:** contradicted.   3. **tainted:** diseased.   5. **guess not:** cannot guess.   6. **in an hour:** i.e., a full hour.   7. **exhibit:** present.   9. **dispatch:** prompt settlement.   10. **devices:** contrived complaints.   12. **Betimes:** early.   13. **sort:** rank.   **suit:** such as owe attendance or are followed by a retinue.   17. **unpregnant:** unapt.   19. **body:** person.

The law against it! But that° her tender shame   20
Will not proclaim against her maiden loss,
How might she tongue° me! Yet reason dares her no,°
For my authority bears of a credent bulk°
That no particular scandal once can touch
But it confounds the breather.° He should have lived,   25
Save that his riotous youth, with dangerous sense,°
Might in the times to come have ta'en revenge
By° so receiving a dishonored life
With ransom of such shame. Would yet he had lived!
Alack, when once our grace we have forgot,   30
Nothing goes right; we would, and we would not.   *Exit.*

ACT 4, SCENE 5°

Enter Duke [in his own habit] and Friar Peter.

DUKE:
    These letters at fit time deliver me.°   [*Giving letters.*]
    The Provost knows our purpose and our plot.
    The matter being afoot, keep° your instruction,
    And hold you ever to our special drift,°
    Though sometimes you do blench° from this to that   5
    As cause doth minister.° Go call at Flavius' house,
    And tell him where I stay. Give the like notice
    To Valencius, Rowland, and to Crassus,
    And bid them bring the trumpets° to the gate;
    But send me Flavius first.   10
FRIAR PETER: It shall be speeded° well.   [*Exit.*]

Enter Varrius.

DUKE:
    I thank thee, Varrius. Thou hast made good haste.
    Come, we will walk. There's other of our friends
    Will greet us here anon. My gentle Varrius!   *Exeunt.*

---

20. **But that:** were it not that.   22. **tongue:** i.e., reproach, accuse.   **dares her no:** i.e., frightens her to say nothing.   23. **bears . . . bulk:** bears such a huge credibility.   25. **But . . . breather:** without its confuting the person who speaks.   26. **sense:** passion, intention.   28. **By:** for, because of.   ACT 4, SCENE 5. Location: Outside the city.   1. **me:** for me.   3. **keep:** keep to.   4. **drift:** plot.   5. **blench:** deviate.   6. **minister:** prompt, provide occasion.   9. **trumpets:** trumpeters.   11. **speeded:** accomplished, expedited.

Act 4, Scene 6°

Enter Isabella and Mariana.

ISABELLA:
To speak so indirectly I am loath.
I would say the truth, but to accuse him so,
That is your part. Yet I am advised to do it,
He says, to veil full purpose.
MARIANA: Be ruled by him.
ISABELLA:
Besides, he tells me that if peradventure°   5
He speak against me on the adverse side,
I should not think it strange, for 'tis a physic°
That's bitter to sweet end.

Enter [Friar] Peter.

MARIANA:
I would Friar Peter —
ISABELLA: O, peace, the Friar is come.
FRIAR PETER:
Come, I have found you out a stand° most fit,   10
Where you may have such vantage on the Duke
He shall not pass you. Twice have the trumpets sounded.
The generous° and gravest citizens
Have hent° the gates, and very near upon°
The Duke is entering. Therefore hence, away!   *Exeunt.*   15

Act 5, Scene 1°

Enter Duke, Varrius, lords, Angelo, Escalus, Lucio, [Provost, officers, and] citizens at several° doors.

DUKE:
My very worthy cousin,° fairly met!
Our old and faithful friend, we are glad to see you.
ANGELO, ESCALUS:
Happy return be to Your Royal Grace!

ACT 4, SCENE 6. Location: Near the city gate.   5. **peradventure:** perhaps.   7. **physic:** remedy.
10. **stand:** place to stand.   13. **generous:** highborn.   14. **hent:** reached, occupied.   **very
near upon:** almost immediately now.   ACT 5, SCENE 1. Location: The city gate.   s.d. *several*:
separate.   1. **cousin:** fellow nobleman. (Addressed to Angelo.)

DUKE:
Many and hearty thankings to you both.
We have made inquiry of you, and we hear   5
Such goodness of your justice that our soul
Cannot but yield you forth to° public thanks,
Forerunning more requital.°

ANGELO:
You make my bonds° still greater.

DUKE:
O, your desert speaks loud, and I should wrong it   10
To lock it in the wards of covert bosom,°
When it deserves with characters° of brass
A forted° residence 'gainst the tooth of time
And razure° of oblivion. Give me your hand,
And let the subject° see, to make them know   15
That outward courtesies would fain° proclaim
Favors that keep° within.° Come, Escalus,
You must walk by us on our other hand,
And good supporters are you.

Enter [Friar] Peter and Isabella.

FRIAR PETER:
Now is your time. Speak loud, and kneel before him.   20

ISABELLA: [*kneeling*]
Justice, O royal Duke! Vail your regard°
Upon a wronged — I would fain have said a maid.
O worthy prince, dishonor not your eye
By throwing it on any other object
Till you have heard me in my true complaint   25
And given me justice, justice, justice, justice!

DUKE:
Relate your wrongs. In what? By whom? Be brief.
Here is Lord Angelo shall° give you justice.
Reveal yourself to him.

ISABELLA: O worthy Duke,
You bid me seek redemption of the devil.   30

---

7. yield . . . to: call you forth to give you.   8. more requital: further reward.   9. bonds: obligations.   11. To lock . . . bosom: i.e., to keep it locked up in my heart.   12. characters: writing, letters.   13. forted: fortified.   14. razure: effacement.   15. the subject: those who are
subjects.   16. fain: happily (as also in line 22).   17. keep: reside.   within: i.e., in the heart.
21. Vail your regard: look down.   28. shall: who shall.

Hear me yourself; for that which I must speak
Must either punish me, not being° believed,
Or wring redress from you.
Hear me, O, hear me, hear!

ANGELO:
My lord, her wits, I fear me, are not firm.   35
She hath been a suitor to me for her brother
Cut off by course of justice.

ISABELLA: [*standing*]   By course of justice!

ANGELO:
And she will speak most bitterly and strange.°

ISABELLA:
Most strange, but yet most truly, will I speak.
That Angelo's forsworn, is it not strange?   40
That Angelo's a murderer, is 't not strange?
That Angelo is an adulterous thief,
An hypocrite, a virgin-violator,
Is it not strange, and strange?

DUKE:
Nay, it is ten times strange.   45

ISABELLA:
It is not truer he is Angelo
Than° this is all as true as it is strange.
Nay, it is ten times true, for truth is truth
To th' end of reck'ning.

DUKE: Away with her! Poor soul,
She speaks this in th' infirmity of sense.°   50

ISABELLA:
O prince, I conjure thee, as thou believ'st
There is another comfort than this world,
That thou neglect me not with that opinion°
That I am touched with madness. Make not° impossible
That which but seems unlike.° 'Tis not impossible   55
But one the wicked'st caitiff° on the ground
May seem as shy,° as grave, as just, as absolute°
As Angelo; even so may Angelo,

---

32. **not being:** if I am not.   38. **strange:** strangely.   47. **Than:** than that.   50. **in . . . sense:**
out of a sick mind, out of the weakness of passion.   53. **with that opinion:** out of a supposition.   54. **Make not:** do not consider as.   55. **unlike:** unlikely.   56. **But one the wicked'st
caitiff:** but that the most wicked villain.   57. **shy:** quietly dignified.   **absolute:** flawless.

In all his dressings,° characts,° titles, forms,
Be an archvillain. Believe it, royal prince,   60
If he be less, he's nothing;° but he's more,
Had I more name for badness.
DUKE: By mine honesty,
If she be mad — as I believe no other —
Her madness hath the oddest frame of sense,°
Such a dependency of thing° on thing,   65
As e'er I heard in madness.
ISABELLA: O gracious Duke,
Harp not on that, nor do not banish reason
For inequality,° but let your reason serve
To make the truth appear where it seems hid,
And hide° the false seems° true.   70
DUKE:
Many that are not mad
Have, sure, more lack of reason. What would you say?
ISABELLA:
I am the sister of one Claudio,
Condemned upon the act of fornication
To lose his head, condemned by Angelo.   75
I, in probation° of a sisterhood,
Was sent to by my brother; one Lucio
As then° the messenger —
LUCIO: That's I, an 't like° Your Grace.
I came to her from Claudio and desired her
To try her gracious fortune with Lord Angelo   80
For her poor brother's pardon.
ISABELLA: That's he indeed.
DUKE: [to Lucio]
You were not bid to speak.
LUCIO: No, my good lord,
Nor wished to hold my peace.
DUKE: I wish you now, then.

---

59. **dressings:** ceremonial robes.   **characts:** insignia of office.   61. **If . . . nothing:** i.e., even if he were less than an archvillain, he would be worthless.   64. **frame of sense:** form of reason.   65. **dependency . . . on thing:** coherence.   67–68. **do . . . inequality:** i.e., do not assume lack of reason on my part because of the inconsistency between my story and Angelo's refutation, or because of the inequality in our reputations.   70. **hide:** put out of sight, remove from consideration.   **seems:** that seems.   76. **in probation:** i.e., a novice.   78. **As then:** being at that time.   **an 't like:** if it please.

Pray you, take note of it. And when you have
A business for yourself, pray heaven you then   85
Be perfect.°
LUCIO: I warrant° your honor.
DUKE:
The warrant's for yourself. Take heed to 't.
ISABELLA:
This gentleman told somewhat of my tale —
LUCIO: Right.   90
DUKE:
It may be right, but you are i' the wrong
To speak before your time. — Proceed.
ISABELLA: I went
To this pernicious caitiff deputy —
DUKE:
That's somewhat madly spoken.
ISABELLA: Pardon it;
The phrase is to the matter.°   95
DUKE:
Mended again.° The matter;° proceed.
ISABELLA:
In brief, to set the needless process by,°
How I persuaded, how I prayed and kneeled,
How he refelled° me, and how I replied —
For this was of much length — the vile conclusion   100
I now begin with grief and shame to utter.
He would not, but by gift of my chaste body
To his concupiscible° intemperate lust,
Release my brother; and after much debatement°
My sisterly remorse° confutes° mine honor,   105
And I did yield to him. But the next morn betimes,°
His purpose surfeiting,° he sends a warrant
For my poor brother's head.
DUKE: This is most likely!

---

86. **perfect:** prepared.   87. **warrant:** assure. (The Duke, however, quibbles in line 88 on the meaning "judicial writ.")   95. **to the matter:** to the purpose.   96. **Mended again:** set right. **The matter:** i.e., proceed to the main point.   97. **to set . . . by:** not to dwell on unnecessary details in the story.   99. **refelled:** refuted, repelled.   103. **concupiscible:** lustful.   104. **debatement:** argument, debate.   105. **remorse:** pity. **confutes:** confounds, silences.   106. **betimes:** early.   107. **surfeiting:** becoming satiated.

ISABELLA:
O, that it were as like° as it is true!

DUKE:
By heaven, fond° wretch, thou know'st not what thou speak'st,   110
Or else thou art suborned° against his honor
In hateful practice.° First, his integrity
Stands without blemish. Next, it imports no reason°
That with such vehemency he should pursue
Faults proper to himself.° If he had so offended,   115
He would have weighed° thy brother by himself
And not have cut him off. Someone hath set you on.
Confess the truth, and say by whose advice
Thou cam'st here to complain.

ISABELLA: And is this all?
Then, O you blessèd ministers above,   120
Keep me in patience, and with ripened time
Unfold° the evil which is here wrapped up
In countenance!° Heaven shield Your Grace from woe,
As I thus wrongèd hence unbelievèd go!   [*She starts to leave.*]

DUKE:
I know you'd fain be gone. An officer!   125
To prison with her. Shall we thus permit
A blasting° and a scandalous breath to fall
On him so near us? This needs must be a practice.
Who knew of your intent and coming hither?

ISABELLA:
One that I would were here, Friar Lodowick.   [*Exit under guard.*]   130

DUKE:
A ghostly father, belike. Who knows that Lodowick?

LUCIO:
My lord, I know him; 'tis a meddling friar.
I do not like the man. Had he been lay,° my lord,
For certain words he spake against Your Grace
In your retirement,° I had swingèd° him soundly.   135

---

109. **like:** likely. 110. **fond:** foolish. 111. **suborned:** induced to give false testimony. 112. **practice:** machination, conspiracy. 113. **imports no reason:** i.e., makes no sense. 115. **proper to himself:** of which he himself is guilty. 116. **weighed:** judged. 122. **Unfold:** disclose. 122–23. **wrapped . . . countenance:** concealed by means of authority, as well as by Angelo's hypocritically composed features and his partiality or favoritism. 127. **blasting:** blighting. 133. **lay:** not a cleric. 135. **In your retirement:** during your absence. **had swinged:** would have beaten.

DUKE:
Words against me? This'° a good friar, belike!
And to set on this wretched woman here
Against our substitute! Let this friar be found.

[*Exit one or more attendants.*]

LUCIO:
But yesternight, my lord, she and that friar,
I saw them at the prison. A saucy friar,   140
A very scurvy fellow.

FRIAR PETER:
Blessed be Your Royal Grace!
I have stood by, my lord, and I have heard
Your royal ear abused. First, hath this woman
Most wrongfully accused your substitute,   145
Who is as free from touch or soil with her
As she from one ungot.°

DUKE:
We did believe no less.
Know you that Friar Lodowick that she speaks of?

FRIAR PETER:
I know him for a man divine and holy,   150
Not scurvy, nor a temporary meddler,°
As he's reported by this gentleman;
And, on my trust, a man that never yet
Did, as he vouches, misreport Your Grace.

LUCIO:
My lord, most villainously, believe it.   155

FRIAR PETER:
Well, he in time may come to clear himself;
But at this instant he is sick, my lord,
Of a strange fever. Upon his mere request,°
Being come to knowledge° that there was complaint
Intended 'gainst Lord angelo, came I hither,   160
To speak, as from his mouth, what he doth know
Is true and false, and what he with his oath
And all probation° will make up full clear,
Whensoever he's convented.° First, for this woman,

---

136. **This'**: this is.   147. **ungot**: unbegotten.   151. **temporary meddler**: meddler in temporal
affairs.   158. **Upon . . . request**: solely at his request.   159. **Being . . . knowledge**: he having
learned.   163. **probation**: proof.   164. **convented**: summoned.

To justify this worthy nobleman,   165
So vulgarly° and personally accused,
Her shall you hear disprovèd to her eyes,°
Till she herself confess it.
DUKE: Good Friar, let's hear it.
                              [*Friar Peter goes to bring in Mariana.*]
Do you not smile at this, Lord Angelo?
O heaven, the vanity° of wretched fools!   170
Give us some seats.   [*Seats are provided.*]
                  Come, cousin Angelo,
In this I'll be impartial. Be you judge
Of your own cause.   [*The Duke and Angelo sit.*]

Enter Mariana, [veiled].

                  Is this the witness, Friar?
First, let her show her face, and after speak.
MARIANA:
Pardon, my lord, I will not show my face   175
Until my husband bid me.
DUKE: What, are you married?
MARIANA: No, my lord.
DUKE: Are you a maid?
MARIANA: No, my lord.   180
DUKE: A widow, then?
MARIANA: Neither, my lord.
DUKE: Why, you are nothing then, neither maid, widow, nor wife?
LUCIO: My lord, she may be a punk,° for many of them are neither maid,
    widow, nor wife.   185
DUKE:
Silence that fellow. I would he had some cause
To prattle for himself.°
LUCIO: Well, my lord.
MARIANA:
My lord, I do confess I ne'er was married,
And I confess besides I am no maid.   190
I have known° my husband, yet my husband
Knows not that ever he knew me.

---

166. **vulgarly:** publicly.   167. **to her eyes:** i.e., to her face.   170. **vanity:** folly.   184. **punk:** harlot.   187. **To . . . himself:** to speak in his own defense. (The Duke hints that there might well be charges pending against Lucio.)   191. **known:** had sexual intercourse with.

LUCIO: He was drunk then, my lord; it can be no better.
DUKE: For the benefit of silence, would thou wert so too!
LUCIO: Well, my lord.   195
DUKE:
   This is no witness for Lord Angelo.
MARIANA:
   Now I come to 't, my lord.
   She that accuses him of fornication
   In selfsame manner doth accuse my husband,
   And charges him, my lord, with such a time°   200
   When, I'll depose,° I had him in mine arms
   With all th' effect° of love.
ANGELO: Charges she more than me?°
MARIANA: Not that I know.
DUKE: No? You say your husband?   205
MARIANA:
   Why, just,° my lord, and that is Angelo,
   Who thinks he knows that he ne'er knew my body,
   But knows he thinks that he knows Isabel's.
ANGELO:
   This is a strange abuse.° Let's see thy face.
MARIANA:
   My husband bids me. Now I will unmask.   [She unveils.]   210
   This is that face, thou cruel Angelo,
   Which once thou swor'st was worth the looking on;
   This is the hand which, with a vowed contract,
   Was fast belocked° in thine; this is the body
   That took away the match° from Isabel,   215
   And did supply thee at thy garden house
   In her imagined person.
DUKE: [to Angelo]   Know you this woman?
LUCIO: Carnally, she says.
DUKE: Sirrah, no more!   220
LUCIO: Enough, my lord.
ANGELO:
   My lord, I must confess I know this woman,

---

200. with . . . time: with doing the deed at just the same time.   201. depose: testify under
oath.   202. effect: manifestations.   203. Charges . . . me: does she (Isabella) bring charges
against persons besides myself.   206. just: just so.   209. abuse: deception.   214. fast
belocked: firmly locked.   215. match: assignation.

And five years since there was some speech of marriage
Betwixt myself and her, which was broke off,
Partly for that° her promisèd proportions°   225
Came short of composition,° but in chief
For that her reputation was disvalued
In levity.° Since which time of five years
I never spake with her, saw her, nor heard from her,
Upon my faith and honor.
MARIANA: [*kneeling*]   Noble prince,   230
As there comes light from heaven and words from breath,
As there is sense in truth and truth in virtue,
I am affianced this man's wife as strongly
As words could make up vows; and, my good lord,
But Tuesday night last gone in 's garden house   235
He knew me as a wife. As this is true,
Let me in safety raise me from my knees,
Or else forever be confixèd° here,
A marble monument!
ANGELO:
I did but smile till now.   240
Now, good my lord, give me the scope° of justice.
My patience here is touched.° I do perceive
These poor informal° women are no more
But° instruments of some more mightier member
That sets them on. Let me have way, my lord,   245
To find this practice out.
DUKE: Ay, with my heart,
And punish them to your height of pleasure. —
Thou foolish friar, and thou pernicious woman,
Compact° with her that's gone, think'st thou thy oaths,
Though they would swear down each particular saint,°   250
Were testimonies against his worth and credit
That's sealed in approbation?° — You, Lord Escalus,
Sit with my cousin; lend him your kind pains
To find out this abuse, whence 'tis derived.

---

225. **for that:** because. **proportions:** dowry. 226. **composition:** agreement. 227–28. **disvalued in levity:** discredited for lightness. 238. **confixèd:** firmly fixed. 241. **scope:** full authority. 242. **touched:** injured, affected. 243. **informal:** rash, distracted. 244. **But:** than. 249. **Compact:** in collusion. 250. **swear . . . saint:** call down to witness every single saint. 252. **sealed in approbation:** ratified by proof.

There is another friar that set them on;   255
Let him be sent for.   [*The Duke rises; Escalus takes his chair.*]
FRIAR PETER:
   Would he were here, my lord! For he indeed
   Hath set the women on to this complaint.
   Your Provost knows the place where he abides,
   And he may fetch him.
DUKE: Go do it instantly.   [*Exit Provost.*]   260
   And you, my noble and well-warranted cousin,
   Whom it concerns to hear this matter forth,°
   Do with your injuries as seems you best,°
   In any chastisement. I for a while
   Will leave you; but stir not you till you have   265
   Well determined° upon these slanderers.
ESCALUS:
   My lord, we'll do it throughly.°   *Exit* [*Duke*].
   Signor Lucio, did not you say you knew that Friar Lodowick to be a dis-
   honest person?
LUCIO: *Cucullus non facit monachum;*° honest in nothing but in his clothes,   270
   and one that hath spoke most villainous speeches of the Duke.
ESCALUS: We shall entreat you to abide here till he come, and enforce
   them° against him. We shall find this friar a notable° fellow.
LUCIO: As any in Vienna, on my word.
ESCALUS: Call that same Isabel here once again. I would speak with her.   275
   [*Exit an attendant.*] Pray you, my lord, give me leave to question. You shall
   see how I'll handle her.
LUCIO: Not better than he, by her own report.
ESCALUS: Say you?
LUCIO: Marry, sir, I think, if you handled her privately,° she would sooner   280
   confess; perchance publicly she'll be ashamed.
ESCALUS: I will go darkly° to work with her.
LUCIO: That's the way, for women are light° at midnight.

Enter Duke [*disguised as a friar*], *Provost, Isabella,* [*and officers*].

ESCALUS: Come on, mistress. Here's a gentlewoman denies all that you
   have said.
                                                                                 285

---

262. **forth:** through.   263. **Do . . . best:** respond to the wrongs done you as seems best to you.
266. **determined:** reached judgment.   267. **throughly:** thoroughly.   270. *Cucullus . . .*
monachum: a cowl doesn't make a monk.   272–73. **enforce them:** forcefully urge your charges.
273. **notable:** notorious.   280. **if . . . privately:** (with sexual suggestion, punning on Escalus'
use of *handle* in line 277).   282. **darkly:** subtly, slyly.   283. **light:** wanton, unchaste.

LUCIO: My lord, here comes the rascal I spoke of, here with the Provost.

ESCALUS: In very good time. Speak not you to him till we call upon you.

LUCIO: Mum.

ESCALUS: Come, sir, did you set these women on to slander Lord Angelo?
They have confessed you did.   290

DUKE: 'Tis false.

ESCALUS: How? Know you where you are?

DUKE:
Respect to your great place! And let the devil
Be sometimes honored for his burning throne!°
Where is the Duke? 'Tis he should hear me speak.   295

ESCALUS:
The Duke's in us, and we will hear you speak.
Look you speak justly.

DUKE:
Boldly, at least. But O, poor souls,
Come you to seek the lamb here of the fox?
Good night to your redress! Is the Duke gone?   300
Then is your cause gone too. The Duke's unjust,
Thus to retort° your manifest° appeal,
And put your trial in the villain's mouth
Which here you come to accuse.

LUCIO:
This is the rascal. This is he I spoke of.   305

ESCALUS:
Why, thou unreverend and unhallowed friar,
Is 't not enough thou hast suborned these women
To accuse this worthy man, but, in foul mouth
And in the witness of his proper ear,°
To call him villain? And then to glance from him   310
To th' Duke himself, to tax him with° injustice?
Take him hence. To th' rack with him! We'll touse° you
Joint by joint, but we will know his purpose.
What, "unjust"?

DUKE: Be not so hot. The Duke
Dare no more stretch this finger of mine than he   315
Dare rack his own. His subject am I not,

293–94. let . . . throne: i.e., may all authority be respected, even the devil's. (Said sardonically.)
302. retort: turn back.   manifest: obviously just.   309. in . . . ear: within his own hearing.
311. tax him with: accuse him of.   312. touse: tear.

Nor here provincial.° My business in this state
Made me a looker-on here in Vienna,
Where I have seen corruption boil and bubble
Till it o'errun the stew;° laws for all faults,   320
But faults so countenanced° that the strong statutes
Stand like the forfeits° in a barber's shop,
As much in mock as mark.°

ESCALUS: Slander to th' state!
Away with him to prison.

ANGELO:
What can you vouch against him, Signor Lucio?   325
Is this the man that you did tell us of?

LUCIO: 'Tis he, my lord. — Come hither, Goodman Baldpate.° Do you
know me?

DUKE: I remember you, sir, by the sound of your voice. I met you at the
prison, in the absence of the Duke.   330

LUCIO: O, did you so? And do you remember what you said of the Duke?

DUKE: Most notedly,° sir.

LUCIO: Do you so, sir? And was the Duke a fleshmonger, a fool, and a
coward, as you then reported him to be?

DUKE: You must, sir, change° persons with me ere you make that my re-   335
port. You indeed spoke so of him, and much more, much worse.

LUCIO: O thou damnable fellow! Did not I pluck thee by the nose for thy
speeches?

DUKE: I protest I love the Duke as I love myself.

ANGELO: Hark how the villain would close° now, after his treasonable   340
abuses!

ESCALUS: Such a fellow is not to be talked withal. Away with him to prison!
Where is the Provost? Away with him to prison! Lay bolts° enough upon
him. Let him speak no more. Away with those giglots° too, and with the
other confederate companion!°   [The Provost lays hands on the Duke.]   345

DUKE: [to Provost]   Stay, sir, stay awhile.

ANGELO: What, resists he? Help him, Lucio.

LUCIO: Come, sir, come, sir, come, sir; foh, sir! Why, you bald-pated, lying

---

317. **provincial:** subject to the religious authority of this province or state.   320. **stew:** (1) stew-pot (2) brothel.   321. **countenanced:** allowed.   322. **forfeits:** cautionary displays, or lists of rules and fines for handling razors, etc., which barbers (who also acted as dentists and surgeons) hung in their shops.   323. **As . . . mark:** as often flouted as observed.   327. **Goodman Bald-pate:** (Lucio refers to the tonsure he assumes this "friar" must have.)   332. **notedly:** particularly.   335. **change:** exchange.   340. **close:** come to terms, compromise.   343. **bolts:** iron fetters.   344. **giglots:** wanton women.   345. **confederate companion:** i.e., Friar Peter.

rascal, you must be hooded, must you? Show your knave's visage, with a
pox to you! Show your sheep-biting° face, and be hanged an hour!° Will 't   350
not off?

    [He pulls off the friar's hood, and discovers the Duke. Angelo and Escalus rise.]

DUKE:

    Thou art the first knave that e'er mad'st a duke.

    First, Provost, let me bail these gentle three.°

    [*To Lucio.*] Sneak not away, sir, for the Friar and you

    Must have a word anon. — Lay hold on him.   355

LUCIO:

    This may prove worse than hanging.

DUKE: [*to Escalus*]

    What you have spoke I pardon. Sit you down.

    We'll borrow place of him. [*To Angelo.*] Sir, by your leave.

                      [He takes Angelo's seat. Escalus also sits.]

    Hast thou or word,° or wit, or impudence,

    That yet can do thee office?° If thou hast,   360

    Rely upon it till my tale be heard,

    And hold no longer out.°

ANGELO: [*kneeling*]   O my dread lord,

    I should be guiltier than my guiltiness

    To think I can be undiscernible,

    When I perceive Your Grace, like power divine,   365

    Hath looked upon my passes.° Then, good prince,

    No longer session hold upon my shame,

    But let my trial be mine own confession.

    Immediate sentence then and sequent° death

    Is all the grace I beg.

DUKE: Come hither, Mariana.   370

    Say, wast thou e'er contracted to this woman?

ANGELO:

    I was, my lord.

DUKE:

    Go take her hence and marry her instantly.

    Do you the office,° Friar, which consummate,°

    Return him here again. Go with him, Provost.   375

---

350. **sheep-biting:** knavish (from the action of wolves or dogs that prey on sheep). **hanged an
hour:** (A sardonic way of saying "hanged.") 353. **gentle three:** i.e., Mariana, Isabella, and
Friar Peter. 359. **or word:** either word. 360. **office:** service. 362. **hold . . . out:** then per-
sist no longer. 366.° **passes:** actions, trespasses. 369. **sequent:** subsequent. 374. **Do . . .
office:** you perform the service. **consummate:** being completed.

Exit [Angelo, with Mariana, Friar Peter, and Provost].

ESCALUS:
My lord, I am more amazed at his dishonor
Than at the strangeness of it.

DUKE: Come hither, Isabel.
Your friar is now your prince. As I was then
Advertising° and holy° to your business,
Not changing heart with habit, I am still   380
Attorneyed at° your service.

ISABELLA: O, give me pardon,
That I, your vassal, have employed and pained°
Your unknown sovereignty!

DUKE: You are pardoned, Isabel.
And now, dear maid, be you as free to us.°
Your brother's death, I know, sits at your heart;   385
And you may marvel why I obscured myself,
Laboring to save his life, and would not rather
Make rash remonstrance° of my hidden power
Than let him so be lost. O most kind maid,
It was the swift celerity of his death,   390
Which I did think with slower foot came on,
That brained° my purpose. But peace be with him!
That life is better life past fearing death
Than that which lives to fear. Make it your comfort,
So° happy is your brother.

Enter Angelo, Mariana, [Friar] Peter, [and] Provost.

ISABELLA: I do, my lord.   395

DUKE:
For this new-married man approaching here,
Whose salt° imagination yet hath wronged
Your well-defended honor, you must pardon
For Mariana's sake. But as he adjudged your brother —
Being criminal, in double violation   400
Of sacred chastity and of promise-breach
Thereon dependent,° for your brother's life —

---

379. **Advertising:** attentive.   **holy:** virtuously dedicated.   381. **Attorneyed at:** serving as agent in.   382. **pained:** put to trouble.   384. **free to us:** i.e., generous in pardoning me.   388. **rash remonstrance:** sudden manifestation.   392. **brained:** dashed, defeated.   395. **So:** thus.   397. **salt:** lecherous.   401–02: **promise-breach . . . dependent:** i.e., breaking his promise made in return for the yielding up of chastity.

The very mercy of the law° cries out
Most audible, even from his proper° tongue,
"An Angelo for Claudio, death for death!"   405
Haste still° pays haste, and leisure answers leisure;
Like doth quit° like, and measure still for measure.
Then, Angelo, thy fault's thus manifested,
Which, though° thou wouldst deny, denies thee vantage.°
We do condemn thee to the very block   410
Where Claudio stooped to death, and with like haste.
Away with him!
MARIANA: O my most gracious lord,
I hope you will not mock me with a husband!
DUKE:
It is your husband mocked you with a husband.
Consenting to the safeguard of your honor,   415
I thought your marriage fit;° else imputation,°
For that° he knew° you, might reproach your life
And choke your good to come. For° his possessions,
Although by confiscation they are ours,
We do instate and widow you withal,°   420
To buy you a better husband.
MARIANA: O my dear lord,
I crave no other, nor no better man.
DUKE:
Never crave him; we are definitive.°
MARIANA: [*kneeling*]
Gentle my liege —
DUKE: You do but lose your labor.
Away with him to death! [*To Lucio.*] Now, sir, to you.   425
MARIANA:
O my good lord! Sweet Isabel, take my part!
Lend me your knees, and all my life to come
I'll lend you all my life to do you service.
DUKE:
Against all sense you do importune her.

---

403. **The very . . . law:** i.e., even mercy itself.   404. **his proper:** its own.   406. **still:** always.
407. **quit:** requite.   409. **though:** even if.   **vantage:** i.e., any advantage. (Angelo must suffer the same penalty as Claudio.)   416. **fit:** appropriate.   **imputation:** accusation, slander.   417. **For that:** because.   **knew:** had sexual relations with.   418. **For:** as for.   420. **instate . . . withal:** grant to you the estate appropriate to a widow.   423. **definitive:** firmly resolved.

Should she kneel down in mercy of this fact,°   430
Her brother's ghost his pavèd bed° would break,
And take her hence in horror.

MARIANA: Isabel,
Sweet Isabel, do yet but kneel by me!
Hold up your hands, say nothing; I'll speak all.
They say best men° are molded out of faults,   435
And, for the most,° become much more the better
For being a little bad. So may my husband.
O Isabel, will you not lend a knee?

DUKE:
He dies for Claudio's death.

ISABELLA: [*kneeling*]   Most bounteous sir,
Look, if it please you, on this man condemned   440
As if my brother lived. I partly think
A due sincerity governed his deeds,
Till he did look on me. Since it is so,
Let him not die. My brother had but justice,
In that he did the thing for which he died.   445
For Angelo,
His act did not o'ertake his bad intent,
And must be buried° but as an intent
That perished by the way. Thoughts are no subjects,°
Intents but merely thoughts.

MARIANA: Merely, my lord.   450

DUKE:
Your suit's unprofitable.° Stand up, I say.   [*They stand.*]
I have bethought me of another fault.
Provost, how came it Claudio was beheaded
At an unusual hour?

PROVOST:
It was commanded so.   455

DUKE:
Had you a special warrant for the deed?

PROVOST:
No, my good lord, it was by private message.

---

430. **in . . . fact:** pleading mercy for this crime.   431. **pavèd bed:** grave covered with a stone slab.   435. **best men:** even the best of men.   436. **most:** most part.   448. **buried:** i.e., forgotten.   449. **no subjects:** i.e., not subject to the state's authority.   451. **unprofitable:** worthless.

DUKE:
　For which I do discharge you of your office.
　Give up your keys.
PROVOST:　　　　　　　Pardon me, noble lord.
　I thought it was a fault, but knew it not,°　　　　　　　　460
　Yet did repent me after more advice;°
　For testimony whereof, one in the prison,
　That should by private order else have died,
　I have reserved alive.
DUKE:　What's he?　　　　　　　　　　　　　　465
PROVOST:　His name is Barnardine.
DUKE:
　I would thou hadst done so by Claudio.
　Go fetch him hither. Let me look upon him.　　　　[Exit Provost.]
ESCALUS:
　I am sorry one so learnèd and so wise
　As you, Lord Angelo, have still° appeared,　　　　　　　470
　Should slip so grossly, both in the heat of blood
　And lack of tempered judgment afterward.
ANGELO:
　I am sorry that such sorrow I procure,
　And so deep sticks it in my penitent heart
　That I crave death more willingly than mercy.　　　　　175
　'Tis my deserving, and I do entreat it.

　Enter Barnardine and Provost, Claudio [muffled],° [and] Juliet.

DUKE:
　Which is that Barnardine?
PROVOST:　　　　　　　This, my lord.
DUKE:
　There was a friar told me of this man. —
　Sirrah, thou art said to have a stubborn soul
　That apprehends no further than this world,　　　　　　480
　And squar'st° thy life according. Thou'rt condemned;
　But, for° those earthly faults, I quit° them all,
　And pray thee take this mercy to provide
　For better times to come. — Friar, advise him;

460. **knew it not:** was not sure.　461. **advice:** consideration.　470. **still:** always.　**s.d. *muffled*:** wrapped up so as to conceal identity (as also in line 485).　481. **squar'st:** regulates.　482. **for:** as for.　**quit:** pardon.

I leave him to your hand. — What muffled fellow's that?   485
PROVOST:
   This is another prisoner that I saved,
   Who should have died when Claudio lost his head,
   As like almost to Claudio as himself.   [*He unmuffles Claudio.*]
DUKE: [*to Isabella*]
   If he be like your brother, for his sake
   Is he pardoned, and for your lovely sake,   490
   Give me your hand and say you will be mine;
   He is my brother too. But fitter time for that.
   By this Lord Angelo perceives he's safe;
   Methinks I see a quickening in his eye.
   Well, Angelo, your evil quits° you well.   495
   Look that you love your wife, her worth worth yours.°
   I find an apt remission° in myself;
   And yet here's one in place° I cannot pardon.
   [*To Lucio.*] You, sirrah, that knew me for a fool, a coward,
   One all of luxury,° an ass, a madman —   500
   Wherein have I so deserved of you
   That you extol me thus?
LUCIO: Faith, my lord, I spoke it but according to the trick.° If you will
   hang me for it, you may; but I had rather it would please you I might be
   whipped.   505
DUKE:
   Whipped first, sir, and hanged after.
   Proclaim it, Provost, round about the city,
   If any woman wronged by this lewd fellow —
   As I have heard him swear himself there's one
   Whom he begot with child — let her appear,   510
   And he shall marry her. The nuptial finished,
   Let him be whipped and hanged.
LUCIO: I beseech Your Highness, do not marry me to a whore. Your High-
   ness said even° now I made you a duke; good my lord, do not recompense
   me in making me a cuckold.   515
DUKE:
   Upon mine honor, thou shalt marry her.
   Thy slanders I forgive and therewithal

---

495. **quits:** rewards, requites.   496. **her . . . yours:** see to it that you are worthy of her worth,
since she deserves no less.   497. **apt remission:** readiness to show mercy.   498. **in place:**
present.   500. **luxury:** lechery.   503. **trick:** fashion.   514. **even:** just.

Remit thy other forfeits.° — Take him to prison,
And see our pleasure herein executed.°
LUCIO: Marrying a punk, my lord, is pressing to death,° whipping, and   520
hanging.
DUKE:
Slandering a prince deserves it.   [*Exeunt officers with Lucio.*]
She, Claudio, that you wronged, look you restore.
Joy to you, Mariana! Love her, Angelo.
I have confessed her, and I know her virtue.   525
Thanks, good friend Escalus, for thy much goodness;
There's more behind° that is more gratulate.°
Thanks, Provost, for thy care and secrecy;
We shall employ thee in a worthier place.
Forgive him, Angelo, that brought you home   530
The head of Ragozine for Claudio's;
Th' offense pardons itself. Dear Isabel,
I have a motion° much imports your good,
Whereto if you'll a willing ear incline,
What's mine is yours, and what is yours is mine. —   535
So, bring° us to our palace, where we'll show
What's yet behind,° that's meet you all should know.   [*Exeunt.*]

FINIS

517–18. **and therewithal . . . forfeits:** i.e., and therefore will not have you whipped and hanged.
519. **see . . . executed:** i.e., see that my order be carried out that Lucio marry Kate Keepdown
(see 3.2.160–61).   520. **pressing to death:** i.e., by having heavy weights placed on the chest. (A
standard form of executing those who refused to plead to a felony charge.) Lucio wryly complains that marrying a whore is as bad as death by torture.   527. **behind:** in store, to come.
gratulate: gratifying.   533. **motion:** proposal (which).   536. **bring:** escort.   537. **What's yet
behind:** what is still to be told.

TEXTUAL NOTES FOR MEASURE FOR MEASURE

Copy text: the First Folio. Act and scene divisions are from the Folio except as indicated below.
ACT 1, SCENE 1. 76. s.d.: [at line 75 in F]
ACT 1, SCENE 2. 47. s.p. [and elsewhere] Mistress Overdone: *Bawd.* 66. s.d.: [after line 46 in F]. 68. s.p. [and elsewhere] Pompey: *Clo.* 92. [F begins *"Scena Tertia"* here], 110. morality: mortality.
ACT 1, SCENE 3. [F labels as *"Scena Quarta"*]. 20. steeds: weedes. 27. Becomes more: More. 54. s.d. Exeunt: *Exit.*
ACT 1, SCENE 4. [F labels as *"Scena Quinta"*]. s.d. [and elsewhere] Isabella: *Isabell.* 2. s.p. [and throughout] Francisca: *Nun.* 5. sisterhood: Sisterstood. 17. stead: steed. 54. givings-out: giuing-out. 61–62. mind, study, and fast. / He: minde: Studie, and fast / He. 72. He's: Has.
ACT 2, SCENE 1. 12. your: our. 39. breaks: brakes. 118. s.d.: [at line 117 in F].
ACT 2, SCENE 2. 63. back again: againe. 104. ere: here.
ACT 2, SCENE 3. 41. law: Loue.
ACT 2, SCENE 4. 9. sere: feard. 17. s.d. Enter Servant: [after line 17 in F]. 30. s.d. Enter Isabella: [after line 30 in F]. 53. or: and. 75. craftily: crafty. 76. me be: be. 94. all-binding: all-building.
ACT 3, SCENE 1. 29. thee sire: thee, fire. 31. serpigo: Sapego. 52. me to hear them: them to heare me. 68. Though: Through. 91. enew: emmew. 96. damned'st: damnest. 131. penury: periury. 191. advisings. To . . . good a: aduisings, to . . . good; a. 203. by oath: oath.
ACT 3, SCENE 2. 0. [not marked as a new scene in F]. 6. law a: Law; a. 7. on: and. 21. eat, array: eate away. 41. it clutched: clutch'd. 62. bondage. If . . . patiently, why: bondage if . . . patiently: Why. 90–91. ungenerative: generatiue. 122. dearer: deare. 177. See: Sea.
ACT 4, SCENE 1. 1. s.p. Boy: [not in F]. 18. s.d. Isabella: *Isabell.* 46. s.d.: [after line 45 in F]. 58. quests: Quest. 61. s.d. Enter . . . Isabella: [after line 61 in F].
ACT 4, SCENE 2. 31–34. If . . . thief: [assigned in F to *Clo.*]. 42. yare: y'are. 44. s.d.: [at line 43 in F]. 56. s.d. Enter Duke: [after line 56 in F]. 84. This . . . man: [assigned in F to *Duke*]. lordship's: Lords. 85. s.p. Duke: *Pro.* 102. s.p. Provost: [not in F].
ACT 4, SCENE 3. 79. s.d.: [at line 78 in F]. 80. Varrius: *Angelo.* 87. well: weale.
ACT 4, SCENE 4. 4. redeliver: reliuer. 12. proclaimed. Betimes: proclaim'd betimes. 16. s.d.: [at line 15 in F].
ACT 4, SCENE 5. 6. Flavius': *Flauia's.*
ACT 5, SCENE 1. 14. me: we. 34. hear!: heere. 173. s.d. Enter Mariana: [after line 173 in F]. 174. her face: your face. 267. s.d.: [at line 266 in F]. 283. s.d.: [at line 281 in F]. 395. s.d. Mariana: *Maria.* 419. confiscation: confutation. 476. s.d. Juliet: *Iulietta.* 537. that's: that.

PART TWO

Cultural Contexts

CHAPTER I

Governance

——————————— >< ———————————

Shakespeare was deeply concerned with questions of governance through-out his career as a dramatist. In his portrayal of Richard II, a man who finds himself paralyzed in the face of an insurrection by his nobles and who relies on God and nature itself to defend his crown for him, Shakespeare shows the harmful effects a weak king can have on the stability of his kingdom. He also shows us bustling kings like Richard III and Macbeth, who murder their way to the crown, and who wreak a different kind of havoc in their respective countries, undermining the very social and institutional structures that prop up the monarchy. Then there are princes like Henry V or *The Tempest*'s Prospero, who encounter great personal and political adversity during their rule but who overcome their troubles and ultimately triumph and emerge as shrewd and powerful leaders of their peoples. *Measure for Measure* likewise is a play steeped in issues of governance, and its leading figure, Duke Vincentio, has strong affinities with Prospero, Henry V, and even Malcolm, who comes to power at the end of *Macbeth*, or Edgar, who emerges as the new ruler at the end of *King Lear*. All of them belong to a category of rulers who restore order to society but who do so in a style of governance profoundly different from their predecessors or, in the case of Prospero and *Measure for Measure*'s Duke, in a way distinct from their own prior ruling practices. Indeed, the man who publicly renders legal

FIGURE 4 *King James I of England and VI of Scotland.*

judgments and engineers an ingenious ending to all the troubles and conflicts in *Measure for Measure*'s final act has seemingly nothing in common with the man who, at the beginning of the play, does not like to stage himself to the people's eyes, who has let Vienna's laws "slip" for fourteen years, and who has lost the respect of his subjects.

Although quite a few of Shakespeare's plays engage the question of governance, it is particularly suitable that *Measure for Measure* should, for it was composed around the time that England experienced a profound governmental and dynastic shift. Elizabeth I died at Richmond Palace on March 24, 1603, ending the Tudor dynasty, which had held sway in England since the coronation of Henry VII in 1485. With the death of the last Tudor monarch, the English crown passed to Elizabeth's cousin, King James VI of Scotland, a member of the House of Stuart. It was for this new king that *Measure for Measure* was performed at Whitehall Palace on December 26, 1604. James too was descended from Henry VII (through Margaret Tudor, daughter of Henry VII), but his Scottish ancestry combined with Elizabeth's refusal to name her successor had made him a likely, but certainly not inevitable, successor to the English throne. When a peaceful transition of power made James king of England in March 1603, it ended a period of great anxiety and uncertainty. Those who knew about the Wars of the Roses from Shakespeare's plays or Holinshed's monumental history, or who remembered the strife and bloodshed surrounding the brief reign of Jane Grey and the accessions of Mary and Elizabeth, were fully aware that things could have turned out very differently. What is more, the final years of Elizabeth's reign had been fraught with social and economic difficulties. Shakespeare's London was also visited by the plague in 1593, killing 15,000 of its citizens. In 1603, when London was a city of just over 200,000 people, the epidemic returned to wipe out roughly 36,000. James's official entry into the city, which was supposed to be a glorious event with pageants and fanfare, had to be postponed because it was thought too dangerous for the king to be exposed to his infected subjects. For many, things were not much better on the economic front. The 1590s saw a number of bad harvests, leading to famine and occasional riots. What is more, the queen's refusal to settle the succession question, even as she aged and was clearly past childbearing age, left her subjects to wonder how England's dynastic future would unfold. Historians have speculated about the reasons for Elizabeth's reluctance to name her successor, some of them arguing that Elizabeth felt she might become irrelevant, or even expendable, to her own court.[1] But whatever her

---

[1] In 1561, she told the Scottish ambassador, "Assuredly, if my successor were known to the world, I would never esteem my state to be safe" (Hayward 85).

Crounes haue their compasse, length of dayes their date,
Triumphes their tombes, felicitie her fate:
Of more then earth, can earth make none partaker,
But knowledge makes the KING most like his maker.

Simon Passæus sculp: Lond.   Ioh: Bill excudit.

FIGURE 5 *James I, frontispiece illustration in* Workes *(London 1616).*

reasons, it is doubtless correct that the queen opted to risk "instability after her death for the sake of stability in her own lifetime" (Haigh 21). This prospect of instability may well have been on the mind of the extremely popular and powerful Earl of Essex and his followers when they attempted what amounted to a *coup d'état* against Elizabeth in 1601, reminding Londoners just how suddenly and seriously the political status quo could be challenged.

In short, the English had plenty to worry about during the last years of the queen's reign. It is hard to estimate what famine, disease, and political uncertainty do to the collective psyche of a nation, but we can fairly surmise from a wide range of contemporary accounts that the English breathed a collective sigh of relief when the transfer of power from Elizabeth to James appeared peaceful, and, by all accounts, that they looked forward with genuine anticipation to James's arrival in London. Many traveled north to meet the new king and greet (as well as petition) him as he made his way down from Scotland to London. James was so touched by his reception that he referred to it in his first address to the English Parliament on March 19, 1604.

> Shall I ever, nay, can I ever be able, or rather so unable in memory, as to forget your unexpected readiness and alacrity, your ever memorable resolution, and your most wonderful conjunction and harmony of your hearts in declaring and embracing me as your undoubted and lawful king and governor? Or shall it ever be blotted out of my mind, how at my first entry into this kingdom, the people of all sorts rid and ran, nay rather flew to meet me, their eyes flaming nothing but sparkles of affection, their mouths and tongues uttering nothing but sounds of joy, their hands, feet, and all the rest of their members' gestures discovering a passionate longing, and earnestness to meet and embrace their new sovereign.
>
> ("A Speech" 132–33)

The people looked to James, rightly or wrongly, as the harbinger of a new era of stability and prosperity (see Fig. 4, p. 118). Addressing the king directly, on his journey into England in 1603, the poet Samuel Daniel spoke for those who looked on the recent past with dismay and to the future with great optimism.

> Only the joy of this so dear a thing
>   Made me look back unto the cause, whence came
> This so great good, this blessing of a King;
>   When our estate so much requir'd the same,
> When we had need of power for well-ordering
>   Of our affairs: need of a spirit to frame

The world to good, to grace and worthiness,
Out of this humor of luxuriousness:

And bring us back unto ourselves again,
    Unto our ancient native modesty,
From out these foreign sins we entertain,
    These loathsome surfeits, ugly gluttony;
From this unmanly and this idle vein
    Of wanton and superfluous bravery;
The wreck of gentry, spoil of nobleness;
And square us by thy temperate nobleness.
                    (Nichols 131; see also Richard Martin's speech, p. 175)

Yet, despite these high expectations, it is also true that most of the people knew very little about James's style and character, which made many uncertain about what kind of king of England James would make. Elizabeth had enjoyed an unusually long reign (from 1558 until 1603), and when James assumed the throne the overwhelming majority of his new English subjects had experienced the rule of only one monarch. To many, James was a mystery. In the years immediately preceding the death of the queen, James had met in Scotland, often clandestinely, with representatives of different English political and religious factions, each of whom hoped to win the potential future king of England to their cause. Catholics hoped that he would extend to them religious tolerance, while Puritans thought he might help them bring about more drastic reforms in the Church of England. Some urged James to pursue war with Spain; others hoped that he would make peace with the most powerful Catholic nation. Trying not to offend any one faction, James made assurances to nearly all of them, and, as a consequence, remained somewhat of a question mark to his new subjects.

English curiosity about the new king is evidenced by multiple London printings in 1603 of James's two treatises on the theory and practice of kingship, which he penned while king of Scotland. One of them, *The True Law of Free Monarchies*, is an elaborate exposition of the theory of the divine right of kings, and the other, entitled *Basilikon Doron*, is a book of advice to James's young son, Henry, on how to be an effective monarch (see Fig. 5, p. 120). *Basilikon Doron* was printed first in Edinburgh in 1598 and again in revised form in 1603. The 1603 edition was taken to London when Elizabeth's death seemed imminent, and went through several printings in the weeks following her March 24 passing (Sommerville 268n. 1). *The True Law*, likewise, was reprinted at least four times (Sommerville 282n. 468). Clearly, the English were eager to learn more about their new king.

There were even those, as the poet Samuel Daniel wrote, who feared "the humors of a future prince" (Nichols 124). In 1604 that fear took expression in a debate in the House of Commons over "The Apology Directed to the King's Most Excellent Majesty." In "The Apology" the House is eager to disabuse the monarch of certain "misinformations" about the rights and privileges of the Commons. Possibly counteracting the new king's pronounced tendency to assert his royal prerogative at will, the Commons gently reminded him that "our privileges and liberties are our right and due inheritance, no less than our very lands and goods; that they cannot be withheld from us, denied or impaired, but with apparent wrong to the whole state of the realm . . ." (Kenyon 31).[2] With this debate, the multiple printings of James's writings, and a general sense of expectation, curiosity, and apprehension in the air, it can be no accident that *Measure for Measure* concerns itself intensely with questions of governance.

The issue of governance is central both to *Measure for Measure* and to any effort to historicize the play. *Measure for Measure* presents us with several figures of authority — but principally the Duke and Angelo — and implicitly asks us to consider what makes for a good and/or effective ruler. Clearly, we are asked to evaluate the Duke's governance of Vienna "this fourteen years" (1.3.21), as well as his controversial decision to put the "precise" Angelo in charge during his "absence." And, like the Duke, we may be curious "what figure" of the Duke Angelo will bear (1.1.17). Will he be an incorruptible voice of justice, as he intends to be, or will he reveal, as the Duke suspects, that "his appetite / Is more to bread than stone" (1.3.52–53). And if Angelo proves corruptible would this be a significant issue for the administration of justice? Does a ruler have to be virtuous to dispense justice? Or is it acceptable (or even unavoidable), as Angelo tells Escalus, that the law cares not if one thief sends another thief to the gallows? What is more, should a prince temper justice with mercy or should he enforce the letter of the law so as to set an unambiguous example for all the people, as Angelo seems to want to do in sentencing Claudio to death? (See Figs. 6 and 7.) How far can or should a prince go in governing his subjects? Should he spy on his own people, as the Duke does? Should he empower a deputy to do the dirty work for him? Should he be allowed to use laws against fornication to prop up his authority?[3] And

---

[2] Kenyon observes that, contrary to the opinion of other historians, this document should not be seen as the first milestone "along the road to rebellion" against Charles I in 1641 but as "neurotically defensive" (25). Either way, the document registers actual or imagined infringements by the king on the rights of his subjects. James's own writings were ambiguous on the issue of royal prerogative. James frequently insists that the king is above (or prior to) the law, but in one of the excerpts from *The True Law of Free Monarchies* included in this section, he also protests it to be a king's duty "to maintain the whole country and every state therein in all their ancient privileges and liberties."

[3] See Dollimore, who argues that the anxiety over rampant sexuality in Vienna is nothing but a ruse that allows the Duke to reassert his authority over his subjects.

FIGURE 6 *"The Wicked Man Is Moved to Mercy by No Entreaty" (Improbus à nullo flectitus obsequia), from Claude Paradin,* The Heroicall Devises of M. Claudius Paradin, Whereunto Are Added the Lord Gabriel Symeons and Others *(1562). The text accompanying this emblem remarks that "Those that are so cruel, so hard-hearted, so austere and wicked, that although a man give them all obedience, yet will not vouchsafe to show him any compassion, are worthy truly to have for their symbol the image of death."*

what is the ruler's relationship to the law? Is he above the law and entitled to apply or ignore it as he sees fit, or is he bound by it and merely its servant and enforcer? Must subjects obey their prince if he acts tyrannically (as Angelo does toward Isabella), or may they disobey or thwart him? And, finally, whence does the ruler's power originate? Is his power divine in nature, as Angelo at one point suggests; that is, does power come from God, or is it simply the product of a skillful politician's actions? Is a ruler an agent of God or a manipulator of men, or can he be both?

The King James Version of *Measure for Measure*

But before we take up the question of governance directly, we should say a few words about a longstanding critical crux that has become inextricably linked to it, namely the play's topicality. Earlier we suggested that there may be a connection between *Measure for Measure*'s interest in governance and the dynastic shift that occurred in England at the time of its composition. But the nexus is both older and more specific than that. At least as far back as 1766, critics have argued that *Measure for Measure* has a special connection to King James I, and that James's *Basilikon Doron*, in particular, may have been a source for Shakespeare's play. This is an example of what Richard Levin has called occasionalism, an approach that "interprets plays as compositions directed at a special audience," in this case at King James (167). *Measure for Measure* was performed before James on December 26, 1604, at Whitehall, and some have insisted that Duke Vincentio is directly modeled on James. This so-called King James Version[4] of *Measure for Measure* looks for suggestive parallels between Shakespeare's Duke and the life and writings of James. The Duke, for instance, confesses that he "has ever loved the life removed" (1.3.8) and says of himself that even an envious person would have to admit that he is "a scholar" (3.2.118). Some critics suggest that this is an intentional compliment to James, who fancied himself a philosopher and a scholar. The Duke also professes to love the people but adds that he does "not like to stage [himself] to their eyes" (1.1.68, 69). James, too, often expressed his love for his subjects and observed, with apparent regret, that kings are placed "upon a public stage, in the sight of all the people; where all the beholders are attentively bent to look and pry in the least circumstance of their secretest drifts" (James I, *Basilikon Doron* 4). Some critics push the association even further and argue that the Duke's distaste of displaying himself in public displays refers to James's well-known fear of crowds and large assemblies, stemming from his days as a young boy in Scotland, when he witnessed the mortal wounding of his grandfather, who received his injury while defending the young James from kidnappers. This and other events, such as the assassination of his father when James was only one, left such an impression on the young king that for most of his life, he apparently wore "doublets quilted for stiletto proof" to ward off would-be assassins (Weldon, qtd. in Houston 117). Furthermore, that the Duke goes among his subjects in disguise is purported to remind us of James's other grandfather, James V of Scotland, who moved among his subjects incognito.

As suggestive as some of these examples and arguments may appear, one can muster at least as many striking differences between James and the Duke as there are supposed similarities. James, for instance, in his *Basilikon Doron*, constantly speaks out against "Papists" and the "Popish Church" even though the Duke (disguised as a friar) claims to have come from the

---

[4] We borrow the term from Richard Levin, who coined the phrase and who did an extensive analysis of the James–*Measure for Measure* connection (171–93).

pope and even hears confession (Levin 186–87). This makes for an odd or even inexplicable dissimilarity. James speaks out in favor of marrying early, but the Duke of Vienna has so far lived his life as a bachelor. James argues that a ruler should always marry someone of his own social rank, but the Duke proposes marriage to a commoner at the end of the play. James tells his son in *Basilikon Doron* that "willful murder" is a crime that a ruler should never forgive (23), but the Duke sees fit to pardon Barnardine the murderer. James says that a ruler should speak plainly and "use a natural and plain form" of speech, whereas the Duke speaks poetically and, at times, ornately.

Despite these and other examples that cast further doubt on the occasionalist readings of *Measure for Measure*, we should not altogether dismiss the possibility of meaningful links between the king and the play. It is possible that audiences noted the apparent similarities between James and the Duke, regardless of other differences, and thought them significant. Furthermore, while we do not encounter any direct quotations from James's *True Law of Free Monarchies* or *Basilikon Doron* in *Measure for Measure*, it is clear that James and Shakespeare grapple with some of the same political ideas. Shakespeare might have read James's writings, but it is just as likely that Shakespeare read some of the widely available political treatises that may have influenced James's thoughts on kingship. James's views on such issues as divine right of kings, absolutism, royal prerogative, and resistance theory, are hardly original. All of them had been part of England's political discourse in one form or another ever since the Middle Ages, and some of them, including divine right of kings and royal prerogative, had become hot topics of discussion in the last decade of Elizabeth's reign. In fact, from plays such as *Richard II, Henry V,* and *Julius Caesar* (to name only the best-known ones) it is clear that Shakespeare was thinking about monarchy, republicanism, divine right, absolutism, resistance theory, and related issues several years before James became king of England. The writings and ideas of historians such as Raphael Holinshed, Edward Hall, Plutarch, and political and/or religious thinkers such as Cicero, Thomas Elyot, Erasmus, William Tyndale, John Aylmer, Robert Filmer, George Buchanan, Richard Bancroft, and Machiavelli circulated widely in early modern culture, and it is reasonable to assume that Shakespeare and James drew on them independently.[5]

Setting aside the question of direct influence, let us examine some of the

---

[5] John Aylmer, *Harbor for Faithful and True Subjects* (1599), Stephanus Junius Brutus, *Vindiciae Contra Tyrannos* (1579), George Buchanan, *De Jure Regni apud Scotus* (1579), Richard Hooker, *Laws of Ecclesiastical Polity* (1594), Mathew Sutcliffe, *De Presbyterio* (1591), Richard Bancroft, *Dangerous Positions and Proceedings* (1593).

salient ideas about governance that one encounters in Shakespeare's play and early seventeenth-century thought.

Divine Right of Kings and Absolutism

Already implied in medieval ideas of kingship, the essence of the early seventeenth-century theory of the divine right of kings is that the monarch derives from God (as opposed to the people or some other source) his power to rule. The reason that God has granted such power to a single individual is that human beings, by virtue of their fallen nature, are incapable of good self-government.[6] If they are to conduct themselves so that they may merit salvation, they need the guidance of the monarch and his or her laws. In some accounts, the people themselves, aware of their sinfulness and eager for their salvation, ask God to place an earthly lord over them. This view dates back centuries before James became king of England, but it gained greater prominence and social and religious urgency in the period of the Reformation following the break with Rome. The removal of the pope from English life as the final arbiter of all ecclesiastical affairs on earth required that the one who would thereafter fulfill this role — the monarch — would be perceived as having special legitimacy and authority to carry out this important function. Hence, in 1531 Henry VIII bestowed on himself the title of Supreme Head of the Church of England, and in 1534 pushed through the *Act for the Submission of the Clergy and Restraint of Appeals*, which made it illegal for appeals to be made to the "the bishop of Rome," and the *Supremacy Act*, which gave the king the legal "authority to reform and redress all errors, heresies, and abuses" in the the Church of England (Stephenson and Marcham 306–07, 311–12). For his attempt to place himself at the head of the church, Henry found support in a variety of places. Among them were the writings of the Lutheran theologian William Tyndale, who asserted in *The Obedience of a Christian Man* (1528) that God "in all lands has put kings, governors, and rulers in His own stead, to rule the world through them" (*Doctrinal Treatises* 1: 174–75, qtd. in Ridley 198). Tyndale continues, "God has made the king in every realm judge over all, and *over him there is no judge*. He that judges the king, judges God, and he that lays hands on the

---

[6] Sommerville observes that divine right extended beyond monarchy to other forms of government such as aristocracy and democracy. In those forms of government, too, "the powers of the governor were derived from God alone" (12). For the purposes of our discussion, however, we will focus solely on divine right monarchy.

king, lays hands on God. And he that resists the king, resists God, and *damns* God's law and ordinances" (Tyndale fol. xxvii; emphasis added).

If the monarch has no judge over him (other than God), it places him in a position of absolute power vis-à-vis his subjects. Henry VIII broke with Rome and papal authority not to increase his power over his English subjects but rather to gain independence from Rome and to nullify Rome's objection to his divorce from his first wife, Catherine of Aragon. On the whole, however, Henry was content to rule within the parameters of English law, even if that limited his "discretionary powers" (Elton 13). It was not until the last decade of Elizabeth I's reign that "clerics were expressing nakedly absolutist ideas [and] not until the succession of James I that an English sovereign gave unequivocal support to such views" (Sommerville 115). While still king of Scotland, James seized on the idea of divine right to expound a full-fledged theory of royal absolutism that claims not only that the king's power stems directly from God but that the king is *therefore* above the law. In his *True Law of Free Monarchies,* James puts it thus: "Kings are called Gods by the prophetical King David, because they sit upon God his throne in the earth, and have the count of their administration to give unto him" (p. 149). And furthermore, "the king is above the law . . . yet a good king will not only delight to rule his subjects by the law, but even will conform himself in his own actions thereunto . . . [but] where he sees the law doubtful or rigorous, he may interpret or mitigate the same . . . upon causes only known to him" (p. 153). In a 1610 speech to Parliament, James made it very clear that he would from time to time explain himself to his subjects, but that he was absolutely under no legal or moral obligation to do so:

> [I]t is sedition in subjects, to dispute what a King may do in the height of his power: But just Kings will ever be willing to declare what they will do, if they will not incur the curse of God. I will not be content that my power be disputed upon: but I shall ever be willing to make the reason appear of all my doings, and rule my actions according to my Laws.
> ("Speech to the Lords and Commons" 184)

The years between 1603 and 1625 reveal that the English Parliament played a greater role than James's declarations would indicate, but on the threshold of his English reign it would not have been unwarranted for people to conclude that James took very seriously both the divine origins and the absoluteness of his power.

The most conspicuous moment in *Measure for Measure*'s exploration of divine right rule occurs in the final scene when Angelo, who now perceives that the mysterious friar is really Duke Vincentio (and that his transgressions are known to the Duke), falls to his knees and says,

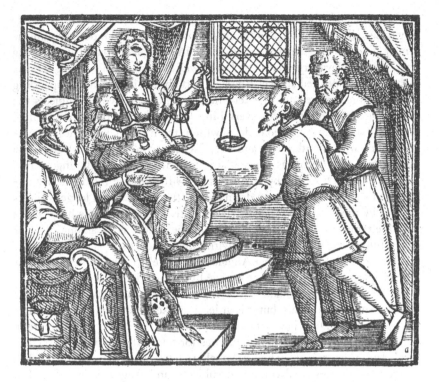

FIGURE 7 *"Description of Justice," from Stephen Bateman,* A Crystal Glass of Christian Reformation *(London, 1585).*

> O my dread lord,
> I should be guiltier than my guiltiness
> To think I can be undiscernible,
> When I perceive Your Grace, like power divine,
> Hath looked upon my passes. Then, good prince,
> No longer session hold upon my shame,
> But let my trial be mine own confession.
> Immediate sentence then and sequent death
> Is all the grace I beg.   (5.1.363–69)

If we consider that the Duke is more interested in reestablishing his ducal authority over his Viennese subjects than he is in stemming the supposed tide of unchecked sexuality (which is not unreasonable because he conveniently forgets about the anti-fornication statutes at the end of the play), then we can see that Angelo's words play right into his hand. Although the Duke is of course not a monarch, Angelo here attributes to him the divine right of kings. Before the people of Vienna, Angelo ascribes to him the ability to see all, to know all, and the power to punish all who deserve punishment. The Duke's supposed omniscience in particular would have struck a chord with playgoers. Elizabeth I was well known for her secret service, whose spies operated all over England and abroad in search of impending insurrection and treason. She very much wanted to give her subjects the impression that her eyes saw everything. To underscore the point, she had herself painted in a gorgeous dress which, upon closer inspection, is embroidered with countless ears and eyes. No one who saw the portrait would doubt that the queen was a formidable foe. Angelo, by attributing omniscience to the Duke and by requesting a swift sentence for his newly uncovered crimes, demonstrates dramatically that "liberty" no longer "plucks justice by the nose" (1.3.29) and that while the Duke may once have "loved the life removed" from his subjects (1.3.8), he is now again among his subjects, fully aware of, and impatient with, their misdeeds.

It is difficult to say whether Angelo is genuinely in awe of the Duke or is merely playing the Duke's game to save his own neck. It is certainly possible that Angelo, in recognizing his own sinfulness, suddenly perceives the Duke's supposed divinity, but it is at least as likely that Angelo now understands that the Duke has meticulously arranged the action to culminate in his own reemergence as Vienna's unquestionable authority figure. If the latter is true, then it would behoove Angelo to be a willing player in the Duke's stage play. Princes need compliant subjects, and Angelo is just that. But either way, playgoers and readers realize that Angelo's attribution of divinity to the Duke is just that, an attribution. We know how the Duke *really* got his information: he dressed himself up as a friar to pry into his subjects' innermost secrets and desires — and there is nothing particularly divine about that. As such, Shakespeare is treating the issue of divine right and the spectacle of rule in a twofold way. He shows how powerful and impressive, and maybe even God-like, the Duke can *appear* to his subjects, but he also shows us how that impression is largely the product of stagecraft. It is not altogether clear how Shakespeare would like us to judge the Duke and his presumed divinity. To all the citizens of Vienna, minus Isabella, Mariana, and anyone else who participated in the Duke's escapade, it could certainly appear that Angelo speaks the truth: the Duke who was thought to be far from home suddenly, almost magically reappears to save the day. Does this mean that Shakespeare is promoting the image of the prince as ruler by divine right and showing its effectiveness? Even Isabella and Mariana, who know virtually all aspects of the Duke's plan, do not show any sign that they consider him a hypocrite. But they, too, like Angelo, stand to gain from playing their parts in the Duke's play: Mariana gets her husband and

Isabella gets her brother back and a marriage proposal from the Duke. But what about the average playgoer? Would he embrace the Duke's purported divinity or deem him exposed as a political construct? Would he view the Duke as an authentic force for good or an actor who, to use Angelo's words, can use his office and its trappings to "wrench awe from fools" (2.4.14).

If we look at the Duke's actions cynically or pragmatically, we enter the world of Machiavelli's *The Prince*. But before we do, we want to say to anyone who wishes to brush aside the Duke's manipulative tendencies, that Shakespeare could easily have given a more idealized portrait of this man. We only have to look at the example of Thomas Middleton's *The Phoenix*, a play written at roughly the same time (and perhaps slightly before) Shakespeare's *Measure for Measure*. This play presents us with an unabashedly positive image of a prince in disguise.[7] Treasonous courtiers persuade the duke of Ferrara to send his son, Prince Phoenix, abroad, ostensibly to gain valuable experience, but actually to get him out of the way. Prince Phoenix agrees to leave Ferrara, but stays behind in disguise to protect his old and infirm father from the power-hungry traitors that surround him and to learn more about what else ails his father's dukedom. What is more, in contrast with Duke Vincentio, who moves about the city alone, Prince Phoenix has a trusted servant with him at all times who serves as an observer and as a choral voice of praise and support. In a brief soliloquy, the servant calls Phoenix a

> Wonder of all princes, precedent, and glory,
> True phoenix, made of an unusual strain.
> Who labors to reform is fit to reign.
> How can that king be safe that studies not
> The profit of his people?   (Middleton, *The Phoenix* 1.1.57–61 [see p. 178])

Prince Phoenix does not go among the people in disguise to prop up his own power or make up for his own neglect, as does Duke Vincentio. The prince's commitment to his father and the people of Ferrara seems absolutely genuine. Middleton makes certain that his audience immediately gets the association between Prince Phoenix and James I by stating in the play's opening lines that the duke has ruled Ferrara for forty-five years, the exact number of years Elizabeth governed England before her death. In fact, the image of Prince Phoenix corresponds closely to the benevolent and thoroughly optimistic portrayal of James I that we see in the welcoming speech of Richard Martin (p. 175), the poem of Samuel Daniel (p. 121), and Ben Jonson's epigram "To King James" (p. 176). Addressing James at

---

[7] See Kamps.

Stamford Hill in 1603, Martin welcomed the new king with words similar to those used by Middleton: "out of the ashes of this phoenix [Elizabeth I] wert thou, King James, born for our good, the bright star of the north" (Nichols 129).

So why would Shakespeare's play not simply reflect the same optimism about governance that we read in the words of his contemporaries? Why would he portray Duke Vincentio in a way that might bring Machiavelli to mind in his audiences? Is it possible that Shakespeare was less enthusiastic about the new king, or that he was generally more skeptical about the nature of royal power than were many of his contemporaries?

Machiavelli

In *Basilikon Doron* (see p. 154), James explains to his young son and heir to the English throne the difference between a good king and a bad king.

> A good king, thinking his highest honor to consist in his due discharge of his calling, employs all his study and pains, to procure and maintain, by the making and execution of good laws, the welfare and peace of his people; and as their natural father and kindly master, thinks his greatest contentment stands in their prosperity, and his greatest surety in having their hearts, subjecting his own private affections and appetites to the weal and standing of his subjects, ever thinking the common interest his chiefest particular: whereby the contrary, an usurping tyrant, thinking his greatest honor and felicity to consist in attaining *per fas, vel nefas* [by lawful or unlawful means] to his ambitious pretences, thinks ever himself sure, but by dissention and factions among his people, and counterfeiting the saint while he once creep in credit, will then (by inverting all good laws to serve only for his private affections) frame the common-weal ever to advance his particular: building his surety upon his people's misery: and in the end (as step-father and an uncouth hireling) make up his own hand upon the ruins of the republic. (*Basilikon Doron* 20)[8]

In popular as well as political discourse of the period, the "tyrant" of James's account was routinely identified with Niccolò Machiavelli's figure of "the prince." The political thought of the Italian Machiavelli was soundly reviled in Shakespeare's time. In Shakespeare's *Henry VI, Part 3* (c. 1592), the wicked Richard of Gloucester, proud of his ability to do harm, crows that he will "set the murderous Machiavel to school" (3.2.193). In Christopher Marlowe's *The Jew of Malta* (c. 1590), a character named Machiavel appears on stage

[8] See also the extract from Barnaby Riche's *Adventures of Brusanus* (1592), p. 157.

and announces his atheism and claims involvement in the St. Bartholomew Massacre in Paris in 1572, in which many Protestants were slaughtered. He then announces his intention to come to England to "frolic with his friends" and cause similar mayhem (Prologue 4). These representations of Machiavelli are crude stereotypes that do not reflect in any way the subtlety of Machiavelli's political thought, but they are loosely based on a crucial insight in *The Prince* that runs directly against the grain of most popular and state-sanctioned conceptions of the *good* prince.

The good prince of medieval and early Renaissance discourse is a virtuous, truthful, and devoutly Christian man who loves his subjects and who labors ceaselessly for their well-being. And the English expected James I to be such a prince, as is indicated in the words of Samuel Daniel (quoted earlier) and in the welcoming speech of Richard Martin (see p. 175), who addressed James at Stamford Hill in 1603. However, in his short treatise *The Prince* (1532), a volume of political advice dedicated to the Italian Duke Lorenzo de' Medici, Machiavelli argues that a ruler who wishes to govern successfully ought not to act out of a sense of moral or religious conviction but in whatever way the situation at hand requires. "A ruler who wishes to maintain his power," he writes, "must be prepared to act immorally when this becomes necessary" (*The Prince*, 1995, 55). Machiavelli similarly suggests that a prince ought to portray himself to his subjects as religious, but that he need not *be* religious, and that it may be necessary to deceive his subjects or make false promises to them. This position is often perverted by early seventeenth-century political pundits. In his posthumously published *Maxims of State* (1640), for instance, Sir Walter Raleigh urges rulers not to be "too light, inconstant, hard, cruel, effeminate, fearful, and dastardly," and instead to be "religious, grave, just, [and] valiant" (pp. 172–73). This advice, Raleigh insists, is contrary to "the false doctrine of . . . Machiavellian policy" which holds it "far the better means to keep the people in obedience than [to incite] love and reverence of the people towards the prince" (p. 173). What Machiavelli actually says is that "it is desirable [for a prince] to be *both* loved and feared" but that it is "difficult to achieve both and, if one of them has to be lacking, it is much safer to be feared than loved" (*The Prince* 59; emphasis added). It is safer because "the dread of punishment is always effective, whereas love, which is "sustained by a bond of gratitude" is easily cast aside when "men are excessively self-interested." And Machiavelli is quick to add, "a ruler must make himself feared in such a way that, even if he does not become loved, he does not become hated." So whereas Raleigh describes Machiavelli's prince as hard, cruel, and dastardly (among other things), Machiavelli actually says that the prince need not be any of those things to be feared by his subjects. We may well ask, are Raleigh and other

English detractors correct to insist that Machiavelli encourages princes to behave immorally or cruelly, or does *The Prince* only advocate deceitful or violent behavior only when political necessity requires it? Are we dealing with a fair-minded reading of a political discourse, or are we witnessing a conflict between calculating pragmatism and Christian morality?

Despite vitriolic rejections of Machiavelli's political thought, his ideas may well have been put into practice. The prologue from *The Jew of Malta*, from which we already quoted, accuses people of publicly condemning yet privately embracing Machiavelli's ideas:

> To some perhaps my name is odious,
> But such as love me guard me from their tongues,
> And let them know that I am Machiavel,
> And weigh not men, and therefore not men's words.
> Admired I am of those that hate me most.
> Though some speak openly against my books,
> Yet will they read me and thereby attain
> To Peter's chair; and when they cast me off,
> Are poisoned by my climbing followers.   (Prologue 5–13)

This portrayal of men who secretly read Machiavelli and benefit from his wisdom is of course still negative, but it also claims that Machiavelli is studied carefully and taken seriously by at least some in positions of power. Shakespeare's portrayal of the murderous Richard III is a case in point. Carefully stage-managing his appearance before a group of London citizens who, he hopes, will ask him to be England's next king, Richard positions himself between two bishops — "Two props of virtue for a Christian prince" — and carries "a book of prayer in his hand" (3.7.98). Audiences and readers of *Richard III* know that the Duke of Gloucester's piety is just a cynical charade, but we may well ask ourselves if Shakespeare's Duke of Vienna could be not a caricature of the Prince but an authentic Machiavel, a calculating politician whose deceptions and manipulations do not reach the level of excess that makes Richard III ultimately so despicable.

Is there an analogy between Machiavelli's view that princes should avoid being *perceived* as tyrants and the Duke's decision to appoint Angelo to put strictness back in Vienna's statutes and bite in its laws (*Measure for Measure* 1.3.19–43)? The strategy certainly seems to pay off for the Duke: it allows him to reassert his authority *and* it makes him seem more benevolent, merciful, and just than the corrupt and cruel Angelo. But is this a legitimate strategy? Raleigh condemns it and ascribes it to (his caricature of) the wicked Machiavellian politician when he says, "All rewards and things grateful [are] to come from himself [the tyrant], but all punishments, exactions, and things ungrateful from his officers and public ministers. And when he has effected what he would by them, if he see the people discontented withal, to make them a sacrifice to pacify his subjects" (29). Barnaby Riche's *The Adventures of Brusanus, Prince of Hungary* (1592), which may have been a source for *Measure for Measure*, wrestles with the same question, albeit from a slightly different vantage point. Although not attributing Machiavellian motives to the prince, the wise Dorestus asks rhetorically, "What profit is it for a prince himself to be honest, and those that should administer justice under him to be dissolute, for a prince to be true, and his officers false, for a prince to be gentle and his officers cruel?" (p. 159). Judging by his actions, how does Vienna's Duke answer this question?

Anxiety

If at the heart of Machiavelli's *The Prince* lies desire to manipulate others for the enhancement of the ruler's power, then we should inquire further how such manipulation is accomplished. Force and intimidation are powerful tools in a prince's arsenal, but he also has more subtle means at his disposal, namely the arousal and management of anxiety in his subjects. The ruling elite of England, influential critic Stephen Greenblatt asserts, "believed that a measure of insecurity and fear was a necessary, healthy element in the shaping of proper loyalties, and [that] Elizabethan and Jacobean institutions deliberately evoked this insecurity" (135–56). The reasons for this are not very different from the reasons given by Vienna's Duke when he impresses upon Friar Thomas that "fond fathers," who only show their children the rod and do not use it, will see that their authority "Becomes more mocked than feared" (1.3.23, 26, 27). However, if a prince governs solely by means of the rod, he will, as Machiavelli observes, be seen as a tyrant and be more than likely to incur the hatred of his people. Therefore it is in the prince's interest to strike a productive balance between the anxiety he arouses in his subjects and the measure of mercy and comfort he affords them. What is the proper balance between anxiety and safety? It will depend on the circumstances but as a general rule the right balance is that which ensures the subjects' obedience. Greenblatt, for instance, describes how in 1603 James I used an apparently treasonous plot against him to cultivate and manage anxiety in his subjects (136). The plot, known as the Bye Plot, was a far-fetched scheme by the priest William Watson and other Catholics to capture the king and force him to grant religious toleration for all English Catholics. It may also have been part of the plan to depose James and replace him with his niece, Arbella Stuart. But the plot went awry, and a number of alleged conspirators were arrested and imprisoned. Greenblatt reports that Watson and another priest "were tortured horribly," and afterward their dismembered bodies were displayed on the city gates as a warning to the public. A week later, another conspirator, a man named George Brooke, was put to death. After a few more days passed, it was the turn of Lords Grey and Cobham and Sir Gervase Markham to climb the scaffold. Markham, Greenblatt writes,

> ... who had hoped for a reprieve, looked stunned with horror. After a delay, the sheriff told him that since he seemed ill prepared to face death, he would be granted a two-hour reprieve; similar delays were granted Grey and Cobham. The prisoners were then assembled together on the scaffold, "looking strange one upon the other," wrote Dudley Carlton, who witnessed the scene, "like men beheaded, and met again in the other world." At this point the sheriff made a short speech, asking the condemned if the judgments against them were just. When the wretches assented, he proclaimed that the merciful king had granted them their lives. (136)

It is not clear whether James meant to grant the condemned clemency all along or whether he had a change of heart. Greenblatt points out that when Brooke was beheaded a few days earlier and the executioner had held his head aloft and cried out, "God save the king!" no one except the sheriff had echoed his call. If there is a link between the two events, we can suggest that James at first was eager to punish the main culprits in the conspiracy as harshly as possible in order to assert his power and discourage future acts of treason (137). But when the crowd failed to repeat "God save the king!" after the Brooke execution, he saw that the public was beginning to doubt the king's justice, and further beheadings, rather than enhancing the king's authority, might have made him appear a cruel tyrant.

What is noteworthy, however, is that Grey, Cobham, and Markham are not spared the ordeal of having to contemplate their imminent death (see Fig. 8). They are brought to the brink of execution twice, only to be told in the end that they will not die. This spectacle arouses and manages anxiety in the condemned as well as in the hearts of all observers, and enhances the king's authority. By leading the three men to the executioner's block, the king demonstrated to all that he had the power to kill them if he wanted to, regardless of the feelings of his subjects, but that he was a benevolent prince who listened to this people, and who would show mercy when appropriate. In other words, by putting the condemned and the onlookers through a fake execution, the king raised their anxiety and apprehension to a fever pitch, and, after holding them in this state of fear and torment for a couple of

FIGURE 8 *Man Praying as He Confronts His Death, from Isaac Ambrose,* Prima and Ultima: First and Last Things or Regeneration *(London 1640).*

hours, he was also the agent who removed that fear and anxiety to the relief of all.

The observer of the executions, Dudley Carlton, recognized that the entire spectacle had much in common with a stage play (Greenblatt 136). And, indeed, *Measure for Measure* emulates the dynamic we see in the aftermath of the Bye Plot. One could argue that the agent who threatened death and then gave life in the Bye Plot incident is split into two figures in *Measure for Measure:* Angelo and the Duke. But we could just as easily say that Angelo, whose character is known well enough by the Duke, is merely a puppet in the Duke's plan to regain authority among Vienna's citizens. What is more, we could even look at the entire justice machinery in *Measure for Measure* as a system of relations that arouses and manages anxiety in its subjects.

On a less abstract level, however, we can point to the way in which the disguised Duke allows Claudio to believe that he will be executed, even though the Duke has seemingly no intention of letting him die for the sin of fornication. After eavesdropping on the conversation in which Isabella tells her brother that he may live if she sleeps with Angelo, the disguised Duke comes forward to say that Angelo was only testing Isabella's virtue, and that Claudio should abandon all hope of escape. "I am confessor to Angelo," he tells them, "and I know this to be true; therefore prepare yourself to death. Do not satisfy your resolution with hopes that are fallible. Tomorrow you must die. Go to your knees and make ready" (3.1.166–69). In addition to seeking a religious compliance from Claudio, the Duke wants him to accept the absoluteness of Angelo's power, much like James wants the Bye Plot conspirators to feel the reality of their impending deaths.

Along similar lines, the Duke deliberately does not inform Isabella that he has saved her brother's head from the block. He himself tells us why:

> She's come to know
> If yet her brother's pardon be come hither.
> But I will keep her ignorant of her good,
> To make her heavenly comforts of despair
> When it is least expected. (4.3.94–98)

He intends first to intensify her anguish (even though there is no apparent need for it), and then to quell it when it suits his purposes. What are the Duke's purposes? Maybe he hopes that a grateful Isabella will accept his proposal of marriage after she learns that the Duke saved her brother after all. But the intent "To make her heavenly comforts of despair" also suggest that the Duke is seeking to project himself to Isabella (and anyone else) as a God-like prince. He is planning to bring Claudio back from the dead, and to do what only God can do, to bring heavenly comforts to one who has abandoned all hope. The Duke could have allowed Isabella in on his secrets, told her that Claudio was still alive, and gone along with the plan without significant alteration. So why not make Isabella, the woman he apparently hopes to marry, a full partner actor in his grand scheme?

Is it possible that the Duke is not in search of co-conspirators but is instead determined to manipulate people's thoughts and feelings? Might this give him greater control over his subjects' lives than do the laws designed to govern their actions? If this is so, does it help to explain why the Duke, after initially proclaiming his intent to put the bite back in Vienna's laws, conveniently ignores the anti-fornication statute and gives no indication by the play's end that he wishes to restore it to prominence? Are the Duke's efforts aimed at renewing the integrity of the law or at restoring the prince's power to intervene in the legal system as he sees fit, thus establishing his superiority to the law of the land?[9] James himself of course repeatedly asserted his preeminence over English law, claiming that there were "no legal limits" to a king's power (Kenyon 8), leading one critic to summarize the peculiar matrix of tensions and competing interests in the play as follows:

> *Measure* puts on stage, through the exaggerations of the comic lens, a justification of the king's justice. . . . The criminal law inspired terror, with harsh arbitrary statutes inconsistently enforced. It was administered by corrupt judges and merciless prosecutors, who arranged public spectacles of bloody executions *pour encourager les autres*. Only the king's justice, coming from an absolute ruler like the duke or James, who operates above the law, penetrates all pretenses, is concerned for all the people, and is able to temper strictness with mercy, can turn leaden law into something that vaguely resembles golden justice. (Kernan 67).

In this view, it is paramount that if the prince is to care for "all the people" and ensure a just society, he must operate "above the law" and see through whatever hindrances his subjects place in his way; he must have complete knowledge of their thoughts and actions to rule them to their benefit. But how can a prince legitimately combine the commonplace qualities attributed to "a good king" in *Basilikon Doron* and the more controversial secretive and manipulative traits commonly associated with Machiavelli? How do we reconcile them?

[9] Leah Marcus suggests that James I acted in a manner similar to the Duke. In an effort to bypass the authority of many of London's ancient customs, ordinances, and privileges, James first asserts his reverence for them and desire to strengthen them (allaying fears among city fathers that the new monarch intends to meddle in local politics), but over time the king "acts indirectly and through intermediaries to assert his own ultimate jurisdiction over the city's customary privileges of policing its territories within the walls" (178).

One way to approach the question is to say that while we may discern Machiavellian traits in the practices of Shakespeare's Duke, it is possible that early seventeenth-century audiences would have recognized the Duke's manipulations but that they would not have deemed them "Machiavellian." Raleigh's *Maxims of State* (1642), as noted earlier, is a treatise of political advice that explicitly rejects Machiavelli's political views, but it also advocates a number of ideas central to Machiavelli's thought. Raleigh observes, for example, that a prince ought to behave himself in such a way that the people will love him *in order that* he "need not greatly fear home conspiracies" (p. 172). The notion that the people's love is not a good in itself but rather a *means* to safeguard the prince's power is purely pragmatic and Machiavellian in nature. Raleigh also advises the prince to visit the courts and palaces of justice from time to time so "that he may seem to have a care of justice among his people," and to "bestow many benefits and graces" upon the capital of his empire so that he may travel and be assured that the people back home are "sure and faithful unto him" (p. 172). The first piece of advice places the prince's image above his substance, and the second points to a system of patronage, or even bribery, intended to secure the prince's place in power.

In his *Maxims of State,* Raleigh advances another fascinating circumstance that may resonate with *Measure for Measure.* Discussing how princes may establish their control over annexed territories, he advises that when princes visit their new territories they should consider punishing "lieutenants and inferior governors" who have ruled harshly or incompetently in their prince's name. Punishing them will make examples of these bad administrators and will conveniently win the prince "the people's hearts" (38). The people will rejoice in the correction or removal of the oppressive "lieutenants and inferior governors" and the prince will be considered a fair and just ally of the people. For our purposes, what is most noteworthy about this passage is that Raleigh advises the prince to punish oppressive deputies not because they are oppressive but because correcting them will enhance the image of the prince in the eyes of the people. If the people believe the prince to be a just man who has their welfare in mind, they will be ruled and controlled more easily.

Now, the city of Vienna is obviously not annexed foreign territory, but the Duke does find himself, by his own admission, in a situation in which he wants to reassert his princely control over a city that no longer respects his authority. And we may wonder if a careful reading of Raleigh's text leads to a plausible connection between his advice to princes to appoint deputies to gain dominance over newly gained territories and the Duke's appointment of Angelo to discipline Vienna's unruly subjects. Allowing Angelo to rule oppressively for a brief period, the Duke then reemerges, much like Raleigh's prince, to punish his deputy and regain "the people's hearts." We may view Raleigh's advice as manipulative and even cynical, but the author would probably not share our view. Does that mean that a Renaissance prince could engage in *some* secretive behavior and manipulation of his subjects, without incurring their contempt or losing their trust? James I seems to have thought so, as he made clear to Prince Henry when he urged him to spy on his subjects. Likewise, William Willymat, in describing the duties of all good Christian subjects to their prince, writes in *A Loyal Subject's Looking-Glass* (1604) that "Kings, princes, and governors do use oftentimes for diverse causes to disguise their purposes with pretences and colors of other matters, so that the end of their drifts and secret purposes are not right seen into nor understood at the first, this to be lawful the word of God does not deny" (58).[10] According to Willymat, whose text is dedicated to Prince Henry, all subjects live perpetually in a state of ignorance about their prince's doings, and they should therefore refrain from judging him.

One thing we can say for certain is that by putting the Duke's secret statecraft on display, Shakespeare enables audiences to adopt a cynical stance vis-à-vis their prince. With the performance of *Measure for Measure*, the theater becomes an institution that displays and celebrates the grandeur and genius of princes. But by reenacting that grandeur, by bringing it to life for ordinary Londoners on the public stage, it is also made less mysterious, divine, and unique than it was before. The very performance of the prince's power tells everyone that it is, or can be understand as, a performance. We do not *know* what the Duke's subjects ultimately think of his ruling practices (unless, of course, we are inclined to believe the rakish Lucio, who does not have a lot of credibility), but it is tempting to imagine a time shortly after the end of the play when various characters who have been subjected to the "friar's" tricks may realize that they have been lied to by their prince — and that they may be lied to again. Therefore, even if Isabella, Mariana, Claudio, Angelo, and Vienna's citizens ultimately agree that the Duke's motives are noble and the outcome desirable, they certainly learned a great deal about *how* the Duke rules them. That knowledge should make it harder for the Duke to manipulate them a second time, and therefore it could weaken his power over them. Could such knowledge ultimately lead to opposition?

---

[10] See also the extract from chapter 20 of Barnaby Riche's *The Adventures of Brusanus, Prince of Hungary* (1592), p. 157. In chapter 20, King Leonarchus, who like *Measure for Measure*'s Duke has traveled among his own people in disguise, emphasizes how important it is for princes to know what goes on in their realms.

Resistance

Whether subjects could legally oppose their prince was part of ongoing political discourse in the late sixteenth and early seventeenth centuries. In the world of Machiavellian *realpolitik,* possible resistance to a prince's authority was a political reality. Indeed, it is precisely Machiavelli's aim to give a prince effective tools and statecraft to minimize the chance of rebellion, treasonous action, military opposition, or other forms of resistance to his rule. Machiavelli views such opposition as an undesirable but inevitable result of particular tendencies in human nature and the potentially uneasy interaction between prince and subjects. In the context of a divine right monarchy, however, resistance to the crown was viewed not simply as another aspect of political reality but as an intervention in God's order. As we would expect, opinions on the subject varied.

The *Vindiciae Contra Tyrannos,* published in 1579 under the pseudonym Stephanus Junius Brutus, insisted that subjects did not have to obey their prince if such obedience were to constitute a violation of God's law. The two men who are contracted by Macbeth to kill Banquo and his son Fleance, for instance, would not be committing a crime against their king if they refused to murder on his behalf because such a murder is against God's law. *Vindiciae* further affirms the justness and even the duty of subjects to resist a tyrannical prince. George Buchanan, a Scotsman who had served as King James I's childhood tutor, similarly defended the subjects' right to remove from power or kill a tyrant. In *De Jure Regni apud Scotus, A Dialogue Concerning the Due Privilege of Government in the Kingdom of Scotland* (1579; trans. 1680), Buchanan argues that when a king takes a coronation oath and vows to govern justly, he enters into a covenant with his people. If he subsequently rules tyrannically and without regard for the law of the land, he breaks that covenant and is no longer entitled to the obedience of his subjects and forfeits his life to any subject who wants to take it (see p. 169). What these texts and others such as John Ponet's *A Short Treatise of Politic Power* [1556] have in common is a belief that a human being's highest accountability is to God and not to the monarch.

On the other side of the issue we find writers such as William Tyndale who, as noted earlier, refuses to distinguish between the will of God and that of the monarch. Tyndale concludes that "He that judges the king, judges God, and he that lays hand on the king, lays hands on God. And he that resists the king, resists God, and damns God's law and ordinances" (Tyndale, *Obedience* fol. xxvii). James I saw things very much the way Tyndale did. In *The True Law of Free Monarchies,* James dealt with the issue of tyrannical kings by explaining that God sometimes sends "a wicked king . . .

for a curse to his people, and a plague for their sins: but that it is lawful to them to shake off that curse at their own hand, which God has laid on them, that I deny, and may do so justly" (79). In short, both the good king and the tyrant rule their subjects in God's name, and both do God's will. To resist either is to resist God.

How is all this relevant to *Measure for Measure*, a play in which no one actually contests a prince's right to rule as he sees fit? Curiously enough, it is the Duke himself who introduces the concept of "resistance" into the action when he sets into a motion a plan to circumvent the authority of his deputy, Angelo. It is easy to see how undermining the authority of the corrupt Angelo ultimately enhances the Duke's own authority, but that is only a part of the story. Once Angelo falls prey to his desire for Isabella and offers his depraved bargain, he becomes the kind of tyrant who sacrifices lawfulness and the rights of his subjects for his personal pleasures. Would King James counsel Vienna's citizens to be passively obedient because it must somehow be God's will that Angelo behaves like a tyrant? Would he maintain that Isabella must somehow deserve punishment for reasons known only to God? And what would Buchanan's point of view be? Would he insist that Isabella is justified in opposing Angelo (as she almost does when she threatens to expose him publicly) or even in killing him (as her counterpart Epitia considers doing in Cinthio's *Gli Hecatommithi*, one of Shakespeare's possible sources for the play)?[11] The Duke himself appears carefully to straddle the line between advocating divine right absolutism and defending resistance to tyrannical princes. And in doing so he may ultimately undermine both positions.

One of the first things the Duke does in the play is bestow upon Angelo his "absolute power" (1.3.13) and to tell Angelo, "Your scope is as mine own, / So to enforce or qualify the laws / As to your soul seems good" (1.1.65–67). Angelo is therefore for the time being Vienna's rightful ruler, not a pretender whose actions are by definition illegitimate. When Angelo proves himself a tyrant, the Duke does not simply remove him from power, as he could have done easily at any time. Rather, he enlists the help of Isabella, Mariana, the Provost, and various others to start plotting against Angelo. Not only does he conjure up the infamous bed-trick, he also saves Claudio's neck from the axe, thereby circumventing the death sentence pronounced by the city's legitimate ruler on an admitted lawbreaker. Whatever we think of the moral connotations of the Duke's actions (many have expressed serious reservations about his efforts to trick Angelo into having sex with Mariana), we cannot escape their legal ramifications, especially when we recognize

---

[11] For a discussion of the *Hecatommithi*, see the general introduction in this volume.

that Isabella, Mariana, and the Provost participate in the Duke's schemes of resistance without knowing that they are helping the "real" Duke. Apparently convinced that Angelo's actions are somehow unacceptable, all three of them freely assist an ordinary friar to thwart the legitimate ruler of Vienna. But this of course aligns the Duke with voices such as Buchanan's and sets him squarely against King James on the issue of resistance to tyrannical princes, creating an odd contradiction for those who wish to see the Duke as a version of James I. The Duke "teaches" Isabella and the Provost — and possibly his audience — how one may oppose an unjust ruler. But that is not all there is to it.

It is true that the disguised Duke repeatedly upholds Angelo's authority to interpret the law any way he wants to, even though he apparently does not think that Claudio should be put to death for fornication. In this respect, the Duke conforms to King James's claim that subjects are *never* authorized to rise against their prince, even if that prince is a brutal tyrant who abuses his subjects. The Duke, for instance, ultimately sets aside the verdict against Claudio, but when he counsels Claudio in prison he never indicates that he finds the law against fornication unduly harsh or Angelo's enforcement of it unreasonable. Rather, he urges Claudio to accept his fate, whatever it is. "Be absolute for death," he tells Claudio. "Either death or life / Shall thereby be the sweeter" (3.1.5–6). He urges Claudio to accept that he has no control over the situation; Angelo will either have him executed or he will pardon him. Likewise, he defends Angelo to Claudio by telling him, "Angelo had never the purpose to corrupt her; only he hath made an assay of her virtue to practice his judgment with the disposition of natures" (3.1.163–65) — even though he knows that this is not true. When the Duke "returns" home in the final act, he defends Angelo publicly against Isabella's charges without any effort whatsoever to investigate her accusations. He dismisses Isabella's allegations and has her carried off to prison: "Shall we thus permit / A blasting and a scandalous breath to fall / On him so near us?" (5.1.126–28). The message to the general public in Vienna is clear: legitimate authority is unassailable, and those who challenge it will pay a heavy price.

The Duke's behavior is ultimately paradoxical. In order to regain effective authority over his subjects, he supports a law against fornication that he then sets aside, and he defends the authority of a deputy whom he urges his subjects to resist. He defends the very things he undermines, and subverts the very principle of authority he hopes to establish. Angelo is never meant to be anything other than a temporary ruler of Vienna, and his removal from power at play's end is therefore hardly a genuine deposition, nor is the death sentence against him a tyrannicide. But the way in which the final scene unfolds, we — and even more so the citizens of Vienna — are led to believe that Angelo is removed from power not because his predetermined term of governance is up but because he has been a tyrannical prince; he has been judged unfit to rule. Nothing in *Measure for Measure* discourages playgoers from extrapolating how the removal of a short-lived tyrant like Angelo might apply to other princes.

Slander

Taken aback by the critical words spoken about him by his own soldiers, Shakespeare's Henry V bitterly laments that all princes are "subject to the breath / Of every fool" (*Henry V* 4.1.231–32). Henry sounds whiney and even unfair — the soldiers who criticized him are hardly fools — but he nonetheless echoes governmental anxiety about unregulated speech of citizens of Shakespeare's England. Among scholars, there are legitimate arguments about the effectiveness of Elizabethan and Jacobean censorship,[12] but there is no doubt that the governments of Elizabeth and James sought to regulate public speech and artistic expression. The gruesome example of the mutilation of John Stubbes, who had his right hand cut off for expressing his views on a possible marriage between Elizabeth I and the French Duke of Alençon, is an extreme instance of the monarch's fear of becoming the object of unregulated public discourse. There were laws against such discourse, and, in general, matters of politic and religious controversy were deemed off limits. This anxiety about public discourse extended to the theater, which was regulated by the Master of the Revels — the monarch's official censor — and which was prohibited from discussing current or recent politics and religion, and from representing any living prince, foreign or domestic, on the stage. James I also showed himself sensitive to the issue in *Basilikon Doron* (excerpted in this section), when he urged his son not to permit anyone to "judge and speak rashly of their prince" or any members of the royal family, living or deceased. Indeed, James ranked the slandering of princes with other offenses such as "witchcraft, willful murder, incest . . . sodomy, poisoning, and false coin" — all of which he deemed "unpardonable crimes."

Now, as critics have observed, Lucio is the only character in *Measure for Measure* who is punished by the Duke at play's end. Angelo's death sentence is revoked, as we may have expected it would be all along, and his marriage to Mariana is certainly less a legal punishment than a social and comedic

[12] See the work of Patterson and of Dutton, among others.

FIGURE 9 *Man in the Stocks for "Seditious Libel," in* Roxburgh Ballads, *vol. 5, parts 1–2 (1883).*

solution. Why is Lucio punished and Angelo not? The answer lies probably less in what they *did* than in what they *say* at the moment of their judgment, and *how* they say it. At the outset of this section, we quoted Henry V's reference to his soldiers as slandering fools. Michael Williams, one of those soldiers, indeed calls his king an outright liar, and although his criticism of Henry is far more credible (and therefore more dangerous) than Lucio's salacious gossip about the Duke, it is Williams who is ultimately rewarded by the king with a glove full of crowns, while Lucio is sentenced to marry a prostitute he got pregnant and to be flogged because "slandering a prince deserves it" (5.1.522). Why? Lucio remains defiant and argumentative with

FIGURE 10 *"Maledicentia" (Slander), in Andrea Alciati,* Emblematum Libellus.

the Duke in the final scene (5.1.499–522), whereas Williams begs the king's pardon and acknowledges the king's authority (*Henry V* 4.8.54–55).[13] When confronted with the king directly, Williams allows his speech to be regulated; Lucio, who quarrels with the justice of his sentence, does not (for images of how slander and libel were perceived, see Figs. 9 and 10). Many of us would rather see Angelo whipped than Lucio, but the latter cannot subdue his slanderous mouth to the Duke's agenda, while Angelo lauds the Duke as a "pow'r divine" and fully embraces that power and its justice when he says, "my penitent heart . . . crave[s] death more willingly than mercy. / 'Tis my deserving, and I do entreat it" (5.1.474–76). That is quite different from Lucio's "I beseech Your Highness, do not marry me to a whore. Your

---

[13] Williams of course also insists that he has done nothing wrong, and that the king should not appear in disguise among his soldiers if he doesn't want to hear what they really think of him (4.8.50–54), but Henry wisely bypasses this issue and rewards him as a noble king would an honest yet humble soldier.

Highness said even now I made you a duke; good my lord, do not recompense me in making me a cuckold" (5.1.513–15). That Angelo is actually guilty of sexual coercion and attempted murder, whereas Lucio has only indulged in unflattering speech and engaged in (as far as we can tell) consensual sex with lots of women, seems not to matter. What matters is that Lucio continues to be his irrepressible, comic self, while Angelo's reckless disobedience has, by all outward appearance, been suppressed. Lucio must therefore be whipped some (presumably to make him compliant), while Angelo is judged ready to resume the life of a compliant subject.

This may, as we observed in our introduction to this volume, elicit moral outrage from the likes of Samuel Taylor Coleridge, John Dryden, William D'Avenant, and others, but it seems to be the way that Shakespeare wanted it. Shakespeare appears to have been more interested in exploring a set of difficult ideas and practices — governance among them — than in having *Measure for Measure* easily conform to any particular dramatic genre. We hope the excerpts from sixteenth- and early seventeenth-century texts gathered in the following section will shed light on what early modern people thought about questions of governance, and on the cultural and ideological climate in which *Measure for Measure* was written and received. They should help reveal the play to be the dramatization of complex and sometimes troublesome social issues that it is.

→ KING JAMES I

From The True Law of Free Monarchies *1598, 1603*

James Charles Stuart was born at Edinburgh Castle in 1566 to Henry Stuart (Lord Darnley), and Mary Queen of Scots. After the murder of his father and forced abdication of his mother, James was crowned king of Scotland in 1567 at the age of one, though he would not govern the nation until almost twenty years later. During his childhood he received instruction from various outstanding tutors, the Calvinist George Buchanan most prominent among them. James was fluent in Greek and Latin, as well as in a number of modern languages. Encouraged by Buchanan, James developed a life-long passion for reading, learning, and writing. Among his most outstanding writings are *Basilikon Doron* (1598) and *The True Law of Free Monarchies* (1598).

King James I, *The True Law of Free Monarchies or The Reciprocal and Mutual Duty Betwixt a Free King and His Natural Subjects* (Edinburgh, 1598; reprinted, London, 1603. Our text is taken from the 1603 London edition), B3r–B5r, C6v–C7r, C8v–Dv, Dr–D2v, D3v–D4r.

In *The True Law*, James discourses on the origins of monarchical power, the king's legal obligations to his subjects, his relationships to the law, as well as his relationship to God. Because *The True Law* was written in 1598, we must keep in mind that when James refers to "our kingdom" he is referring to Scotland and not to England. It is fair to say, however, that James's ideas on kingship changed very little when he became monarch of England. He remained a firm believer in divinely sanctioned absolute power, patriarchalism, the king's *a priori* position vis-à-vis the law, and the royal prerogative. Although other critics have done so, we are not suggesting that Shakespeare's Duke Vincentio is a version of, or role model for, King James. Nor are we keen to argue that Shakespeare must have read James's writings before he wrote *Measure for Measure*, although some of the ideas expressed by James also emerge in Shakespeare's play. They probably share an interest in certain key concepts because the ideas on governance were part of a wider cultural context that predates James's texts and Shakespeare's play. Other literary and political texts of the period — some of which are included in this section — do certainly bear this out.

The Place and Office of the King

Kings are called gods[1] by the prophetical King David[2] because they sit upon God his throne in the earth, and have the count[3] of their administration to give unto him. Their office is to minister justice and judgment to the people,[4] as the same David says; to advance the good and punish the evil,[5] as he likewise says; to establish good laws to his people and procure obedience to the same,[6] as diverse good kings of Judah did; to procure the peace of the people,[7] as the same David says; to decide all controversies that can arise among them,[8] as Solomon did; to be the minister of God for the weal[9] of him that doth well; and, as the minister of God, to take vengeance upon them that do evil,[10] as St. Paul says. And, finally, as a good pastor, to go out and in before his people,[11] as is said in the first of Samuel; that through the prince's prosperity the people's peace may be procured,[12] as Jeremiah says.

And therefore in the coronation of our own kings, as well as of every Christian monarchy, they give their oath, first to maintain the religion presently professed within their country, according to their laws, whereby it is established, and to punish all those that should press to alter or disturb profession thereof.

---

[1] **Kings are called gods:** Psalms 82:6.   [2] **King David:** the second king of Judah and Israel; the father of King Solomon and assumed writer of the Psalms.   [3] **count:** account.   [4] **Their ... people:** Psalms 101.   [5] **advance ... evil:** Psalms 101.   [6] **establish ... same:** 2 Kings 18, 2 Chronicles 29, 2 Kings 22 and 23, 2 Chronicles 34 and 35.   [7] **procure ... people:** Psalms 72.   [8] **decide ... them:** 1 Kings 3.   [9] **weal:** welfare.   [10] **take ... evil:** Romans 13:4.   [11] **go ... people:** 1 Samuel 8.   [12] **that ... procured:** Jeremiah 29.

And next, to maintain all the lowable[13] and good laws made by their predecessors; to see them put into execution, and the breakers and violators thereof to be punished, according to the tenor of the same. And lastly to maintain the whole country and every state therein in all their ancient privileges and liberties, as well against foreign enemies as among themselves; and shortly to procure the weal and flourishing of his people, not only in maintaining and putting to execution the old lowable laws of the country, and by establishing of new (as necessity and evil manners well require) but by all other means possible to foresee and prevent all dangers that are likely to fall upon them; and to maintain concord, wealth, and civility among them; as a loving father and careful watchman, caring for them more than for himself, knowing himself to be ordained for them, and they not for him; and therefore countable[14] to that great God, who placed him as his lieutenant over them, upon the peril of his soul to procure that weal of both souls and bodies, as far as in him lieth, of all them that are committed to his charge. And this oath in the coronation is the clearest civil and fundamental law whereby the king's office is properly defined.

By the law of nature the king becomes a natural father to all his lieges[15] at his coronation. And as the father of his fatherly duty is bound to care for the nourishing, education, and virtuous government of his children, even so is the king bound to care for all his subjects.[16] As all the toil and pain that the father can take for his children will be thought light and well bestowed by him, so that the effect thereof redound[17] to their profit and weal; so ought the prince to do towards his people. As the kindly father ought to foresee all inconvenients and dangers that may arise towards his children, and though with the hazard of his own person press to prevent the same, so ought the king towards his people. As the father's wrath and correction upon any of his children that offendeth ought to be by a fatherly chastisement seasoned with pity, as long as there is any hope of amendment in them, so ought the king towards any of his lieges that offends in that measure.

And shortly, as the father's chief joy ought to be in producing his children's welfare, rejoicing at their weal, sorrowing and pitying at their evil, to

---

[13] lowable: laudable, permissible. [14] countable: accountable. [15] lieges: subjects. [16] And as the father . . . subjects: Here James draws a direct analogy between the patriarchal authority of the father in the early modern family (in which the spouse and children had no independent political power and were largely subsumed into the identity of the father) and his own nearly absolute power over his subjects. James's contention resonated with many — but not all — of his subjects because many embraced the idea of the patriarchal family and believed strongly in the authority of the father on the basis of both biblical grounds and natural law. [17] redound: return.

hazard for their safety, travel for their rest, wake for their sleep, and, in a word, to think that his earthly felicity and life standeth and liveth more in them, nor in himself; so ought a good prince think of his people.

[In the section that follows, James describes the relation of the monarch to the law. The essence of James's argument is that the king is prior to the law and therefore not subject to the law.]

Now, as for the describing the allegiance that the lieges owe to their native king out of the fundamental and civil law, especially of this country,[18] as I promised, the ground must first be set down of the first manner of establishing the laws and form of government among us, that the ground being first right laid, we may thereafter build rightly thereupon.

Although it be true (according to the affirmation of those that pride themselves to be the scourges of tyrants) that in the first beginning of kings rising among the gentiles in the time of the first age, diverse commonwealths and societies of men chose out one among themselves who, for his virtues and valor being more eminent than the rest, was chosen out by them and set up in that room[19] to maintain the weakest in their right, to throw down oppressors, and to foster and continue the society among men, which could not otherwise but by virtue of that unity be well done. Yet these examples are nothing pertinent to us because our kingdom and diverse other monarchies are not in that case, but had their beginning in a far contrary fashion.

For as our chronicles bear witness, this isle, and especially our part of it, being scantily inhabited but by very few, and they as barbarous and scant of civility as number, there comes our first King Fergus,[20] with great number with him, out of Ireland, which was long inhabited before us, and making himself master of the country by his own friendship and force, as well as of the Ireland-men that came with him, as of the countrymen that willingly fell to him, he made himself king and lord, as well as of the whole lands, as of the whole inhabitants within the same. Thereafter he and his successors, along while after their being made kings, made and established their laws from time to time, and as the occasion required.

So the truth is directly contrary in our state to the false affirmation of such seditious writers as would persuade us that the laws and state of our country were established before the admitting of a king; whereby the contrary ye see it plainly proved that a wise king coming in among barbares[21]

---

[18] **this country:** James refers here to his native Scotland but later in *The True Law* applies the same argument to England. [19] **room:** dominion. [20] **Fergus:** legendary king of Scotland (third century B.C.E.). [21] **barbares:** barbarians.

first established the estate and form of government, and thereafter made laws by himself, and his successors according thereto.

The kings therefore in Scotland were before any estates or ranks of men within the same, before any parliaments were holden[22] or laws made; and by them was the land distributed (which at the first was whole theirs),[23] states erected and discerned, and forms of government devised and established. And so it follows of necessity that the kings were the authors and makers of the laws, and not the laws of the kings. . . .

And according to these fundamental laws already alleged,[24] we daily see that in the Parliament (which is nothing else but the head court of the king and his vassals) the laws are but craved by his subjects and only made by him at their rogation,[25] and with their advice. For albeit the king make daily statutes and ordinances, enjoining such pains thereto as he thinks meet, without any advice of parliament or estates, yet it lies in the power of no parliament to make any kind of law or statute without his scepter be put to it for giving it the force of law. And although diverse changes have been in other countries of the blood royal and kingly house, the kingdom being reft[26] by conquest from one to another, as in our neighbor country in England (which was never in ours), yet the same ground of the king's right over all the land and subjects thereof remaineth alike in all other free monarchies, as well as in this. For when the Bastard of Normandy[27] came into England and made himself king, was it not by force and with a mighty army? Where he gave the law and took none, changed the laws, inverted the order of government, set down the strangers[28] his followers in many of the old possessor's rooms, as at this day well appeareth a great part of the gentlemen in England being come of the Norman blood, and their old law, which to this day they are ruled by, and written in his language, and not in theirs. And yet his successors have with great happiness enjoyed the crown to this day. Whereof the like was also done by all them that conquested them before.

. . . And as ye see it manifest that the king is overlord of the whole land, so is he master over every person that inhabiteth the same, having power over the life and death of every one of them. For although a just prince will not take the life of any of his subjects without a clear law, yet the same laws whereby he taketh them are made by himself or his predecessors. And so the

---

[22] **holden:** held. [23] **whole theirs:** That is, all land at first belonged to kings. [24] **laws already alleged:** In a passage omitted here, James points to various Scottish laws that define the king's relationship to his subjects. [25] **rogation:** formal petition. [26] **reft:** bereft, robbed. [27] **Bastard of Normandy:** duke of Normandy, who invaded England in 1066 and became King William I (the Conqueror). [28] **strangers:** foreigners; i.e., William's French followers.

power flows always from himself; as by daily experience we see, good and just princes will from time to time make new laws and statutes, adjoining the penalties to the breakers thereof, which before the law was made had been no crime to the subject to have committed. Not that I deny the old definition of a king and of a law, which makes the king to be a speaking law,[29] and the law a dumb king;[30] for certainly a king that governs not by law can neither be countable to God for his administration, nor have a happy and established reign. For albeit it be true that I have at length proved that the king is above the law, as both the author and giver of strength thereto, yet a good king will not only delight to rule his subjects by the law but even will conform himself in his own actions thereunto, always keeping that ground that the health of the commonwealth be his chief law. And where he see the law doubt-some or rigorous,[31] he may interpret or mitigate the same; lest otherwise *summum ius* be *summa iniuria.*[32] And therefore general laws made publicly in parliament may, upon known respects to the king, by his authority be mitigated and suspended upon causes only known to him. . . .

[Feeling that he has sufficiently established the king's a priori *relationship and superiority to the law, James moves on to describe the kind of loyalty subjects therefore owe the monarch. Using various analogies, James argues that just as it is inconceivable that the people would remove a local magistrate or provost, or that a congregation would remove its pastor, or that pupils would remove their schoolmaster, so the king cannot be removed by his subjects.]*

If these[33] I say (whereof some are but inferior, subaltern[34] and temporal magistrates, and none of them equal in any sort to the dignity of a king) cannot be displaced for any occasion or pretext by them that are ruled by them, how much less is it lawful upon any pretext to control or displace the great provost and great schoolmaster of the whole land; except by inverting the order of all law and reason, the commanded may be made to command their commander, the judged to judge their judge, and they that are governed to govern their time about their lord and governor.

And the agreement of the law of nature in this our ground with the laws and constitutions of God and man already alleged, will by two similitudes[35] easily appear. The king towards his people is rightly compared to a father of children, and to the head of a body composed of divers members. For as

---

[29] **speaking law:** the law is what the king says it is.   [30] **law . . . king:** even when the king is personally silent, the law is still the king speaking.   [31] **doubt-some or rigorous:** doubtful or extremely strict.   [32] *summum . . . iniuria:* law pushed to extremes is extreme injustice.   [33] **these:** The examples mentioned in our summary.   [34] **subaltern:** subordinate.   [35] **similitudes:** similarities.

fathers, the good princes and magistrates of the people of God acknowledged themselves to their subjects. And for all other well-ruled commonwealths, the style of *Pater Patriae*[36] was ever, and is commonly used to kings.
And the proper office of a king towards his subjects agrees very well with
the office of the head towards the body, and all members thereof. From the
head, being the seat of judgment, proceedeth the care and foresight of guid-
ing, and preventing all evil that may come to the body, or any part thereof.
The head cares for the body, so does the king for his people. As the discourse and direction flows from the head, and the execution according
thereunto belongs to the rest of the members, every one according to their
office,[37] so it is betwixt a wise prince and his people. As the judgment coming from the head may not only employ the members, every one in their
own office, as long as they are able to do it; but likewise in case any of them
be affected with any infirmity, must care and provide for their remedy, in
case it be curable; and if otherwise, gar[38] cut them off for fear of infecting of
the rest: even so it is betwixt the prince and his people. And as there is ever
hope of curing any diseased member by the direction of the head, as long as
it is whole; but by the contrary, if it be troubled, all the members are partakers of the pain: so is it betwixt the prince and his people.

[36] *Pater Patriae:* father of the fatherland.   [37] office: function.   [38] gar: to cause to be done (i.e.,
cause the incurable members to be cut off).

→ KING JAMES I

From Basilikon Doron   *1598*

If King James's *The True Law of Free Monarchies* (1598) is his theoretical statement on the duties and powers of a king, then *Basilikon Doron*[1] is his very concrete advice to his eldest son, Prince Henry, on how to put these theories into
practice once he succeeds his father as King of England and Scotland. The book
was originally supposed to remain secret, and the first edition consisted of only
seven copies. Word of the book's existence got out, however, and, giving in to
popular pressure and disturbed by the distribution of flawed, pirated copies,
James granted permission for an authorized version of his "Kingly Gift" to be
published. When James succeeded to the English crown in 1603, *Basilikon*

[1] *Basilikon Doron:* the kingly gift.

King James I, *Basilikon Doron. Or His Majesty's Instructions to His Dearest Son, Henry the Prince.*
(Edinburgh, 1598; reprinted, London, 1603. Our excerpts are taken from the 1603 London edition), 29–33, 52–53.

Doron went through several London printings to satisfy English curiosity. That the book had not been intended for public consumption may account for the frankness of James's advice to young Henry. The king's very practical suggestions on how his son should fashion a public, royal persona, and in what manner he should interact with his subjects, are especially revealing.

Book 2

Of a King's Duty in His Office.

[In the first excerpt, James I urges Prince Henry to enforce laws from the beginning of his reign. Subsequently, James gives his son a list of unpardonable crimes, and also urges him not to let go unpunished any slanders aimed at members of the royal family.]

And as for the execution of good laws, whereat I left, remember that among the differences that I put betwixt the form of the government of a good king and an usurping tyrant, I show how a tyrant would enter like a saint while he found himself fast underfoot, and then would suffer his unruly affections to burst forth. Therefore be ye contrary at your first entry into your kingdom, to that *Quinquennium Neronis*,[2] with his tender-hearted wish, *Vellum nescirum literas*,[3] in giving the lawful execution against all breakers thereof but exception. For since ye come not to your reign *precario*,[4] nor by conquest, but by right and due descent, fear no uproars for doing of justice, since you may assure yourself the most part of your people will ever naturally favor justice, providing always that ye do it only for love to justice, and not for satisfying any particular passions of yours, under color thereof;[5] otherwise, how justly that ever the offender deserve it, ye are guilty of murder before God. For ye must consider that God ever looketh to your inward intention in all your actions.

And when ye have by the severity of justice once settled your countries and made them know that ye can strike, then may ye thereafter all the days of your life mix justice with mercy, punishing or sparing as ye shall find the crime to have been willfully or rashly committed, and according to the bypast behavior of the committer. For if otherwise ye kyth[6] your clemency at the first, the offences would soon come to such heaps, and the contempt of

---

[2] *Quinquennium Neronis:* the (first) five years of (Emperor) Nero's reign.   [3] *Vellum nescirum literas:* I wish that I had never learned to write. (Words spoken by Nero when asked to sign his first execution warrant. Cicero, *De Clementia*, 2.1.2.)   [4] *precario:* on sufferance (allowed or tolerated but not supported).   [5] **under color thereof:** under pretense of justice.   [6] **kyth:** make known.

you grow so great, that when ye would fall to punish, the number of them to be punished would exceed the innocent; and ye would be troubled to resolve whom at[7] to begin; and against your nature would be compelled then to wark[8] many, whom the chastisement of few in the beginning might have preserved. But in this, my over-dear bought experience may serve you for a sufficient lesson. For I confess, where I thought (by being gracious at the beginning) to win all men's hearts to a loving and willing obedience, I by the contrary found the disorder of the country and the loss of my thanks to be all my reward.

But as this severe justice of yours upon all offenses would be but for a time (as I have already said), so is there some horrible crimes that ye are bound in conscience never to forgive, such as witchcraft, willful murder, incest (especially within the degrees of consanguinity[9]), sodomy, poisoning, and false coin.[10] As for offenses against your own person and authority, since the fault concerneth yourself, I remit to your own choice to punish or pardon therein, as your heart serveth you, and according to the circumstances of the turn[11] and the quality[12] of the committer.

Here would I also eike[13] another crime to be unpardonable, if I should not be thought partial, but the fatherly love I bear you will make me break the bounds of shame in opening it unto you. It is, then, the false and unreverent writing or speaking of malicious men against your parents and predecessors. Ye know the command of God's law, "Honor your father and mother," and consequently, [since] ye are the lawful magistrate, suffer not both your princes and parents to be dishonored by any; especially since the example also toucheth yourself in leaving thereby to your successors the measure of that which they shall mete out again to you in your like behalf. I grant we have all our faults, which, privately betwixt you and God, should serve you for examples to meditate upon and mend in your person, but should not be a matter of discourse to others whatsoever. And since ye are come of as honorable predecessors as any prince living, repress the insolence of such, as under pretense to tax a vice in a person seeks craftily to stain the race, and to steal affection of the people from their posterity. . . .

But unto one fault is all the common people of the kingdom subject, as well burgh as land,[14] which is to judge and speak rashly of their prince: setting the common-weal upon four props,[15] as we call it; ever weary of the

---

[7] whom at: with whom.   [8] wark: to cause physical pain for.   [9] consanguinity: blood relationship.   [10] false coin: counterfeiting money.   [11] turn: act of ill will.   [12] quality: character, disposition; also social rank.   [13] eike: add.   [14] burgh as land: in town as well as the in countryside.   [15] setting . . . props: James seems to suggest that gossip or slander places the kingdom on weak foundations.

present estate and desirous of novelties. For remedy whereof (besides the execution of the laws that are to be used against unreverent speakers) I know no better mean then so to rule as may justly stop their mouths from all such idle and unreverent speeches; and so to prop[16] the weal[17] of your people with care of their good government; that justly, Momus[18] himself may have no ground to grudge at; and yet so to temper and mix your severity with mildness that as the unjust railers may be restrained with a reverent awe; so the good and loving subjects may not only live in security and wealth but be stirred up and united by your benign courtesies to open their mouths in the just praise of your so well-moderated regiment.

[16] prop: support.   [17] weal: wealth, happiness.   [18] Momus: the Greek god of mockery; a fault-finder.

→ BARNABY RICHE

From The Adventures of Brusanus, Prince of Hungary
1592

Born in Essex circa 1540, Barnaby Riche came to the writing of prose romances in the early 1570s, following the example of John Lyly's popular *Euphues*. Before that, during the reign of Mary, however, Riche was a soldier of fortune and saw action against France in the low countries. His *Riche His Farewell to Military Profession* (1581) served as an important source for Shakespeare's *Twelfth Night*.

The sprawling prose romance *The Adventures of Brusanus* tells many colorful stories, but principally that of King Leonarchus, who assumes the disguise of a merchant to secretly observe life at court and in his realm. His son, Prince Dorestus, assumes his father's place but refuses the crown and believes that his father is alive and will return. The king in disguise and some friends he has made on his travels are arrested on trumped up charges of treason and brought before Dorestus for judgment. Dorestus speaks eloquently on the subject of justice and the duties of a prince and dismisses the false charge of treason. King Leonarchus is so impressed with his son's wisdom that he throws off his disguise and reveals to him the acts of corruption he has observed on his travels.

Barnaby Riche, *The Adventures of Brusanus, Prince of Hungary, Pleasant for All to Read, and Profitable for Some to Follow* (London, 1592), 25–26, 35, 41–42.

THE TWELFTH CHAPTER.

Dorestus sits in judgment, Gloriosus[1] accuses Castus.[2]

The next day, he [Prince Dorestus], being accompanied with the nobles that were in the court, came into the common place of justice, usually called by the name of the House of Reformation. This House of Reformation was a very large room where the kings of Epirus in the ancient time were accustomed personally to sit, at the least three times every week, to hear suitors and to dispatch all manner of causes[3] and controversies that were between their subjects, and to minister justice to as many as were to demand it. And in this House of Reformation it was ever accustomed that if there were many suitors the complaints of the poor were ever heard before the requests of the rich. The prince being come to this place, after that he had given reverence to the throne of majesty wherein his father had been accustomed to sit, then sitting himself down in the next seat, the noblemen likewise everyone taking his place, the prisoners were brought to the bar, where Gloriosus was likewise ready to inform. But before they did proceed to the hearing of the matter,[4] the young prince delivered these words: "They make themselves guilty of great injustice who, being appointed of God to persecute the wicked with the sword drawn, will yet keep their hands clean from blood, whereas the wicked in the meantime commits [sic] all manner of sin, and that uncontrolled. And it is no less cruelty to punish no offense, than not to forgive any, the one being an abuse of clemency, the true ornament of a sovereign, and the other to turn authority into tyranny. Nevertheless, magistrates in the execution of justice ought to take great heed, lest by over-great severity, they hurt more than they heal, for the seat of a judge that is too severe seemeth to be a gibbet[5] already erected. We must then diligently note that as it is the duty of all magistrates to chastise and to punish every malefactor, so likewise they must beware, lest under pretense of exercising justice they fall into another kind of injustice through overmuch rigor, for too much severity causeth men to be misled for cruelty, and belongeth rather to beastly and savage nature than to the nature of man; for clemency and compassion never ought to be separated from good and just sentence, which is to hold small faults excused, or but lightly to punish them (provided always that justice be not violated) for as the wise man saith, that it was ill to be

---

[1] Gloriosus: a vain, arrogant, and unethical courtier. [2] Castus: a gentleman who is critical of corruption at the court. [3] causes: issues, typically legal ones. [4] matter: the legal issue before the court. [5] gibbet: gallows.

subject to a prince under whom nothing was tolerated, but worse where all things were left at random. . . ."

THE SEVENTEENTH CHAPTER.

Dorestus proceeds to judgment . . .

Dorestus willing a seat to be prepared, caused Brusanus to sit down next unto himself, and being thus settled, Dorestus, minding to proceed in justice, delivered these words: "The office of a good prince is to defend the commonwealth, to help the innocent, to aid the simple, to correct the offender, to relieve the poor, to honor the virtuous, to punish the vicious, to bridle the ambitious, and by justice to give everyone his own. And commonwealths are not lost for that[6] princes live in pleasure, but because they have no care of justice. Neither do people murmur when the prince doth recreate his person, but when he is slack to redress wrongs. O, that princes did know what it were to take charge of a kingdom, he should find that to be just in himself were honor to his person, but to minister justice is profit to the whole commonwealth; it is not therefore enough for him to be virtuous in his own person, but he is also bound to root all vices from amongst his people. But what profit is it for a prince himself to be honest, and those that should administer justice under him to be dissolute, for a prince to be true, and his officers false, for a prince to be gentle and his officers cruel? And hath it not been often known that where the prince himself hath been careful, those that he hath put most in trust, have been negligent? . . ."

THE TWENTIETH CHAPTER.

[King] Leonarchus discourseth what experience he hath gathered in his late travels, and first of the infections of his own court.

As it is the nature of vice to put on a vizard, to disguise and cover itself with those shows that belong only unto virtue, and being thus clothed with the help of corruptible pleasures, it yoketh base-minded men (whose care is only set upon the desire of earthly things) which it presenteth before their eyes as their felicity, seeking to defend itself by reason, which although they be altogether vain and frivolous, yet of great weight, in regard of the weak

---

[6] for that: because.

flesh of men, which easily suffereth itself to be a bond-slave to sin: we are therefore to take good heed that we suffer not ourselves to be surprised by so dangerous an enemy, nor to give him any access or entrance into us. To know then the causes of evil is the readiest way to cure them, for a disease known is half cured, and many kingdoms are brought to ruin by diverse causes, which if they were known to their princes and governors, they might easily be prevented by providence and reason. The prince that is careful to see and inquire for the damages of his realm, it may be said (if he provide not for them) that he can do no more, but to him that is negligent to warn them (if he do not provide) it may be said he will do no more. This hath been the cause that thus disguised as you see, I have traveled through mine own dominions to see the demeanors of my subjects, that by gathering a platform of common report, I might be the better able to reform a common mischief; for the surest councilors that belongeth to a prince, be his own eyes and his ears, which must be always vigilant; and it is not decent that princes should be lords over many and should communicate privately with few. By my travels in the country I have bettered my experience, to learn the follies of my own court . . .

→ NICCOLÒ MACHIAVELLI

From The Prince

1532

Niccolò Machiavelli (1469–1527) was born in the Italian city of Florence. Educated at the University of Florence, Machiavelli became active in the world of politics and rose to the post of secretary of the foreign relations committee of the Florentine republic. Best known among Machiavelli's writings is *The Prince*, a text of political advice dedicated to Lorenzo de' Medici, Duke of Urbino, and ruler of Florence. Although *The Prince* was not translated into English until 1640, there is ample evidence that many of its ideas — some in highly distorted form — circulated in English political and popular discourse. In Shakespeare's time, Machiavelli was generally reviled and vilified because of his political pragmatism and putative atheism, but that did not stop some from putting his ideas into practice.

Niccolò Machiavelli, *The Prince, Also the Life of Castruccio Castracani of Lucca and the Means Duke Valentine Us'd to Put to Death Vitellozzo Vitelli . . .* (1532; translated into English by E. D.; London, 1640. Excerpts are taken from the 1640 edition), 48–50, 128–32, 135–41.

CHAPTER 7

Of new Principalities gotten by fortune and other men's forces.

[In this section, Machiavelli relates how a private citizen who becomes a ruler should "fasten his roots in those estates which other's arms or fortune bestowed on him" (Machiavelli 43). This way the ruler may build a strong foundation for his power in the future. Machiavelli discusses the example of Cesare Borgia, Duke of Milan, who, after conquering Romagna[1] with the military aid of others and assassinating his political rivals, implemented a political strategy reminiscent of the Duke's in Measure for Measure.*]*

These heads[2] being plucked off,[3] and the partisans made his friends, the duke had laid very good foundations to build his own greatness on, having in his power Romagna with the Duchy of Urbino, and gained the hearts of those people by beginning to give them some relish of their well-being. And because this part is worthy to be taken notice of, and to be imitated by others, I will not let it escape. The duke, when he had taken Romagna, finding it had been under the hands of poor lords who had rather pillaged their subjects than chastised or amended them,[4] giving them more cause of discord than of peace and union, so that the whole country was fraught with robberies, quarrels, and all other sorts of insolencies, thought the best way to reduce them to terms of pacification and obedience to a princely power was to give them some good government; and therefore he set over them Remirro de Orco, a cruel, hasty man, to whom he gave an absolute power.

This man in a very short time settled peace and union amongst them with very great reputation. Afterwards, the duke thought such excessive authority served not so well to his purpose, and doubting[5] it would grow odious, he erected a civil judicature[6] in the midst of the country, where one excellent judge did preside. And hither every city sent their advocates and because he knew the rigors past had bred some hatred against him, to purge the minds of those people, and to gain them wholly to himself, he purposed to show that if there was any cruelty used it proceeded not from any order of his but from the harsh disposition of his officer.[7] Whereupon laying hold on him, at this occasion he caused his head to be struck off one morning early in the market place at Cesena, where he was left upon a gibbet, with a

---

[1] **Romagna:** region in northern Italy.   [2] **heads:** i.e., Borgia's political opponents.   [3] **plucked off:** removed (actually, as Skinner reports, Borgia had his opponents strangled, not beheaded [Skinner and Price 25n]).   [4] **amended them:** forgave them their faults.   [5] **doubting:** fearing.   [6] **civil judicature:** a civil tribunal.   [7] **officer:** i.e., Remirro de Orco, Borgia's deputy.

bloody sword by his side, the cruelty of which spectacle for a while satisfied and amazed those people. . . .

CHAPTER 17.

Of Cruelty and Clemency, and whether it is better to be beloved or feared.

Defending afterwards unto the other fore-alleged qualities, I say that every prince should desire to be held pitiful[8] and not cruel. Nevertheless ought he beware that he ill[9] uses not this pity. Cesare Borgia was accounted cruel, yet had his cruelty redressed the disorders in Romagna, settled it in union and restored it to peace and fidelity; which if it be well weighed we shall see was an act of more pity than that of the people of Florence, who, to avoid the term of cruelty, suffered Pistoia[10] to fall to destruction. Wherefore a prince ought not to regard the infamy of cruelty, for to hold his subjects united and faithful, for by giving a very few proofs of himself the other way,[11] he shall be held more pitiful than they who through their too much pity suffer disorders to follow, from whence arise murders and rapines[12]; for these are wont to hurt an entire universality[13] whereas the executions practiced by a prince hurt only some particular. And among all sorts of princes, it is impossible for a new prince to avoid the name of cruel because all new states are full of dangers; whereupon Virgil by the mouth of Dido excuses the inhumanity of her kingdom, saying, *"Res dura, et regni novitas me talia cogunt moliri, et late fines custode tueri."*[14] My hard plight and new state force me to guard my confines all about with watch and ward.

Nevertheless ought he be judicious in his giving belief to any thing, or moving himself thereat, not make his people extremely afraid of him; but proceed in a moderate way with wisdom and humanity, that his too much confidence make him not unwary, and his too much distrust intolerable. From hence arises a dispute, whether it is better to be beloved or feared. I answer, a man would wish he might be the one and the other[15]; but because hardly can they subsist both together, it is much safer to be feared than be loved, being that one of the two must needs fail; for, touching men, we may say this in general: they are unthankful, unconstant,[16] dissemblers,[17] they

---

[8] **pitiful:** merciful. [9] **ill:** inappropriately. [10] **Pistoia:** a village in Tuscany. [11] **by giving . . . way:** by behaving cruelly on occasion. [12] **rapines:** taking away by force the property of another. [13] **universality:** state or community. [14] *Res dura . . . tueri:* E. D. offers a translation in the next sentence. **Dido,** founder and queen of Carthage. For the quotation given here, see Virgil's *Aeneid,* Bk. 1, 11. 793–95. [15] **answer . . . other:** Skinner and Price translate from the Italian as follows: "My view is that it is desirable to be both loved and feared" (59). [16] **unconstant:** fickle, disloyal. [17] **dissemblers:** people who conceal something under false pretenses.

avoid dangers and are covetous of gain; and whilst thou doest them good, they are wholly thine, their blood, their fortunes, lives, and children are at thy service, as is said before, when the danger is remote; but when it approaches they revolt. And that prince who wholly relies upon their words, unfurnished of all other preparations,[18] goes to wrack,[19] for the friendships that are gotten with rewards,[20] and are not by the magnificence and worth of the mind, are dearly bought indeed; but they will neither keep long, nor serve well in time of need; and men do less regard to offend one that is supported by love than by fear. For love is held by a certainty of obligation which, because men are mischievous, is broken upon any occasion of their own profit. But fear restrains with a dread of punishment which never forsakes a man. Yet ought a prince cause himself to be beloved in such a manner that if he gains not love he may avoid hatred, for it may well stand together that a man may be feared and not hated, which shall never fail if he abstain from his subjects' goods and their wives. And whensoever he should be forced to proceed against any of their lives, do it when it is to be done upon a just cause, and apparent conviction. But above all things forbear to lay his hands on other men's goods; for men forget sooner the death of their father than the loss of their patrimony. Moreover, the occasions of taking from men their goods do never fail,[21] and always he that begins to live by rapine finds occasion to lay hold upon other men's goods; but against men's lives they are seldomer found and sooner fail. . . .

CHAPTER 18.

In what manner Princes ought to keep their words.

How commendable in a prince it is to keep his word, and live with integrity, not making use of cunning and subtlety,[22] everyone knows well. Yet we see by experience in these our days that those princes have affected great matters who have made small reckoning of keeping their words, and have known by their craft to turn and wind[23] men about, and in the end have overcome those who have grounded upon[24] the truth. You must then know there are two kinds of combating or fighting, the one by right of laws, the other merely by force. That first way is proper to men, the other is also common to beasts; but because the first many times suffices not, there is a

---

[18] **preparations:** defenses.   [19] **wrack:** ruin.   [20] **rewards:** financial rewards.   [21] **occasions . . . fail:** there will always be pretexts for confiscating a person's property.   [22] **subtlety:** trickery.   [23] **turn and wind:** to deceive skillfully (to manage according to one's pleasure).   [24] **grounded upon:** relied upon.

necessity to make recourse to the second; wherefore it behooves a prince to know how to make good use of that part which belongs to a beast, as well as that which is proper to a man.

   This part has been covertly showed to princes by ancient writers, who say that Achilles[25] and many others of those ancient princes were entrusted to Chiron the centaur,[26] to be brought up under his discipline. The moral of this, having for their teacher one that was half beast and half man, was nothing else but that it was needful for a prince to understand how to make his advantage of the one and the other nature, because neither could subsist without the other. A prince, then, being necessitated to know how to make use of that part belonging to a beast, ought to serve himself of the conditions[27] of the fox and the lion[28]; for the lion cannot keep himself from snares, nor the fox defend himself against the wolves. He had need then be a fox that he may beware of the snares, and a lion that he may fear[29] the wolves. Those that stand[30] wholly upon the lion understand not well themselves. And therefore a wise prince cannot, nor ought not keep his faith given when the observance thereof turns to disadvantage, and the occasions that made him promise are past. For if men were all good, this rule[31] would not be allowable; but being they are full of mischief, and would not make it good to thee, neither art thou tied to keep it with them. Nor shall a prince ever want[32] lawful occasions to give color[33] to this breach. Very many modern[34] examples hereof might be alleged wherein might be shown how many peaces concluded, and how many promises made, have been violated and broken by the infidelity of princes. And ordinarily things have best succeeded with him that hath been nearest the fox in condition.[35]

   But it is necessary to understand how to set a good color[36] upon this disposition, and to be able to feign and dissemble thoroughly; and men are so simple[37] and yield so much to the present necessities that he who hath a mind to deceive shall always find another that will be deceived. I will not conceal any one of the examples that have been of late. Alexander VI[38] never did anything else than deceive men, and never meant otherwise, and always found whom to work upon; yet never was there man would protest more

---

[25] Achilles: the great warrior in Homer's *Iliad*. Also a student of Chiron.   [26] Chiron the centaur: a creature from Greek mythology with the upper part of a human being and the lower part of a horse. The wise medicine man among the centaurs, Chiron was the educator of heroes and children of the gods.   [27] conditions: characteristics.   [28] fox . . . lion: in the animal fables, the fox signifies guile and discretion, the lion courage and strength.   [29] fear: frighten. [30] stand: rely.   [31] this rule: i.e., that rulers should sometimes break their promises.   [32] want: lack.   [33] to give color: to give a seemingly good or plausible appearance.   [34] modern: contemporary (to Machiavelli).   [35] that . . . condition: that imitates the fox the best.   [36] color: appearance.   [37] simple: naïve.   [38] Alexander VI: Rodrigo Lanzol y Borgia (1431–1503), who was pope from 1492 to 1503.

effectually,[39] nor aver anything with more solemn oaths, and observe them less than he. Nevertheless, his cozenages[40] all thrived well with him; for he knew how to play this part cunningly. Therefore is there no necessity for a prince to be endued[41] with all these above written qualities,[42] but it behooves well that that he seem to be so; or, rather, I will boldly say this, that having these qualities, and always regulating himself by them, they are hurtful; but seeming to have them, they are advantageous; as to seem pitiful, faithful, mild, religious, and of integrity, and indeed to be so, provided withal thou be of such a composition that if need require thee to use the contrary thou canst, and knows how to apply thyself thereto. And it suffices to conceive this, that a prince, and especially a new prince, cannot observe all those things for which men are held good; he being often forced for the maintenance of the state to do contrary to his faith, charity, humanity, and religion. And therefore it behooves him to have a mind so disposed as to turn and take the advantage of all winds and fortunes; and as formerly I said, not forsake the good while he can, but to know how to make use of the evil upon necessity.

A prince then ought to have a special care that he never let fall any words but what are all seasoned with the five above-written qualities; and let him seem to him that sees and hears him, all pity, all faith, all integrity, all humanity, all religion; nor is there any thing more necessary for him to seem to have than this last quality, for all men in general judge thereof, rather by the sight than by the touch; for every man may come to sight of him, few come to the touch and feeling of him; every man may come to see what thou seemest, few come to perceive and understand what thou art; and those few dare not oppose the opinion of many who have the majesty of state to protect them. And in all men's actions, especially those of princes wherein there is no judgment to appeal unto,[43] men forbear to give their censures till the events and end of things.[44] Let a prince therefore take the surest courses he can to maintain his life and state: the means shall always be thought honorable and commended by everyone, for the vulgar[45] is overtaken with the appearance and event of a thing; and for the most part of people they are but the vulgar; the others that are but few take place where the vulgar have no

---

[39] **effectually:** earnestly, ardently.   [40] **cozenages:** deceptions.   [41] **endued:** endowed.   [42] **qualities:** all the prince's good qualities are listed in chapter 15. They are: generosity, mercifulness, loyalty, boldness, affability, moderation, moral rectitude, devoutness, and flexibility. Here, in chapter 18, Machiavelli seems to reduce them to five main qualities: "all pity, all faith, all integrity, all humanity, all religion" (mercy, trustworthiness, compassion, moral uprightness, religiousness).   [43] **there . . . unto:** i.e., there is no authority higher than the prince to which anyone with a complaint against the prince can appeal.   [44] **events . . . things:** outcome (results).   [45] **the vulgar:** the common people.

subsistence.[46] A prince there is in these days, whom I shall not do well to name, that preaches nothing else but peace and faith; but had he kept the one and the other, several times had they taken him from his state and reputation.

[46] **the others . . . subsistence:** E. D.'s translation here is unclear. Price's modern translation from the Italian runs as follows: "the few [that is, those who are able to see the prince for what he truly is] are isolated when the majority and the government are one" (63).

➔ HUGH LATIMER

From The First Sermon upon the Lord's Prayer   *1552*

Hugh Latimer (1485–1555) was an English Protestant Bishop and religious reformer who was burned at the stake during the reign of Queen Mary. In the introduction to the Governance section, we discussed how a prince might arouse and manage anxiety in his subjects for the purpose of controlling their beliefs and feelings. In his chapter on *Measure for Measure,* Stephen Greenblatt uses the text of a sermon by the Protestant martyr Hugh Latimer to illustrate how authority figures in early modern England cultivated and managed anxiety in their subjects (Greenblatt, *Shakespearean Negotiation* 129–38). We reproduce the relevant portion of Latimer's sermon here in order to suggest a similarity between the strategies followed by Latimer and *Measure for Measure*'s Duke (especially in his treatment of the imprisoned Claudio who is awaiting execution).

Here I have occasion to tell you a story which happened at Cambridge. Master Bilney[1] (or rather Saint Bilney that suffered death for God's word sake[2]) the same Bilney was the instrument whereby God called me to knowledge,[3] for I may thank him, next to God, for that knowledge that I have in the word of God. For I was as obstinate a papist as any was in England, insomuch that when I should be made Bachelor of Divinity, my whole oration went against Philip Melanchthon[4] and against his opinions. Bilney heard me at that time and perceived that I was zealous without

[1] **Bilney:** Thomas Bilney, whose religious views played a crucial role in Latimer's conversion in 1524, was burned for heresy in Norwich in 1531.   [2] **for . . . word:** for the sake of God's word. [3] **knowledge:** correct understanding of God's truth.   [4] **Philip Melanchthon:** German-born theologian (1497–1560) who became a protegé of Martin Luther at the University of Wittenberg.

Hugh Latimer, *Fruitful Sermons Preached by the Right Reverend Father and Constant Martyr of Jesus Christ, M. Hugh Latimer . . .* (London, 1578), 126v–127v.

knowledge, and he came to me afterward in my study and desired me, for God's sake, to hear his confession. I did so, and, to say the truth, by his confession I learned more than before in many years. So from that time forward I began to smell the word of God, and forsook the school doctors[5] and such fooleries.

Now after I had been acquainted with him, I went with him to visit the prisoners in the Tower at Cambridge, for he was ever visiting prisoners and sick folk. So we went together and exhorted them as well as we were able to do, moving them to patience and to acknowledge their faults. Among other prisoners, there was a woman which was accused that she had killed her child, which act she plainly and steadfastly denied and could not be brought to confess the act, which denying gave us occasion to search for the matter, and so we did. And at the length we found that her husband loved her not, and therefore he sought means to make her out of the way. The matter was thus.

A child of hers had been sick by the space of a year and decayed as it were in a consumption.[6] At the length, it died in harvest time. She went to her neighbors and other friends to desire their help to prepare the child to the burial, but there was nobody at home; every man was in the field. The woman, in a heaviness and trouble of spirit, went and, being herself alone, prepared the child to burial. Her husband, coming home, not having great love towards her, accused her of the murder. And so she was taken and brought to Cambridge. But as farforth[7] as I could learn through earnest inquisition, I thought in my conscience the woman was not guilty, all the circumstances well considered.

Immediately after this, I was called to preach before the king,[8] which was my first sermon that I made before his majesty, and it was done at Windsor, where his majesty, after the sermon was done, did most familiarly talk with me in a gallery. Now when I saw my time, I kneeled down before his majesty, opening the whole matter, and afterwards most humbly desired his majesty to pardon that woman. For I thought in my conscience she was not guilty, else I would not for all the world sue for a murderer. The king most graciously heard my humble request, insomuch that I had a pardon ready for her at my return homeward.

In the mean season that same woman was delivered of a child in the Tower at Cambridge, whose godfather I was, and Mistress Cheke[9] was godmother. But all that time I hid my pardon and told her nothing of it, only

---

[5] school doctors: school theologians. [6] consumption: a wasting away of the body. [7] as farforth: to the extent. [8] king: Edward VI, king of England from 1547 to 1553. [9] Mistress Cheke: mother of the English humanist Sir John Cheke.

exhorting her to confess the truth. At the length the time came when she looked to suffer. I came, as I was wont to do, to instruct her. She made great moan to me and most earnestly required me that I would find the means that she might be purified before her suffering. For she thought she should have been damned if she should suffer without purification. Where Master Bilney and I told her that that law was made unto the Jews, and not unto us, and that women lying in childbed be not unclean before God. Neither is purification used to that end that it should cleanse from sin, but rather a civil and politic law, made for natural honesty['s] sake, signifying that a woman before the time of her purification, that is to say, as long as she is a green woman,[10] is not meet[11] to do such acts as other women, nor to have company with her husband. For it is against natural honesty and against the commonwealth. To that end purification is kept and used, not to make a superstition or holiness of it, as some do which think that they may not fetch neither fire nor anything in that house where there is a green woman, which opinion is erroneous and wicked. For woman (as I have said before) be as well in the favor of God before they be purified as after. So we travailed with this woman till we brought her to a good trade,[12] and at length showed her the king's pardon and let her go.

This tale I told you by this occasion that though some women be very unnatural and forget their children, yet when we hear anybody so report, we should not be so hasty in believing the tale but rather suspend our judgments till they know the truth.

[10] green woman: a woman who has recently given birth.   [11] meet: appropriate.   [12] trade: understanding.

→ GEORGE BUCHANAN

From A Dialogue Concerning the Due Privilege of Government in the Kingdom of Scotland *1579*

George Buchanan (1506–1582) was among the sixteenth century's most learned Scotsmen. Educated at the Universities of Paris and St. Andrews, Buchanan rose to prominence as a Latin scholar, a successful poet, a political thinker, a teacher to the influential French essayist Michel de Montaigne, and a mentor to royalty, including Mary, Queen of Scots, and, from 1570 to 1578, as tutor to her young son James VI of Scotland (who in 1603 also became king of England).

George Buchanan, *De Jure Regni apud Scotus, A Dialogue Concerning the Due Privilege of Government in the Kingdom of Scotland* (Edinburgh, written in Latin, 1579; trans. 1680), 126–27.

Buchanan's Protestant leanings and his public disapproval of the notorious murder of Queen Mary's husband, the Englishman Lord Darnley, forced a permanent split between the queen and her former teacher, but Buchanan regained favor with the Protestant James VI, in whose administration he served. This is not to say, however, that James and Buchanan saw eye to eye on all issues. *De Jure Regni apud Scotus*, for instance, supports James's rule of Scotland, but Buchanan's views on the people's right to resist and even remove a wicked ruler differ sharply from the views that James would express in his *True Law of Free Monarchies* (1598).

BUCHANAN: . . . But I suppose you know what the law doth permit, namely to kill any way a thief stealing by night, and also to kill him if he defend himself when stealing by day. But if he cannot be drawn to compare to answer but by force, you remember what is usually done, for we pursue by force and arms such robbers as are more powerful than that by law they can be reached. Nor is there almost any other cause of all the wars betwixt nations, people, and kings than those injuries which, while they cannot be determined by justice, are by arms decided.

MAITLAND: Against enemies indeed for these causes wars use to be carried on, but the case is far otherwise with kings, to whom by most sacred oath interposed we are bound to give obedience.

BUCHANAN: We are indeed bound, but they do first promise that they shall rule in equity and justice.

MAITLAND: It is so.

BUCHANAN: There is then a mutual pact betwixt the king and his subjects.

MAITLAND: It seems so.

BUCHANAN: Doth not he who first recedes from what is covenanted, and doth contrary to what he hath covenanted to do, break the contract and covenant?

MAITLAND: He doth.

BUCHANAN: The bond then being loosened, which did hold fast the king with the people, whatever privilege or right did belong to him, by that agreement and covenant who loseth the same, I suppose is lost.

MAITLAND: It is lost.

BUCHANAN: He then with whom the covenant was made becometh as free as ever he was before the stipulation.

MAITLAND: He doth clearly enjoy the same privilege and the same liberty.

BUCHANAN: Now if a king do those things which are directly for the dissolution of society, for the continuance whereof he was created, how do we call him?

MAITLAND: A tyrant, I suppose.

BUCHANAN: Now a tyrant hath not only no just authority over a people, but is also their enemy.

MAITLAND: He is indeed an enemy.

BUCHANAN: Is there not a just and lawful war with an enemy for grievous and intolerable injuries?

MAITLAND: It is forsooth[1] a just war.

BUCHANAN: What war is that which is carried on with him who is the enemy of all mankind, that is, a tyrant?

MAITLAND: A most just war.

BUCHANAN: Now a lawful war being once undertaken with an enemy and for a just cause, it is lawful not only for the whole people to kill the enemy, but for every one of them.

MAITLAND: I confess that.

BUCHANAN: May not every one out of the whole multitude of mankind assault with all the calamities of war a tyrant who is a public enemy, with whom all good men have a perpetual warfare?

[1] forsooth: in truth.

→   SIR WALTER RALEIGH

From The Prince, or Maxims of State   *c. 1612*

Few Elizabethans personify the idea of the "renaissance man" as well as Sir Walter Raleigh (1554–1618). Born into an ancient but not particularly wealthy family in Devonshire, Raleigh rose to fame, fortune, and a position of considerable political power at the court of Queen Elizabeth. He was a lauded poet, a member of Parliament, a veteran of dangerous military campaigns (including the defeat of the Spanish Armada), and one of the earliest English explorers of the New World. Although Raleigh at times had a turbulent relationship with Queen Elizabeth (and paid for it with a stint in the Tower in 1592), it is clear that the queen liked him, and she continued to bestow great honors on him until the end of her life.

Raleigh did not fare so well in the court of King James I. He lost his lucrative wine-licensing patent in 1603, and was stripped of various titles, such as the lieutenancy of Cornwall and governorship of Jersey, granted to him by Elizabeth. Later in the same year, Raleigh was implicated in a plot to kill James I, and

Walter Raleigh (attributed), *The Prince, or Maxims of State written by Sir Walter Raleigh, and presented to Prince Henry* (London, 1650), 20, 21, 22, 25–26, 28–29, 30, 33, 38, 45, 46–47, 50–51. (*The Prince* was published in 1642 but written sometime before the death of Prince Henry in 1612.)

spent the years from 1603 to 1616 in the Tower, only to be let out briefly in 1616 and 1617 to make voyages on the king's behalf to Guiana. After a failed attempt to escape to France in 1618, Raleigh was arrested and beheaded at Whitehall. Just before his execution, Raleigh is supposed to have asked to see the axe and to have said, "This is sharp Medicine, but it is a Physician for all Diseases."

The text reproduced here — *The Prince*, or *Maxims of State* — may or may not have been written by Raleigh, but it was attributed to him many times in the course of the seventeenth century. *Maxims of State* reveals a political conservatism and pragmatism, combined with a noticeable lack of original political thinking, that characterizes some of Raleigh's other writings, most notably his *History of the World* (1614). The following excerpts from *Maxims* are of potential interest to readers of *Measure for Measure* for two reasons: first, because they deal directly with questions of governance that may help us contextualize Shakespeare's Duke and Angelo; and, second, because *Maxims* stands in an uneasy relationship to some of the central ideas of Machiavelli's *Prince*, which it emphatically rejects but to which it also seems deeply indebted. Raleigh's *Maxims*, therefore, may give us a glimpse of how Machiavelli was sanitized for English consumption and how playgoers may have interpreted Shakespeare's Duke Vincentio in a way that makes him less controversial.

General Rules

[The prince is] to take heed that no magistrate be created or continued contrary to the laws and policy of [the] state. As that in a senate there be not created a perpetual dictator, as Caesar in Rome. In a kingdom, that there be no senate or convention of equal power with the prince in state matters, as in Poland.

[The prince is] to create such magistrates as love the state as it is settled, and take heed of the contrary practice, as to advance popular persons in a kingdom or aristocracy. And, secondly, to advance such as have skill to discern what doth preserve and what hurteth or altereth the present state.

[The prince is] to that end to have certain officers to pry abroad, and to observe such as do not live and behave themselves in fit sort, agreeable to the present state, but desire rather to be under some other form or kind of government. . . .

[The prince is] to take heed of small beginnings, and to meet with them even at the first, as well touching the breaking and altering of laws, as of other rules which concern the continuance of every several state. For the disease and alteration of a commonwealth doth not happen all at once, but grows by degrees, which every common wit cannot discern, but[1] men expert on policy.

---

[1] **but:** only.

Kingdoms Hereditary Are Preserved
by the Ordering

Himself,[2] *viz.*[3] by the tempering and moderation of the prince's power and prerogative.[4] For the less and more temperate their power and state is, the more firm and stable is their kingdom and government because they seem to be further off from a master-like and tyrannical empire; and less unequal in condition to the next degree[5] — to wit, the nobility — and so less subject to grudge and envy. . . .

People, *viz.* so to order and behave himself that he be loved and reverenced of[6] the people. For that the prince need not greatly fear home conspiracies or foreign invasion if he be firmly loved of his own people. The reason for that the rebel can neither hope for any forces for so great enterprise, nor any refuge being discovered and put to flight if the multitude affect their prince. But the common people once offended, [the prince] hath cause to fear every moving, both at home and abroad. This may be effected by the prince if he use means and art of getting the favor of the people, and avoid those things that breed hatred and contempt, *viz.* if he seem as a tutor or a father to love the people, and to protect them; if he maintain the peace in his kingdom, for that nothing is more popular nor more pleasing to the people than is peace.

If he [the prince] show himself oftentimes graciously, yet with state[7] and majesty to his people, and receive complaints of his suppliants,[8] and such like.

If he sit himself sometimes in open courts and place of justice that he may seem to have a care of justice among his people. If he bestow many benefits and graces upon that city which he maketh the seat of his empire, and so make it sure and faithful unto him, which [i.e., the city] is fit to be in the middle of his kingdom, as the heart in the middle of the body, or the sun in the middle of heaven,[9] both to divide himself more easily into all the parts of his dominions; and least the furthest parts at one end move while the prince is in the other (if he go in progress many times to see the provinces, especially those that are remote). . . .

If he avoid all such things as may breed hatred or contempt of his person, which may be done if he show himself not too light, inconstant, hard, cruel,

---

[2] **Himself:** the prince.   [3] *viz.:* namely.   [4] **prerogative:** a term used to describe a monarch's extra-legal powers.   [5] **degree:** rank or social class.   [6] **of:** by.   [7] **with state:** with the dignity that behooves his high office.   [8] **suppliants:** petitioners.   [9] **sun . . . heaven:** probably a reference to the Ptolemaic conception of the universe, in which the sun is positioned in the centrally located fourth of the seven heavenly spheres.

effeminate, fearful, and dastardly, etc. But contrariwise [show himself] religious, grave, just, valiant, etc., whereby appeareth the false doctrine of the Machiavellian policy, with far the better means to keep the people in obedience than [to incite] love and reverence of the people towards the prince.[10] . . .

The prince himself is to sit sometimes in place of public justice, and to give an experiment of his wisdom and equity, whereby great reverence and estimation is gotten, as in the example of Solomon,[11] which may seem the reason why our kings of England had their King's Bench[12] in place of public justice, after the manner of the ancient kings that sat in the gate;[13] where for better performing of this princely duty some special causes may be selected, which may thoroughly be debated and considered upon by the prince in private with the help and advice of learned council, and so be decided publicly, as before is said by the king himself. At least the king is to take accompt[14] of every minister of public justice, that it may be known that he hath a care of justice and doing right to this people, which makes the justicers[15] also to be careful in performing of their duties.

KINGDOMS NEW GOTTEN OR PURCHASED BY FORCE ARE PRESERVED BY THESE MEANS

[In this section, Raleigh advises Prince Henry how to control annexed foreign territories. On the surface, Raleigh's subject has nothing to do with the governance of Shakespeare's Vienna. However, if we view Vienna as a territory lost to Duke Vincentio's administrative control, we can view the appointment of Angelo in light of the "lieutenants and inferior governors" discussed in Raleigh's account.]

They [the people of annexed territories] conceive that they have refuge by the prince's presence if they be oppressed by the lieutenants and inferior governors, where it will be convenient for the winning of the people's hearts that some example be made of punishing such as have committed any violence or oppression.

---

[10] false doctrine . . . prince: What Machiavelli actually wrote is this: "My view is that it is desirable to be *both* loved and feared; but it is difficult to achieve both and, if one of them has to be lacking, it is much *safer* to be feared than loved" (qtd. in Sommerville, *King James* 59; emphases added). Also note that Raleigh says that a prince must "show himself" in a way that his subjects will love him, which recalls the same kind of self-fashioning that Machiavelli recommends to rulers.   [11] Solomon: King of Israel noted for his wisdom.   [12] King's Bench: court of law (so called because the sovereign used to sit there on a raised bench).   [13] gate: place of judicial assembly (dating back to biblical times).   [14] accompt: account.   [15] justicers: justices.

Because being present, he [the prince] seeth and heareth what is thought and attempted; and so may quickly give remedy to it, which, being absent, he cannot do, or not do in time.

SOPHISMS[16] OF A BARBAROUS AND PROFESSED TYRANNY

[In this section, Raleigh observes that "sophisms of tyrants are rather to be known than practiced . . . by wise and good princes." It can be argued that some of these so-called sophisms are practiced in Measure for Measure.*]*

[Tyrants are] to have their beagles[17] or listeners in every corner and parts of the realm, especially in places that are more suspect, to learn what every man saith or thinketh, that they may prevent all attempts and take away such as mislike[18] their state.

SOPHISMS OF THE SOPHISTICAL OR SUBTLE TYRANT, TO HOLD UP HIS STATE

[A tyrant is] to make show of a good king by observing a temper and mediocrity[19] in his government and whole course of life. To which end, it is necessary that this subtle tyrant be a cunning politician or a Machiavellian at the least, and that he be taken so to be for that it maketh him more to be feared and regarded, and it is thought thereby, not unworthy for to govern others.

[A tyrant is] to make show not of severity but of gravity by seeming reverent, and not terrible in his speech and gesture and habit, and other demeanor. . . .

All rewards and things grateful [are] to come from himself [i.e., the tyrant], but all punishments, exactions,[20] and things ungrateful to come from his officers and public ministers. And when he hath effected what he would by them, if he see the people discontented withal, to make them a sacrifice to pacify his subjects.

[A tyrant is] to pretend great care of religion and of serving God (which hath been the manner of the wickedest tyrants) for that people do less fear any hurt from those whom they think virtuous and religious, nor attempt likely to do them hurt, for they think that God protects them. . . .

---

[16] **sophisms:** clever and plausible but fallacious arguments or reasoning.   [17] **beagles:** trusty servants, spies.   [18] **mislike:** dislike.   [19] **mediocrity:** avoidance of extremes.   [20] **exactions:** excessive demands, extortion.

[A tyrant is] to procure that other great persons be in the same fault or case with them, that for that cause they be forced to defend the tyrant for their own safety.

→ RICHARD MARTIN

From A Speech Delivered to the King's Most Excellent Majesty, in the Name of the Sheriffs of London and Middlesex *1603*

Richard Martin (1570–1618) was born at Otterton in Devonshire and educated at Oxford University and the Inner Temple. He was elected to Parliament in 1601, where he earned a reputation as an outstanding speaker, and he counted King James among the admirers of his wit and eloquence (Nichols 128).

But let England be the school wherein your Majesty will practice your temperance and moderation; for there flattery will essay to undermine or force your Majesty's strongest constancy and integrity. Base assentation,[1] the bane of virtuous princes, which (like Lazarus's dogs) licks even princes' sores, a vice made so familiar to this age by long use, that even pulpits are not free from that kind of treason — a treason, I may justly call it, most capital, to poison the fountain of Wisdom and Justice, whereat so many kingdoms must be refreshed.

Nor can I be justly blamed to lay open to a most skillful and faithful physician our true griefs; nay, it shall be the comfort of my age to have spoken the truth to my Lord the King, and, with a heart as true to your Majesty as your own, to make known to an uncorrupted king the hopes and desires of his best subjects, who (as if your Majesty were sent down from heaven to reduce the Golden Age) have now assured themselves that this island (by strange working and revolution now united to your Majesty's obedience) shall never fear the mischiefs and misgovernments which other countries

---

[1] **assentation:** immediate and flattering or hypocritical assent.

Richard Martin, "A Speech Delivered to the King's Most Excellent Majesty, in the Name of the Sheriffs of London and Middlesex" (1603), in *The Progresses, Processions, and Magnificent Festivities of King James the First, His Royal Consort, Family, and Court*, vol. 1, ed. John Nichols (London, 1828), 130–31.

and other times have felt. Oppression shall not be here the badge of authority, nor insolence the mark of greatness. The people shall every one sit under his own olive tree and anoint himself with the fat thereof, his face not grinded with extorted suits, nor his marrow sucked with most odious and unjust monopolies. Unconscionable lawyers and greedy officers shall no longer spin out the poor man's cause in length to his undoing and the delay of justice. No more shall bribes blind the eyes of the wise, nor gold be reputed the common measure of men's worthiness. Adulterate gold, which can guild a rotten post, make Balaam[2] a bishop, and Issachar[3] as worthy of a judicial chair as Solomon, where he may wickedly sell that justice which he corruptly bought! The money changers[4] and sellers of doves, I mean those which traffic the living of simple and religious pastors, shall your Majesty whip out of the Temple and Commonwealth; for no more shall church livings be pared to the quick,[5] forcing ambitious churchmen (partakers of this sacrilege) to enter in at the window by simony and corruption, which they must afterwards repair with usury, and make up with pluralities.

[2] **Balaam:** in biblical times, a diviner in the Babylon region (today's Iraq) who succumbed to earthly riches and betrayed Israel. [3] **Issachar:** a son of Jacob and Leah (Gen. 30:18) from whom one of the twelve tribes of Israel is descended. [4] **money changers . . . Commonwealth:** the reference is to Matt. 21:12 in which Jesus casts the moneylenders out of the Temple in Jerusalem. The author draws an analogy between James's purifying influence in England and Christ's expulsion of sinners from the house of God. [5] **for . . . pluralities:** Under James's purifying influence, Martin predicts, the income of church officials will be raised and no longer tempt churchmen to resort to various undesirable practices to earn a living.

➜ BEN JONSON

Epigram 35. To King James   *1616*

A prominent playwright and poet, Ben Jonson (1573?–1637) was a self-made man of humble origins. Although he was stepson of a bricklayer, Jonson had the good fortune of attending prestigious Westminster school, sponsored by an anonymous benefactor. There Jonson studied with the famous historian, antiquarian, philologist, and classicist William Camden and developed a deep love for learning and a fervent respect for the texts of Greek and Roman antiquity. Although Jonson did not graduate from Westminster and did not go on to the universities of Oxford or Cambridge (as many Westminster students did), he

Ben Jonson, *The Works of Benjamin Jonson* (London, 1616), 778.

became a towering literary figure of his age, and wrote masques[1] that were performed before King James at court. Jonson steadfastly believed that there was a profound and reciprocally beneficial relationship between learning and governance. He wrote in his commonplace book that "Learning needs rest. . . . Sovereignty gives it. Sovereignty needs counsel, learning affords it." Hence Jonson always sought the patronage of the powerful, including James, in return for the benefits of his wisdom, often in the form of poetry. In his epigrams, he routinely characterizes members of the royal court, including the king, in order to praise or criticize them. Epigram 35, reproduced below, may give us the impression that Jonson was sometimes little more than a sycophant with a poetic gift, but we must heed his own words on this score: "Who e're is rais'd, / For worth he has not, He is tax'd, not prais'd" (Epigram 65. "To My Muse").

Who would not be thy subject, *James,* t'obey
 A Prince, that rules by'example, more than sway?
Whose manners draw, more than thy powers constrain.
 And in this short time of thy happiest reign,
Hast purg'd thy realms, as[2] we have now no cause
 Left us of fear, but first our crimes, then laws.
Like aids 'gainst treasons[3] who hath found before?
 And than in them, how could we know god more?
First thou preserved wert,[4] our king to be,
 And since, the whole land was preserv'd for thee.[5]

---

[1] **masque:** an extravagant form of courtly entertainment that involved actors (who sometimes were members of the court) and dancers who wore masks. A masque generally included allegorical and/or mythological characters and relied more on music, elaborate costumes, and spectacle than on plot. [2] **as:** so that. [3] **treasons:** James had been the object of treasonous plots before his coronation. [4] **wert:** was. [5] **whole land . . . thee:** probably a reference to the devastating London plague of 1603.

→ THOMAS MIDDLETON

From The Phoenix   *1603–1604*

Born in London to a well-to-do bricklayer who donned a coat of arms, Thomas Middleton (1580–1627) was educated at Queen's College, Oxford, though he probably did not graduate. There is reason to believe that Middleton came from "a moderate Puritan background" (Heinemann 51). The author of many popular plays, Middleton is perhaps best known for his city comedies full of splendid humor and biting social satire. His *The Phoenix* (1603–04) is such a satirical play, and, written around the time that Shakespeare composed *Measure for Measure*, portrays a prince who goes among the people of Ferrara to discover deceit and corruption. Middleton's Prince Phoenix is certainly a far less complex and dark figure than Shakespeare's Duke Vincentio, but this may in itself be instructive if we allow that theatrical representations are at least in part reflections of the concerns, beliefs, and anxieties of paying customers. As such, the largely optimistic portrayal of a prince in disguise in one play and a far more troubling duke in another may be an indication of the range of feelings aroused in early Jacobean playgoers by intrusive authority figures.

SCENE I

PHOENIX: The duke my father has a heavy burden
    Of years upon him.
FIDELIO: My lord, it seems so, for they make him stoop.
PHOENIX: Without dissemblance he is deep in age,
    He bows unto his grave. I wonder much   5
    Which of his wild nobility it should be
    (For none of his sad[1] council has a voice in't)
    Should so far travel into his consent
    To set me over[2] into other kingdoms
    Upon the stroke and minute of his death?   10
FIDELIO: My lord, 'tis easier to suspect them all,
    Than truly to name one.
PHOENIX: Since it is thus,
    By absence I'll obey the duke my father,
    And yet not wrong myself.

[1] sad: serious, grave.   [2] set me over: send me.

Thomas Middleton, *The Phoenix* (1603–04), ed. Lawrence Danson and Ivo Kamps, in *The Complete Works of Thomas Middleton*, ed. Gary Taylor (Oxford: Oxford UP, forthcoming), 1.75–140.

FIDELIO: Therein, my lord,
You might be happy twice.
PHOENIX: So shall it be; 15
I'll stay at home, and travel.
FIDELIO: Would your grace
Could make that good.
PHOENIX: I can. And indeed a prince need not travel farther than his own
kingdom, if he apply himself faithfully, worthy the glory of himself and
expectation of others. And it would appear far nobler industry in him to 20
reform those fashions that are already in his country than to bring new
ones in, which have neither true form nor fashion; to make his court an
owl,[3] city an ape,[4] and the country a wolf preying upon the ridiculous
pride of either. And therefore I hold it a safer stern[5] upon this lucky
advantage, since my father is near his setting, and I upon the eastern hill 25
to take my rise, to look into the heart and bowels of this dukedom, and in
disguise mark all abuses ready for reformation and punishment.
FIDELIO: Give me but leave unfeignedly to admire you,
Your wisdom is so spacious and so honest.
PHOENIX: So much have the complaints and suits[6] of men seven, nay, sev- 30
enteen years neglected, still[7] interposed[8] by coin and great enemies, pre-
vailed with my pity, that I cannot otherwise think but there are infectious
dealings in most offices, and foul mysteries[9] throughout all professions.
And therefore I nothing doubt but[10] to find travel enough within myself,
and experience, I fear, too much. Nor will I be curious[11] to fit my body to 35
the humblest form and bearing, so the labor may be fruitful: for how can
abuses that keep low come to the right view of a prince? Unless his looks
lie level with them, which else will be longest hid from him, he shall be
the last man sees 'em.
For oft between king's eyes and subject's crimes 40
Stands there a bar of bribes; the under office
Flatters him next above it, he the next,
And so of most, or many.
Every abuse will choose a brother:
'Tis through the world, this hand will rub the other. 45

---

[3] owl: Because of its nocturnal habits, the owl was a symbol of solemn stupidity. [4] ape: foolish mimic. [5] safer stern: safer course ("stern" here standing for a ship's helm or rudder). [6] suits: pleas. [7] still: always. [8] interposed: opposed, obstructed. [9] mysteries: secrets (with a pun: "professions" were also called "mysteries"). [10] nothing doubt but: expect. [11] Nor . . . curious: I will not be too finicky.

FIDELIO: You have set down the world briefly, my lord.
PHOENIX: But how am I assured of faith in thee?
   Yet I durst trust thee.
FIDELIO: Let my soul be lost
   When it shall loose[12] your secrets; nor will I
   Only be a preserver of them, but,   50
   If you so please, an assister.
PHOENIX: It suffices.
   That king stands surest who by his virtue rises
   More than by birth or blood; that prince is rare,
   Who strives in youth to save his age from care.
   Let's be prepared — away.   55
FIDELIO: I'll follow your grace;

                                            Exit Phoenix

   Thou wonder of all princes, precedent,[13] and glory,
   True phoenix, made of an unusual strain.
   Who labors to reform is fit to reign.
   How can that king be safe that studies not   60
   The profit of his people?

---

[12] **loose:** tell.   [13] **precedent:** worthy example.

CHAPTER 2

Marriage, Sex, and Society

>‹

Marriage à la Mode

Marriage in the Renaissance was not merely *a* social institution, but, some would argue, *the* social institution upon which all others depended. From a biblical perspective, marriage is the first human social act. It is the source of relational connections, creating extended kinship ties between families and within families. It is the prior contract that permits a religiously and governmentally sanctioned sexual consummation, which in turn provides the children through whom the future of individuals, countries, and the human race is secured. Above all it is the foundation of property relations, since estates and wealth are transmitted by marriage, and through marriage legitimate heirs to property are produced: in the words of Thomas Becon, "only matrimony maketh children to be certain and giveth true and undoubtful heirs" (*Works* 678v). By extension, because thrones and titles are inherited through legitimate births only, princes, kings, and, of course, dukes rely on marriage as the basis of their own authority to rule.

The problem explored in *Measure for Measure* is that marriage is far from a simple institution, since the functions it serves are so complex, and its expressions and formal constraints vary so greatly. Different forms of

English law recognized different kinds of marriage and marriage ceremonies, leading to confusion about how one married legally, and when
exactly one's children would be considered legitimate. In act 1 of the play,
Claudio is perplexed by his arrest for fornication, since, as he tells Lucio,

> upon a true contract
> I got possession of Juliet's bed.
> You know the lady; she is fast my wife,
> Save that we do the denunciation lack
> Of outward order. (1.2.118–22)

As far as Claudio is concerned, he and Juliet are married, and not merely in
secret — hence the remark, "You know the lady," suggesting that Lucio and
perhaps other friends are aware that Juliet is Claudio's legal wife. The only
complication is Juliet's dowry, "remaining in the coffer of her friends, / From
whom we thought it meet to hide our love / Till time had made them for us"
(1.2.124–26). In order to receive her dowry, Claudio and Juliet are attempting
to win the approval of her "friends," the relatives who have been charged
with her care since the (assumed) death of her parents. But Angelo, representing the law of Vienna, has determined that this form of spousal does
not constitute marriage, and he punishes Claudio for fornication, a crime
identical to the wholesale sexual license being practiced in Vienna's brothels. How did such a gap of understanding about what constitutes marriage
evolve?

In England there were two separate sources of tradition and law governing marriages, and each had undergone extensive change and adaptation
by the time Shakespeare wrote *Measure for Measure*. English *common law*,
the code of civil practices and accepted contractual rules amassed over
England's long history, was modified during the reign of Henry III in the
thirteenth century to reject "spousals" made merely by spoken vow between
the parties marrying, a form of marriage that had been accepted in *church
law* since the twelfth century. Common law emphasized the public nature
of true marriage contracts, requiring "banns" or public announcements
placed weeks in advance so that marriages might be approved by the larger
social group; following this public announcement, a ceremony with witnesses was necessary to guarantee that the marriage was legal. Thus, T. E.,
the author of *The Law's Resolutions of Women's Rights*, which is excerpted in
this section (see p. 205) notes that marriage is a three-part process: "The first
beginning of marriage . . . is when wedlock by words in the future tense is
promised and vowed, and this is but *sponsio* or *sponsalia*. The full contract of
matrimony is when it is made by words, *de praesenti* in a lawful consent . . .
yet matrimony is not accounted consummate until there go with the con-

sent of mind and will conjugation of body." Canon, or church law, had different origins and so different outcomes: it was, for instance, revised in 1604 to exclude clandestine marriages, that is, marriages that occurred without witnesses and without parental consent, which might describe Claudio's pre-contract with Juliet. Until 1604, however, clandestine or secret marriages were accepted (in contrast, T. E. points out that secret spousals are sometimes "tolerated" where they can lead to full marriage, but never "esteemed"). For ecclesiastical law, marriage was primarily a matter between God and the marrying parties — consent of parents, external public announcements, and other requirements were secondary. When Claudio tells Lucio that he and Juliet merely "the denunciation lack / Of outward order," he suggests that he sees the public form of marriage necessary to the civil law as a formality unrelated to the union's legal status. According to canon law, they have a marriage *de futuro* with a possible condition attached — the acquisition of her dowry. Henry Swinburne, the codifier of the canon law regarding spousals, agrees that this form of marriage is legal as long as the conditions are not impossible to achieve.

The Puritan writer William Perkins delineates in his *Christian Economy* (see p. 209) the traditional parts of what constitutes a publicly recognized marriage when he distinguishes between the contract *per verba futuro* (a verbal promise to marry in the future) and the contract *per verba de praesenti* (the exchange of words such as "I do take thee to my wife" and "I do take thee to my husband" in the present). But he then makes a somewhat convoluted point when he conflates a couple's promise of marriage in the *future* with an intent to bind themselves in the *present*, and argues that a promise made to marry in the future ("I will take thee, etc.") made in good conscience before God "is indeed a contract made *for the present time* before God." One could argue that the case articulated here by Perkins describes the circumstances of the vows exchanged between Claudio and Juliet described in *Measure for Measure*, and that the confusion Perkins exhibits was not unusual given the complexity of the various modes of marriage accepted in civil and church law.

Later in *Measure for Measure* we hear of another interrupted nuptial, this one between Angelo and Mariana. According to the Duke, "She should this Angelo have married, was affianced to her by oath, and the nuptial appointed; between which time of the contract and limit of the solemnity, her brother Frederick was wrecked at sea, having in that perished vessel the dowry of his sister" (3.1.203–06). Hearing that her dowry was no longer on offer, Angelo abandoned Mariana, "swallowed his vows whole, pretending in her discoveries of dishonor" (3.1.213), and left her to mourn and pine for him. Like Claudio and Juliet, Mariana and Angelo were pre-contracted, probably with a verbal promise. Perkins suggests that, while Angelo's actions here may be cold-hearted, they are not precisely wrong: he mentions the failure of a promised dowry to be produced as a just cause upon which the other party may back out of a promise of marriage *per verba futuro*. Furthermore, when the Duke arranges the bed-trick that substitutes Mariana for Isabella, insisting that it is "no sin" because of "the justice of [Mariana's] title to him [Angelo]" (4.1.69–70) his argument would be, in Perkins' view, self-serving and incorrect.

Henry Swinburne's 1686 *Treatise of Spousals,* parts of which we have excerpted here (see p. 214), attempts to fully outline all the eventualities involved in betrothals covered by canon or church law in the latter part of the seventeenth century. Most of his observations come from exactly the kinds of cases represented by the many partial marriages in *Measure for Measure,* and the detail with which he inundates his readers suggests that such cases were legion and even more perplexing than Claudio and Juliet's or Angelo and Mariana's. In fact, Swinburne's publisher opines in his preface that the "Questions and Difficulties, that arise about it [the spousal], are of the greatest Variety and Niceness." He further insists that the only difference between the spousal *de praesenti* and legal marriage is the "greater solemnity" of the marriage and its "Benediction of the Minister." While Puritans like Perkins tried to "circumvent the official system" so as to avoid "superstitious" practices, like the use of wedding rings (Marcus 174), the Church of England found these tokens, gestures, and signs important to the legality of the ceremony, and Swinburne's treatise tries to cover them all.

Thus, in the centuries before the Marriage Act of 1753 finally regularized the form of legal marriage, the overlaps and differences between English civil and ecclesiastical law continued to make the legal standing of some marriages problematic.

This does not explain, however, why there is such a rash of unmarried women in the play: Juliet is betrothed but not yet (according to the state's interpretation of its laws) formally and publicly married; Isabella is a novitiate; Mariana is at first betrothed but jilted and finally in the same position as Juliet, publicly known to be no virgin, but not quite married either. Mistress Overdone has apparently been married nine times, but has no husband at present. We hear indirectly about other women who are not married, like Kate Keepdown, the whore Lucio has gotten pregnant and abandoned, or the nameless prostitutes who staff Mistress Overdone's house. The only legitimately married woman mentioned is Mistress Elbow, but her husband's testimony that she is a "suspected" woman who has been found entertaining herself in a brothel with Froth leads us to wonder whether she can be counted a "proper" wife.

The men are in no better condition: Angelo wants a sexual union with Isabella rather than a legal marriage to Mariana; the Duke, who, in Lucio's words, "had some feeling of the sport" is not yet married either. Nor are Claudio or Lucio. In a typical Shakespearean comedy, this would be unremarkable, since young single folk are the stuff of happy endings, but in this play the focus is on the ways in which sexual desire or its absence interrupts and defers marriage rather than promotes it. So the play is not just about how legal marriages are made, but about what human nature does to the process of finding and securing a spouse.

Renaissance approaches to marriage differed from medieval versions at least in theory due to the effects of the Reformation in the early sixteenth century. Catholicism valued marriage highly, including it among the sacraments, but valued celibacy more. While marriage fulfilled the biblical injunction to "increase and multiply," the apostle Paul declared marriage to be the resort for weaker mortals (1 Corinthians 7), and provided the basis for a priestly caste of celibates. With the Reformation in England, monasteries were dissolved, and the life they represented was thoroughly criticized: priests, nuns, and monks had since Chaucer's day been the target of satires aimed at their corruption and indulgence in secret vices, but with the additional pressure of justifying a wholesale religious transformation antimonastic literature became more intense and more common. English Protestants soon came to think of themselves as saving marriage from the grasp of sinful, warped celibates of the old evil Church, restoring it to its role as a mirroring of God's love for and union with human beings through Christ. Hence the new marriage ceremony in the *Book of Common Prayer*, reproduced in this section, mentioned the role of marriage in remedying lust, but foregrounded far more its role in bringing man into closer imitation of Christ. The "Homily of the State of Matrimony" (1547, 1563), one of a series of official sermons disseminated by the Anglican Church, reminds listeners that marriage "is instituted of God to the intent that man and woman should live lawfully in a perpetual friendly fellowship, to bring forth fruit, and to avoid fornication" (*Certain Sermons or Homilies* 239), repeating the new hierarchy that placed the intellectual and spiritual comfort of marriage at the top.

Marriage thus took on greater significance in the lives of Protestants as part of the path to righteousness. The first step along that path was controlling the desires of the body through their sanctified expression in the marriage bed. *A Book of Christian Prayers*, a text filled with daily prayers to be said on specific occasions or at times of need, includes the "Prayer against the Flesh," in which the speaker entreats God for strength to subordinate the "brutish and filthy" body to the "sovereignty" of reason (see p. 221). The prayer notes the origin of fleshly sin in Eve's first rebellion in Paradise, and then quickly moves on to define the "brutish" body as female and the mind as male, which, in the same way that Eve rejected the authority of Adam (and extension of God), rejects the controlling mind of man: "she" (the body) thus becomes an "unkind and lewd bondservant" to her master. The master/servant, male/female binaries outlined in the "Prayer against the Flesh" reflect widespread assumptions about the nature of women at the time. Joseph Swetnam's 1615 tract *The Arraignment of Lewd, Idle, Froward and Unconstant Women* summarized centuries of popular antifeminist attitudes when Swetnam claimed "she was no sooner made, but straightaway her mind was set upon mischief," or proposed that "women are called the hook of all evil, because men are taken by them, as fish is taken with the hook" (1, 15). Helkiah Crooke writes in his *Microcosmographia* (1618) that "females are more wanton and petulant than males . . . because of the impotency of their minds; for the imaginations of lustful women are like the imaginations of brute beasts . . ." (276). While women had their defenders as well as their detractors, popular sentiment held that women were deceivers and seducers in the tradition of their mother, Eve, the instruments by which the Devil entered men's lives.

The way to control temptations of the flesh was, by extension of both logics — the one that has the body feminized in contrast to masculine intellect, and the one that holds Eve responsible for man's descent into mortal sin — to control women, especially women's bodies. But women are, according to most early modern thought on the subject, the weaker sex, more prone to give in to their appetites. Aristotle observes that woman is more imperfect than man in all things, leading her to greater susceptibility to the emotions and other irrational behaviors; thus, controlling her lusts and desires is more difficult, since she presumably lacks that degree of internal self-discipline men can claim. This may be why early modern treatises exhorting maids to chastity and wives to fidelity abound: they answer a certain anxiety about how well men can in fact regulate women's deeds.

Control over women in *Measure for Measure* is likewise supposed to be achieved by rendering all women intelligible in relation to a marital union with a rational male. When the Duke confronts Mariana in act 5, he reflects this imperative to define all women in terms of marital and sexual status:

DUKE: What, are you married?
MARIANA: No, my lord.
DUKE: Are you a maid?
MARIANA: No, my lord.
DUKE: A widow, then?

MARIANA: Neither, my lord.

DUKE: Why, you are nothing, then, neither maid, widow, nor wife?

(5.1.177–83)

A maid is a woman who is a virgin, and so potentially marriageable; all three terms, maid, widow, and wife, describe a woman via some marital role (Fig. 11). Lucio reminds the Duke, however, that another possibility exists: that a woman may play outside the rules, or as Lucio puts it, "My lord, she may be a punk [prostitute] for many of them are neither maid, widow, nor wife." And since so many of the women in the play do reject, resist, or merely side-step the usual roles of maid, widow, and wife, the specter of women's rampant sexual promiscuity continues to subvert the play's attempts to "measure" it.

FIGURE 11 *Frontispiece, Samuel Rowlands,* 'Tis Merrie When Gossips Meet, *1602. Rowland's work, a dialogue amongst three women who represent the three conditions or stages of women's lives, repeats the assumptions behind the Duke's speech to Mariana in act 5, scene 1.*

Renaissance playgoers believed that women were highly sexual, and likely as the "weaker sex" to give in to their passions; marriage served as a control over this tendency to stray. Husbands were to "master" their wives, educate them in their duties and keep them on the straight and narrow. The marriage ceremony in the *Book of Common Prayer* (see p. 216) points out that the husband is the "head" of the wife in the same way that Christ is the head of the Church; in submitting to him, the wife gains many things, prominent among them the relief from the sins of her body, to which she is "naturally" inclined. Of course, this notion of marriage as a prison to contain the illicit behaviors to which women are prone breeds a double anxiety among men: how does one absolutely secure a young woman's chastity before marriage? And how certain can any man be after marriage that the wife he supposedly controls is genuinely behaving herself?

What is at stake in the policing of women's sexuality is not only sin and spiritual uncleanness. Women's bodies are the site of reproduction. As long as their chastity before and within marriage can be ascertained, the children they produce are a benefit, continuing the species, creating more souls for God (a major goal, repeated in the marriage ceremony, homilies, conduct literature, and sermons), and providing heirs to the estates of their husbands. If women stray before marriage, however, they may produce bastard children who become a burden on the state — without legal fathers from whom they can inherit, these children will have to rely on the provisions made for them through charity. In his *Book of Matrimony* (1564), Thomas Becon summarizes the condition of the bastard child thus:

> And it is the common sentence and judgement of lawyers that he hath an uncertain father and a naughty mother which is not born in matrimony. For he is base-born and is the son of the people, yea rather the son of no man, which is the child of a woman not lawfully married. (*Works*, 678)

Of course, to some extent the much-repeated Renaissance fear that bastard children will tax the economic well-being of the community is a fiction, since the great majority of children born during the Renaissance were to the poor and middling classes, where inheritance was not an issue; mothers and children of the lower and middle classes had to work to support themselves anyway, and were as likely to end up a drain on charity for reasons of natural debility, or in times of economic disaster, as for bastardy. Rather the fear seems to be of children who *have no place*, who do not easily and recognizably fit into the social order. These children might become the future bawds, pimps, cheats, whores, bandits, and vagabonds who inspired so much fear and fascination in the period (see Chapter 3, "The Underworld").

Early modern views on pregnancy before marriage were not entirely consistent, however; while the sin of fornication was much decried, and bastard children born outside the official period of marriage were deplored and barred from inheriting estates or titles, there was considerable local and practical tolerance for pregnancies incurred *while* a marriage was being contracted. Bridal pregnancy appears to have been fairly common in early modern England, particularly among members of the lower classes. As Martin Ingram reports, "couples with serious matrimonial intentions were allowed a good deal of license in their courtship behavior and often commenced sexual relations before they were wed" (162). Richard Adair observes that in the parish of Lamplugh (Cumberland), 60 percent of brides were pregnant in the early years of the seventeenth century (92). "In early modern England generally, at least one fifth of all brides were with child by the time they got married in church" (Ingram 219). Adair further notes that despite "the exploitation of litigation for defamation from the mid-sixteenth century onwards, and the acute sensitivity to slurs on sexual honor, the accusation of pre-nuptial pregnancy (as opposed to plain fornication) virtually never appears in the records" (92). While early modern Englishmen and women should not be described as libertines (unlike Lucio, most early seventeenth-century Londoners would not consider sex before marriage a mere "game of tick-tack"), it seems fair to observe, as Ingram does, that many displayed tolerance for activities that fell short of "blatant sexual immorality" (167). Given the limited evidence (see the selections in this chapter) it appears that sexual intercourse between two people who planned to get married was not viewed as the moral equivalent of fornication. Another Shakespeare play illustrates this flexible perspective on premarital sex: in *Much Ado about Nothing*, when Claudio accuses his betrothed, Hero, of sexual infidelity at the beginning of their marriage ceremony, Leonato, the bride's father, says to Claudio, "if you, in your own proof, / Have vanquish'd the resistance of her youth, / And made defeat of her virginity —" (4.1.44–46). The reason for Leonato's suggestion is clear: one might argue that Hero embraced Claudio "as a husband" and that this fact lessens the sin of fornication. According to Swinburne's *A Treatise of Spousals*, the rape of a woman by her betrothed converts the spousals into matrimony, since the consummation of the marriage is accomplished, by canon or ecclesiastical law, and the marriage complete.

In Shakespeare's hometown of Stratford, sexual transgressions were also punished, but not nearly in as extreme a fashion as we see in *Measure for Measure*'s Vienna. In 1608, one Thomas Burman got Susanna Aynge pregnant. Burman confessed to the act and "received the inevitable injunction to go through a white sheet penance on two successive Sundays. He asked for mitigation and the judge allowed him to make complete satisfaction by payment of two shillings to the poor" (Brinkworth 75). Shakespeare himself obtained a marriage license to wed Anne Hathaway in November 1582, but his first child was born only six months later in May 1583. He may have wed his wife prior to gaining the license, or the marriage may have been the result of her pregnancy — we have no way of knowing. But it seems likely that Shakespeare had some personal knowledge and experience of the vagaries of marriage laws and premarital sex.

However, it is true that by the late sixteenth and early seventeenth centuries, "the church courts became increasingly rigorous" (Ingram 221) about policing bridal pregnancies. The 1563 Council of Trent had rendered invalid for Catholics marriages by spousals (or pre-contracts, as Claudio and Juliet's marriage) alone. And English common law did not recognize the legitimacy of children conceived out of wedlock even if their parents married after the child's birth. "Civil law [that is, the law of contracts], on the other hand, made distinctions among kinds of bastards predicated in part on the intention of the copulating pair regarding matrimony and, like canon law, allowed for the post-matrimonial legitimation of hitherto illegitimate children." The problem of children conceived by rape can be instructive about confusions over marriage, legitimacy, and the various versions of law: in common law, a child born of the rape of an unmarried woman was illegitimate. But, if the raped woman married before the child was born, the child would become the husband's lawful heir.

If you get the feeling that it could be quite difficult to judge the legitimacy of a child, or the validity of a marriage in early modern England, then you're recognizing what ordinary people like Claudio and Juliet had to contend with. When the Duke (as friar) asks Juliet whether her "most offenseful act" was committed "mutually," her affirmation may be less an admission of guilt than a statement of simple fact: as she says, she loves the man who made her pregnant as much as herself, injecting a little resistance into her apparent submission to the friar's judgment. Even within the play, views differ on whether Juliet's pregnancy is really so awful: Angelo calls her a "fornicatress" (2.2.26), but Lucio describes her condition as the result of plenteousness and good husbandry (1.4. 43–44), and even the Provost is willing to blame her youth and be gentle with her.

The Duke calls Juliet's sin "of heavier kind" than Claudio's (2.3.29). He remarks on the simple fact that women show with their bodies that they have strayed sexually; but he also echoes the more antifeminist sentiments of early modern writers about women's essentially sinful, tempting nature, prone to passion and too weak or irrational to control their own desires. As

FIGURE 12   *Henry Singleton,* Measure for Measure *(London, 1798), act 2, scene 1. Constable Elbow tries to explain what crime Pompey and Froth have led Mistress Elbow to commit.*

we have seen, marriage is supposed to contain this side of women's character, but marriage is too complex to secure easily, and besides, so many women in the play are sexually active outside marriage: Juliet, Kate Keepdown (whom we learn has also conceived an illegitimate child by Lucio), Mistress Overdone, and the many prostitutes she must employ. And if women stray *within* marriage, then men will find themselves ruling over a cuckoo's nest, in which some other man's fledgling draws off their time, attention, and finally their worldly possessions. Paranoia about women's fidelity thus did not end, but intensified with marriage.

Mistress Elbow generates just such paranoia in her husband when she visits a brothel with Froth, leading her husband, Constable Elbow, to arrest Froth and Pompey as bawds in act 2, scene 1 (see Figs. 12 and 13). Moreover, her condition — pregnant — would have made the Renaissance audience find her behavior a bit easier to believe. As in Juliet's case, Mistress

Elbow's pregnancy is a visual reminder that she has known "mutual pleasure." According to early theories of generation, women could conceive only when the right amount of "heat" was generated in the act of sex. Heat came from stimulation, the degree of which could be judged by the amount of pleasure a woman took in copulating. Galen, the accepted classical authority for much reproductive knowledge in the period, teaches that the female is an "imperfect" version of the male because "colder" by nature; the male provides the form of the child in his semen, while the female provides the material or body matter. Orgasm is necessary to raise enough heat in a woman so that she might conceive, her cold nature being an obstacle to the process (Culpeper, 57–58). So according to this theory both Juliet and Mistress Elbow know what it is to experience pleasure; and in Claudio's words, their "mutual entertainment" is written on their very bodies in "character too gross" (1.2.127, 128). Mistress Elbow's presence in the brothel, then, signifies not so much Pompey's and Froth's guilt, as her own guilty desires, satisfied only by stewed prunes and sex with strangers. She is clearly not an encouraging figure in a play concerned with containing women's sinful natures.

Of all the notions in the play, Angelo's concept of sin, marriage, and reproduction may be most significant and disturbing. In keeping with his role as the "man of stricture" (1.3.12), the abstinent man whose "blood is very snow broth" (1.4.57–8), Angelo does not comprehend or forgive the weaknesses of the flesh. For him, enforcing the letter of the law on marriage is a means of protecting the state's interests. Children born out of wedlock are, he repeatedly emphasizes, unlawfully "coined":

> Ha? Fie, these filthy vices! It were as good
> To pardon him that hath from nature stolen
> A man already made, as to remit
> Their saucy sweetness that do coin heaven's image
> In stamps that are forbid: 'Tis all as easy
> Falsely to take away a life true made,
> As to put metal in restrainèd means
> To make a false one.   (2.4.42–49)

Angelo's language in this speech is the language of money, of minting coins and counterfeiting. To him, fornication is an evil because it steals from the state the right to control the generation of legitimate children. By Angelo's logic, the true "father" with the right to determine who and when subjects may marry is the monarch, and any who defy him are stealing his authority; just as the king oversees the creation of coins, guaranteeing their validity, so Angelo believes the monarch must regulate human "coining" or reproduction through legal marriage. This sentiment is found elsewhere in Shake-

FIGURE 13 *Illustration from "The Female Ramblers,"* Roxburgh Ballads. *A tavern scene, with ladies entertaining a young gallant with drink and dice. Taverns were often assumed to be meeting-places for prostitutes and their customers — hence Froth's name, which refers to his favorite pastime, but also has sexual connotations, or Pompey's occupation as both tapster and pimp.*

speare's works: Duke Theseus in *A Midsummer Night's Dream* tells the disobedient Hermia that she is "but as a form in wax / by [her father] imprinted," and it is therefore her father's choice whether to "leave the figure or disfigure it" (1.1.49–61). The idea is that Hermia is like a coin struck by her father, and he may melt her down (kill her) if he so chooses.

Shakespeare may well have had in mind an actual coin, the Henrician or Elizabethan "angel," a gold coin with the head of the monarch stamped into the metal, when he named Angelo. One of the edicts issued by James I early in his reign was an order concerning the weighing of metal coins: it was the crown's responsibility to assure that the measuring of various kinds of goods was regularized (Powers). Through the connection between Angelo's name, coinage, and the king's authority, the audience might have been reminded that Angelo too is being measured to see what character he bears. The Duke's early allusion to the parable of the talents (1.1. 30–36) should have been warning enough, indicating that Angelo would answer to his own master what "credit and use" he had generated out of his natural talents.

True to his discourse of coins and metals, Angelo couches his offer to Isabella in terms of her yielding the "treasures" of her body to him, to "redeem" her brother. He transforms her impassioned speech about mercy

(2.2.115–28) into a tit-for-tat exchange, her virginity for her brother's life, making concrete and gross what she intended as spiritually uplifting: "Lawful mercy / Is nothing kin to foul redemption" (2.4. 113–14). Angelo justifies the theft he is attempting by calling Isabella to task for refusing the "natural" role of a woman:

> Be that you are,
> That is, a woman; if you be more, you're none.
> If you be one, as you are well expressed
> By all external warrants, show it now
> By putting on the destined livery.   (2.4. 135–39)

Punning on her choice to become a nun (she's not a woman, she's a "none/nun"), Angelo locates Isabella as unnatural because she, unlike other women in the play, is not weakly sexual, but as rigidly virtuous as he once thought he was. He further suggests that only by engaging in sexual intercourse does a woman become a woman. Since he is not offering her marriage, the "destined livery" she should exchange for her habit would be something like either the finery of the prostitutes in Mistress Overdone's brothel, or the mourning weeds Mariana wears for him. Both are acceptable where the nun's habit is not, because both signal openness to the act of procreation — or fornication. In sum, Angelo's frosty blood (which has given him no sense of compassion for the weaknesses of the flesh, but also no armor against them) leads him ultimately to devalue both reproduction *and* marriage, which he believes he defends.

Understanding Isabella

Isabella has been much misunderstood throughout *Measure for Measure*'s critical history: G. Wilson Knight accuses her of "lacki[ing] human feeling"; she has "sex inhibitions" that she cannot face, and "sees her own soul and sees it as something small, frightened, despicable" (93). For critics who had this opinion, Isabella's final position, on her knees begging for Angelo's life, is a just punishment for one too proud, too cold, too superior. Arthur Kirsch believes that "she herself offers unconscious sexual provocation," because she has not accepted herself "as a woman" (186), thereby echoing one of Angelo's arguments against her. On the opposing side, some nineteenth-century critics celebrated Isabella as a paragon of chastity, and her angry attack on Claudio as a noble and pure position on chastity (Dowden 125; Stevenson 88–89). Late-twentieth-century critics have had less interest in defending or criticizing Isabella as if she were a real person, which of course she isn't, but it is hard to escape the feeling, as David Stevenson puts it, that "a partial not-liking of Isabella is written into the play" (83).

Critical confusion about how to read Isabella stems from her complexly layered public position and her equally complex private feelings. We must, then, consider what it means that Isabella has chosen to become a nun — that is, what it means in Catholic Vienna, but also what it means to Protestant English playgoers. We must also understand what her chastity means to her, to Angelo, and to the moral economy of the play. Finally we should not omit a thorough exploration of Isabella's character: she, after all, gives the play's most moving speech on mercy, and her character fascinates not one but two men in the play — first Angelo, and then the Duke, who proposes marriage to her after presumably being captivated by her virtues.

Act I introduces Isabella as an aspiring novitiate. The order of nuns Isabella wishes to join, whose rules she discusses with Francesca, is the Poor Clares. St. Clare's story is, suitably, about determined resistance in the pursuit of a religious life; it emphasizes her quiet implacability on a number of issues, including her original vocation, her sisterly love for St. Francis of Assisi, her defense of the convent at Damiano from the marauding Saracens, and especially her order's "liberty of absolute poverty" in the face of Church opposition. St. Clare was born to a noble family of Assisi in 1194, but became a follower of St. Francis, joining the Franciscan order in 1212, at the age of seventeen. She did so without the knowledge of her parents, who were gentry of the local community, which led to well-intentioned familial interventions meant to restrain her from her vocation. She even foiled their attempts to haul her out of the church where she took her vows. In sum, she pitted her spiritual integrity against her family's desire to have her follow the traditional path for women by marrying and raising children.

Clare was the first female saint to create a religious rule, and she was canonized only two years after her death, making her also one of the most quickly sainted women ever. However, Clare's vision was to maintain a separate and relatively independent existence for her own order, one devoted to poverty and a restrictive set of practices, a vision that did not always agree with Church hierarchy and its treatment of the female orders, or with the Church's efforts at reforming the priesthood. When the independence of the Poor Clares was challenged by changes in Church structure that threatened their subsumption under Benedictine authority, Clare vehemently protested, claiming special status based on grants by Pope Gregory IX. She was successful in her defense, convincing Pope Innocent IV to confirm his predecessor's grants, a fact that attests to her ability to argue faith and privilege in the face of a repressive and not very sympathetic Church leadership (see Fig. 16, p. 249).

While anecdotes about the firmness of her devotion are standard fare for hagiographic or saints' biographies, their importance to *Measure for Measure* lies in the image of the stoic and unyielding Clare who rejects all the usual trappings of a young woman's life, and not coincidentally rejects the roles appointed her by her society. Isabella's desire to commit herself to the order of Poor Clares stands in direct opposition to the play's repeated categorizations of women as "maid, widow, wife" or "punk," and thus makes her descent into the maelstrom of negotiation over Claudio's life an even more significant loss of autonomy. Of course in choosing the conventual life, Isabella, like Clare, substitutes the patriarchal authority of God and Church for the worldly patriarchy of marriage, family, and the state. Yet, again in imitation of Clare's choices, Isabella's decision is potentially subversive of her culture's ideologies of gender. When the Duke offers Isabella his hand in marriage at the play's close, his offer is thus complex: he seeks to replace God as her potential spouse, and would return her to a world where women are, as wives and mothers, vehicles for patrilineal transmission of wealth, something the Poor Clares emphatically repudiated in their quest for absolute poverty.

Such an interpretation of Isabella as a resistant and subversive figure, however, must be tempered and complicated by the play's indeterminate location. If indeed we read the play as simply occurring in Catholic Vienna, then Isabella's choices have the same moral weight as Clare's. But if we imagine that "Vienna" is meant to mirror Protestant London, then the implications of Isabella's choices might be quite different. As we have seen, post-Reformation England did not hold celibacy for men or women in esteem. Although England had its own houses of the Poor Clares, these were closed along with the greater and lesser monasteries during the mid-to-late 1530s. A Protestant audience might have condemned Isabella's desire to join such a restrictive female community as a perverse rejection of her "proper" and "natural" duties as wife and mother. Indeed, Isabella's conversation with Francesca about her perception that the order's rules are not stringent enough would likely have resonated with a Protestant audience as perverse indeed, given that the Clares were very strict in comparison to other Catholic female orders. Lucio's remark that he holds her "as a thing enskied and sainted" (1.4.34) would, in the same context, appear sarcastic, a reflection on Isabella's overly refined sensibilities and self-deluding faith in her own superiority over her more worldly counterparts. To the Protestant theatergoer, then, Isabella might appear a foil to Angelo, sharing some of his qualities.

Isabella's reaction to Angelo's proposition that she exchange her virginity for her brother's life does not help us sympathize with her and has been a stumbling block for generations of the play's readers and viewers. At first her indignation is fully understandable, fitting for a young woman who has committed her body to Christ. But by the time she announces, infamously, "Then, Isabel, live chaste, and, brother, die / More than our brother is our chastity" (2.4.185–86), she has lost some of the audience's approval, gained when she so ardently defended her brother before Angelo. While it is possible to defend Isabella on the grounds that her brother would have trouble living with himself were he to demand she sacrifice her body and soul to the soulless Angelo, it is a weak defense, and quickly overwhelmed by her impassioned denunciation of poor Claudio when he seeks to live:

> O faithless coward, O dishonest wretch!
> Wilt thou be made a man out of my vice?
> Is't not a kind of incest, to take life
> From thine own sister's shame? (3.1.139–42)

Essentially, she accuses him of prostituting her for his own gain. Yet the literary record and even the religious tradition do not seem to support her outrage. Tales of women who sacrifice their virtue to save a loved one, often a husband or brother, are relatively plentiful in Shakespeare's day. In Geraldi Cinthio's "Story of Epitia," one of Shakespeare's sources, the pursued innocent does surrender her body to her pursuer. (See p. 228.) Epitia's brother is condemned by the acting ruler, Juriste, for a far worse offense — the actual rape of a maiden. Epitia pleads for him nonetheless, and is eventually convinced to surrender her virginity to Juriste. So far from being reviled by the Emperor or others when her situation comes to light, Epitia is deemed "honest" and her honor restored with a marriage.

Augustine, in fact, writes about a related case in which a wife, with her husband's consent, allows herself to be ravished to save his life. Saint Augustine clearly feels such a case does not deserve the same level of blame that ordinary fornication does: he sees the disposal of the wife's body as properly authorized by her husband, and so "man's moral sense is not so ready to condemn what happened in this woman's case." In book 1, chapter 16 of his *City of God*, Augustine elaborates on issues of chastity and rape, again allowing exceptions for what we might call "special circumstances" — in this case, the rape of nuns and other Christian women during the sack of Rome:

> Let this, therefore, in the first place, be laid down as an unassailable position, that the virtue which makes the life good has its throne in the soul, and thence rules the members of the body, which becomes holy in virtue of the holiness of the will; and that while the will remains firm and unshaken, nothing that another person does with the body, or upon the body, is any fault of the person who suffers it, so long as he cannot escape it without sin. (52–53)

While it is true that Isabella would, paradoxically, have to consent to her own rape if she were to sleep with Angelo, and it is true that she has no immediate husband to give her authority to surrender her virginity without reproach, these examples still suggest that her hard-line position is not fully supported by a variety of precedents. Her declaration to Claudio that "might but my bending down / Reprieve thee from thy fate, it should proceed" (3.1.146–47) does align her with Angelo's cold, unyielding nature, and sets her in opposition to the accommodations the play wishes to find.

Perhaps we should not be asking, though, whether Isabella is right or wrong, but why the play puts her, and us, in the position of having to answer such questions. Shakespeare significantly changed his source materials to lighten the "crime" committed by Claudio and to change its nature; he also transformed the sister-by-blood of the sources into a woman who is both familial and spiritual sister. These alterations draw our attention away from the simple equation of Isabella's virginity with her brother's life. Is Claudio's future as a loving husband and father more or less important than Isabella's commitment to God? That is, do human social roles balance equally against spiritual purity? If we answer that Isabella's chastity, even though it is in service to a supposedly higher spiritual "marriage," is worth less than her brother's life, would that change how we evaluate, for example, a prostitute's need to sell her body to preserve her *own* life? If we decide that Isabella's future nuptials to Christ (requiring her pure body and mind) are of greater value than Claudio's life and role as father, don't we then set the right of an abstract and deified husband-to-be and father in conflict with an earthly husband and father-to-be?

By understanding Isabella fully, then, we come to recognize the play's deliberate and persistent complexity in its treatment of female chastity. We don't necessarily find any fixed answers to the questions her character raises, but that may not be the play's goal. The play's conclusion in itself would argue as much: after allowing Isabella to be publicly doubted when she accuses Angelo, after forcing her to bend that unbending knee to plead for Angelo's life, and after subjecting her to the certainty that her brother was executed despite her intervention, the Duke proposes marriage to her: "Give me your hand and say you will be mine" (5.1.491) he offers, and later as all exit, "Dear Isabel / I have a motion much imports your good, / Whereto if you'll a willing ear incline, / What's mine is yours, and what is yours is mine" (5.1.532–35). What about Isabella has attracted the Duke? When did a match with her become a good idea? And what could her response be? The play's ending has perplexed both critics and directors — especially the latter, since *some* kind of response seems called for on Isabella's part. But what would it be? Does she smile happily and take the Duke's hand? Does she look

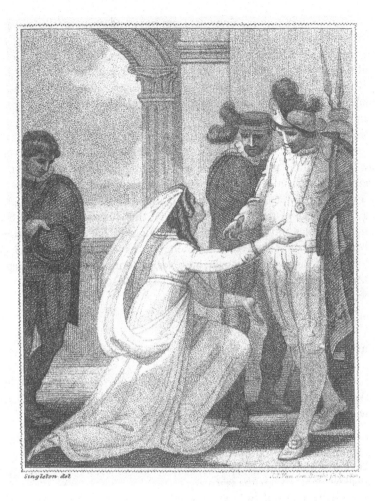

FIGURE 14 *Henry Singleton,* Measure for Measure *(London, 1798), act 5, scene 1.*
Isabella pleads eloquently and passionately for Claudio's life.

coldly on his attempt to drag her away from her commitment to the Poor
Clares? Does the audience feel cheered by this turn of events? Pleased that
another woman is being given a "proper" role as wife and future mother?
Or uneasy that Isabella is being finally forced into the economy of sexual
exchange in Vienna? If Isabella were to remain true to the example of St.
Clare, she would resist this attempt to force her away from a spiritual union
and into a fleshly one: Clare herself, after all, withstood the "torment" of her

"worldly friends in order to draw her from her good purpose." But the play's Protestant English and comedic imperatives are different, involving weddings and the restoration of social harmony through the balanced linking of all the single characters. Even Lucio must marry, although his fate is the equivalent of "pressing to death, whipping, and hanging" (5.1.520–21). Would Isabella say the same about her own fate in marriage if she were given speech?

Isabella is silent in the concluding moments of the play, leaving these questions unresolved. If she does in any way gesture her assent, however, we may consider her "pre-contracted" to the Duke as Juliet was to Angelo: Swinburne's *Treatise of Spousals* makes it clear that there are numerous ways for a woman (or man for that matter) to signal consent to a marriage contract, and not all of them are verbal. In fact the sheer abundance of Swinburne's examples and permutations would suggest that silent gestures were fairly common, or at least common enough to have caused some legal speculation about their validity. Again, however, a silent gesture does not register on the playscript, leaving us at the very last still struggling to understand Isabella.

Chastity and Eloquence

The reason Angelo falls for Isabella is that she is a passionate and eloquent speaker, as well as a pure woman: "She speaks, and 'tis such sense / That my sense breeds with it" (2.2.147–48) (see Fig. 14, p. 199). He muses later,

> Can it be
> That modesty may more betray our sense
> Than woman's lightness? Having waste ground enough,
> Shall we desire to raze the sanctuary
> And pitch our evils there? (2.2.175–79)

Angelo's words perhaps inadvertently conjure the story of St. Clare defending the altar at Damiano against the marauding Saracens, preserving the sanctuary of the Clares from other men bent on its desecration (see Figure 29). Certainly they attest to the power of Isabella's combined virtues, her chaste body and her lovely speech. That power is an important part of the play's treatment of chastity and lewdness from the outset. As Lucio knocks at the gates of the convent, Sister Francisca notes that "When you have vowed, you must not speak with men / But in the presence of the prioress; / Then if you speak you must not show your face, / Or if you show your face, you must not speak" (1.4.10–13). This is far more information than we need in order to understand why Francisca can't open the door herself!

The rules Francisca describes reflect attitudes toward women's beauty, temptation, and the seductions of speech that extend beyond the convent walls. Women's speech is much discussed — and much denounced — in early modern conduct literature. Juan Luis Vives advises, "Full of talk I would not have her, no not among maids" (*Instruction* I, chapter 12). Puritan preacher Henry Smith writes, "As it becometh her [a good wife] to keep home, so it becometh her to keep silence" (*Preparative* 25). And Thomas Becon asserts, "For there is nothing that doth so much commend, avaunce, set forth, adorn, deck, trim and garnish a maid as silence" (*Catechism*, in *Works* 536). The thinking behind these kinds of remarks is that a woman who speaks much puts her reputation at risk: the willingness to speak out or discourse at any length indicates a lack of self-discipline and self-control. Speaking too much shows a woman to be "open" to intercourse — and the meaning of that term slips from verbal to sexual very quickly in the Renaissance imagination. When all the metaphors and advice used to encourage young women to virtue revolve around guarding, enclosing, protecting, and limiting themselves, opening the mouth to speak takes on negative and sexualized connotations.

Thus Isabella's reluctance to venture from the convent to plead her brother's case, and her initial reticence before Angelo are part of every good maiden's armor against the possible pitfalls of public speech and conduct. Lucio has to egg her on, acting the role of pimp with encouragements like "you are too cold," "Ay touch him," "O to him, to him wench! He will relent; / he's coming (2.2.49, 75, 129–30)."

But from Francisca's instruction we get a remarkably repressive picture of what constitutes acceptable behavior in Isabella's world, even for an already repressive early modern culture: the idea that if one speaks at all at the same time that one's face is showing goes far beyond mere conduct manual rhetoric. For the Clares, as for many other orders, women are to be utterly absent as speaking participants in the world. If they do have to speak, they must do so as disembodied voices with identities, barely even there as full human beings. *The Nun's Rule*, which was written for medieval convents centuries before Shakespeare created *Measure for Measure*, seems nonetheless still to apply to Viennese nuns (and perhaps, by extension, for all truly virtuous women of this culture). Even while confessing her sins to her fellow religious, a nun must keep herself contained, partially absent, as if the linguistic openness of confession were in itself a terrible temptation: "hear his [your confessor's] words and sit quite still, that, when he parteth from you, he may not know either good or evil of you, nor know any thing either to praise or to blame you." *The Nun's Rule* (see p. 241) repeatedly turns to the image of the Virgin Mary, who spoke little as the exemplar for female religious; Eve, on the other hand, "held a long conversation with the serpent," and so damned humanity. The *Rule* offers a warning about women's speech, having advised the nun to avoid speaking with anyone alone without a third party present: "This is not said in respect of you, dear sisters, nor of any such as you; — no, but because the truth is disbelieved, and the innocent often belied, for want of a witness" (p. 242). In its warning, *The Nun's Rule* seems prescient of Isabella's predicament at the end of *Measure for Measure*. When she attempts to accuse Angelo, she is disbelieved by all present. Only when the Duke is revealed are her words validated.

Yet there is an alternate tradition regarding women's speech, exemplified by Christine de Pisan's *Book of the City of Ladies* and especially her story of Saint Catherine of Alexandria (see p. 238). Women's eloquence can be transformative, its power capable of converting souls to Christianity. Where virtuous speech is combined with a strong and pure body, women seem undefeatable. De Pisan's story recounts Catherine's intervention in the pagan sacrifices of the Emperor Maxentius — in a verbal replay of Christ's more physical rampage in the temple, she argues before the emperor that his rites are misguided, leaving him "completely amazed and utterly speechless." When he challenges her to debate a host of philosophers, they are all converted by her eloquence, leaving the emperor in a rage. He threatens and tortures her, including having her placed between two razored wheels (which is where we get the term "Catherine wheels" for cartwheels), but to no avail. He finally offers to marry her, but she has vowed to marry no man, and so in the end he has her beheaded. While Catherine's story is not identical to Isabella's, it stands as a counterpoint to the tradition of blaming women for eloquence and engagement in verbal intercourse. Without Catherine's vehement arguments against pagan sacrifice, the many converts she gains would be lost to God; and without them, she would not have entered the ranks of the saints. She is meant as a model to other women to show the righteousness of women's speech in defense of Christian values. Isabella's eloquence in *Measure for Measure* is likewise directed at educating Angelo in merciful Christian behavior.

De Pisan's purpose is, as she notes at the beginning of the *Book of the City of Ladies*, to remedy the long history of male writings that revile women as monstrous. Cast into despair by her readings in such male-authored texts, which make her hate her own sex, de Pisan has a vision that leads her to write a history of great and good women. Her work is clearly polemical and instructive. Its translation in 1521 into English by Brian Anslay may not have given it a wide readership, yet the sentiments and the stories in de Pisan's work do resonate in early modern texts defending women, and Shakespeare may well have known many of the arguments in such texts even if he did not know de Pisan's work in particular.

Mariana and the Play's Resolutions of Women's Rights

If Isabella has been much misunderstood by past generations of critics, then Mariana may be the most misunderstood by recent generations of readers and playgoers. Her constancy toward the faithless Angelo, her willingness to submit to the bed-trick, and her desire to become his wife and keep him alive despite his pursuit of Isabella don't sit well with women — or men — of our own time. Why on earth doesn't she just get herself another, better husband?

Mariana's case involves both legal and moral issues attendant on the fashioning of marriage contracts. The Duke tells her not to fear the consequence of the bed-trick, since "He is your husband on a precontract; / To bring you thus together, 'tis no sin, / Sith that the justice of your title to him / Doth flourish the deceit" (4.1.68–71). Initially she is, unlike Juliet, a virgin, but one whose reputation has been compromised by Angelo's maneuverings to escape the match. Without either dowry (lost with her brother at sea) or her reputation for chastity and honor, Mariana is unlikely to be able to make another advantageous marriage. The Duke clearly takes the ecclestiastical court's position that the consummation of an oath-based betrothal will make the marriage legal, rather than constitute fornication (possibly an appropriate position for one who wears the habit of a friar, but clearly divergent from the civil laws of Vienna; when he resumes his role as Duke in act 5, Vincentio calls for her to be quickly and officially married by Friar Peter; so despite his claims to the contrary, the betrothal plus the sexual consummation of Mariana's match is not enough). And besides, as the Duke notes, Mariana is even more in love with Angelo than ever, and might well pine away from sorrow without him. When we first meet her, she is listening to a song about the contradictions inherent in passionate love: "O, take those lips away . . . But my kisses bring again, bring again" (4.1.1–5). Her self-destructive passionate attachment to her faithless fiancé (which she calls her "brawling discontent" [4.1.9]) most resembles Claudio's view of desire as the poison to which humans are inexorably drawn even at peril of their lives. Although the virginal Mariana lives in a "moated grange," a secluded farm far from the city's corrupting influences (and her name echoes that of the Virgin Mary, resonating with both her virginity and her function as a quasi-divine instrument in the Duke's plan), her character too is influenced by the same forces that drive city-dwellers to the brothels, or drive Angelo to defile Isabella.

Through the bed-trick, the play gives Mariana certain rights over Angelo that she does not have without it: in the denouement she is given an instant marriage, title to all Angelo's worldly possessions, and the power to determine whether he lives or dies. Her situation differs from Juliet and Claudio's in that she has maintained her virginity, and only sacrifices herself on the friar's advice to control Angelo's illicit actions. Mariana is supposed to be the play's remedy or corrective; through her virginal body, and her faithful desire, all the play's murky dangers can be put right. Right, that is, if you value marriage above all else. Mariana's apparent folly in continuing to desire Angelo may thus not be her own personal folly, but a byproduct of the play's drive to enforce universal and legal marriage on all. At the play's conclusion, Mariana also seems to infuse the mere shell of legality with emotion when she begs the Duke not to punish Angelo for Claudio's supposed murder. She could, in the Duke's phrase, "buy a better husband" with Angelo's property once widowed, but chooses instead to give Angelo the chance to become genuinely — that is, humanely and imperfectly — virtuous: "They say best men are molded out of faults, / And, for the most, become much more the better / For being a little bad" (5.1.435–37). If the bed-trick indicated that all women are the same in the dark, Mariana's pleading in act 5 insists that not all men are alike for those who love them. Against the contrary examples of Lucio's forced marriage to Kate Keepdown and Isabella's possible and possibly forced marriage to the Duke, Mariana's relationship to Angelo looks surprisingly like the model of companionate and affective marriage so celebrated by English Protestantism. Whether this resolves the trouble modern audiences have with her character, however, is not clear. Nor is it impossible that Shakespeare's audiences felt some of the same reservations about her in the end.

We should not be distracted, however, by the way that the play offers Mariana her heart's desire from the insidiousness of the overall conclusion. If marriage becomes easier to achieve by the play's end, it has not become easier to understand as a legal entity. Claudio and Juliet are still violators of the civil law; Lucio and Kate Keepdown do not promise a marriage of fidelity and longevity, and their child would still, by most legal rubrics, remain a bastard; and the Duke and Isabella do not seem precisely a marriage made in heaven — in fact, heaven might be a tad provoked that the

Duke has usurped its privileges with this young novitiate. A woman like Mariana might gain the right to her role as wife, but Isabella has lost some degree of control over her life. Both have been sexually compromised, Mariana in fact and Isabella in reputation after her public declaration that Angelo deflowered her. Whether the brothels will continue to operate seems a foregone conclusion, despite Mistress Overdone's arrest, and Pompey's conversion to executioner. As a means for containing sexuality, marriage has failed many times over by the play's conclusion, and has not been rehabilitated by the Duke's dispensations. In sum, marriage remains a problem as much as a solution to the social and sexual ills of the play's world.

→ **T. E.**

From The Law's Resolutions of Women's Rights   *1632*

A compendium of information on women's legal status, also often called "The Women's Lawyer," edited by the anonymous T. E., this work offers (as it notes on its title page) "a methodical collection of such statutes and customs, with the cases, opinions, arguments and points of learning in the law, as do properly concern women."

The Second Book.

Now that I have brought up a woman, and made her an inheritor, taken her out of ward,[1] helped her to make partition,[2] etc., me thinks she should long to be married: *Fœmina appetit virum, sicut materia formam.*[3] And I did not mean when I begun, to produce any vestal virgin, nun, or new Saint Bridget.[4] Following therefore my first intention, I will begin to instruct women grown, first such as are, or shortly shall be wives, and then widows.

---

[1] **taken . . . Ward:** discussed wardship (the practice of awarding care of an orphaned child to another).   [2] **make partition:** legally divide property.   [3] *Foemina . . . formam:* woman craves man just as matter craves form.   [4] **Saint Bridget:** fourteenth-century Swedish princess, visionary, and founder of the Order of Brigittines.

T. E., *The Law's Resolutions of Women's Rights: Or, The Law's Provision for Women* (Printed by the assignes of John More, esq. and are to be sold by John Grove: London, 1632), 51–57, 62–64.

Section I. Of Marriage, According to the Civil and Common Law.

Marriage is defined to be a conjunction of man and woman, containing an inseparable connection, and union of life. But as there is nothing that is begotten and finished at once, so this contract of coupling man and woman together, hath an inception first, and then an orderly proceeding. The first beginning of marriage (as in respect of contract, and that which law taketh hold on) is when wedlock by words in the future tense is promised and vowed, and this is but *sponsio*, or *sponsalia*. The full contract of matrimony is when it is made by words, *de praesenti*[5] in a lawful consent, and thus two be made man and wife existing without lying together, yet matrimony is not accounted consummate, until there go with the consent of mind and will conjunction of body.

Section II. Of Sponsion or First Promising.

The first promising and inception of marriage is in two parts, either it is plain, simple and naked, or confirmed and born by giving of something: the first is, when a man and woman bind themselves simply by their word only to contract matrimony hereafter; the second, when there is an oath made, or somewhat taken as an earnest or pledge betwixt them on both parts, or on one part, to be married hereafter. There is not here to be stood upon, the age definitively set down for making of marriage irrevocable, but all that are seven years old (betwixt whom matrimony may consist) may make sponsion and promise. But if any that is under the age of seven, begin this vow and betrothing, it is esteemed as a mist, and vanisheth to nothing.

Section III. Of Public Sponsion.

This sponsion (in which as it stands, is no full contract of matrimony, nor any more, save only an obligation, or being bound in a sort to marry hereafter) may be public or secret: public, either by the parties themselves, present together, or by message or letters when they be distant from one another. Neither is there herein any curious form of paction or stipulation required, but only by words, howsoever expressed, a plain consent and agreement of the parties, and by the civil law, (with which the ancient

---

[5] *de praesenti:* in the present.

canons concorded) or their parents; if the contractors were *sub potestate parentum*,[6] the like reasons seemeth to be for consent of tutors, etc. But it is now received a general opinion that the good will of parents is required, in regard of honesty, not of necessity, according to the canons which exact necessarily, none other consent but only of the parties themselves, whose conjunction is in hand, without which the conclusion of parents is of none effect: note further, that *sponsalia* may be made pure or conditional, and whatsoever is else adjected[7] (as earnest, pledge, or such like) is but accidental.

Section IIII. Of Secret Sponsion.

Those spousals which are made when a man is without witness, *Solus cum sola*[8] are called secret promising or desponsation, which though it be tolerated, when by liquid and plain probation[9] it may appear to the judge, and there is not any lawful impediment to hinder the contract, yet it is so little esteemed of (unless it be very manifest) that another promise public made after it shall be preferred and prevail against it. The cause why it is misliked is the difficulty of proof for avoiding of it, when for offence her just cause of refusal, the one or other party might seek to go loose, and perhaps cannot, but must stand haltered from any other marriage, and the judge in suspense what to determine.

Section X. Of Matrimony Contracted in the Present Time, and Who May Contract.

Those which the Latins called *puberes*, that is, they which are come once to such state, habit and disposition of body that they may be deemed able to procreate, may contract matrimony by words of the time present, for in contract of wedlock, *pubertas*, is not strictly esteemed by number of years, as it is in wardship, but rather by the maturity, ripeness, and disposition of body. There is further required in them which contract matrimony, a sound and whole mind to consent, for he that is mad, without intermission of fury, cannot marry. But he that is deaf and dumb, may contract matrimony, *quia*

---

[6] *sub potestate parentum:* under parental authority.   [7] adjected: appended.   [8] *Solus cum sola:* alone, by himself.   [9] liquid . . . probation: proof in court that there is no hindrance to the contract.

non verbis tantum sed num & signis sensa mentis exprimuntur,[10] and as they which are *impuberes,* cannot for infirmity of age, make any firm knot of wedlock, so likewise they which by coldness of nature, or by enchantment, are impotent, be forbidden to contract.

The impediments ecclesiastical, as vows, compaternity and spiritual kindred, I will not meddle with. But come to kindred of blood, which containeth a principal let and prohibition of marriage.

Section XVIII. What Words Are Requisite.

There needs no stipulation or curious form of contract in wedlock making, but such words as prove a mutual consent and sufficient, and it may be made by letters. If question rise about words, *recurrendum est ad communem intellectum, & usum loquendi, & indubio pro matrimonie iudicandum*[11] for there is more doubtfulness in constructing words, *ut res magis valeat quam perea,*[12] etc.

Section XIX. The Accidents of Marriage.

Those things which are of solemnity or benevolence, as provision of dower, earnest, giving pledges, nuptial benediction, etc., are not of the essence of matrimony which is made by consent, for though dower cannot consist without marriage, yet marriage may very well stand without dower. And so it is of all donations *proper nuptias.*[13] In only one case written instruments are required in making of marriage, and that is where a man marrieth her whom he hath held a long time as concubine; here *instrumenta dotalia*[14] are behooveful, that the children had before marriage, may be esteemed legitimate. But this holdeth not in England.

---

[10] *quia . . . exprimuntur:* because the mind's intentions are expressed not only in words, but in nods and signs.   [11] *recurrendum . . . iudicandum:* one must have recourse to popular intention and parlance, and undoubtedly the judgment is in favor of marriage.   [12] *ut . . . perea:* in order that the thing may flourish rather than perish.   [13] *proper nuptias:* by or because of marriage. [14] *instrumenta dotalia:* items of dowry.

Section XXI. The Consummation . . . of Marriage.

When to the consent of mind, there is added copulation of body, matrimony is consummate, the principal end whereof is propagation or procreation. But where the course after going is not observed, there riseth no lawful offspring, the children which are had are not in power and commandment of them which beget or bear them, neither are they taken by law for any other, than *vulgo questiti*.[15] Otherwise it is in lawful wedlock, the knot whereof is so straight and indissoluble, that they which are yoked therein, cannot the one without the consent of the other, (neither was it ever permitted) abdicate themselves, or enter into religion, for Saint Paul in the above titled epistle and chapter, sayeth plainly, that the husband hath not power of his own body, etc. And there cannot chance any fetidity or uncleanness of body so great, as that for it a man and wife ought perpetually to be segregated, yea so unpartable be they, that law sayeth, they may not utterly leave *coniugalem consuetudinem*,[16] though one of them have the very leprosy itself.

And here is moved a question not impertinent, that is, whether a woman be bound to follow her husband wheresoever he goeth, if he require it, whereunto it is answered by Bartall and by some other, that if the wife before she married knew the negotiations and occasions of her husband would be such, that he must of necessity ever be traveling, she is bound, and in the contract seemeth to have consented to go with him at commandment, but if after the bargain made he take up a new trick of *circumvagare*[17] she may let him go when he list and tarry at home when she will.

[15] *vulgo questiti:* sought by the crowd.   [16] *coniugalem consuetudinem:* marriage custom.   [17] *circumvagare:* to beat around the bush (literally to wander around).

→ **WILLIAM PERKINS**

From Christian Economy   *1609*

A famous Puritan preacher and author, William Perkins (1558–1602) was educated at Cambridge University. He authored the *Christian Economy* in Latin in the 1590s. The text was translated into English by Thomas Pickering and published by Felix Kyngston in 1609. Perkins's view on what constitutes a marriage

William Perkins, *Christian Economy; or, A Short Survey of the Right Manner of Erecting and Ordering a Family According to the Scriptures* (London, 1609), 18–23, 68–72.

is fairly typical for the period and speaks to both the betrothal of Claudio and Juliet and the broken contract between Mariana and Angelo.

CHAPTER 4.

Of the Contract.

Marriage hath two distinct parts, the first is the beginning; the second, the accomplishment or consumption thereof.

The beginning is the contract or espousals;[1] the end or accomplishment[2] is the solemn manifestation of the contract by that which properly we call marriage. *What man is there that hath betrothed a wife, and hath not taken her? Let him go and return again unto his house, lest he die in battle and another man take her.*[3] *When his mother Mary was betrothed to Joseph before they came together, she was found with child of the Holy Ghost.*[4]

Between the contract and the marriage, there ought to be some certain space or distance[5] of time. The reasons whereof may be these:

First, a business of so great importance as this is would be rashly or unadvisedly attempted, but should rather be done by degrees in process of time, according to that saying, not so ancient as true. *Actions of weight, before resolution, require mature deliberation.* Secondly, that during such space inquiry may be made whether there be any just cause which may hinder the consummation of marriage; considering that before the parties come and converse together, what is amiss may be remedied and amended, which to do afterward will be too late. Thirdly, in these cases, persons espoused must have regard of honesty as well as of necessity; not presently upon the contract seeking to satisfy their own fleshly desires, after the manner of brute beasts, but proceeding therein upon mature deliberation.

The contract is a mention or mutual promise of future marriage before fit and competent judges and witnesses.

The best manner of giving this promise is to make it *in words touching the present time,*[6] and simply without any exception or condition expressed or

---

[1] contract or espousals: the formal "plighting of troth" between a man and a woman; a promise of marriage (also spousals). [2] accomplishment: sexual consummation, completion. [3] *What . . . her:* Deuteronomy 20:7. [4] *When . . . Holy Ghost:* Matthew 1:18. The quotations from the books of Deuteronomy and Matthew are meant to support the point immediately following, which is that there should be a period of time between the marriage contract and the marriage itself. [5] space or distance: a reasonable period of time for reflection and deliberation. [6] in words . . . time: *(per verba de praesenti),* as when the couple exchanges words such as "I do take thee to be my wife" and "I do take thee to be my husband."

conceived. For by this means it comes to pass that the bond is made the surer, and the ground or foundation of future marriage the better laid. And hence alone it is that the persons betrothed in scripture are termed man and wife. Jacob speaking of Rachel, who was only betrothed unto him, says to Laban, *"Give me my wife."*[7] *If a maid*[8] *be betrothed to a husband, and a man find her in the town and lie with her, then shall ye bring them both unto the gates of the city and shall stone them to death, the maid because she cried not being in the city, and the man because he hath humbled his neighbor's wife.*[9] *Joseph fear not to take Mary thy wife.*[10]

Now if the promise be uttered in the words, *for time to come,*[11] it doth not precisely bind the parties to performance. For example, if one of them says to the other, "I will take thee," etc., and not, "I do take thee," etc., by this form of speech the match is *not made but only promised* to be made afterward. But if, on the other side, it is said, "I do take thee," and not, "I will take thee," by these terms the marriage at that very instant is begun, though not in regard of fact, yet in regard of right and interest, which the parties have each in another in deed and in truth. And this is the common opinion of the learned. Yet notwithstanding, if the parties contracting shall say each to other, "I will take thee to," etc., with intention to bind themselves at the present, the bond is in conscience precisely made before God, and so the contract is indeed made *for the present* time before God. True it is that he which standeth to his promise made, as much as in him lieth, doth well; yet if the promise hath or conceiveth some just cause why he should afterward change his purpose, the contract expressed in terms for the time to come, though it were formerly made and confirmed by oath, must notwithstanding give place to the contract made for time present.

Those espousals which are made upon condition which is honest, possible, and belonging to marriage, do cease or depend so far forth as the condition annexed ceaseth or dependeth. For example, if the one party promiseth to marry the other upon condition that his or her kinsman will yield consent to the match, or upon condition of a dowry that she shall bring unto him, suitable to her education[12] and the family whereof she cometh, these conditions being kept or not kept, the promise does likewise stand or not stand.[13]

But those conditions which are necessarily understood, or which may certainly be kept and come to pass, do neither hinder nor suspend marriage.

---

[7] *"Give ... wife.":* Genesis 29:21. [8] maid: virgin. [9] *If ... wife:* Deuteronomy 22:23. [10] *Joseph ... wife:* Matthew 1:20. [11] for time to come: *(per verba de futuro),* a verbal promise to marry in the future. [12] education: social station. [13] these conditions ... stand: This appears to speak directly to the broken contract between Angelo and Mariana.

As this: "I promise thee marriage if I live," or, "I promise to marry thee if the sun rise tomorrow."

Again, conditions that are either impossible or dishonest are not to be accounted as promises annexed in way of marriage. Of which sort are these, "I will be thy wife if thou wilt take unto thee wings and fly," or, "If thou wilt bring an untimely birth."

Furthermore, if the parties betrothed do lie together before the condition (though honest and appertaining to marriage) be performed, then the contract for time to come is, without further controversy, sure and certain. For where there hath been a carnal use of each other's body, it is always presupposed that a mutual consent, as touching marriage, hath gone before.

CHAPTER 6.

Of Consent in the Contract.

The second thing required to the making of a contract is the free and full consent of the parties, which is indeed the very soul and life of the contract. And this consent standeth in the approbation[14] or, as we commonly call it, the sure-making[15] of the parties contracted.

Consent in this case is twofold, either of the man and the woman, or of the parents.

Touching the first, that the man and the woman may yield free consent each to other, it is necessary that in respect of understanding their judgment should be sound; and in regard of will, their choice should be free. And here sundry cases are to be resolved.

1. CASE. When the contract flows not from the will and good liking of the parties, but is forced and compelled, what is then to be done?

ANSWER. If the espousals have been made through force or fear, I mean, such as may befall a constant and resolute man, and which hath been wrought upon good knowledge and consideration; then are they of no moment and, in truth, mere nullities; because there is wanting to them the free and voluntary accord and assent of both parties. Nevertheless, if afterward they shall grow to a new consent, or both yield to an after-acceptation[16] of that which was formerly made, the espousals shall then stand in force; without further exception or contradiction.

---

[14] approbation: official approval.   [15] sure-making: betrothal.   [16] acceptation: acceptance.

2. CASE. But how if consent be past, and in process of time it appears to the espoused persons that they have erred, either in choice or consent, or both?

ANSWER. There is a threefold error in consent: the one of the person,[17] the other of ability or estate[18] of the person, the third of the quality.[19]

Error in respect of the person is when one person is taken for another, or when the contract is made between two whereof the one was taken to be such a party as afterwards he proved not to be. Now where this error is committed, it is a plain case: there was no consent, and therefore the contract, upon certain knowledge thereof, is quite frustrate.[20] For the knowledge of the party is the ground of consent and belongs consequently to the very substance of marriage.

Nevertheless, if, the error being once known, the parties have secret society,[21] one with another, and have either again consented or grown to an after-acceptation of the consent before made, the contract may and doth stand in full force. For example, Jacob, by the deceit of Laban, had taken Leah for Rachel, to his wife.[22] So says the text: *When the evening was come Laban took Leah his daughter and brought her to him, and he went in unto her, but when the morning was come, behold, it was Leah.*[23] Now by the judgment of the best divines, Jacob might justly have renounced Leah, if he would, because Laban had given her unto him for Rachel, and so deceived him; yet he would not use extremity, but kept her as his wife.[24]

If it be said, there was an error in the person, therefore no consent, and so Leah was not his lawful wife, but Rachel. I answer that Jacob did renew his consent afterward, and that renewed consent following upon their knowing[25] one of another made her his wife, though in extremity and rigor[26] she was not. Again, Rachel was indeed the party to whom he was espoused by the former contract; and therefore, upon their mutual agreement afterward, she also became his wife. So says the Holy Ghost, *Fulfill seven years for her, and we will also give thee Rachel for thy service, etc. Then Jacob did so, and Laban gave him Rachel his daughter to be his wife.*[27]

---

[17] person: identity. [18] ability or estate: financial position. [19] quality: virginity. [20] frustrate: rendered null and void. [21] secret society: sexual intercourse. [22] Jacob . . . wife: Rachel (Laban's younger daughter) had been promised to Jacob in return for Jacob's service to Laban for a period seven years (Genesis 29:9–29). [23] *When . . . Leah:* Genesis 29:23, 25. [24] extremity: extreme means (to seek redress from Laban). See Genesis 29:27–29. [25] knowing: knowing each other sexually. [26] extremity and rigor: in the strictest sense. [27] *Fulfill . . . wife:* Genesis 29:27–28.

→ HENRY SWINBURNE

From A Treatise of Spousals
1686

Although it was first published late in the seventeenth century, Henry Swinburne's *Treatise of Spousals* offers a useful digest of legal debates throughout the period over the various forms and content of spousals (betrothals or precontracts). Swinburne (1560?–1623) was commissary of the exchequer and judge of the consistatory court (responsible for cases involving church lands and property) at York; his unfinished work excerpted here is concerned with the definition of spousals under ecclesiastical or church law.

Section IV

Of the great importance of the first Division or Distinction betwixt Spousals *de futuro* and Spousals *de praesenti*.[1]

When we shall view the small difference betwixt those words, whereby spousals *de futuro*, or *de praesenti* are contracted, it cannot but seem strange that from so small a difference of forms, so great diversity of effects should proceed: for in truth, so very little (very often) is the odds betwixt the form of words of these two contracts, that the best learned are at greatest variance whether such words make spousals *de futuro* or *de praesenti*. Neither is it unknown to the youngest students in this faculty that words of future time do not evermore import spousals *de futuro;* neither words of present time always spousals *de praesenti*. Again, that some words are so untoward that it is a question whether they make any kind of spousals at all, and contrariwise, some words so flexible that they may easily be stretched to make, either the one or the other. . . .

. . . Understand therefore that man and that woman which do contract spousals *de futuro* as "I will take thee to my wife; I will take thee to my husband," are not very husband and wife, neither so reputed in law, excepted they may by mutual agreement dissolve those spousals and safely match themselves elsewhere; or if but one of them alone shall renounce and thereupon adventure indeed to marry otherwise, or to contract spousals *de praesenti* with some other person, in these cases by the laws civil and ecclesi-

---

[1] *de futuro . . . de praesenti:* literally, future versus present betrothals.

Henry Swinburne, *A Treatise of Spousals, or Matrimonial Contracts: Wherein All the Questions Relating to That Subject Are Ingeniously Debated and Resolved* (London: 1686), 11–14, 194–95, 203–04.

astical this marriage or contract *de praesenti* shall stand firm and lawful, notwithstanding the precontract of spousals *de futuro*. The reason is because like as when a man doth promise he will sell his land, the land is not thereby sold in deed, but promised to be sold afterwards; so while the parties do promise only that they will take or will marry they do not thereby presently take or marry, but deferring the accomplishment of that promise until another time the knot in the meantime is not so surely tied but that it may be loosed, while the matter is in suspense and unperfect. But that woman and that man which have contracted spousals *de praesenti*, as "I do take thee to my Wife" and "I do take thee to my husband," cannot by any agreement dissolve those spousals, but are reputed for very husband and wife in respect of the substance and indissoluble knot of matrimony, and therefore if either of them should in fact proceed to solemnize matrimony with any other person, consummating the same by carnal copulation, and procreation of children, this matrimony is to be dissolved as unlawful, the parties marrying to be punished as adulterers, and their issue in danger of bastardy.

The reason is because here is no promise of any future act, but a present and perfect consent, the which alone maketh matrimony, without either public solemnization or carnal copulation; for neither is the one nor the other of the essence of matrimony but consent only.

Section XIV

Of Public and Private Spousals.

Others are of another opinion, holding the contract for firm and indissoluble [when made in private]; for the confirmation whereof they allege a very round text extant in the body of the law. The words are these: *Clandestina conjugia contra leges quidem siunt, contracta tamen dissolve non possunt*, Secret marriages are done indeed against the law, but being contracted cannot be dissolved; yielding this reason, that because these solemnities are not of the substance of spousals or of matrimony, but consent only; for (as another text saith), *sufficit nudus consensus ad constituenda sponsalia*, Naked consent is sufficient to make spousals.

Section XV

Of Contracting Spousals by Signs.

It is an old and tough controversy, whether words be necessary in contracting spousals or matrimony, wherein diverse do hold the affirmative at least as touching the church (which doth not otherwise determine of that which is conceived inwardly, but that which is expressed outwardly) . . . Others nevertheless hold the negative, by reason of another text, which saith *sufficit ad matrimonium solus illorum consensus, de quorum conjunctionibus agitur,* Their consent alone is sufficient for matrimony, of whose conjunction there is any ado; and it followeth in the same place that he or she which cannot speak may contract matrimony, the reason there yielded is this, *Quod verbis non potest, Signis valeat declarari,* That which cannot be expressed by words, may be declared by signs.

→ CHURCH OF ENGLAND

Of Matrimony
1559

This familiar ceremony was the Church's public solemnization of marriage; it requires public announcement of the impending union to ensure that both parties are truly free to marry, and establishes the centrality of marriage to the spiritual health of mankind. In its emphasis on gestures (the holding of hands), tokens (the exchange of the ring), and words, the ceremony fulfills legal, as well as spiritual, requirements.

The Form of Solemnization of Matrimony.

First, the banns[1] must be asked three several Sundays or holy days in the time of service, the people being present after the accustomed manner.

And if the persons that should be married, dwell in divers parishes, the banns must be asked in both parishes, and the curate of the one parish shall not solemnize matrimony betwixt them, without a certificate of the banns being thrice asked, from the curate of the other parish. At the day appointed for solemnization of mat-

---

[1] **Banns:** the banns, or proclamations, read publicly of intent to marry.

Church of England, *The Book of Common Prayer, and Administration of the Sacrament and Other Rites and Ceremonies of the Church of England* (1559; London: Robert Barker, 1607).

rimony, the persons to be married shall come into the body of the church, with their friends and neighbors. And there the priest shall say thus:

Dearly beloved friends, we are gathered together here in the sight of God, and in the face of his congregation, to join together this man and this woman in holy matrimony, which is an honorable estate, instituted of God in paradise, in the time of man's innocency, signifying unto us the mystical union that is betwixt Christ and his church: which holy estate Christ adorned and beautified with his presence, and first miracle[2] that he wrought in Cana of Galilee, and is commended of St. Paul to be honorable among all men, and therefore is not to be enterprised nor taken in hand unadvisedly, lightly, or wantonly, to satisfy men's carnal lusts and appetites, like brute beasts that have no understanding, but reverently, discreetly, advisedly, soberly, and in the fear of God, duly considering the causes for which matrimony was ordained. One was the procreation of children, to be brought up in the fear and nurture of the Lord, and praise of God. Secondly, it was ordained for a remedy against sin, and to avoid fornication, that such persons as have not the gift of continency, might marry, and keep themselves undefiled members of Christ's body. Thirdly, for the mutual society, help, and comfort, that one ought to have of the other, both in prosperity and adversity: into the which holy estate these two persons present come now to be joined. Therefore, if any man can show any just cause, why they may not lawfully be joined together, let him now speak, or else hereafter forever hold his peace.

And also speaking to the persons that shall be married, he shall say:

I require and charge you (as you will answer at the dreadful day of judgment, when the secrets of all hearts shall be disclosed) that if either of you do know any impediment, why ye may not be lawfully joined together in matrimony, that ye confess it. For be ye well assured, that so many as be coupled together otherwise than God's word doth allow, are not joined together by God, neither is the matrimony lawful.

At which day of marriage, if any man do allege and declare any impediment, why they may not be coupled together in matrimony, by God's law or the laws of this realm, and will be bound, and sufficient sureties with him to the parties, or else put in a caution to the full value of such charges as the persons to be married do sustain, to prove his allegation: the solemnization must be deferred, unto such time as the truth be tried. If no impediment be alleged then shall the curate say unto the man: N., Wilt thou have this woman to thy wedded wife, to live together

---

[2] first miracle: John 2:1–11.

after God's ordinance in the holy estate of matrimony? Wilt thou love her, comfort her, honor and keep her in sickness and in health? And forsaking all other, keep thee only unto her, so long as you both shall live? *The man shall answer:* I will.

Then shall the priest say to the woman: N., Wilt thou have this man to thy wedded husband, to live together after God's ordinance, in the holy estate of matrimony? Wilt thou obey him and serve him, love, honor, and keep him in sickness and in health? And forsaking all other, keep thee only unto him, so long as you both shall live? *The woman shall answer:* I Will.

Then shall the minister say: Who giveth this woman to be married to this man?

And the minister receiving the woman at her father's or friend's hands, shall cause the man to take the woman by the right hand, and so either to give their troth to other, the man first saying: I, N. take thee N. to my wedded wife, to have and to hold from this day forward, for better, for worse, for richer, for poorer, in sickness and in health, to love and to cherish, till death us depart, according to God's holy ordinance: and thereto I plight thee my troth.

Then shall they loose their hands, and the woman taking again the man by the right hand, shall say: I N. take thee N. to my wedded husband, to have and to hold from this day forward, for better, for worse, for richer, for poorer, in sickness and in health, to love, cherish, and to obey, till death us depart, according to God's holy ordinance: and thereto I give thee my troth.

Then shall they again loose their hands, and the man shall give unto the woman a ring, laying the same upon the book, with the accustomed duty to the priest and clerk. And the priest taking the ring, shall deliver it unto the man to put it upon the fourth finger of the woman's left hand. And the man taught by the priest shall say: With this ring I thee wed, with my body I thee worship, and with all my worldly goods I thee endow. In the name of the Father, and of the Son, and of the Holy Ghost. Amen.

Then the man leaving the ring upon the fourth finger of the woman's left hand, the minister shall say: Let us pray. O eternal God, creator and preserver of all mankind, giver of all spiritual grace, the author of everlasting life, send thy blessing upon these thy servants, this man and this woman, whom we bless in thy name, that as Isaac and Rebecca lived faithfully together, so these persons may surely perform and keep the vow and covenant betwixt them made (whereof this ring given and received is a token and pledge) and may ever remain in perfect love and peace together, and live according unto thy laws, through Jesus Christ Our Lord, Amen.

Then shall the priest join their right hands together, and say: Those whom God hath joined together, let no man put asunder.

Then shall the minister speak unto the people: Forasmuch as N. and N. have consented together in holy wedlock, and have witnessed the same before God and this company, and thereto have given and pledged their troth either to other, and have declared the same by giving and receiving of a ring, and by joining of hands, I pronounce that they be man and wife together. In the name of the Father, of the Son and of the Holy Ghost. Amen.

↦ A Selection of Court Cases Concerned with Sex *1508–1623*

The church court entries gathered here offer an instructive glimpse into the church's treatment of fairly common moral offenses such as fornication and premarital pregnancy. First, it is noteworthy that these cases came before church courts and not before secular courts. The secular courts generally heard cases dealing with moral offenses only if they included violence, and were thus deemed serious crimes. The church courts were not allowed to hand down death sentences, and those who came before it were rarely imprisoned (Hair 22). Typically, the church courts would impose fines or demand that the offender perform an act of public penance, and leave it at that. Angelo's decision, therefore, to arrogate Claudio's case to his secular authority and pronounce a death sentence, appears in stark contrast to what the early modern men and women would have witnessed in their own lives. What is more, although Claudio and Juliet's case is unique in *Measure for Measure,* we can be sure that premarital sex was hardly a rare occurrence in early modern England. Paul Hair calculates that between the years 1450 and 1640 somewhere around one to three million moral/sexual offenses were brought before church courts, but even this number does not give an accurate picture of the frequency of moral/sexual offenses because such offenses were often difficult to prove in a court of law and often did not come to trial (Hair 25). The incidence of premarital sex, in particular, must have been much higher than the number of extant court cases because parish registers reveal that (after the year 1538) "about one third of all brides were pregnant at marriage" (Hair 25). Needless to say, it would have been impractical and undesirable for the church courts to charge all these newlyweds.

The italicized portions are Paul Hair's summaries of the original entries.

Paul Hair, ed., *Before the Bawdy Court: Selections from Church Court and other Records Relating to the Correction of Moral Offences in England, Scotland, and New England, 1300–1800* (London: Elek, 1972), 53, 55–56, 93–94, 105–06, 111, 119, 120.

CHARLBURY, OXFORDSHIRE, 1584. William White of Charlbury for keeping together with Mary Gillett in one house . . . *and the said Mary Gillett who appeared and replied to the charge* that she does and has used the company of William White who is contracted to her before sufficient witness and means to marry her as soon as he is out of service. Verdict: dismissed.

ST. IVES, HUNTINGDONSHIRE, 1530. *On the 25th of April 1530 in a chapel at St. Ives before his lordship the chancellor sitting judicially, appeared in person Joan Martyn of Owton and alleged that Robert Blundell had made a contract of marriage with her and that he had known her and impregnated her; and Robert Blundell being present admitted that he had known and impregnated her and even that he had said to her,* "I will marry thee and if thou wilt let me have ado[1] with thee and she said certain I will never have none but you," and upon that they had ado together. *Then the lord chancellor adjudged Robert husband and Joan wife and ordered them to solemnize their matrimony before the 1st of August next, under pain of major excommunication.*

WARRINGTON, LANCASHIRE, 1592. *Against Peter Holbroke and Susan Middleton, fornicators. Excommunicated.* [Later . . .] *He appears and confesses* and says he is to marry the woman presently and that the time is appointed. *Wherefore his lordship absolved him and also the woman, and decreed that should the marriage be duly solemnized they confess their fault before the Rector of Warrington and the wardens there, and if they do not marry they must do the usual penances, and they are to certify before the Feast of St. Bartholomew concerning the solemnization and also the confessions.*

SANDFORD, OXFORDSHIRE, 1584. *John Stacie of Sanford for incontinence with a maid servant in the house of his father . . . appears, is sworn and replies* to the charge that there has been good will and motion of marriage between this respondent and Jane Bannister but no perfect contract because the friends[2] of this respondent and the same Jane have not yet concluded; *he denies carnal knowledge and that this is common fame; dismissed.*

WISTOW, HUNTINGDONSHIRE, 1518. *John Campion and Joan Wilson are accused of incontinency.* [In court, they] *appear and claim that they are betrothed and that they intend to marry, and his lordship warns them that they must be married before Michaelmas. They pay 8d.[3]* [the fee for citation].

---

[1] **ado:** sexual intercourse.   [2] **friends:** relatives (most likely the parents).   [3] **8d:** eight pence, eight times the price of admission to the pit to watch a play in the public playhouse in Shakespeare's day.

OTTERHAMPTON, SOMERSET, 1623. *Against John Duddridge. Presented* that he and Jane Vinobles did lie together on Christmas Eve last in fornication or incontinency. *He appeared . . . and alleged pre-contract. Order to produce proof.* [Later,] *he appeared without proof. Public penance once in church.* [Later,] *a certificate of penance produced, dismissed, 4d* [fees].

LONDON, 1508. *Joan Cokes is charged with the crime of fornication with William Cokes, and keeps her as his wife. She is cited to appear on the 24th of February but his lordship holds the case over till they are married when it will be dismissed. William Cokes appears and swears to marry Joan before the St. John Baptist day next.*

→ RICHARD DAY

From A Book of Christian Prayers   *1602*

Books of daily prayers were popular fare in the Renaissance: lavishly decorated with marginal illustrations, such books were often given as gifts. *A Book of Christian Prayers* promises in its epistle to the reader to inspire "zeal and knowledge in hearty prayer."

A PRAYER AGAINST THE FLESH

O savior of mankind, we feel (alas to your great grief we feel) that our spirit is clogged with the flesh, a reasonable thing with a brutish and filthy thing. While man was in innocency, reason made the spirit a sovereign: but now the sinfulness that we have received by the inheritance from our first parents, that matched the rebellious flesh against her superior and ruler, the mind. And the more gentleness that is used towards this most unkind and lewd bondservant the body: so much the worse and more wicked doth it become. If we follow it, it carryeth us into destruction, turning us away from God, to her own earthiness and rottenness. O how unseemly an encounter is

---

Richard Day, *A Book of Christian Prayers, Collected out of the Ancient Writers, and Best Learned in Our Time; Worthy to Be Read with an Earnest Mind of All Christians in These Dangerous and Troublesome Days, That God for Christ's Sake Will Yet Still Be Merciful unto Us* (London, 1602; 1608), 120.

FIGURE 15 *"Great Grief Assails the Lecherous Mind" from Stephen Bateman,* A Crystal Glass of Christian Reformation *(London, 1585).*

this, wherein the flesh being matched against the spirit, (that is to say, the bondslave against his Lord) striveth with him for victory and preeminence; sometime getting the upper hand, so as his master is not able erewhiles[1] to repress his boldness, malapertness,[2] and lustiness: because he bare with him too long and too often.

---

[1] **erewhiles:** formerly.   [2] **malapertness:** impudence.

→ JUAN LUIS VIVES

From Instruction of a Christian Woman 1592

Juan Luis Vives was born in Valencia in 1492, but his family soon left to settle in Paris, where he was given a comprehensive humanist education. In 1523, having gained a reputation as an educator and philosopher, he was offered a post at Oxford by Cardinal Wolsey. His *Instruction of a Christian Woman*, dedicated to his country-woman Queen Catherine of Aragon for her daughter Mary (later Queen Mary I), had caught the attention of Henry VIII and his court, leading them to offer Vives royal patronage by making him Mary's tutor. Vives was eventually caught in the quagmire of Henry's long affair with Anne Boleyn and his efforts to divorce his first wife, writing in defense of Catherine for which Vives earned arrest and banishment. Once away from England, he took the prudent course and refrained from criticizing Henry or aiding Catherine. He continued to write, however, until his death in 1540, by which time he had amassed a number of popular works on devotion, education, political economy, and philosophy. Many of his writings advocate education for women — Vives believed that women were fully capable of intellectual achievement. *The Instruction of a Christian Woman* also argued that marriage was more properly based on intellectual companionship than procreation, a position that was undoubtedly inspired in part by Catherine's problems in her marriage to Henry. Vives was no feminist, however; he advocated restrictive codes of behavior for women, as did most of his contemporaries, especially where sexual chastity was concerned. The excerpts here address the ideal of virginity for unmarried women.

CHAPTER 6.

The Instruction of Virginity.

Now will I talk altogether with the maid herself, which hath within her a treasure without comparison, that is the pureness both of body and mind. Now so many things come unto my remembrance to say, that I wote[1] not where is best to begin: whether it were better to begin where as Saint Augustine doth, when he will entreat of holy virginity. All the holy church is a virgin, masters unto one husband Christ, as Saint Paul writeth unto the Corinthians. Then what honor be they worthy to have, that be the members

---

[1] wote: know.

Juan Luis Vives, *A Very Fruitful and Pleasant Book Called Instruction of a Christian Woman*, made first in Latin, by the right famous clerk M. Luis Vives, and translated out of Latin into English, by Richard Hyrde (London: Printed by John Danter, dwelling in Hosier-Lane near Holburne Conduit, 1592), 52–60. (Copy found on Early English Books Online from British Library.)

of it which keep the same office in flesh, that the holy church keepeth in faith, which followeth the mother of her husband and Lord: for the church is also a mother and a virgin. Nor there is nothing that our Lord delighteth more in, than virgins, nor wherein angels more gladly abide and play with. For they be virgins also themselves, and their Lord, which would have a virgin unto his mother and a virgin to his dear disciple, and the church his spouse a virgin. And also he marrieth unto himself other virgins, and goeth unto marriages with virgins. And whither soever he goeth, that lamb without spot which made us clean with his blood, a hundred and forty thousand virgins follow him. It is written in the canticles:[2] *Our sister is a little one, and hath no breasts.* Whether that be the saying of Christ or angels to the soul: in whom standeth the very virginity pleasant unto God. All glory of the king's daughter is inward, sayeth David in the Psalm.[3] There is that golden clothing, there is that garment set and powdered with so many virtuous and precious stones. Be not proud, maid, that thou art holy of body, if thou be drunken in mind, nor because no man hath touched thy body, if many men have pierced thy mind. What availeth it, thy body being clean, when thou bearest thy mind and thy thought infected with a foul and a horrible blot? O thou maid, thy mind is withered by burning with man's heat: nor thou frettest not with holy love, but hast dried up all the good fatness of the pleasures of paradise. Therefore art thou the foolish maid and hast no oil, and while though runnest to the cellar, art shut forth: and as our Lord in the Gospel threateneth, when thou comest again, and knockest, thou shalt be answered, Who art thou? I know thee not.[4] ... I pray thee, understand thine own goodness, maid, thy price cannot be esteemed, if thou join a chaste mind unto a chaste body, if thou shut up both body and mind, and seal them with those seals that none can open; but he that hath the key of David,[5] that is thy spouse, which resteth so in thee, as in a temple most clean and goodly. Thinkest thou this any final thing, that thou mayest receive only by pureness that thing, which cannot be comprehended in this whole world. How glad is a woman, if she bear in her womb a child which shall be a king: But thou bearest a king already not only in thy womb, but also in thy mind, which is more goodly. Yea, and such a king, in whose garment this title of virginity is written: *King of all kings, and lord of all lords, of whom prophets have prophesied, and his reign is the reign of all worlds, whose reign the angel told should have no end.* Let us now lift up ourselves above the common people: and let us dispute this most goodly matter with Saint Augustine, but yet so that thou mayest perceive us, and doubtless thou shalt perceive us better

---

[2] **canticles:** hymns or songs.   [3] **Psalm:** Psalm 45.   [4] **Who . . . not:** Matthew 25:1–13.   [5] **key of David:** Revelation 3:7.

than we shall ourselves. For we speak of thy goodness, which thou art not ignorant of; and we show thee that thing that thou hast within thee. The holy virgin Mary conceived first in her mind our lord Christ, and after in her body. And it was a more honorable, noble, and excellent thing to conceive in mind, than in body. Wherefore thou art partner of the more excellent conception. O happy art thou, that are marvelously mother to an excellent and marvelous child. Our Lord in the Gospel, when the woman said: *Blessed be the womb that bare thee, & the breasts that thou suckest.* He answered, *Nay, but blessed be they that hear the word of God, and keep it.*[6] And when the Jews told him that his mother and brethren tarried him without, he asked them, *Who is my mother and my brethren?* And pointing his hand towards his disciples: *Those be* (saith he) *my brethren and mother, and who so else obeyeth the commandments of my father.*[7] Wherefore virgins, and all holy souls, engender Christ spiritually. Howbeit corporally only one virgin did bear God and man: which is spouse and also father unto all other virgins. O thou maid, thinkest thou this but a small thing, that thou art both mother, spouse and daughter to that God, in whom nothing can be, but it must be thine, and thou mayest with good right challenge for thine: For both thou gettest, and art gotten and married unto him. If thou wouldst have a fair spouse, it is said by him, *Thou art beautiful above the children of men, grace is diffused in thy lips.*[8] . . . Now think with what diligence this pearl[9] ought to be kept, that maketh thee like unto the church, like unto the virgin Mary, sister unto angels, mother unto God, and the spouse of Christ, beside worldly honors, which ought to have no place, or very little place in a Christian body's heart? But yet also they as it were fasten their eyes upon a virgin. How pleasant and dear unto every body is a virgin? How reverend a thing, even unto them that be ill and vicious themselves. And among those foul and filthy gods of the pagans, they say, that *Sibill,* whom they all called mother, was a virgin. And *Diana* was the most favored of the gods, because she was a perpetual virgin. Also three things made *Pallas* honorable: virginity, strength, and wisdom: and she was feigned to be bred of *Jupiter's*[10] brain, whom they called the greatest prince of the gods, of which nothing might grow, but pure, chaste, and wise: So that they thought virginity and wisdom were joined together. And they dedicated the number of seven both to chastity and to wisdom; and said that the muses, whom they called the

---

[6] Blessed . . . keep it: Luke 11:27.   [7] Who is . . . my father: Matthew 12:48–50.   [8] Thou art . . . lips: Psalm 45.   [9] pearl: Matthew 13:45. The pearl of great price, which represents heaven, inspires the wealthy merchant to sell all he has in order to purchase it.   [10] Sibill . . . Diana . . . Pallas . . . Jupiter: Sibill is a female prophet; Diana is the goddess of chastity; Pallas, also Athena, is goddess of wisdom, who sprang full-grown from the head of Jupiter, or Zeus, her father.

rulers of all sciences, were virgins. And in the Temple of *Apollo, Delphicus,* the wise woman, which inspired with the heavenly spirit, showed things to come unto them, that demanded to know, was ever a virgin. Saint Jerome sayeth, that all the *Sibilles,* whom *Varro* sayeth, were ten in number, were virgins. At Rome there was a Temple of *Vesta,* unto whom virgins did minister, which were called *Vestales:* and all the senators would rise and reverence them, every officer gave them the way, and they were in great honor with all the people of Rome.

Virginity was ever an holy thing, even amongst thieves, breakers of sanctuary, ungracious livers, murderers, and also among wild beasts. Saint Tecla, as Saint Ambrose sayeth, altered the nature of wild beasts with the reverence of virginity.

Virginity hath so much marvelous honor in it, that wild lions regard it.

→ ST. AUGUSTINE

From The Lord's Sermon on the Mount *394*

Augustine of Hippo, author of the *Confessions* and *The City of God,* is one of the most important figures in early Christianity. Born in 354 C.E. in Tagaste in Northern Africa, Augustine lived through some of the most troubled times for both the Roman Empire and the early Christian church. Although baptized a Christian by his mother, Augustine took a long and wandering path to full participation in the religion. While studying in Carthage, he was exposed to the Eastern dualist philosophy of the Manicheans; later, as a professor of rhetoric in Milan, Augustine was fascinated by ancient Greek philosophy. The influence of his mother, Monica, and Ambrose, at the time Bishop of Milan, combined with illness and disillusionment with other philosophies, finally led Augustine to dedicate himself to Christianity. In the latter part of his life, Augustine witnessed not only numerous internal controversies in the Church, but also the Church's fate during the Vandals' attacks on Carthage and Northern Africa, and during the Goths' sack of Rome. His works thus not only detail his own journey toward the Christian faith, but attempt to explain and defend his own vision of Christianity against internal and external foes. His *De Sermone Domini in Monte Secundum Matthaeum* is a work of biblical exegesis written in 394, one year before Augustine was made Bishop of Hippo. In the following selection, Augustine discusses the kinds of complicated situations that might be reasons

---

St. Augustine, *De Sermone Domini in Monte Secundum Matthaeum,* trans. by John J. Jepson, in *St. Augustine, The Lord's Sermon on the Mount* (Westminster, Md.: Newman Press, 1948), excerpted in *Narrative and Dramatic Sources of Shakespeare,* ed. Geoffrey Bullough, Vol. 2, *The Comedies, 1597–1603* (New York: Columbia UP, 1958), 418–19.

for separation, including examples like the one that is excerpted here. His example provides many of the same circumstances that occur in Isabella's case, raising some questions about how unforgivable it would be were she to give her body to Angelo.

Book I, Chapter 16

But yet whether the words of the Apostle:[1] "The wife hath not power of her own body, but the husband; and in like manner the husband also hath not power of his own body, but the wife," can bear the construction that with his wife's permission, who has the power of her husband's body, her husband can have intercourse with another woman who is not the wife of another nor separated from her husband: such a supposition must not be made; otherwise it would appear that with her husband's consent a woman could do this too, — a thing which the universal moral sense rejects.

And yet some cases can happen where it might appear that a wife also, with her husband's consent, would be obligated to do this for the sake of her husband himself. Such a thing is said to have happened at Antioch about fifty years ago in the time of Constantius.

Acindynus was then governor, a man who was also of consular rank. When he demanded of a man the payment of a pound of gold to the imperial treasury, acting upon I know not what motive, he did a thing which is very often fraught with danger in those public officials to whom anything and everything is allowed, or rather, is thought by them to be allowed: he threatened with oaths and stormy language to put the man to death if he did not pay the aforesaid gold by a certain date which he had fixed. And so he was kept in harsh confinement and he was unable to rid himself of the debt, the dread day began to draw ominously near.

Now, he happened to have a very beautiful wife; but she was without money to come to her husband's aid. When a certain wealthy man, infatuated by the woman's beauty, had learned of her husband's plight, he sent her word that he would give her a pound of gold if for a single night she would agree to have intercourse with him. Whereupon, knowing that not she had power over her own body, but her husband, she reported back to him that for her husband's sake she was ready to comply, provided her husband, the conjugal master of her body to whom all her chastity was owed, decided — thus disposing of a matter properly his own — that for his life's sake this should be done. He was grateful and told her to do this; not at all deeming the intercourse to be adultery because there was no lust on her part, and

---

[1] the words of the Apostle: 1 Corinthians 7:4.

again her great love for her husband demanded it, at his own bidding and will. The woman went to the mansion of the rich man, and did what the lecher wished; but she gave her body only to her husband, who was asking, not as at other times, to lie with her, but to live. She received the gold; but he who gave it, surreptitiously took back what he had given and substituted a duplicate bag with earth in it. When the woman discovered it, she was already back at her home. She rushed into the street to publish aloud what she had done, animated by the same tender affection for her husband by which she had been driven to do it. She protests to the governor, tells him the whole story, shows how she has been victimized. And then the governor first pronounces himself guilty because by his threats it had come to this, and, as if passing sentence on another, decides that "a pound of gold should be paid into the imperial treasury from the property of Acindynus"; but that the woman should be installed as the mistress of the piece of land whence she had received earth in place of gold.

Out of this story I make no argument of any sort. Let each one pass judgement as he wishes. The account is taken from no divine source. But when the incident is told, man's moral sense is not so ready to condemn what happened in this woman's case at the behest of her husband, as we were shocked before when the case itself was being suggested without any illustration.

→ G. B. GIRALDI CINTHIO

From The Story of Epitia 1583

Giovanni Battista Giraldi, also known as Cinthio (1504–1573), Italian author, provided the stories for *Othello* and *Measure for Measure* in his *Gli Hecatommithi*, or *One Hundred Tales* (1565). In contrast with Shakespeare's Isabella, Cinthio's heroine Epitia does surrender her virginity to save her brother, and marries Juriste, the man who betrayed them both. Shakespeare modifies Epitia's story further to complicate the tale's issues of marriage, fornication, and punishment. Shakespeare would have known Cinthio's story through its translation by George Whetstone into his *Heptameron of Civil Discourses* (1582) and his play *Promos and Cassandra* (1578).

G. B. Giraldi Cinthio, "The Story of Epitia" from *Gli Hecatommithi*, in *Narrative and Dramatic Sources of Shakespeare*, ed. Geoffrey Bullough, Vol. 2, *The Comedies, 1597–1603* (New York: Columbia UP, 1958), 420–30.

BOOK 8, CHAPTER 5

[Gli hecatommithi, *or the one hundred stories of M. Giovanni Battista Giraldi Cinthi, noble Ferrarese; in which, besides delightful material, we recognize the most useful moral precepts for living a virtuous life, and for likewise arousing our minds to greater wisdom.]*

While this great Lord, who was a rare example of courtesy, magnanimity and singular justice, reigned happily over the Roman Empire, he sent out his ministers to govern the states that flourished under his rule. And among them he sent to govern Innsbruck one of his intimates, a man very dear to him named Juriste. Before sending him he said: "Juriste, the good opinion I have formed of you while you have been in my service makes me send you as Governor to this noble City of Innsbruck. I could instruct you about many things concerning your rule there but I shall limit myself to one thing only, which is: that you keep Justice[1] inviolate, even if you have to give sentence against me who am your overlord. And I warn you that I could forgive you all other faults, whether you did them through ignorance or through negligence (though I wish you to guard against this as much as possible), but anything done against Justice could never obtain pardon from me. If therefore you do not feel it incumbent on you to behave in this way I urge you (since every man is not good for every thing) do not take up this charge, but rather remain here at Court, where I hold you dear, in your accustomed duties; for otherwise, once you are Governor of that City you might oblige me to do against you that which, if I had to do it on behalf of Justice, would give me the utmost unhappiness." And hereupon he was silent.

Juriste was more pleased with the office to which the Emperor called him than sound in knowledge of his own nature. He thanked his master for the proof of his favour and said that he was always animated by the desire to serve Justice, but that he would preserve her the more ardently henceforth, since the Emperor's words were like a torch which had fired him to it all the more keenly; that he would bend his mind to succeed in his new charge so that his master could not but praise him. The Emperor rejoiced at Juriste's words and said to him. "Truly you will give me cause only to praise you if your deeds prove as good as your words." And having the letters patent given to him which were already made out, he sent him on his way.

Juriste began to rule over the City with great prudence and diligence, taking the utmost care and deliberation to ensure that the balance of Justice

---

[1] Justice: personified in the traditional fashion as a woman holding scales and blindfolded; as below when Juriste "balances" her.

should be rightly poised not only in judgements but also in the bestowal of offices, in the reward of Virtue and the punishment of Vice. For a long time his moderation gained him great favour from his master and earned him the approval of all the people. And he would have been thus happily celebrated above all others if his government had continued in that fashion.

It happened that a young man of the region, called Vico, violated a virgin, a citizen of Innsbruck, and complaint was made to Juriste. He immediately had the young man arrested, and on his confessing that he had done violence to the maiden, condemned him to death in accordance with the law of that City by which such a criminal was to be beheaded even if he were willing to take his victim for his wife.

The young man had a sister, a virgin not more than eighteen years old, who besides being adorned with extreme beauty, had a very sweet way of speaking and a charming presence together with all feminine goodness. This lady, whose name was Epitia, was smitten with grief on hearing that her brother was condemned to die, and resolved to see whether she could, if not liberate him, at least soften the penalty; and having been, with her brother, under the tutelage of an old man whom their father had kept in the house to teach them both Philosophy (though her brother had followed its precepts but ill) she went to Juriste and prayed him to have compassion on her brother, because of his youth (he was no more than sixteen years old) which made him deserving of pardon, and because of his inexperience of life, and the violent impulse that Love had in his heart. She argued that many wise men held the opinion that adultery committed through the violence of Love, and not undertaken to do injury to a woman's husband, deserved a less penalty than if committed with injurious intent; that the same might be said in her brother's case, who had done the deed for which he was condemned not out of malice but spurred by ardent love; that he was ready and willing to marry the girl, and do whatever else the law might demand; and that although the law might declare that such a settlement did not apply to a man who violated virgins, yet Juriste, being the wise man he was, could mitigate the severity of his attitude, which was more rigorous than Justice demanded; for he was in that City through the authority he held from the Emperor, as the living law, and His Majesty in his equitable fairness showed himself rather merciful than savage in his judgements. She claimed that if the law might be alleviated in any case, it should be in offences done for love, especially where the honour of the injured lady remained unharmed, as it would in her brother's case, who was very willing to make her his wife. She believed that the law had been thus severely framed to strike terror rather than to be rigorously carried out, for it would be (she pleaded) cruel to punish with death a crime which could be honourably and religiously recompensed to the satisfaction of the injured party. Thus she sought, with many other reasons, to induce Juriste to pardon the poor youth.

Juriste, whose ears were no more delighted by Epitia's sweet way of talking than his eyes were charmed by her great beauty, was eager to hear and see more of her; so he asked her to repeat her plea. Taking this for a good augury the lady spoke again with even greater force, and now, overcome by Epitia's graceful speech and rare loveliness he was smitten with lustful desire, till it came into his mind to commit against her the same crime for which he had condemned Vico to death. He said: "Your pleadings have so much helped your brother that whereas his head should have been cut off tomorrow, the execution will be deferred until I have considered the reasons you have given me. If I find that they enable me to give your brother his freedom, I shall give him to you the more willingly because I should have been grieved to see him led out to his death through the rigour of the hard law which has imposed it."

At these words Epitia took good hope and thanked him for showing himself so courteous, telling him that she would be eternally obliged, believing that she would find him no less generous in liberating her brother than she had found him in prolonging his life. She added that she firmly hoped that if he considered the things she had said, he would complete her happiness by freeing Vico. Juriste repeated that he would give them every consideration, and that if at all possible without offending Justice he would not fail to fulfil her wishes.

So Epitia departed, full of hope, and went to her brother whom she informed of what she had done with Juriste and how much hope she had obtained from the first interview. In his desperate situation this was very welcome to Vico, and he prayed her to beg for his release. His sister promised to make every effort to that end.

Juriste meanwhile, in whose mind the form of Epitia had deeply impressed itself, turned all his thoughts — lascivious as they became — towards enjoying her, and he waited eagerly for her to come back and speak to him. After three days she returned and asked him courteously what he had decided. As soon as he saw her Juriste felt himself aflame. He said: "Welcome, lovely maiden; I have not failed to examine diligently all that your arguments could do in your brother's cause, and I have myself searched for others so that you might rest content; but I find that every thing points to his death. For there is a universal law, that when a man sins, not through ignorance, but negligently, his crime cannot be excused, since he ought to know that all men without exception should live virtuously; he who sins in neglect of this principle deserves neither pardon nor pity. Your brother was in this position; he must have been fully aware that anybody who raped a virgin deserved to die; so he must die for it, nor can I reasonably accord him mercy. Nevertheless, for your sake, whom I long to please, if, in your great love for your brother, you are willing to let me enjoy your favours, I am disposed to allow him his life and change the death penalty to one less grave."

At these words Epitia's cheeks blushed fiery red and she replied: "My brother's life is very dear to me, but still dearer is my virtue, and I would much sooner try to save him by giving up my life than by losing my honour. Set aside this dishonourable suggestion of yours; but if by any other means of pleasing you I can win back my brother I shall do so very gladly." "There is no other way," said Juriste, "and you should not behave so coyly, for it might easily happen that our first coming-together would result in your becoming my wife." "I do not wish," said Epitia "to put my honour in danger." "But why in danger?" asked Juriste. "You may well become my wife though now you cannot think it could ever be. Think well upon it, and I shall expect your answer tomorrow." "I can give you my answer at once," she said, "Unless you take me for your wife, if you really mean that my brother's release depends on that, you are throwing your words to the wind." Again Juriste replied that she should think it over before returning with her answer, considering who he was, what power he had, and how useful he could be not only to her but to any of her friends, since he had in his hand both Reason and Authority.

Epitia left him, deeply disturbed, and went to her brother. She described to Vico all that had passed between her and Juriste, affirming that she did not want to lose her honour even to save his life, and tearfully she begged him to prepare himself patiently to endure the lot which either Fate or his own ill-fortune had brought upon him. At this Vico began to weep and entreat his sister not to consent to his death, since she could obtain his release in the manner proposed by Juriste. "Can you wish, Epitia," he said, "to see me with the executioner's axe on my neck, and my head struck off; to see the head of him who came from the same womb, born of the same father, who grew up and was taught side by side with you, thrown on the ground by the executioner? Ah, sister! may the motions of Nature in our blood and the love we have always shared be so strong in you that, since it is in your power to do so, you will free me from so shameful and wretched an end. You can atone for my error; do not be miserly in your aid. Juriste has told you that he might make you his wife, and why should you disbelieve that it would be so? You are very beautiful and adorned with all the graces which Nature can give to a lady. You are noble and charming; you have an admirable gift of speech, virtues any one of which could endear you — I will not say to Juriste only — but to the Emperor of the whole world. You have no right to doubt that Juriste would want you as his wife. Thus you may save your honour, and at the same time save the life of your brother."

Vico wept as he spoke, and Epitia wept with him. She embraced him and did not leave him until, overcome by his tears, she had been persuaded to promise that she would surrender herself to Juriste, provided that he were willing to save Vico's life and confirm her hope of becoming his wife.

Having come to this decision with her brother the maiden went back to Juriste and told him that the hope he had given her of marrying her after their first embraces, and her wish to free Vico not only from death but from any other punishment for his error, had induced her to place herself entirely at his disposal; for both these reasons she was willing to surrender herself, but above all she requested him to promise the safety and release of her brother.

This made Juriste think himself the happiest of men since he would be able to enjoy so lovely and charming a maiden. He told her that he would repeat the promise he had previously made her and that she would receive her brother free from prison the morning after he had been with her. So having dined together Juriste and Epitia went to bed and the false villain took his full pleasure of the lady. But before he went to lie with the virgin, instead of setting Vico free, he ordered him to be beheaded at once. The lady in her anxiety for her brother's release thought only of the hour of daybreak, and never did the sun seem so to delay bringing in the day as on that night.

When morning was come, Epitia, betaking herself from Juriste's embrace, prayed him in the sweetest way to fulfil the hope he had raised of making her his wife, and meanwhile to send Vico to her, freed from prison. He replied that it had been delightful for him to be with her, that he was pleased that she had entertained the hope he had given her, and that he would send her brother to her at home. So saying he called for the gaoler[2] and said: "Go to the prison, remove thence the lady's brother, and take him to her house."

Hearing this Epitia went home full of joy, expecting her brother's liberation. The gaoler had Vico's body put on a bier, set the head at its feet, and covering it with a pall had it carried to Epitia, himself going before. Entering the house he called for the young lady, and "This," he said, "is your brother whom my lord Governor sends you freed from prison." With these words he had the bier uncovered and offered her brother in the way you have heard.

I do not believe that tongue could tell or human mind could comprehend the nature and depth of Epitia's anguish on being thus offered her brother's corpse when she was so joyfully expecting to see him alive and released from

[2] gaoler: jailer

all penalties. I think, ladies, that you will recognize that the wretched lady's pain surpassed any ordinary grief. But she shut it deep in her heart, and whereas any other lady would have begun to weep and cry aloud, she, whom Philosophy had taught how the human soul should bear itself in every kind of fortune, showed herself unmoved. She said to the gaoler: "You will tell your lord — and mine — that I accept my brother in the way in which he has been pleased to send him to me; and although he has not wished to fulfil my desire, I remain content to have fulfilled his; and thus I make his will my own, assuming that what he has done he must have done justly. I send him my respects, offering myself as always ready to do his will."

The gaoler took back Epitia's message to Juriste, telling him that she had shown no sign of discomposure at so horrible a spectacle. Juriste was happy at this, reflecting that he could have had his will of the maid no more satisfactorily even if she had been his wife and if he had sent her Vico alive.

But Epitia, when the gaoler had departed, fell upon the body of her dead brother, weeping bitterly, complaining long and grievously, cursing Juriste's cruelty and her own simplicity in giving herself to him before he had released her brother. Shutting herself up alone in her room, urged on by just anger she began to say to herself: "Will you tolerate it, Epitia, that this ruffian has taken your honour and, after promising to restore your brother alive, has sent him to you dead and in so miserable a state? Will you suffer him to boast of having deceived your simplicity with two such tricks, without giving him condign punishment?" And inciting herself thus to revenge she thought: "My simplicity opened the way for this scoundrel to achieve to the full his dishonest desires. I resolve that his lasciviousness shall give me a way of revenge; and although to seek vengeance will not restore my brother alive, yet it will be a way of removing my vexation of spirit." And in such a turmoil of ideas her mind closed with the thought that Juriste would send for her again to lie with him; going whither she resolved to carry concealed about her a knife and to take the first opportunity she might find of killing him, whether he were awake or asleep; and if she found it possible to cut off his head she would carry it to her brother's tomb and consecrate it to him. But then, thinking it over more maturely she saw that even if she managed to kill the deceiver, it could easily be presumed that she, as a fallen woman and eager therefore for every kind of evil, had done it in an impulse of fury, not because he had failed to keep his word. Then because she had heard how great was the justice of the Emperor (who was then at Villaco) she determined to go and find him, and to complain to his Majesty of the ingratitude and injustice shown her by Juriste, for she felt sure that the best and most just of Emperors would wreak the heaviest of punishments on that false man for his injustice and ingratitude.

So clad in mourning weeds Epitia set out alone on the journey, reached Maximian, sought audience with him, and having obtained it threw herself at his feet, and, suiting her mourning garb with a sad voice she said, "Most Sacred Emperor, I am impelled to appear thus before you by the tyrannous ingratitude and incredible injustice shown me by Juriste, your Imperial Majesty's Governor in Innsbruck, hoping that you will so exercise your Justice that no other wretch will have to suffer such pain as the infinite misery I have received from Juriste by the wrong he has done me — no greater wrong was ever heard — and that no arrogant man will do what he has done to me, that is, miserably assassinated me (if I may be allowed to use that word before your Majesty), so that, however bitterly he be punished for it, that cannot equal the cruel and unheard of shame done me by this wicked man, giving me proof at once of both his injustice and his ingratitude."

And now, bitterly sobbing and sighing, she told his Majesty how Juriste (giving hope of becoming his wife and freeing her brother) had robbed her of her virginity, and then had sent her her brother dead on a bier with his head at his feet; and here she gave so great a cry, and so bedewed her eyes with tears, that she moved the Emperor and the Lords about him so that they stood like men cast down for very pity.

But although Maximian had great compassion on her, nonetheless having given one ear to Epitia (whom at the end of her plaint he made rise to her feet), he kept the other open for Juriste. He sent the lady away to rest and ordered Juriste to be summoned at once, instructing both the messenger and the others who had been present, as they held his favour dear, to say no word about it to Juriste.

Juriste, who never in the least expected that Epitia would go to the Emperor, came quite gaily, and on reaching his Majesty's presence, having made his reverence, asked what was wanted of him. "You shall know that at once," said Maximian, and straightway had Epitia summoned. When Juriste saw that she whom he had so grievously injured was there, he was overcome by conscience, and so lost his self-possession that, his vital spirits ebbing, he began to tremble all over. Seeing this, Maximian knew for certain that the lady had spoken nothing but the truth and turning towards him he said with severity appropriate to so atrocious a thing: "Hear what this young woman complains about you." And he bade Epitia lay bare her complaint. She told them the whole story in due order and at the end, weeping as before, she asked for Justice.

When Juriste heard the accusation he tried to jest and flatter the lady, saying: "I should never have believed that you whom I love so much would have come to accuse me thus before his Majesty." But Maximian would not let him cajole her and said: "This is no time for wooing; answer the accusation which she has made against you." Juriste then abandoned a manner which could do him harm. "It is true," he said, "that I had this woman's brother beheaded for having raped and done violence to a virgin and I did that so as not to violate the sanctity of the law, but (as your Majesty so strongly recommended me) to preserve Justice, since without offence against Justice he could not be allowed to live."

Here Epitia spoke: "If you assert that you sought Justice, why did you promise to give him back to me alive, and why, under that promise, and giving me hope that you would marry me, did you rob me of my virginity? If my brother deserved to feel the severity of Justice for one crime, you then deserved it twice as much." Juriste stood there like a dumb man, whereupon the Emperor: "Does it seem to you, Juriste," he said, "that this was to serve Justice, or rather to have so injured her as almost to slay her by using towards this gentle lady the greatest ingratitude ever used by a scoundrel? But you shall not go scot free, believe me!" Juriste now began to beg for mercy, and Epitia on the other hand to demand Justice again.

Realizing the girl's honesty and Juriste's villainy the Emperor deliberated how best to save her honour and preserve Justice, and having resolved in his own mind what he should do, he desired Juriste to marry Epitia. The girl did not want to consent, saying that she could not believe that she would ever receive from him anything but outrages and betrayals. But Maximian insisted that she accept what he had resolved.

Having married Epitia Juriste believed that he had put an end to his woes, but it turned out otherwise, for as soon as Maximian had given the lady leave to return to her inn, he turned to Juriste who had remained there, and said to him: "Your crimes were two in number, and both very grave; first, to have deflowered that young woman by means of such a trick that it must be said that you have done violence to her; second to have killed her brother contrary to your given word; which also deserves death. Since you were disposed to violate Justice, surely it would have been more fitting to keep faith with his sister, since in your dissolute lust you had promised him to her, rather than to dishonour her and then send him to her, as you did, a corpse. Since you have atoned for the first crime by marrying the lady you violated, so in amends for the second I ordain that as you had her brother's head cut off, so shall your own be."

The depth of Juriste's misery when he heard the Emperor's judgment can be easier imagined than described. He was handed over to the Sergeants to be executed next morning in accordance with the sentence. After this Juriste was fully prepared for his doom, expecting nothing else but death at the hands of the executioner.

Meanwhile however Epitia, who had been so ardently against him, when she heard of the Emperor's sentence was moved by her natural benignity and decided that it would be unworthy of her, since the Emperor had ordered Juriste to be her husband and she had accepted him, if she consented that he be slain on her account. That, she thought, could be attributed rather to a craving for revenge than to a desire for Justice. And so, bending all her thoughts to the salvation of the wretched man she went to the Emperor, and obtaining permission to speak, began thus: "O most sacred Emperor, the injustice and ingratitude shown by Juriste against me induced me to beg for justice against him from your Majesty. And you, with regard to the two crimes he has committed, have proceeded most justly against the one — which was making a treacherous theft of my virginity — by making him take me to wife; and against the other — which was having my brother killed despite his promise to me — by condemning him to death.

"But just as, before I was his wife, I had to desire your Majesty to condemn him to the death which you have most justly assigned him, so now, when according to your pleasure I am bound to Juriste in the sacred bonds of matrimony, I should, if I consented to his death, regard myself as deserving perpetual infamy as a pitiless and cruel woman. That would be a result contrary to your Majesty's intention of preserving both Justice and my honour. Most sacred Majesty, let your good intent find its proper end and my honour remain without blemish. I pray you most humbly and reverently, not to ordain by your Majesty's verdict that the sword of Justice cut so woefully the knot with which you have been pleased to tie me to Juriste. Your Majesty's sentence has given clear proof of your Justice; now may it please you, as I sincerely beg, to manifest your Clemency by giving him to me alive.

"It is, most sacred Majesty, no less praise for him who holds the government of the world as now your Majesty most worthily holds it, to exercise Clemency as to show Justice. For whereas Justice shows that Vices are hateful and punishes them accordingly, Clemency makes a monarch most like to the immortal Gods. If I obtain this singular kindness from your benignity in this gracious act, I, who am your Majesty's most humble servant, shall always devoutly pray God to preserve your Majesty for long and happy years, so that you may long reveal your Justice and Clemency for the benefit of mortals, and to your own honour and immortal glory." And here Epitia put an end to her speech.

It appeared most wonderful to Maximian that she could thrust into oblivion the grave injury she had received from Juriste and pray so warmly for him; and he felt that her generosity merited that he should grant her the life of the wretch who had been so justly condemned to death. So summoning Juriste before him at the very hour when he was expecting to be led out to die, he said to him: "The generosity of Epitia, you evil man, has such power over my will that although your crime deserves to be punished with a double death, not with one alone, she has moved me to spare your life. Your life, I wish you to understand, comes from her; and since she is willing to live with you, joined in the marriage which I ordained, I am willing to let you live with her. But if I shall ever hear that you treat her as anything but a most loving and gracious wife, I shall make you realize what great displeasure that will give me."

With these words the Emperor, taking Epitia by the hand, gave her to Juriste. Together she and Juriste gave thanks to his Majesty for his graciousness and favour towards them; and Juriste, realizing the extent of Epitia's generosity to him, held her ever dear; so that she lived happily with him for the rest of her days.

→ CHRISTINE DE PISAN

From The Book of the City of Ladies   *1431*

Christine de Pisan (1364–1431) was born in Venice, but lived most of her life in France. She arrived at the court of Charles V with her father, where she was given a classical education in ancient languages and literatures. The death of her husband when she was just twenty-five, along with the deaths of her father and her patron, King Charles, left her with three small children, a mother, and a niece to support. Although she was offered places at other courts, she refused to leave France, and instead determined to support herself with writing, which she did successfully for the rest of her life. She was prolific, publishing dozens of books and uncounted poems, ballads, and songs, many of which were extremely popular. She gained a reputation for wisdom and eloquence, and many of her contemporaries compared her to the great male rhetoricians and philosophers of the ancient world. De Pisan often wrote about the condition of women, defending their intellectual and moral capacity. Her *Book of the City of Ladies* is a collection of stories about female heroines of the past meant to inspire women with evidence of their sex's illustrious history.

Christine de Pisan. *The Book of the City of Ladies*, trans. Brian Anslay (London: Henry Pepwell, 1521).

PART III, CHAPTER 3

Of Saint Katherine the Holy Virgin.

To make company with ye virgin queen of heaven — the princess of the City of Ladies — we must lodge with her the blessed virgins and holy ladies in showing how God hath proved the kind of women, by that the same wise[1] that he given unto men he hath given unto women, for to understand in their young and tender age for to be constant and strong in suffering horrible martyrdoms for the holy law, the which been crowned in glory of whom the fair lives been of good example to hear to every woman above all other wisdom. And therefore they shall be ye superlative degree of our City. And first as a right excellent [example] ye blessed Katherine which was daughter of King Costes of Alexandria. This blessed virgin was left to be heir of her father in the age of eighteen years. And notably she governed her and her heritage. She was a Christian woman and all given to God, refusing all other marriages. It happened that in to the city of Alexandria was come the emperor Maxencius the which on a day of great solemnity of his gods had made to array great apparel to make solemn sacrifice. Katherine being in her palace heard the noise of beasts that were arrayed to do sacrifice and great noise of instruments and, as she had sent to know what it was. And it was reported to her that the emperor was in the temple to do sacrifice. Anon she went and began to correct the emperor of his error by many wise words. And as she was a great clerk and had learned sciences she began to prove by good reasons of philosophy that there was but one God, maker of all things, and that he ought to be worshipped and none other. When the emperor heard this maiden that was so noble and of so great authority thus speak — and who was so fair — he was all amarveled[2] and knew not what to say but intended to behold her. So he sent all about to seek philosophers in all the land of Egypt. So there came before him fifty philosophers which held then right evil content when they knew the cause wherefore they were brought thither, and said that little wit had moved them to travel from so far countries to dispute with a maiden. And, to tell shortly, when the day of their dispute yon was come, the blessed Katherine led them forth so with arguments that they were all overcome and could not foil her questions, for which the emperor was passing wrath with them, but all that availed nothing. For by the grace of God and by the holy words of the virgin they were all converted and confessed the name of Jesus Christ, for the which spite the emperor

---

[1] wise: fashion. [2] amarveled: in awe.

made them all to be burnt and the holy maiden comforted them in their martyrdom and assured them to be received in perpetual glory and prayed God that he would keep them in the very faith. And so by her they were put in the number of the blessed martyrs. And such a miracle God showed them that the fire never hurt their bodies, nor their clothes, but that they bode[3] all whole after the fire was done without losing of any hair of their heads, but it seemed that all were alive. The tyrant Maxencius which greatly coveted the holy virgin Katherine for her beauty, began to flatter her that she should turn to his will. But when he saw that it availed nothing he turned him to his menacings and then to torment and made her to be beaten cruelly and after to put her in prison without visiting of any persons for the space of twelve days without meat or drink, trying to have made her die of hunger. But the angels of our lord were with her which comforted her and after the twelve days she was brought before the emperor, and he saw her more fresh and whole than she was before and trowed[4] that she had been visited. So he commanded the keepers of the prison to be tormented, but Katherine, which had pity on them, affirmed that she had no comfort save only from heaven. The emperor knew not what hard torments he might make to torment her. And by the counsel of his provost, he let make wheels full of razors which turned one against another and whatever was in the midst was all cut off, and between these wheels he made pure Saint Katherine, all naked, which [who] always worshipped God with joined hands. Then the angels of God came and defended her, which broke the wheels with so great strength that all the tormentors were slain with them. And when the emperor's wife understood these marvels that God made for Saint Katherine she was converted and blamed the emperor of that that he did, and then she went and visited the holy virgin in the prison and prayed her that she would pray to God for her. For the which spite the emperor made to torment his wife and to draw off her paps and the virgin said to her: "Doubt ye not ye torments noble queen, for this day thou shall be received in the joy without end." And then the emperor made his wife to be beheaded and a great multitude of people that were connected. The emperor required Katherine that she would be his wife and when he saw that she was refusing to all his petitions went and gave his sentence that she would be beheaded. And she made her prayer, praying for all them that had remembrance on her passion and for them that called her name in their tribulations that God might be their help and succor. A voice came from heaven which said that her prayer was heard. So she made an end of her martyrdom and instead of blood there came milk out of her body. And the angels took her holy body

---

[3] **bode:** remained.   [4] **trowed:** believed.

and bore it to the Mount Sinai which is twenty days journey from thence. And there they buried her at the which tomb God hath done many miracles, which I let pass for shortness. And of the same tomb there runneth oil which healeth many sick men and God anon after punished the emperor right horribly.

TARRANT HOUSE CONVENT

From The Nun's Rule

c. 1300

The Nun's Rule, originally the Ancren Wisse, was a medieval (thirteenth or fourteenth century, but possibly based on an even older text) guide for cloistered or secluded nuns, written for a small community of religious women at Tarrant House in Dorset, England. It is a frank discussion of spiritual practices and the need for restraint and self-abnegation, but also deals with the practical life of an anchorite, including domestic arrangements, accounts, and so on.

2: Of Speech

Speaking and tasting are both in the mouth, as sight is in the eyes; but we shall let tasting alone until we speak of your food, and treat, at present, of speaking, and thereafter of hearing, of both in common, in some measure, as they go together.

First of all, when you have to go to your parlour window, learn from your maid who it is that is come; for it may be some one whom you ought to shun; and, when you must needs go forth, make the sign of the cross carefully on your mouth, ears, and eyes, and on your breast also, and go forth in the fear of God to a priest. Say first, "Confiteor," and then "Benedicite,"[1] which he ought to say; hear his words and sit quite still, that, when he parteth from you, he may not know either good or evil of you, nor know any thing either to praise or to blame in you. Some one is so learned and of such wise speech, that she would have him to know it, who sits and talks to him and gives him word for word, and becomes a preceptor, who should be an anchoress,[2] and teaches him who is come to teach her; and would, by her own account, soon be celebrated and known among the wise. — Known she

[1] **Confiteor . . . Benedicite:** introduction and conclusion of confession. [2] **Preceptor . . . anchoress:** she becomes an instructor instead of a recluse.

The Nun's Rule or the Ancrene Riwle, modernized by James Morton, introduction by Abbot Gasquet (New York: Cooper Square Publications, Inc., 1966).

is well,[3] for, from the very circumstance that she thinketh herself to be reputed wise, he understands that she is a fool; for she huntest after praise and catches reproach. For, at last, when he is gone away he will say, "This anchoress is a great talker." Eve, in paradise, held a long conversation with the serpent, and told him all the lesson that God had taught her and Adam concerning the apple; and thus the fiend, by her talk, understood, at once, her weakness, and found out the way to ruin her. Our lady, Saint Mary,[4] acted in a quite different manner. She told the angel no tale, but asked him briefly that which she wanted to know. Do you, my dear sisters, imitate our lady, and not the cackling Eve. Wherefore, let an anchoress, whatsoever she be, keep silence as much as ever she can and may. Let her not have the hen's nature. When the hen has laid, she must needs cackle. And what does she get by it? Straightway comes the chough[5] and robs her of her eggs and devours all that of which she should have brought forth her live birds. And just so the wicked chough, the devil, beareth away from the cackling anchoresses, and swalloweth up, all the good they have brought forth, and which ought, as birds, to bear them up toward heaven, if it had not been cackled. The poor peddler makes more noise to cry his soap than a rich mercer[6] all his valuable wares. Of a spiritual man in whom you place confidence, as you may do, it is good that you ask counsel, and that he teach you a safe remedy against temptations; and in confession shew him, if he will hear you, your greatest and vilest sins, that he may pity you, and out of compassion cry internally to Christ to have mercy upon you, and have you often in his mind and in his prayers. "But be aware and on your guard," saith our Lord, "for many come to you clothed in lambs' fleece, and are raging wolves."[7] Believe secular men little, religious still less. Desire not too much their acquaintance. Eve spoke with the serpent without fear. Our lady was afraid of speaking with Gabriel.

Without a witness, of man or of woman, who may hear you, speak not with any man often or long; and even though it be of confession, in the same house, or where he may look at you, let there be a third person present; except the same third person upon another occasion should fail thee. This is not said in respect of you, dear sisters, nor of any such as you; — no, but because the truth is disbelieved, and the innocent often belied, for want of a witness. Men readily believe the evil, and the wicked gladly utter falsehoods against the good. Some unhappy creature, when she said that she was at

---

[3] Known . . . well: she is well understood.   [4] Saint Mary: the Virgin Mary used as an example of the appropriately silent woman, see Mark 16:8; Luke 1:26–38, 2:49, and 2:51.   [5] chough: crow.   [6] mercer: fabric merchant.   [7] "But be aware . . . wolves": Matthew 7:15.

confession, has confessed herself strangely: therefore the good ought always to have a witness, for two reasons especially: the one is, that the envious may not calumniate[8] them, so that the witness may not be able to prove the accusers false; the other is, to give an example to others, and to deprive the evil anchoress of that unhappy false pretence which I spoke of.

Hold no conversation with any man out of a church window, but respect it for the sake of the holy sacrament which ye see therein, and sometimes take your woman to the window of the house; the other men and women to the window of the parlour, to speak when necessary; nor ought ye but at these two windows . . .

Our dear lady, St. Mary, who ought to be an example to all women, was of so little speech that we do not find anywhere in Holy Writ that she spake more than four times. But, in compensation for her seldom speaking, her words were weighty, and had much force. Her first words that we read of were when she answered the angel Gabriel, and they were so powerful that as soon as she said "Behold the handmaid of the Lord; be it unto me according to thy word";[9] at this word, the Son of God, and very God, became man; and the Lord, whom the whole world could not contain, inclosed himself within the womb of the maiden Mary. Her next words were spoken when she came and saluted Elizabeth, her kinswoman. And what power, thinkest thou, was manifested in those words? What? That a child, which was St. John, began to play in his mother's womb when they were spoken. The third time that she spoke was at the wedding; and there, through her prayer, was water changed into wine. The fourth time was when she had missed her son and afterwards found him. And how great a miracle followed those words! That God Almighty bowed himself to a man! to a carpenter, and to a woman, and followed them, as subject to them, whither soever they would! Take heed now, and learn diligently from this, how great efficacy there is in speaking seldom.

---

[8] caluminate: slander.   [9] "Behold . . .": Luke 1:38; 2:51.

→ FRANCIS DUPUIS

The Life and Legend of the Lady Saint Clare 1563

Clare of Asissi (1194–1253) was born to a wealthy family, but upon hearing the teachings of Francis of Assisi, devoted herself to a life of poverty and seclusion from the world, founding the Order of the Poor Clares, and becoming the first abbess of the monastery at San Damiano. She resisted not only family pressure, but the will of two popes, Count Ugolino, later Gregory IX, who initially attempted to bring her religious house under the control of the Benedictine rule, and Innocent IV, who likewise tried to relax the order's strict observance of absolute poverty. Two of Clare's miracles occurred in the defense of her house from the invading armies of Frederick II in 1234. The first attack saw Clare rising from her sickbed to repel the soldiers scaling the walls of her house. A light from her ciborium (a gold-lined vessel used to hold the sacrament, which she likely picked up to use as a symbol of her faith), it was claimed, blinded the soldiers, who fell in retreat. During a second attack, Clare's prayers were believed to have brought a torrential storm that made an assault impossible. She was canonized in 1255, only two years after her death, for these and other miracles, and for her remarkable success in extending her order far and wide through Europe.

How She Lived in the House of Her Father.

When she was still both young and little, this Clare began to live clearly in the shadow of the world, and as she grew older to shine in prowess of good deeds. Her heart was so docile that she kept in it all the good lessons that her mother taught her. This was no marvel, for the Holy Spirit was in her and embraced her heart. In very truth her body was so pure that it showed plainly it was a vessel full of grace. Her hands were so open to the poor that out of the goods which abounded in the house of her father she relieved the sufferings of many poor folk. And thus from her childhood pity and compassion grew in her heart and her thoughts. For the sufferings of the poor grieved her much. She loved holy prayer so much, and felt so often the sweet fragrance thereof, that little by little she attained to the heavenly life; and for that she had no paternosters[1] on which she could make her devotions, she made heaps of little stones, and thus paid her devotions to Our Lord in orderly manner. And when holy love began first to weigh on her heart, the love and the flower of worldly things seemed to her but smoke and a false painting of short durance, and for this it seemed to her they should be

---

[1] paternosters: rosaries.

Francis Dupuis, *La vie et la legende de madame saincte Claire* (1563), trans. by Charlotte Balfour (London: Longmans, Green, 1910), 39–49, 63–65.

despised. And when the Holy Spirit had taught her, worldly love became to her a hard thing, and it did not draw her, but rather wearied her. She wore a hair shirt secretly beneath her robes, and thus she showed herself in worldly dress without, but within her heart was clothed with God. And when her friends desired greatly to marry her, she would in no wise consent, because she wished to preserve her virginity for Our Lord. Thus she seemed a chamber full of good teaching and of good, sweet-smelling spices, although she knew not of it. But the fragrance was so great in her that it was felt by others. The neighbours praised her often, and the fame of the neighbours' praise and of these good deeds was spread amongst the people.

How She Became Acquainted with Master St. Francis.

When she heard tell of the great fame of Master St. Francis, who was like a man newly renewed with new virtues, and was teaching to the world the way of perfection, by the guidance of the Holy Spirit she desired much to see and hear him. And St. Francis, too, taught by the Holy Spirit, when he heard the fame of this most gracious maiden, desired no less to speak with her; for he would willingly rive[2] her from the world and steal her from earthly things, and give back such noble prey to Our Lord. He went to her and she to him often, and so discreetly, according to the will of God, did they visit each other, that no one perceived it, nor could any rightly think or speak ill of their meetings. For when she went to the man of God, St. Francis, to hear his words so ardent and burning, whose works seemed such works as were beyond the power of all, she went by a very secret way, and took one only companion who was her loyal friend. Then did Master St. Francis admonish her with lively words to despise the world and the deceitful vanity and the dry hope that is in it. And he showed her gently the words of Our Blessed Saviour and Redeemer Jesus Christ. And he admonished her that she should keep her precious virginity and that she should be the spouse of Him who for love of us had willed to become mortal man. And how can I tell you rightly of it all? So well did St. Francis admonish her, her dear father as well as her faithful counsellor, that she consented. And soon she grew to know God and His goodness, and despised like filth the world in comparison with the joys of Paradise. And it was as though her heart began to be completely arrested by the good things of Paradise. And when God had lit within her His holy fire she despised entirely the vain glory and vanity of this world so much that no merriment nor joys of the world

[2] rive: tear, remove.

could hold back or mingle with her good intention. All fleshly delights were hideous to her. And she proposed within her heart never again to have any earthly pleasure, but to make of her body a temple to Our Saviour. And thenceforward she strove with great strength so that she might be the spouse of the King of Paradise. Then she put herself entirely under the counsels of St. Francis, and established him for always as her director and counsellor. And from thenceforward she followed altogether the counsels of St. Francis. And she kept in her heart all the holy words she spoke of sweet Jesus. And although she wished to gain Jesus Christ she wore with great sorrow all the beauty and ornaments of the world. And all that pleases in the world and all the beauty seemed to her like filth.

How St. Francis Took Her out of the World and Put Her into Religion.

St. Francis hastened to take this Clare out of this world full of darkness so that the ways of this world should not corrupt her youth and her good thought. One day before Palm Sunday came this maiden, who became the servant of St. Francis, to him and consulted him much about her conversion when she should leave the world. And St. Francis commanded her that on Palm Sunday she should array herself with palms and ornaments, and that the night after she should tear herself from the world, and be converted with tears to the death and passion of Our Saviour and Redeemer Jesus Christ.

And on the Sunday the maiden went adorned and resplendent amongst the other ladies to the minster. And it happened as though according to a prophecy, for when the others hastened each to take their reeds, this Clare, who was gentle, did not move from her place. And the Bishop came down the two steps and came to her and put a palm into her hand. And she, who desired to flee the world and obey the command of St. Francis, the night after arrayed herself and departed with good and honest companions.

But she wished not to go by a frequented place, so she entered by a door much barred and obstructed with stones. And God gave her such marvellous strength that she opened it with her own hands. And thus she left the city of her friends and relations, and went to the monastery of Our Lady of the Little Portion, there where the Brothers Minor lived then with Master St. Francis. And when she came they received her with great joy. She threw away all the pleasures and lusts of the world, and gave to the world the word of refusal, and bent her head to the brothers for the cutting of her hair, and left all her elegances. For it would not have been right that the last order of virgins should begin to flourish elsewhere but in the monastery of the

Blessed Virgin, Mother of God. And also this was the place where began the order of the Brothers Minor under Master St. Francis, from which one may see that it is the sacred spot where the Virgin Mary, Mother of Mercy, brought to birth one and the other religious order. As soon as the most humble handmaid Clare had taken the habit of penitence before the altar of the Blessed Virgin Mary, and had become the Spouse of Jesus Christ, then Master St. Francis took her to a Church of St. Paul until that God had provided a place where she could live beseemingly.

How She Maintained Herself
against the Assaults of Her Relations.

When the news came to her relations their hearts were tormented, and they maligned her good intention, and all ran together to the place where the virgin was, to tempt her, a thing which could not be. First they wished to drag her out by force, and then afterwards by evil counsel they promised her many things, and prayed her to leave this folly, which set not a good example and appertained not to her lineage. But she clung to the cloths on the altar of her heavenly Father, and showed to them her head all shaven, and affirmed that never would she depart from the service of God. And the more her parents strove to draw her away from her good purpose the greater grew her love of doing right. For the love she had for God gave her grace to suffer peaceably all the cruel things they said to her. And she was tormented by her worldly friends in order to draw her from her good purpose. And they ran together to the place where the virgin was. But for all that her good purpose and courage were not moved nor her fervour; thus she endured words of blame and enclosed her heart in holy thoughts and good hope so that her parents left her in that country.

And after a little she went to the church of St. Angelo in Panso. And when she saw that there she could not have perfect peace, she went to the church of St. Damiano by the counsel of Master Saint Francis. And her mind was possessed with the thought that never for anything she had had, nor for any other thing, would she remove from this place. And it was this church that St. Francis wished so much to repair that he gave to the priest his money to do it. Here he was praying once to Our Saviour when from a cross there came a voice which said to him: "Francis, repair My house which is thus destroyed, as thou seest." In this little house which seemed like a cloister the Lady Saint Clare enclosed herself. And for her the tempest of the world ceased, and she secluded her body as long as she lived. She may be called a silver dove, for thus does the dove make her nest and her walls, and thus did she build herself in with other such little ones, there where she brought forth to God a great company of virgins. And she established her monastery and there founded her order of Poor Ladies in the way of penitence. Her first aim was that those who came after her should know her path and her footsteps. In this narrow cloister she lived in great austerity and great discipline for the space of forty years. And she mortified here the beauty of her body. She was all full of virtues, and Holy Church was filled with the odour of her good life. Well may we say she lived gloriously who sees how many souls she gained to Our Lord. . . .

SOME MIRACLES OF HER PRAYERS, AND FIRST CONCERNING THE SARACENS WHO WERE PUT TO FLIGHT.

Now it is right and reasonable we should tell you of the number of great marvels which God did through her and by the prayers of the Lady St. Clare, who was true and loyal and worthy of great honours. That tempest which was at the time of Frederick the Emperor,[3] by which the Church was in such torment that she had much to suffer in diverse parts of the world, was more heavy in the land of Spoleto than in any other part. And by the command of the Emperor there were established armies and a great company of Christians, Saracens,[4] and archers, like a swarm of flies to destroy many people, and with them castles and cities. The people ran as though mad to the gates of Assisi, and soon the Saracens, full of cruelty and all malice, sought nothing but to shed the blood of the Christians. They came even to the cloisters of the holy Poor Ladies of St. Damiano. The holy ladies were in such great fear that their hearts trembled within them, and they ran lamenting to their holy mother. And she, who was sick, caused herself to be taken to the gates and set before the enemy. And she made them bring before her the body of Our Lord, which was in a monstrance devoutly set and kept. And this holy lady came before Him in prayer and said to Him with tears: "Ah, sweet Lord God, doth it please Thee that these who serve Thee and who have given themselves to Thee, whom I keep for the love of Thee, should fall into the hands of the heathen? O sweet Jesus, I pray thee succour Thy handmaids, for I cannot in this moment succour them." And Our Lord, by a new and special grace, sent her a voice like the voice of a child which said: "I will keep you always." "Ah, sweet Lord God," said she,

---

[3] **Frederick the Emperor:** Frederick II (1194–1250), German King and Holy Roman Emperor, who repeatedly warred with the papacy and was excommunicated twice.   [4] **Saracens:** a general term for Arabs or Moors. Frederick II's Sicilian origins made him more familiar with and more willing to use Muslim warriors to prosecute his wars with Pope Innocent IV.

FIGURE 16 *St. Clare on Her Deathbed Sees a Company of Virgins Wearing Crowns,*
from Andraes Collaert, Icones Sanctae Clarae *(Antwerp, 1630).*

"keep this city, for it gives us our living for the love of Thee." And Our Lord
answered: "The city will take no harm, but always I will defend it." And
when she rose from her prayer, the saint wept and comforted her daughters
full sweetly and said to them: "I command you, sweet sisters, that you be
comforted and have true faith and true hope in God, for the Saracens will

do you no harm." And the Saracens were so much afraid that they fled hastily outside the walls inside which they had entered, and were thus routed by the virtue of the prayer of the virgin Clare. Then she commanded to all those that had heard the voice of which I have told you that they should tell it to no man nor woman in any manner so long as she lived.

CHAPTER 3

The Underworld

Although *Measure for Measure* is set in Vienna, its original audiences would have recognized not a foreign world of crime, prostitution, and punishment, but their own local surroundings: the same neighborhood that housed Shakespeare's Globe theater and many other forms of mass entertainment, such as bear-baiting, cock-fighting, bull-baiting, or fencing, was also the neighborhood occupied by brothels, taverns, thieves, pickpockets, bawds, johns, and not a few prisons. The physical geography of this area is described in John Stow's *Survey of London*, which notes that the "Stews," or red light district, is of long duration and has been treated with some degree of tolerance in most ages. Created during Roman times as the location of soldiers' and citizens' bathhouses, the Stews (the name for which may derive either from variants on the word "estues" or estuary, or from "styes") evolved in Southwark, a city suburb where the Roman legions were quartered. Over the centuries, Southwark retained its position as a marginal neighborhood, just across the river from the center of London — a geographical position that had psychological and social consequences, ensuring its association with escape and a kind of rough freedom from restraint. Bankside, the area along the banks of the river Thames, became known as "The Bears' College" (a reference to bear-baiting, but also to the treatment of newcomers) for the education it gave all frequenters in sinful pursuits.

Walking through the streets on the way to see a play at the Globe or a bull-baiting at the arena next door, the Londoner of the early seventeenth century would have passed block after block of "bawdy houses," many secretly owned by famous figures of the day (Burford 187). Development of Bankside began in earnest in 1570 with increases in London's population, and continued throughout the seventeenth century. Taverns and brothels were attractive investments for landlords, while the availability of land in Southwark made the location suitable for the new amphitheaters; as a result, the theatrical establishment of Shakespeare's day was closely associated with its neighborhood and its neighbors, often in practical ways — both Philip Henslowe, a well-known producer, and Edward Alleyn, the celebrated actor, owned properties that housed brothels on Bankside.

Mistress Overdone, the brothel madam introduced in act 1 of *Measure for Measure*, finds herself shut out of her usual business by Angelo's orders, and forced to turn to other options. According to Elbow, she now "professes a hothouse" (2.1.60) or bathhouse; there was an understood connection between the Stews' historical use as a bathing area and its use for the procurement of sexual pleasure, as well as a connection to the contemporary notion that sweating or "stewing" was a possible cure for the pox or venereal disease (and the hothouse thus the place where one both contracted and remedied the same disease). As did her predecessors in the Stews for centuries before, Mrs. Overdone faces an attempt by the government to control her business, in addition to the usual daily challenges of running a brothel: "What with the war, what with the sweat, what with the gallows, and what with poverty, I am custom-shrunk," she complains, only to hear from Pompey that "All houses in the suburbs of Vienna must be plucked down" (1.2.65–66; 77). Stow records that just such an attempt at regulating prostitution occurred in the reign of Henry II, with the establishment of laws regarding the enticing of custom (that is, procurement), the admission of "any woman of religion, or any man's wife," and other daily aspects of the trade. Henry VIII also tried to "pluck down" the brothels, but the effort was doomed. According to Pompey, the Duke's and Angelo's similar repression of prostitution is also unlikely to succeed: while the suburbs are to be purged, the city brothels will continue to stand, and serve for "seed" to a new generation of suburban stew-houses. Nor need Mistress Overdone worry, since she may simply become a tavern keeper for a time, without ceasing her real business: taverns were notorious hangouts for pimps and the lower class of streetwalker, and so when Pompey advises her "you need not change your trade; I'll be your tapster" (1.2.87–88), he promises to continue as her procurer in what is essentially a front for a new form of the same game.

Southwark's prison was the Clink, which according to Stow was nicely located to receive those who "should brabble, frey, or break the peace on the said bank, or in the brothel houses" (see p. 275). Rather than a world removed from and geographically distant from the underworld of crime, the prison was fully integrated into the community it "served." Early modern prisons were described in several popular texts as whole cities or communities in themselves, mimicking the attributes of the world outside their walls. Geoffrey Mynshul, writing about a debtors' prison, calls it "a *Microcosmus*, a little world of woe," and a "little Commonwealth, although little wealth be common" in it. Such writers often emphasized the paradox of distance involved in going to prison by writing their tales as if they were travel narratives, to an "infernall iland" (Mynshul 13) or a far-off kingdom, despite being right in the middle of London. Thus William Fennor's *The Counter's Commonwealth, or A Voyage Made to an Infernal Island Discovered by Many Captains, Seafaring Men, Gentlemen, Merchants, and Other Tradesmen* (1617) (see p. 302) borrows its title's conventions from the literature of travel and discovery in the late sixteenth and early seventeenth centuries, but in fact belongs with the popular literature describing the lives, language, and practices of rogues, thieves, and vagabonds.

William Fennor was a minor poet with some connection to the stage; he apparently wrote his account of the Wood Street Counter (a sheriff's prison for debtors — "counter" comes from the term "comptor," referring to bill payment) while residing there temporarily in 1616. While Fennor's book was meant as light entertainment, feeding the literate public's endless appetite for insights into the seedy underworld of London, it also launched a serious attack on the abuses commonly found in prisons of all sorts. For some with money, debtors' prison could serve as a refuge from enemies or even from the law itself, but in general conditions were deplorable, and few had the funds to support themselves well. The most impoverished could die of starvation if they had no friends to send them money; the wealthiest could offer enough bribes to secure favors and even occasional release time, making their prison time resemble life outside. Fennor offers a portrait of prison life in which the prison becomes a semi-isolated "commonwealth" all to itself, with its own social distinctions, trades, characters, and so on, a school in which the cleverest students learn to make their stay comfortable and their return to the society more profitable. If we can extrapolate from Fennor's tale to Shakespeare's play, then we might imagine that the world of the Duke's prison works in a similar fashion, with its own long-time residents (Barnardine), its corrupt officials (Pompey, undoubtedly, although the Duke notes that the Provost himself is "gentle"), and its scholars to be instructed (Claudio?).

The keepers of this strange land were a motley and largely unsavory bunch: prison wardens commonly took bribes, shortchanged the prisoners' fare for profit, and engaged in as much vice as they could get away with. Although at least one writer claimed that "our jailers are guilty of felony by an old law of the land if they torment any prisoner" and bragged that English legal punishment was more enlightened than that of any other country, the majority would have disagreed with him (Harrison 187). In Robert Speed's *The Counter-Scuffle*, prisoners revolt against intolerable conditions: a food fight at the Counter is put down, but because of its violence no one will go near the prison to clean (see illustration on p. 311). Speed's first poem is followed, appropriately enough, by "The Counter Rat," detailing the results of the squalor the prisoners must endure. He makes his point clear, however, by naming as the biggest rats the two-legged variety, recounting how these were "caught, how mous'd." Prisoners often tried to buy their food through windows to the outside streets; when the King's Bench prison marshal walled the window through which trade was conducted, prisoners rioted (Salgado 182). If prisoners could not pay for food or a better place to sleep, as Fennor recounts, they ended up in the "The Hole," a dark, dank narrow space where inmates slept on the floor without bedding. Mynshul calls the prisoner an "impatient patient, lingring under the rough hands of a cruel physician," and the keepers "insinuating knaves and mercenary rascals" (38). Newgate prison, where felons and those suspected or convicted of violent crimes were housed, was supposed to be especially poorly administered; the Counter's conditions, awful as Fennor makes them sound, might well have been better than in other prisons. There were some attempts at reform: Stow notes that the Counter at Bread Street had to be moved to Wood Street due to abuses of its keeper, Richard Husband, who "dealt, for his own advantage, hard with the prisoners under his charge" (31) for which he was in turn sent to Newgate. The prison house was, however, his by lease, and so had to be moved and re-established elsewhere. Husband also allowed "thieves and strumpets" to buy a bed in his prison for four-pence to avoid being taken up during searches (131). Prisoners of the Fleet prison complained to the city officials, accusing their warden Joachim Newton of having leased the feeding of prisoners to a couple of extortionists (Newton was also later accused of murder); another warden actually made a special door for his prison through which prisoners who had bribed him for their release could pass (Salgado 174). Such were the wardens entrusted with guarding and caring for the prisoners, and reform measures like the 1601 Poor Law, which levied a tax to support the upkeep of poor prisoners, could do little to remedy the situation. As the Duke remarks in *Measure for Measure*, it is "seldom when / The steelèd jailer is the friend of men" (4.2.70–71).

Shakespeare's plays reflect the low opinion of all law enforcement held by many at the time. Constable Elbow is true to a common literary character type for being bungling and ignorant, if not for the specific trial he suffers with his roving wife. Like Constables Dogberry in *Much Ado about Nothing* and Dull in *Love's Labors Lost*, Elbow is prone to malapropisms — he refers to his wife whom he "detests," and claims Pompey and Froth are "respected" fellows — which must be puzzled out by the higher-class characters in the play. Elbow's situation in itself reflects on his impotence: his wife has, after all, been caught in a bawdy house with Froth.

The main reason representatives of law enforcement were often held in low esteem was that they were unpaid amateur members of the community. While in rural areas, amateur "ward watches" (local preventive patrol units) or "hue and cry" (the notion that all citizens were responsible for aiding in the capture of criminals) might have been quite effective, London was a large and mobile city — in some areas as much as two-thirds of the population was originally from towns and communities at least fifty miles outside the city (McMullan 79) — and so the traditional forms of crime fighting did not work. Twenty-six local ward units were responsible for policing London; the constables serving each were burdened by a host of duties: in addition to enforcing vagrancy laws, keeping the peace, and overseeing a host of civil issues like property disputes, building permits, and so on, constables were also charged with ensuring that apprenticeships were administered properly, mediating wage disputes, and fulfilling myriad other duties. Only gradually did a core group of professional watchmen evolve, and they were often drawn from the ranks of domestic servants and others of like status, giving them little real power over those above them on the social ladder. City marshals were appointed to serve as a centralized body to govern crime fighting in London; but marshals were prone to corruption, since their positions were a source of financial and political patronage that could be bartered and sold. Even those who were honest had to rely on a deficient constabulary, a suspicious and sometimes obstructive public, and vague rules about jurisdiction. James Gryffon's *Song of a Constable* (see p. 314) presents the complaint of an honest and dutiful constable faced with these handicaps. His parish masters "grutch / and twit him" when he tries to do his job; in attempting to apprehend criminals and enforce the law he may find himself "taken up" to be charged and tried. In the courts, "They'll punish the leastest, and favor the greatest, / nought against *them* proceed" (p. 317). The song concludes that only "able men" should become constables, because "knaves and fools in authority do / but themselves and their country disgrace" (p. 317). Clearly Pompey's elevation from arrested bawd to official and paid executioner in *Measure for Measure* is the kind of law enforcement decision that prompted Gryffon's plea.

Social and Moral Geography

The idea of a criminal "class" that is poor, lives on the fringe of society (or in the city's downtrodden center), and is relatively constant is a modern invention (Sharpe 94–120; McMullen 1–6). As Geoffrey Mynshul points out, "Men of all conditions are forced into prison, as all rivers run into the sea" (38), suggesting that the early modern criminal underworld could be inhabited by a fluctuating constituency. There were, however, various criminal archetypes familiar to audiences of the time, and associated assumptions about how and why they came to practice illicit professions. England's hierarchical social structure bolstered the sense that those at the top of society were exempt from scrutiny and punishment, while the poor, especially those who were itinerant or could not be identified as under the control of a "master," were the targets of increasingly severe legal oppression. While radical changes in England's economy and social organization guaranteed that there was an explosion of mobile poor labor, many of whom gravitated toward the cities, fear of civil disturbance and unrest inspired a proliferation of legislation against the poor. Between 1530 and 1572, statutes requiring violent punishment of "masterless men" were established, in some cases allowing for them to be whipped, chained, even branded, and made slaves for life. In 1572 some relief was offered by laws that distinguished between "sturdy beggars" and "respectable" poor (McMullen 38–39). Later laws in 1597 and 1601 modified but did not substantially change these laws. One result was that many more kinds of offenses were made punishable, especially those associated with traveling in search of work; other offenses were upgraded in the type of punishment they required. The entire populace was affected by these laws, some practically, in that they became targets of criminal prosecution, but most psychologically, in that they began to imagine a great mass of potentially disruptive, certainly criminal poor subjects roaming the highways, fields, and city streets of England.

Cony-catchers (a "cony" is a rabbit; the term thus indicates a "snare-setter" or con man, with an additional reference to the word "cunny" or pudendum, and its suggestion of trickery by prostitutes) were the topic of many warning treatises and pamphlets, which we might suspect were as much read for a glimpse into this conniving and clever segment of society as for genuine information. Robert Greene's popular works on the subject offered humorous tales of villains and their marks, giving definitions of the underworld's slang and sounding fair warning to innocents. Thomas Harman's *A Caveat for Common Cursitors, Vulgarly Called Vagabonds* describes "Upright men," "rogues," "doxies," and "bawdy baskets," among other mainly roving opportunistic criminals. (See p. 282.) Bawdy baskets, for instance, were men or women who sold lace, pins, and other sundries from baskets door-to-door; some (but not all) were on the lookout for potential sexual liaisons or quick theft. A high degree of physical mobility made it more likely that legitimate workers looking for new jobs mingled on the roads with actual criminals; for some, a blend of legal and illegal occupations might have been the norm. All, however, were tarred with the same brush, named vagabonds or masterless men, and subject to severe punishments if accused.

More serious were England's infamous highwaymen, also the subject of popular interest. Duels and other forms of violence among the upper classes and gentry brought some sons of wealthy and powerful families through the prison gates. There were murderers in plenty, often sensationalized in ballads, plays and broadsides. And, of course, there were prostitutes, both streetwalkers and the higher-class brothel-kept women. What is significant to our understanding of Shakespeare's audience is the pervasive fascination with all these types of criminals — the hunger for inside information, for "true to life" depictions, for juicy stories. Any member of the audience at *Measure for Measure*, whether highborn or low, whether literate or not, could have been counted on to know something (or to want to know something) about crime and criminals.

While in retrospect historians are able to retrieve a picture of the social and economic changes that created the expectation of crime and the conditions that might have encouraged it, there was no attempt at the time to understand crime as the product of social upheaval and poverty; apart from some few highwaymen and gentlemen duelists, most criminals were assumed to be naturally vicious and to have entered an illegal profession by choice rather than necessity. Punishments were severe for those convicted of even minor offenses, and ranged from the stocks (restraints for the feet and hands) to the pillory (restraints applied to the neck or body) to whipping, branding, transportation to the colonies or hanging for highwaymen and other felons. Barnardine, the drunken prisoner who refuses to be executed in *Measure for Measure*, awaits death for the crime of murder; he might, however, as easily have committed any of a range of crimes, from simple theft or pickpocketing to receiving stolen goods, to warrant the death penalty.

Prostitution, Pox, and Plague

Prostitution held a special place in the constellation of early modern crimes. John Stow's list of rules for the Stews in his *Survey* indicates that the Bankside brothels became established and acknowledged houses of resort, advertising through signage and probably also through the women who lingered in windows or on doorsteps. Prostitution was always presumably illegal, yet many women in the profession were preserved from the law's long arm. In part this was because they provided a service in much demand.

There were at least three general orders of prostitution: McMullen describes the wandering whores as bawdy baskets and doxies who sometimes combined prostitution with other forms of cozenage and crime; these women made alliances with pimps and protectors, worked taverns, docks, and took numerous clients. Housed whores and courtesans had a considerably more stable and profitable existence, forming attachments to a limited number of clients, sometimes becoming an exclusive mistress to a wealthy man. These fortunate few figured prominently in the social life of the wealthy, were discreet, and imitated the manners, dress, and even the accomplishments of aristocratic women (like music and dancing). "Pennyrent whores" and streetwalkers were the most precarious group, sharing tenement lodgings to which they could bring men, or simply living on the streets where they worked.

One infamous brothel of the mid-seventeenth century was Holland House, run by "Britanica Hollandia" (the allegorical name for Elizabeth Holland, a notorious madam), which occupied a former manor in a fashionable "liberty" or suburban neighborhood. Holland House provided a secluded place for high-class whores to entertain their clients — it was surrounded by a moat, and guarded by an armed marshal (see Fig. 17). The women of Holland House would have been well-educated in all aspects of their trade by their madam, and were supported by a legion of maids, servants, seamstresses, and provisioners. Men who entered the house might, as a woodcut from Crispijn de Passe's *Le Mirroir des Plus Belles Dames* (Fig. 18) depicts, have chosen a companion from paintings of the women displayed in the entrance halls or downstairs rooms. Once her price was agreed upon, the courtesan would walk with her visitor in the extensive gardens, entertain him with song and conversation, before moving to a well-appointed room for the ultimate pleasures she had to offer. In its organization and its extensive rules governing its inhabitants' appearance, behavior, and remuneration, Holland House resembles nothing quite so much as a convent — or even a prison. The moat, the drawbridge, the guard, the rules, and the feminine community within the house all resonate with the locations of both Isabella and Mariana in *Measure for Measure*, the one locked within the walls of her nunnery, the other in her "moated grange," and suggest that these two main characters have something in common with the mainly invisible and unnamed whores of the "pulled-down" hothouses like Mistress Overdone's.

FIGURE 17 *Holland House, title page illustration from Nicholas Goodman,* Hollands Leaguer *(London 1632).*

The story of Holland House was told in a popular text, *Hollands Leaguer,* which narrated the life of its madam and her decision — indeed, her desire — to become first a whore and then a brothel-keeper. Born and bred a respectably country girl, the young Dame Hollandia takes off for the city because she feels overlooked and underappreciated: "shee would often say within her selfe, what is beautie, if not seene, what seene, if not admired, what admired if not desired, and why any, or all if not enjoyed" (Goodman 58). She marries to cloak her real goals, and then falls prey to a gallant who "comes with his Legions of inchantments to besiege this Redoute or weak sconce." Having surrendered the fort of her virtue (and from its title

FIGURE 18 *Gallants Choosing Whores at a Brothel, from Crispijn de Passe,* Le Miroir des Plus Belles Dames *(Paris, 1641).*

throughout, *Hollands Leaguer* uses military imagery to depict the fall of its protagonist), the lady determines to become a "bawd" or panderer of others:

> She will no more be a Lais, but a Lena, no more a bewitching whore, but a deceiving bawd, the sins of others shall maintain her sin, she will no more trust herself on the surges, but will traffic by factors and according to the wealth of her wares, so shall be the increase or decrease of her revenues.   (Goodman 67)

Similar works represented authors' "investigations" of the terrible sins and lives of prostitutes: *The Night-Walker: or, Evening Rambles in Search after Lewd Women* concludes that "in our Rambles we find many times that Young Women have been tempted to dishonour their Bodies, that they might have wherewith to maintain their excesses in Apparel" (3). This sentiment is echoed throughout the literature on whores, who figure repeatedly in plays, ballads, and broadsides. Richard West's *The Court of Conscience* (1607) harangued "Punks and Shameless Whores" as the source of robbery among misled youth: "And to bring youth by your alluring words, / To all the mischiefe that the world affords. / To rob and steal to pillfer and purloyne, / Their maisters goods" merely to clothe their "filthy Cancred" bodies (E4r). As regards criminals generally, the belief was that women turned to the trade out of natural vice or wantonness, not out of poverty and lack of options for work. In fact, women had far fewer legitimate trades open to them in early modern England. The closing of monasteries and convents under the reign of Henry VIII had left a disproportionate number of women unemployed and without options, while demographic imbalances made marriage for all young women less likely. As a result, the period in which Shakespeare wrote may have seen a real increase over previous times in the numbers of women who turned to the streets for a living via both theft and prostitution.

The case of Peter Manyfield, who was brought before the church courts on charges of pimping, is perhaps more common than that of Dame Hollandia, who chose her trade: Manyfield was reputed to have "carried away, by stealth and violence against her will, a certain Alice Burle from her parents'

FIGURE 19 *"A Whore Is a Deepe Grave: and an Harlot,"* from Stephen Bateman, A Crystal Glass of Christian Reformation *(London, 1585)*.

house," raped her, and then "sold her to a certain Easterling in the Steelyard" (p. 301). Clearly a number of young women were abducted and forced
into the life; others, fearing starvation and with no legitimate occupation
open to them, turned to the life out of desperate need and were exploited by
their pimps and brothel madams. Richard Lovelace's "The Fair Beggar"
(see p. 295) registers a callousness toward this kind of economic pressure
on women: Lovelace addresses a woman who, from her pathetic dress (a
"thrice-bequeathed gown," "eclipst with earth" [dirt]), sounds like a pennyrent whore but might be any unkempt aspiring prostitute. He offers her an
exchange: she may "sup" and feed her hunger by feeding his "fancy," and
"quench[ing] [his] heat" (p. 296). Lovelace seems unconcerned that the
poverty he means to remedy by "charity" does not really inspire one to
believe his target offers him "love" in the transaction, unless one defines love
purely physically as the act of sex. Contemporaries, however, accepted the
pervasive misogyny that dictated all women were prone to vice, that they fell
into prostitution through their own unruly desires. As Thomas Overbury
put it in his *Characters*, "A very Whore is a woman. She enquires out all the
great meetings which are medicines for her itching [lust]" (29). Samuel
Rowlands' "wife" in *Tis Merrie When Gossips Meet* laments "I could not for
the world have liv'd a Nunne: / Oh, flesh is fraile, we are a sinfull sorte," a
sentiment with which Constable Elbow's wife might have emphatically
agreed. Her visit to Pompey's brothel and her dalliance with Froth, re-
counted by her scandalized husband in act 2, scene 1, appear to stem from
her inherently lustful nature. That she is pregnant, and longing for plums
(that is, has appetites for forbidden fruit), signals that she knows her own
lust and how to satisfy it: according to many early modern medical theories
about conception, a woman needed to be stimulated to orgasm in order to
conceive a child. Hence her pregnancy, like Juliet's, is a visible record of her
carnal desires satisfied.

One of the most virulent attacks on fornication and its fruits is Philip
Stubbes's *Anatomy of Abuses* (see p. 286), which links the "horryble vice"
of whoredom to a litany of other sins which weaken England (code name
"Ailgna" — that is "Anglia" spelled backward — in the *Anatomy*). Written
as a dialogue between Philoponus and Spudeus, the *Anatomy* laments the
lack of proper punishment for adulterers and whores: despite the fact that
whoring in itself "dulleth the spirits, it hurteth the memory, it weakeneth
the whole body . . . it bringeth ulcerations, scabs, scurf, blain, botch, pocks
and biles" (p. 291). Philoponus would add scarring with hot irons on the
face or other visible part of the body, or else poison and certain death to
ensure the avoidance of sin. He apparently agrees with William Harrison's
expressed wish in *The Description of England* that "adultery and fornication

to have some sharper law . . . to be condemned to the galleys; for that punishment would prove more bitter to them" than the usual treatment of public humiliation (189–90). Stubbes conflates simple fornication and ordinary adultery with prostitution when he claims that "so far are some, from suffering condign punishment for this horrible sin, that they get good maintenance with practicing the same," and go "gentlewomenlike . . . in their silks . . . with their fingers clogged with rings" (p. 294). His comingling of adultery with prostitution is not unusual for anti-vice literature of the time, and neither is his emphasis on its source in women's weakness and vanity.

Even the few who defended prostitution in print did so without contradicting prevalent views about women's — and to a lesser degree, man's — essentially sinful nature. To Philoponus's tirade, Spudeus offers the argument some mount in favor of sexual freedom, that Nature and God intended man to procreate, and that "whoredome is a badge of love, a cognizance of amitie, a tutch of lustie youth." Freevill in John Marston's *The Dutch Courtesan* (see p. 297) makes a strong economic case for prostitution to his puritanical friend Malheureux: "every man must follow his trade, and every woman her occupation; a poor decayed mechanical man's wife, her husband is laid up, may not she lawfully be laid down, when her husband's only rising is by his wife's falling?" Ironically, he claims that money spent on whores is better spent than on goods, since goods will age or be lost, but you may get something in return at a brothel — the pox, or syphilis, which will "stick by you as long as you live" (pp. 298–99). Another character in the play, Cocledemoy, notes that only a prostitute gets her living without relying on another's misery; rather, she gives pleasure, which is more than most can claim about "honest" professions. Ultimately, Malheureux falls in love with a prostitute, proving that not even the most righteous man can avoid the sins of desire, while Freevill is reformed and marries a gentleman's daughter. Freevill's perspective is not exactly endorsed by Marston, although his views have some currency in early modern culture. Some writers turned their scorn equally against those who created and profited from prostitution, albeit without letting prostitutes themselves off the hook: West, for instance, excoriates bawds, who lure young countrywomen looking for service into the life, and attacks panderers who "live upon a whores reversion / Upholding them in all their whorish doings," (F2r) distributing blame equally among all.

The "sweat" that deprives Mistress Overdone of a portion of her customers may refer to either the plague, or the pox, which usually indicated syphilis rather than its weaker cousin, gonorrhea (sweating was a common symptom of plague, while it was a supposed cure for pox). In fact, plague and pox were not unrelated illnesses (both seemed associated with populous cities, both were aligned with sin and punishment, both were fatal and terrifying diseases), except for the fact that the wealthy could avoid the plague by fleeing the city where it struck, while pox was an equal-opportunity disease. One author of a treatise on treating the pox notes that because the Italians suffer so many cases of pox, "it has in good part freed them from the Plague" (L. S. 3). It was an accepted fact of early modern sexual life that contracting the pox was a real threat, and the disease early moderns knew was far more virulent than it has become over the centuries. Syphilis, the French disease, or *morbus gallicus*, was a venereal disease that arrived in early modern Europe with a vengeance in the latter part of the fifteenth century. In its early form it caused profound eruptions of suppurating sores all over the body. After appearance of the sores, and painful swelling of the joints, the patient literally rotted away from inside; the disease attacked bone and brain and every other organ, ending in death within months. As the pox spread, however, it probably mutated and became less potent as so many such diseases do, and many people survived initial attacks, experiencing periods of remission. Physicians tried to inform the public that the pox could be contracted from other than sexual sources — L. S., for example, a "doctor of physick" who wrote his *Prothylantinon, or, Some considerations of a notable expedient to root out the French pox from the English nation* in 1673, warns that nursing babies could contract it from infected nurses, and that the practice of open-mouth kissing spread the disease effectively as well. But in the minds of the majority, the pox came from sexual contact with whores. In Thomas Dekker's *The Honest Whore*, Bellafronte complains:

> They [prostitutes] have no issue but foule ugly ones,
> That run along with them, e'ene to their graves:
> For stead of children, they breed rank diseases,
> And all you Gallants, can bestow on them,
> Is that French Infant, which n'ere acts but speaks:
> What shallow sonne and heir then, foolish gallant,
> Would waste all his inheritance to purchase
> A filthy loathd disease . . .

Thomas Dekker's *Lantern and Candlelight, Or The Bellman's Second Night's Walk* (1608) (see p. 276) calls its chapter on the sins of Bankside "The Infection of the Suburbs," playing on the relationship between prostitution, the pox, the locality of Bankside and Southwark, and the more general idea that the sins fostered there could reach into the heart of the city itself. Dekker's work takes us on a tour of some familiar aspects of the trade in sex:

prostitutes bedecking the doors of their houses, "being better to the house than a double sign" (p. 276), landlords (deemed "grand-bawds") who may absent themselves but for earning profits off the brothels, and the pervasive association of whoring with disease, especially plague. Indeed, Dekker warns that the suburbs' harlots will invade the city disguised as puritans, and perform more discreetly that they may the better go unnoticed and unimpeded. Dekker may mean his diatribe literally: Pompey's off-hand comment that a few brothels will "stand for seed" (1.2.79) and the city prostitutes will go unmolested in Vienna suggests that suburban sin and city sin were interdependent. But Dekker's references to punks, or prostitutes, who are squired around by gallants, dress demurely, claim to be married, and know how to manipulate justice, lift his commentary to the level of allegory — he refers to the "goodliest garden" within which is infected by the "stinking weeds" of harlotry. The garden it seems is the city of London in sum, its welfare too much neglected by those who are trusted with its defense (from constables to magistrates to the city leaders and government). Dekker sounds the bell for radical change in individual and communal behavior — but with tongue at least partially in cheek, one suspects, since he made his living writing popular exposés of crime and the underworld.

Dekker did not only write about plague as allegory: a number of his most famous pamphlets were about the Black Death, or the bubonic plague, a very real infection that attacked suburbs and urban centers alike throughout Europe during the Middle Ages and the Renaissance. It might seem strange to include plague in a section on the criminal underworld in *Measure for Measure*, but in the view of many early modern English men and women the plague was inevitably a moral, as well as a health issue. Dekker's image of the infection that spreads from the Stews into the cities describes the presumed course of the many plague outbreaks during the sixteenth and seventeenth centuries, since plague manifested itself most virulently where populations were dense, sanitation was poor, and housing was rudimentary. While there was no clear understanding in the period of the vectors that spread the disease (primarily the black rat, *Rattus rattus*, and its fleas, a fact discovered only in the 1890s), there was a profound understanding of its demographics. The poor died in droves; some of the wealthy did too, but in far fewer numbers, in part because those with money could temporarily escape the location of an outbreak. Perhaps because of its clear preference for the neighborhoods of the marginal — the Stews, Bankside, the liberties generally — most people believed that plague happened to those who through some inherent immorality brought it on themselves. Dekker's *A Rod for Runaways* (1625) calls the plague "God's judgment" on London, and few of his countrymen would have disagreed with him. Thus when Mistress

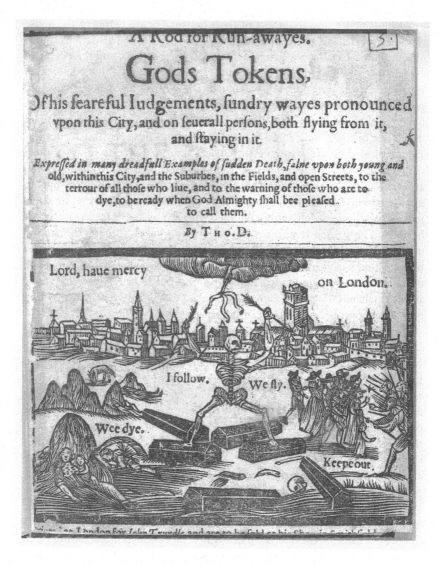

FIGURE 20   *Thomas Dekker, frontispiece from* A Rod for Runaways *(London, 1625).*

Overdone remarks that her customers are disappearing because of the plague, among other causes, she would have confirmed to Shakespeare's audience the sinfulness of her trade, and the general vice-ridden condition of Vienna under the Duke's lax policies. Like so many other cities in

Europe, its embrace of licentiousness was being punished with the divine scourge of disease.

The frontispiece of *A Rod for Runaways* (Fig. 20) comments on the practice of attempting to leave the city to avoid the contagion. In the middle of the engraving, Death stands atop several coffins, hurling arrows after the group of citizens running away; behind is a view of London; in the foreground are dying victims of plague. But the inscriptions, which reads "Lord have mercy on London; We fly; I [that is, Death] follow; wee dye," implies that flight is futile. Dekker was wrong about the effectiveness of escape from the pragmatic point of view, but his point is not to make recommendations about physical health. In fact, he explicitly rejects the idea that plague happens only in overpopulated areas: "We flatter ourselves that the *Pestilence* serves but as a Broome, to sweep Kingdomes of people, when they grow ranke and too full" (Dekker, "A Rod" 143). Instead, plague is God's punishment for man's evil, and running from it while leaving behind only the poorest and most helpless compounds the sin that called it down in the first place.

Despite Dekker's contention that plague has nothing to do with overpopulation, early modern authorities saw places where people gathered in great numbers as a threat during times of plague. The theaters, where high and low were packed in together, were just such venues, and they, along with houses of prostitution where people's very intent was to "mingle" intimately, were targets of official closure during plague outbreaks. Because theaters were also associated in the minds of many with license, sinfulness, and the fomenting of rebellion, there were continual temporary theater closures throughout the seventeenth century. In one proclamation, a 1607 petition of the Lord Mayor of London, we see the attitudes of official London clearly expressed:

> Whereas it pleaseth god that the Infeccion of sicknes is the theis two or three weekes of late somewhat increased in the Skirtes and Confines of this Cittie, and by the untymely heate of this season may spreade further then can hereafter be easilie prevented, My humble desier is that your L[ordshi]p: for the preventinge of soe great a danger will vouchsafe ... First in restrayninge such comon Stage Plaies, as are Daylie shewed and exercised and doe occasion the great Assemblies of all sortes of people in the suburbes and partes adioyninge to this Cittie, and cannot be continiewed but with apparent daunger of the encrease of the sicknes. (Chambers, 339)

Plays were restricted in 1593, a year of constant plague, along with fairs, official celebrations, and other gatherings; plague again curtailed the play season in 1594, 1596, and 1603 (the year of Elizabeth's death and James's accession; plague was anticipated in years of such change on the assumption that it was God's instrument for purging the old, bad ways). So if Shakespeare shows some understanding of Mistress Overdone's suffering during plague years, it may be because his own business could fluctuate with the comings and goings of the disease as well.

In *Measure for Measure*, sexuality is directly connected to plague by Claudio, who remarks on man's propensity for sin, particularly lustful sin: "Our natures do pursue / Like rats that ravin down their proper bane, / A thirsty evil, and when we drink we die" (1.2.105–07). While the Renaissance did not recognize the specific role of *Rattus rattus* in spreading plague bacilli via its fleas, the place of vermin like rats in promoting unhealthful conditions was well known, and rats were poisoned in droves during outbreaks (as were cats, dogs, and other common animals). Claudio's idea that sex is poison reflects a general sense that in Vienna (or London) sex is a generally unhealthy activity for both the body and the soul. To be sure, Claudio's death is threatened because his sexual indulgence has led to Juliet's pregnancy; but the overall tenor of the play aligns sexuality with illicit and sinful behavior, to the point where *all* sex seems to be unlawful fornication. Lucio, ironically, is the only character to provide a healthful understanding of desire and its satisfaction: speaking to Isabella about her brother he reports that

> Your brother and his lover have embraced.
> As those that feed grow full, as blossoming time
> That from the seedness the bare fallow brings
> To teeming foison, even so her plenteous womb
> Expresseth his full tilth and husbandry. (1.4. 40–44)

Lucio's language of "increasing and multiplying," while robustly positive, nonetheless echoes the language Claudio and Pompey applied to fornication and prostitution, with its emphasis on "feeding" and "seeds." Whether the play endorses Lucio's version of sex or not is difficult to tell. The argument that sex is a normal human behavior, natural and sanctioned by God, is found in many Renaissance texts on the subject of marriage, since married people could have sex legally and with no chance of ill effects on the public good in the form of bastard births. And Angelo, the "man of snow" who represses his "natural desires" only to have them manifest as dangerous perversions, might stand as a warning to those who err on the side of a Puritanical rigor. But Lucio is simply not a reliable source for how to think about sex, since he has himself frequented prostitutes and gotten one pregnant. The play, then, seems poised between the idea that sex is like the plague — that it plagues mankind with the constant temptation to sin and suffer disease and death accordingly — and the contradictory idea that

FIGURE 21 *Man Being Led to the Gallows,* a woodcut from Thomas Harmon, A Caveat for Common Cursitors *(London, 1567).*

human sexuality is the very thing that triumphs over disease and death through procreation.

On many levels, then, *Measure for Measure* deals with problems of sinfulness and its manifestation as crime and criminal behavior. It takes its audience on a journey into places that paradoxically seemed both exotic and everyday, from prison cells to brothels, from the Stews to the inner moral crises experienced by so many, both highborn and low. While the play appears to reject the sin of fornication in all its forms, we find a certain

FIGURE 22 *"Barnardine," from Robert Smirke,* Measure for Measure *(London, 1800).*

degree of tolerance for it — for its humorous expression in Elbow's frantic defense of his "much suspected" wife, for the tacit acceptance that the brothels will never truly disappear, for Claudio and Juliet's crime and even Angelo's attempted transgression. In the end, only Lucio is punished, and that simply by enforced marriage to Kate Keepdown (which he insists is as bad as "pressing to death, whipping, and hanging" [5.1.520–21], but which seems relatively benign given the play's other precedents for punishment). Equally, while Angelo and the Duke appear initially to want to purge Vienna of criminals and criminal behaviors, by the play's conclusion most of the inhabitants of Vienna's prison have been released, even the drunken Barnardine (see Figs. 21 and 22). Pompey, the bawd, escapes his sentence by assisting the executioner, Abhorson, although neither seems likely to have much work. Perhaps such an abundance of merciful pardons helped the play's audiences more willingly negotiate the dark and difficult subjects of crime and sexual transgression, but it is equally possible that the play's happy endings failed even in their first appearance to paper over the harsh social realities of crime and punishment London faced in the early seventeenth century.

→ JOHN STOW

From The Survey of London   *1603*

John Stow (1525–1605), by profession a tailor, was a self-educated man and serious historian who, as we can tell from his detailed topographical description of London, took great pride in his native city. Stow documents the history of permitted Stews (brothels) on the bankside of the Thames, and concludes with Henry VIII's order to have them all pulled down. This should not give the impression that Henry's order actually rid Southwark of a flourishing sex trade. The following excerpt describes the borough of Southwark, an area of London outside the city walls on the southern bank of the river Thames that was home to Shakespeare's Globe theater, as well as other playhouses, brothels, gaming houses, prisons, and bear-bating arenas.

John Stow, *The Survey of London* (London, 1603), 405–09.

BRIDGE WARD WITHOUT

The Twenty-sixth in Number Consisting of the Borough of Southwark, in the County of Surrey.

Having treated of the wards in London, on the north side of the Thames (in number 25), I am now to cross over the said river into the borough of Southwark, which is also a ward of London without[1] the walls, on the south side thereof, as is Portsoken[2] on the east, and Farringdon extra[3] on the west.

This borough being in the county of Surrey,[4] consisteth of divers streets, ways, and winding lanes, all full of buildings, inhabited; and, first to begin at the west part thereof, over against the west suburb of the city.

On the bank of the river Thames there is now a continual building of tenements, about half a mile in length to the bridge. Then from the bridge, straight towards the south, a continual street, called Long Southwark, built on both sides with divers lanes and alleys up to St. George's Church, and beyond it through Blackman Street towards New Town (or Newington); the liberties[5] of which borough extend almost to the parish church of New Town aforesaid, distant one mile from London Bridge, and also southwest a continual building almost to Lambeth, more than one mile from the said bridge.

Then from the bridge along by the Thames eastward is St. Olave's Street, having continual building on both the sides, with lanes and alleys, up to Battle Bridge, to Horsedown, and towards Rother Hithe;[6] also some good half mile in length from London Bridge.

So that I account the whole continual buildings on the bank of the said river, from the west towards the east, to be more than a large mile in length.

Then have ye, from the entering towards the said Horsedown, one other continual street called Bermondes High Street, which stretcheth south, likewise furnished with buildings on both sides, almost half a mile in length, up to the late dissolved monastery of St. Savior called Bermondsey. And from thence is one Long Lane (so called of the length), turning west to St. George's Church afore named. Out of the which lane mentioned Long Lane breaketh one other street towards the south and by east, and this is called Kentish Street, for that is the way leading into that country; and so have you the bounds of this borough.

---

[1] without: outside. [2] Portsoken: an area on the eastern side of the city running all the way to the Thames. [3] Farringdon extra: Farringdon without, an area outside ("extra") the city walls west of London. [4] Surrey: county southwest of London. [5] liberties: suburban area outside of the legal and political boundaries of the city. [6] hithe: a small haven or landing place on the river.

The antiquities most notable in this borough are these: first, for ecclesiastical there was Bermondsey, an abbey of black monks,[7] St. Mary Overies, a priory of canons regular, St. Thomas, a college or hospital for the poor, and the Loke, a lazar[8] house in Kent Street. Parish churches there have been six, whereof five do remain; viz.,[9] St. Mary Magdalen, in the priory of St. Mary Overy, now the same St. Mary Overy is the parish church for the said Mary Magdalen, and for St. Margaret on the hill, and is called St. Savior.

St. Margaret on the hill being put down is now a court for justice; St. Thomas in the hospital serveth for a parish church as before; St. George a parish church as before it did; so doth St. Olave and St. Mary Magdalen, by the abbey of Bermondsey.

There be also these five prisons or gaols:[10]

The Clink on the Bank.

The Compter,[11] in the late parish church of St. Margaret.

The Marshalsey.

The King's Bench.

And the White Lion, all in Long Southwark.

Houses most notable be these:

The Bishop of Winchester's House.

The Bishop of Rochester's House.

The Duke of Suffolk's house, or Southwark Place.

The Tabard, an hostery or inn.

The Abbot of Hyde, his house.

The Abbot of St. Augustine, his house.

The Bridge house.

The Abbot of Battaile, his house.

Battaile Bridge.

The Stews[12] on the bank of the Thames.

And the Bear gardens[13] there.

Now, to return to the west bank, there be two bear gardens, the old and new places, wherein be kept bears, bulls, and other beast to be baited; as also

---

[7] black monks: monks of the order of St. Benedict, so called from the color of the habit worn. [8] lazar: a diseased beggar, especially a leper. [9] viz.: namely. [10] gaols: jails. [11] Compter: old spelling for "counter," a debtor prison. [12] Stews: brothels. [13] Bear gardens: arenas for bear-baiting and, occasionally, other forms of entertainments such as interludes and jigs. Bear-baiting is the "sport" of setting hungry dogs to attack a bear chained to a stake.

mastiffs in several kennels, nourished to bait them. These bears and other beasts are there baited in plots of ground, scaffolded about for the beholders to stand safe.

Next on this band was sometime the Bordello, or Stews, a place so called of certain stew-houses privileged there, for the repair of incontinent men to the like women; of the which privilege I have read thus:

In a parliament holden[14] at Westminster, the eighth[15] of Henry the Second, it was ordained by the commons, and confirmed by the king and lords, that divers constitutions for ever should be kept within the lordship or franchise,[16] according to the old customs that had been there used time out of mind: amongst the which these following were some, viz.

That no stew-holder or his wife should let or stay any single woman, to go and come freely at all times when they listed.[17]

No stew-holder to keep any woman to board, but she to board abroad at her pleasure.

To take no more for the woman's chamber in the week than fourteen pence.

Not to keep open his doors upon the holidays.

Not to keep any single woman in his house on the holy days, but the bailiff to see them voided out of the lordship.

No single woman to be kept against her will that would leave her sin.

No stew-holder to receive any woman of religion, or any man's wife.

No single woman to take money to lie with any man, but[18] she lie with him all night till the morrow.

No man to be drawn or enticed into any stew-house.

The constables, bailiff, and others, every week to search every stew-house.

No stew-holder to keep any woman that hath the perilous infirmity of burning,[19] not to sell bread, ale, flesh, fish, wood, coal, or any victuals, etc.

These and many more orders were to be observed upon great pain and punishment. I have also seen divers patents of confirmation, namely, one dated 1345, the nineteenth of Edward the Third. Also, I find that in the fourth of Richard the Second, these stew-houses belonging to William

---

[14] holden: held.   [15] eighth: the eighth year of his reign.   [16] lordship or franchise: a domain or district with an exceptional right granted by the sovereign or government.   [17] listed: desired.
[18] but: except that.   [19] burning: fever, possibly the result of the plague or venereal disease.

Walworth, then mayor of London, were farmed by Froes[20] of Flanders, and spoiled by Walter Tyler, and other rebels of Kent; notwithstanding, I find that ordinances for the same place and houses were again confirmed in the reign of Henry the First, to be continued as before. Also, Robert Fabyan[21] writeth that in the year 1506, the 21st of Henry the Seventh, the said stew-houses in Southwark were for a season inhibited, and the doors closed up, but it was not long, says he, ere the houses there were set open again, so many as were permitted, for (as it was said) whereas before were eighteen houses, from henceforth were appointed to be used but twelve only. These allowed stew-houses had signs on their fronts, towards the Thames, not hanged out, but painted on the walls, as a Boar's head, the Cross keys, the Gun, the Castle, the Crane, Cardinal's hat, the Bell, the Swan, etc. I have heard of ancient men, of good credit, report that these single women were forbidden the rites of the church, so long as they continued that sinful life, and were excluded from Christian burial, if they were not reconciled before their death. And therefore there was a plot of ground called the Single Woman's churchyard, appointed for them far from the parish church.

In the year of Christ 1546, the 37th of Henry Eighth, this row of stews in Southwark was put down by the king's commandment, which was proclaimed by sound of trumpet, no more to be privileged and used[22] as a common brothel, but the inhabitants of the same to keep good and honest rule as in other places of this realm, etc.

The next is the Clink, a gaol or prison for the trespassers in those parts, namely in old time for such as should brabble, frey, or break the peace on the said bank, or in the brothel houses; they were by the inhabitants thereabout apprehended and committed to this gaol, where they were straightly imprisoned.

[20] **Froes:** from "frows" or "vrouwen," Dutch women.   [21] **Robert Fabyan:** (d. 1513), historian and author of *New Chronicles of England and of France* (1516).   [22] **used:** regarded.

→ THOMAS DEKKER

From Lantern and Candlelight

1608

Thomas Dekker (1570?–1641?), popular playwright and pamphleteer, focused most of his writing on the sinfulness of London's citizenry. In addition to "rogue" pamphlets like *Lantern and Candlelight,* a sequel to *The Bellman of London* printed earlier the same year, Dekker wrote a range of works for the stage, both alone and in collaboration with some of the most prominent playwrights of his time. Writing, however, was a chancy career, and Dekker found himself in and out of debtors prison throughout his life. *The Bellman of London* is a trip through the "night world" or underworld of London guided by the Bellman, a kind of watchman who shines his lantern on London's vices. It was the sequel, however, excerpted below, that was by far Dekker's most reprinted and profitable work.

THE INFECTION OF THE SUBURBS

The infernal promoter[1] being wearied with riding up and down the country, was glad when he had gotten the City over his head; but the City being not able to hold him within the freedom, because he was a foreigner, the gates were set wide open for him to pass through, and into the suburbs he went. And what saw he there? More ale-houses than there are taverns in all Spain and France! Are they so dry in the suburbs? Yes, pockily dry. What saw he besides?

He saw the doors of notorious carted bawds[2] like Hell-gates stand night and day wide open, with a pair of harlots in taffeta gowns, like two painted posts, garnishing out those doors, being better to the house than a double sign. When the door of a poor artificer, if his child had died but with one token of death about him, was closer rammed up and guarded, for fear others should have been infected, yet the plague that a whore-house lays upon a city is worse, yet is laughed at; if not laughed at, yet not looked into; or if looked into, winked at.

The tradesman having his house locked up, loseth his customers, is put

---

[1] **infernal promoter:** Lucifer, against whose works in London the pamphlet is a warning.
[2] **carted bawds:** "carting," or being pulled through the streets behind a cart, was a common punishment for procurers.

Thomas Dekker, *Lantern and Candlelight. Or the Bellman's Second Night's Walk in Which He Brings to Light, a Book of More Strange Villanies, Than Ever Were Till This Year Discovered* (London, 1608), H3r-I2v.

from work and undone; whilst in the meantime the strumpet is set on work and maintained (perhaps) by those that undo the other. Give thanks, O wide-mouthed Hell! Laugh Lucifer at this! Dance for joy all you devils!

Beelzebub keeps the register-book of all the bawds, pander and courtesans; and he knows that these suburb sinners have no lands to live upon but their legs: every 'prentice passing by them can say, "There sits a whore." Without putting them to their book they will swear so much themselves. If so, are not constables, churchwardens, bailiffs, beadles and other officers, pillars and pillows to all the villanies, that are by these committed? Are they not parcel bawds[3] to wink at such damned abuses, considering they have whips in their own hands, and may draw blood if they please? Is not the landlord of such rents the grand-bawd, and the door-keeping mistress of such a house of sin, but his under-bawd, since he takes twenty pounds rent every year for a vaulting school, which from no artificer living by the hardness of the hand could be worth five pound? And that twenty pound rent, he knows must be pressed out of petticoats. His money smells of sin: the very silver looks pale, because it was earned by lust.

How happy therefore were cities if they had no suburbs, since they serve but as caves, where monsters are bred up to devour the cities themselves! Would the Devil hire a villain to spill blood, there he shall find him; one to blaspheme, there he hath choice; a pander that would court a matron at her prayers, he's there; a cheater that would turn his own father a begging, he's there; a harlot that would murder her new-born infant, she lies in there!

What a wretched womb hath a strumpet, which being for the most barren of children, is notwithstanding the only bed that breeds up these serpents! Upon that one stalk grow all these mischiefs. She is the cockatrice[4] that hatcheth all these eggs of evils. When the Devil takes the anatomy of all damnable sins, he looks only upon her body. When she dies, he sits as her coroner. When her soul comes to Hell, all shun that there, as they fly from a body struck with the plague here. She hath her door-keeper, and she herself is the Devil's chambermaid. And yet for all this, that she's so dangerous and detestable, when she hath croaked like a raven on the eaves, then comes she into the house like a dove. When her villanies, like the moat about a castle, are rank, thick and muddy with standing long together, then, to purge herself, is she drained out of the suburbs, as though her corruption were there left behind her, and as a clear stream is let into the City.

---

[3] parcel bawds: that is, they participate in the crime (are a parcel with it) by not punishing it.
[4] cockatrice: a mythological serpent able to kill with a glance, and said to be hatched from a cock's egg.

WHAT ARMOUR A HARLOT WEARS COMING OUT OF THE SUBURBS TO BESIEGE THE CITY WITHIN THE WALLS.

Upon what perch then does she sit? What part plays she then? Only the puritan. If before she ruffled in silks, now is she more civilly attired than a midwife. If before she swaggered in taverns, now with the snail she stirreth not out of doors. And where must her lodging be taken up, but in the house of some citizen, whose known reputation she borrows (or rather steals) putting it on as a cloak to cover her deformities? Yet even in that hath she an art too, for he shall be of such a profession, that all comers may enter, without the danger of any eyes to watch them. As for example, she will lie in some scrivener's house, and so, under the color of coming to have a bond made, she herself may write *Noverint universi*.[5] And though the law threaten to hit her never so often, yet hath she subtle defences to ward off the blows. For, if gallants haunt the house, then spreads she these colors: She is a captain or a lieutenant's wife in the Low Countries, and they come with letters, from the soldier her husband. If merchants resort to her, then hoists she up these sails: She is wife to the master of a ship, and they bring news that her husband put in at the Straits, or at Venice, at Aleppo, Alexandria, or Scanderoon, etc. If shopkeepers come to her, with "What do you lack?" in their mouth, then she takes up such and such commodities, to send them to Rye, to Bristol, to York, etc., where her husband dwells. But if the stream of her fortunes run low, and that none but apronmen launch for her there, then keeps she a politic seamstress's shop, or she starches them.

Perhaps she is so politic that none shall be noted to board her. If so, then she sails upon these points of the compass: So soon as ever she is rigged, and all her furniture on, forth she launcheth into those streets that are most frequented; where the first man that she meets of her acquaintance shall, without much pulling, get her into a tavern; out of him she kisses a breakfast and then leaves him. The next she meets does upon as easy pulleys draw her to a tavern again. Out of him she cogs[6] a dinner, and then leaves him. The third man squires her to a play, which being ended, and the wine offered and taken, for she's no recusant[7] to refuse anything, him she leaves too. And being set upon by a fourth, him she answers at his own weapon, sups with him, and drinks upsy-Freeze[8] till the clock striking twelve, and the drawers being drowsy, away they march arm in arm, being at every footstep fearful to

---

[5] *Noverint universi:* "all the people have been made aware," an announcement.   [6] cogs: cheats.
[7] recusant: a term usually applied to English Catholics who refused to conform themselves to the Protestant faith after the Reformation.   [8] upsy-Freeze: a drinking term; freeze-water was water used to dilute wine.

be set upon by the band of halberdiers,[9] that lie scouting in rug-gowns to cut off such midnight stragglers; but the word being given, and "Who goes there?" with "Come before the constable" being shot at them, they prevail presently and come, she taking upon her to answer all the billmen and their leader, between whom and her suppose you hear this sleepy dialogue:

"Where have you been so late?"

"At supper forsooth with my uncle here (if he be well bearded), or with my brother (if the hair be but budding forth), and he is bringing me home."

"Are you married?"

"Yes forsooth."

"What's your husband?"

"Such a nobleman's man, or such a Justice's clerk." And then names some alderman of London, to whom she persuades herself one or other of the bench of brown bills are beholden.

"Where lie you?"

"At such a man's house."

Sic tenues evanescit in auras.[10] And thus by stopping the constable's mouth with sugar-plums, that's to say, whilst she poisons him with sweet words, the punk vanisheth. O Lantern and Candlelight, how art thou made a blind ass, because thou hast but one eye to see withal! Be not so gulled, be not so dull in understanding. Do thou but follow aloof those two tame pigeons, and thou shalt find that her new uncle lies by it all that night, to make his kinswoman one of mine aunts; or if she be not in travail all night, they spend some half an hour together. But what do they? Marry, they do that which this constable should have done for them both in the streets, that's to say, *commit, commit.*

You guardians over so great a princess as the eldest daughter of King Brutus:[11] you twice twelve fathers and governors over the noblest city, why are you so careful to plant trees to beautify your outward walks, yet suffer the goodliest garden within to be overrun with stinking weeds? You are the pruning knives that should lop off such idle, such unprofitable, and such destroying branches from the vine. The beams of your authority should purge the air of such infection; your breath of justice should scatter those foggy vapors, and drive them out of your gates as chaff tossed abroad by the winds.

---

[9] **halberdiers:** carriers of halberds (weapon with an axlike blade and spike on a long shaft). [10] *Sic tenues evanescit in auras:* "so she disappeared into thin air" (*Aeneid* 2:791). [11] **King Brutus:** mythological founder of England.

→ BEN JONSON

From Epigrams

1616

Ben Jonson (1573?–1637), the stepson of a bricklayer, rose to fame and fortune as a celebrated writer of comedies for the public playhouse and a writer of masques and poetry for the court of King James I. In both his plays and poetry, Ben Jonson is well known for his penchant for satire and didacticism. If we think of Shakespeare as the poet of romantic comedy, Jonson is the witty but often hard-edged voice of social satire, exposing vice and duplicity wherever he encounters it. Jonson's "Epigrams," from which the poem that follows is taken, is a collection of short verses that contain clever and critical descriptions of prominent people, places, and social practices, and often conclude with a moralizing "sting" intended to expose or embarrass or educate its subject and the reader. In the dedication of his "Epigrams" to William, Earl of Pembroke, Jonson referred to them as "the ripest of my studies." "On the New Hot-House" tells the brief story of a London brothel that, probably under pressure of the authorities, was closed down, and reopened its doors under a different name while plying the same trade. As Escalus puts it to Pompey the pimp, "Pompey, you are partly a bawd, Pompey, howsoever you color it in being a tapster, are you not?" (2.1.182–83).

EPIGRAM 7. ON THE NEW HOT-HOUSE

Where lately harbor'd many a famous whore,
A purging bill,[1] now fix'd upon the door,
Tells you it is a hot-house.[2] So it ma':[3]
And still be a whore-house. Th'are *synonima.*

---

[1] **purging bill:** a law meant to cleanse.   [2] **hot-house:** a bath-house with hot water supplied, commonly used to treat venereal diseases. Also a brothel.   [3] **ma':** may.

Ben Jonson, *The Works of Benjamin Jonson* (London, 1616), 770.

⇥ KING JAMES I

Proclamation against Inmates   *September 16, 1603*

The Jacobean royal proclamation that follows is one of a number of proclamations issued in the early modern period that addresses the terrible overcrowding that plagued certain London neighborhoods around the turn of the century. Officials recognized that neighborhoods in which citizens were huddled together in small houses and apartments in narrow streets under poor sanitary conditions aided the spread of the plague and other diseases. Moreover, the authorities were also wary of overcrowding because it increased poverty and crime, and created a climate favorable for sedition and rebellion. In this particular proclamation of September 16, 1603, the government addresses the overcrowding issue by trying to stem the influx of people and by ordering the tearing down of buildings to reduce living space.

A PROCLAMATION AGAINST INMATES[1] AND MULTITUDES OF DWELLERS IN STRAIT[2] ROOMS AND PLACES IN AND ABOUT THE CITY OF LONDON, AND FOR THE RAZING AND PULLING DOWN OF CERTAIN ERECTED BUILDINGS.

Whereas it falleth out by woeful experience, that the great confluence and access of excessive numbers of idle, indigent, dissolute and dangerous persons, and the pestering of many of them in small and strait rooms and habitations in the City of London, and in and about the suburbs of the same, have been one of the chiefest occasions of the great plague and mortality, which hath not only most extremely abounded in and about the said city and suburbs thereof, and especially in such strait rooms and places, and amongst persons of such quality, but also from thence hath most dangerously overspread, and infected very many principal and other parts of this realm, (which Almighty God cease at his good pleasure) His Majesty tendering the safety of his loving subjects, and minding, as much as in him lieth, to avoid the continuance or renewing of such mortality, doth by the advice of the Privy Council, not only straightly require and command that His Majesty's good and profitable order and directions already published for

---

[1] inmates: migrant lodgers or subtenants; the term also refers to foreigners, so-called strangers.
[2] strait: narrow, small.

King James I, "By the King. A proclamation against inmates and multitudes of dwellers in strait rooms and places in and about the City of London: and for the razing and pulling down of certain erected buildings," in *Stuart Royal Proclamations, Vol. I: Royal Proclamations of King James I, 1603–1625,* ed. James F. Larkin and Paul L. Hughes (Oxford: Clarendon P, 1973), 47–48.

the staying (if God so please) of the same infection, be carefully, speedily, and duly executed, but also doth straightly prohibit and forbid that no new tenant or inmate or other person or persons be admitted to inhabit or reside in any such house or place in the said city, suburbs, or within four miles of the same, which have been so infected, during the continuance of this plague and mortality, in or about the said city, nor after, until such time and as it shall be thought safe and expedient by the principal officers there for the time being; that is to say, if it be within the said city, by the Alderman of the Ward, or his deputy; if without, then by the next Justice of the Peace. Wherein his Majesty straightly doth charge and require every of the said aldermen and their deputies, and every Justice of the Peace to whom it shall appertain, that they take special care that none of the foresaid rooms, houses or places be hereafter pestered with multitudes of dwellers or with any inmates. And that such of the said rooms, houses, or places as by any proclamation heretofore published,[3] are ordered or appointed to be razed or pulled down, shall forthwith, the same being now void, or as the same shall hereafter become void, be razed and pulled down accordingly. And being one pulled down, that they or any of them at any time afterwards, suffer not any of the same to be newly erected, as they will answer the contrary at their uttermost peril.

Given at his Majesty's Manor of Woodstock, the sixteenth day of September in the first year of our reign of England, France, and Ireland, and of Scotland the seven and thirtieth. God save the King.

[3] any . . . published: On June 22, 1602, Elizabeth I had issued a proclamation prohibiting "further building and subdividing of houses in London" or "within three mile of the city of London." In the same proclamation, the queen also ordered "all sheds and shops to be plucked down that have been builded within the places and precincts aforesaid within seven years last past" (Hughes and Larkin 245–48, 247).

→ THOMAS HARMAN

From A Caveat for Common Cursitors   *1567*

Thomas Harman, a country magistrate, had ample opportunity to study the world of rogues and other criminals. In this work, which shares in the same popular audience that eagerly read Dekker's pamphlets, he recounts some of his

---

Thomas Harman, *A Caveat or Warning for Common Cursitors Vulgarly Called Vagabones, Set Forth by Thomas Harman, Esquire, for the Utility and Profit of His Natural Country* (London, 1567; reprinted 1573, from which this text is taken), F1v-F2v, F4r-G1r.

observations. While Harman focuses on the con-games run by criminals, he gives glimpses of the social conditions that lead to vagabondage and crime. The following selections spotlight the role of women in the criminal underworld.

A Bawdy Basket

These bawdy baskets be also women, and go with baskets and cap-cases on their arms, wherein they have laces, pins, needles, white inkle, and round silk girdles of all colors. These will buy conyskins,[1] and steal linen clothes off on hedges. And for their trifles they will procure of maiden-servants, when their mistress or dame is out of the way, either some good piece of beef, bacon, or cheese, that shall be worth twelvepence for twopence of their toys. And as they walk by the way, they often gain some money with their instrument,[2] by such as they suddenly meet withal. The upright men[3] have good acquaintance with these, and will help and relieve them when they want. Thus they trade their lives in lewd loathsome lechery. Amongst them all is but one honest woman, and she is of good years. Her name is Joan Messenger. I have had good proof of her, as I have learned by the true report of divers.

There came to my gate the last summer, *Anno Domini* 1566, a very miserable man, and much deformed as burnt in the face, blear-eyed, and lame of one of his legs, that he went with a crutch. I asked him where he was born and where he dwelt last, and showed him that thither he must repair and be relieved, and not to range about the country; and seeing some cause of charity, I caused him to have meat and drink, and when he had drunk, I demanded of him whether he was never spoiled of[4] the upright man or rogue.

"Yes, that I have," quoth he; "but yet these seven years, for so long I have gone abroad, I had not so much taken from me, nor so evil handled, as I was within these four days."

"Why, how so?" quoth I.

"In good faith, sir," quoth he, "I chance to meet with one of these bawdy baskets which had an upright man in her company, and as I would have passed quietly by her, 'Man,' saith she unto her mate, 'do you not see this ill-favoured, windshaken, knave?' 'Yes,' quoth the upright man. 'What say you to him?' 'This knave oweth me two shillings for wares he had of me, half a year ago, I think it well.' Said this upright man, 'Sirrah,' saith he, 'pay your debts.' Saith this poor man, 'I owe her none; neither did I ever bargain with

---

[1] conyskins: rabbit skins. [2] with their instrument: play on words, "with their genitals."
[3] upright men: members of roving gangs of con men. [4] spoiled of: robbed by.

her for anything, and as I am advised I never saw her before in all my life.' 'Mercy, God!' quoth she, 'what a lying knave is this! And he will not pay you, husband, beat him surely.' And the upright man gave me three or four blows on my back and shoulders, and would have beat me worse an[5] I had not given him all the money in my purse; and, in good faith, for very fear, I was fain to give him fourteen pence, which was all the money that I had. 'Why,' saith this bawdy basket, 'hast thou no more? Then thou owest me ten pence still; and, be well assured that I will be paid the next time I meet with thee.' And so they let me pass by them. I pray God save and bless me, and all other in my case, from such wicked persons," quoth this poor man.

"Why, whither went they then?" quoth I.

"Into East Kent, for I met with them on this side of Rochester. I have divers times been attempted, but I never lost much before. I thank God there came still company by afore this unhappy time."

"Well," quoth I, "thank God of all, and repair home to thy native country." . . .

A Doxy

These doxies be broken and spoiled of their maidenhead by the upright men, and then they have their name of doxies, and not afore. And afterward she is common and indifferent for any that will use her, as *homo* is a common name to all men. Such as be fair and somewhat handsome, keep company with the walking morts, and are ready always for the upright men, and are chiefly maintained by them, for others shall be spoiled for their sakes. The other inferior sort will resort to noblemen's places, and gentlemen's houses, standing at the gate, either lurking on the back-side about back-houses, either in hedgerows or some other thicket, expecting their prey, which is for the uncomely company of some courteous guest, of whom they be refreshed with meat and some money, where exchange is made, ware for ware. This bread and meat they use to carry in their great hosen; so that these beastly bribering[6] breeches serve many times for bawdy purposes.

I chanced, not long since, familiarly to common with a doxy that came to my gate, and surely a pleasant harlot, and not so pleasant as witty, and not so witty as void of all grace and goodness. I found by her talk that she had passed her time lewdly eighteen years in walking about. I thought this a necessary instrument to attain some knowledge by. And before I would

---

[5] an: if. [6] bribering: thieving.

grope her mind, I made her both eat and drink well. That done, I made her faithful promise to give her some money if she would open and discover to me such questions as I would demand of her, and never to betray her, neither to disclose her name.

"An you should," saith she, "I were undone."

"Fear not that," quoth I. "But I pray thee," quoth I, "say nothing but truth."

"I will not," saith she.

"Then first tell me," quoth I, "how many upright men and rogues dost thou know, or hast thou known and been conversant with, and what their names be?"

She paused awhile, and said, "Why do you ask me, or wherefore?"

"For nothing else," as I said, "But that I would know them when they came to my gate."

"Now, by my troth," quoth she, "then are ye never the nearer, for all mine acquaintance for the most part are dead."

"Dead!" quoth I, "how died they? For want of cherishing, or of painful diseases?"

Then she sighed, and said they were hanged.

"What, all?" quoth I, "And so many walk abroad, as I daily see!"

"By my troth," quoth she, "I know not past six or seven by their names" — and named the same to me.

"When were they hanged?" quoth I.

"Some seven years agone, some three years, and some within this fortnight" — and declared the place where they were executed, which I knew well to be true by the report of others.

"Why," quoth I, "did not this sorrowful and fearful sight much grieve thee, and for thy time long and evil spent?"

"I was sorry," quoth she, "by the mass. For some of them were good loving men. For I lacked not when they had it, and they wanted not when I had it, and divers of them I never did forsake, until the gallows departed us."

"O merciful God!" quoth I, and began to bless me.

"Why bless ye?" quoth she. "Alas! Good gentleman, every one must have a living."

Other matters I talked of. But this may now suffice to show the reader, as it were in a glass, the bold beastly life of these doxies. For such as hath gone any time abroad will never forsake their trade, to die therefore. I have had good proof thereof. There is one notorious harlot of this affinity called Bess Bottomly. She hath but one hand, and she hath murdered two children at the least.

A DELL

A dell is a young wench, able for generation, and not yet known or broken by the upright man. These go abroad young, either by the death of their parents and nobody to look unto them, or else by some sharp mistress that they serve do run away out of service; either she is naturally born one, and then she is a wild dell. These are broken very young. When they have been lain withal by the upright man, then they be doxies, and no dells. These wild dells, being traded up with their monstrous mothers,[7] must of necessity be as evil, or worse, than their parents, for neither we gather grapes from green briars, neither figs from thistles.[8] But such buds, such blossoms, such evil seed sown, will worse being grown.

[7] monstrous mothers: doxies; the wild dells are assumed to be the children of doxies and other whores.   [8] gather . . . thistles: that is, by the fruit you know the tree.

→ PHILIP STUBBES

From Anatomy of Abuses   1583

Philip Stubbes (1555–1610) was a Puritan reformer and author who capitalized on his public's appetite for scandalous fare in order to turn them away from vice and sin. His *Anatomy of Abuses,* first published in 1583, documents the evils of dicing, gaming, theater-going, and other vicious pastimes through a dialogue between Philoponus (whose name means "love of toil") and Spudeus (meaning worthy, of good or excellent character). Philoponus recounts his visit to Ailgna (or Anglia, an alternate name for England, spelled backward). Stubbes describes the anxieties over a national descent into lawlessness and immorality that seem to inspire the Duke and Angelo, albeit in different fashion.

THE HORRIBLE VICE OF WHOREDOM IN AILGNA

PHILOPONUS: The horrible vice of whoredom also is there too much frequented, to the great dishonor of God, the provoking of his judgments against them, the stain and blemish of their profession, the evil example of all the world, and finally to their own damnation for ever, except they repent.

SPUDEUS: I have heard them reason, that mutual coition betwixt man and woman, is not so offensive before God. For do not all creatures (say they)

Philip Stubbes, *Anatomy of Abuses* (London, 1583), 59–68.

as well *reptilia terræ, as volatilia Cæli,* the creeping things upon the earth, as the flying creatures in the air, and all other creatures in general both small and great engender together? Hath not nature and kind ordained them so? And given them members incident to that use?[1] And doth not the Lord (say they) (as it were with a stimule, or prick[2] by his mandate, saying . . . increase, multiply and fill the earth,) stir them up to the same? Otherwise the world would become barren, and soon fall to decay: wherefore they conclude that whoredom is a badge of love, a cognizance of amity, a touch of lusty youth, a friendly dalliance, a redintegration[3] of love, and an ensign[4] of virtue, rather meritorious than damnable: these with the like be the exceptions which I have heard them many times to object, in defense of their carnal pollutions.

PHILOPONUS: Cursed be those mouths, that thus blaspheme the mighty God of Israel and his sacred word, making the same cloaks, to cover their sin withal, worse are they than libertines who think all things lawful, or atheists, who deny there is any God. The devils themselves never sinned so horribly, nor erred so grossly as these (not Christians, but dogs) do, that make whoredom a virtue, and meritorious: but because you shall see their deceptions displayed and their damnable abuses, more plainly discovered, I will reduce you to the first institution of this godly ordinance or matrimony. The Lord our God having created all things in heaven, earth, or hell whatsoever created of every sex, two, male and female of both kinds, and last of all other creatures, he made man after his own likeness, and similitude, giving him a woman, made of a rib of his own body, to be his companion and comforter, and linking them together in the honorable state of venerable wedlock he blessed them both, saying, *crescite, multiplicamini, & replete terra,* increase, multiply, and replenish the earth: whereby it is more than apparent that the Lord, whose name is Jehovah, the mighty God of Israel, is the author of godly matrimony, instituting it in the time of man's innocence in paradise, and that as may seemeth for four causes. First, for the avoidance of whoredom; secondly, for the mutual comfort, and consolation that the one might have of the other in all adversities and calamities whatsoever; thirdly, for the procreation and godly propagation of children in the fear of the Lord, that both the world might be increased thereby, and the Lord also in them glorified; and fourthly, to be a figure or type of our spiritual wedlock betwixt Christ and his church both militant and triumphant. This congression and mutual copulation of those that be thus joined together in the godly

---

[1] **incident to . . . use:** for the purpose of. [2] **stimule, or prick:** stimulus. [3] **redintegration:** renewal. [4] **ensign:** sign.

state of blessed matrimony, is pure virginity, and allowable before God and man, as an action whereto the Lord hath promised his blessing through his mercy, not by our merit, *ex opere operato*,[5] as some shame not to say. All other goings together and coitions are damnable, pestiferous, and execrable. So, now you see, that whereas the Lord sayeth, increase, multiply, and fill the earth, he alludeth to those that are chained together in the godly state of matrimony and wedlock, and not otherwise: for to those that go together after any other sort, he hath denounced his curse and wrath forevermore, as his all-saving word beareth record. And whereas they say that all creatures upon the earth do engender together, I grant it is true. But how? *in suo genere*, in their own kind. There is no creature creeping on the earth, or flying in the air, how irrational soever, that doth degenerate as man doth, but keepeth the same state and other wherein they were made at the first, and so if man did, he should not commit abominable whoredom and filthy sin as he doth. It is said of those that write *de natura animalium*[6] that (almost) all unreasonable beasts and flying fowls after they have once linked and united themselves together to any one of the same kind, and after they have once espoused themselves one to the other, will never after join themselves with any other, till the one be dissolved from the other by death. And thus they keep the knot of matrimony inviolable to the end. And if any one chance to revolt and go together with any other during the life of his first mate, all the rest of the same kind assemble together, as it were in a council or parliament, and either kill or grievously punish the adulterer or adulteress whether ever it be, which law I would God were amongst Christians established. By all which it may appear how horrible a sin whoredom is in nature, that the very unreasonable creatures do abhor it. The heathen people who know not God so much loathe this stinking sin of whoredom that some burn them quick, some hang them on gibbets, some cut off their heads, some their arms, legs and hands, some put out their eyes, some burn them in the face, some cut off their noses, some one part of their body, some another, and some with one kind of torture, and some with another: but none leaveth them unpunished: so that we are sent to school to learn our first rudiments (like young novices or children fear crept out of the shell) how to punish whoredom, even by the unreasonable creatures and by the heathen people who are ignorant of the divine goodness. *God be merciful unto us.*

---

[5] *ex opere operato:* judge the maker by the work.   [6] *de natura animalium:* of the nature of animals.

FIGURE 23 *Taverngoers, from "The Bachelors' Banquet,"* Roxburgh Ballads, *vol. 2 (1874), parts 2 and 3.*

SPUDEUS: I pray you rehearse some places out of the word of God, wherein this cursed vice of whoredom is forbidden, for my better instruction.

PHILOPONUS: Our savior Christ in the eighth of John speaking to the woman, whom the malicious Jews had apprehended in adultery, bade her go her way and sin no more. If it had not been a most grievous sin, he would never have bid her to sin therein no more.

In the fifth of Matthew he sayeth, who so lusteth after a woman in his heart, hath committed the fact already, and therefore is guilty of death for the same. To the Pharisees, asking him whether a man might not put away his wife for any occasion, Christ answered, for no cause, save for whoredom only, inferring that whoredom is so heinous a sin, as for the perpetuation thereof it shall be lawful for a man to sequester himself from his own wife and the wife from her own husband. The apostle Paul sayeth, know you not that your bodies are the members of Christ, shall I then take the members of Christ (sayeth he) and make them the members of an whore? God forbid, know ye not that he who coupleth himself with a harlot is become one body with her? Flee fornication (sayeth he) therefore, for every sin that a man committeth is without the body, but who committeth fornication sinneth against his own body. And in another place: know you not, that your bodies are the temples of the Holy Ghost, which dwelleth within you? And who so destroyeth the temple of God, him shall God destroy.

SPUDEUS: Now am I fully persuaded by your invincible reasons that there is no sin greater before the face of God than whoredom, wherefore, God grant that all his may avoid it.

PHILOPONUS: You have said true, for there is no sin (almost) comparable unto it, for besides that, it bringeth everlasting damnation to all that live therein to the end, without repentance, it also bringeth these inconveniences, with many more, *vidilicet*[7] it dimmeth the sight, it impaireth the hearing, it infirmeth the sinews, it weakeneth the joints, it exhausteth the marrow, consumeth the moisture and supplement of the body, it riveleth[8] the face, appalleth[9] the countenance, it dulleth the spirits, it hurteth the memory, it weakeneth the whole body, it bringeth it into a consumption, it bringeth ulcerations, scabs, scurf, blain, botch, pocks and biles,[10] it maketh hoar hairs, and bald pates: it induceth old age, and in fine, bringeth death before nature urge it, malady enforce it, or age require it.

SPUDEUS: Seeing that whoredom bringeth such sour sauce with it, namely, death everlasting after this life, and so many discomodities besides in this life, I wonder that men dare commit the same so securely as they do nowadays?

PHILOPONUS: It is so little feared in Ailgna, that until every one hath two or three bastards apiece, they esteem him no man, (for that, they call a man's deed) insomuch as every scurvy boy of twelve, sixteen or twenty years of age will make no conscience of it, to have two or three, peradventure half a dozen several women with child at once, and this exploit being done, he shows them a fair pair of heels, and away goeth he, *Euro volocius*, as quick as a bee (as they say) into some strange place where he is not known where how he liveth, let the wise judge, for *coelum non animum mutant qui trans mare currunt*, though they change their place of abode, yet their naughty dispositions they retain still.

Then having estranged themselves thus for a small space, they return again, not to their pristine cursed life I dare say, but unto their country, and then no man may say black is their eye; but all is well, and they as good as Christians as those that suffer them unpunished.

SPUDEUS: The state and condition of that country is most miserable if it be true you report, it were much better that every one had his lawful wife,

---

[7] *vidilicet:* that is to say.   [8] **riveleth:** wrinkle or shrivel.   [9] **appalleth:** make pale.   [10] **scab** . . . **biles:** signs of various diseases, scabbing, and sloughing of skin; **blain** means ulcer; **bile** means boil.

and every woman her lawful husband, as the apostle commandeth, then thus to be drowned in the filthy sin of whoredom.

PHILOPONUS: That is the only salve and sovereign remedy, which the Lord ordained against whoredom, that those who have not the gift of continence might marry, and so keep their vessels undefiled to the Lord. But notwithstanding, in Ailgna there is over great liberty permitted therein: for little infants in swaddling clothes, are often married by their ambitious parents and friends when they know neither good nor evil, and this is the origin of much wickedness, and directly against the word of God, and examples of the primitive age. And besides this, you shall have every saucy boy of ten, fourteen, sixteen or twenty years of age, to catch up a woman and marry her, without any fear of God at all, or respect had, either to her religion, wisdom, integrity of life, or any other virtue, or which is more, without any respect how they may live together with sufficient maintenance for their callings and estate. No no, it maketh no matter for these things, so he have his pretty pussy to huggle[11] withal, it forceth not, for that is the only thing he desireth. Then build they up a cottage, though but of elder poles, in every lane end almost, where they live as beggars all their life. This filleth the land with such store of poor people, that in short time (except some caution be provided to prevent the same) it is like to grow to great poverty and scarceness, which God forbid.

SPUDEUS: I cannot see how this gear should be holpen.[12]

PHILOPONUS: What if a restraint were made, that none (except upon special and urgent causes) should marry before they come to twenty or twenty-four years, or at the least, before they be twenty-four or twenty-eight years old, would not this make fewer beggars than now there are?

SPUDEUS: But if this were established, that should we have more bastards, and of the two I had rather we had many legitimate, than many illegitimate.

PHILOPONUS: The occasion of begetting of many bastards were soon cut off, if the punishment which either God his law doth allow, or else which good policy doth constitute, were aggravated, and executed upon the offenders.

For the punishment appointed for whoredom now is so light that they esteem not of it, they fear it not, they make but a jest of it. For what great thing is it, to go two or three days in a white sheet[13] before the

---

[11] pretty pussy to huggle: pretty girl to hug, with play on "pussy" as "pucelle," occasional name for whore. [12] gear . . . holpen: habit should be changed. [13] go . . . sheet: being humiliated by appearing before the public in a white gown.

congregation, and that sometimes not past an hour or two in a day, having their usual garments underneath, as commonly they have? This impunity (in respect of condign[14] punishment, which that vice requireth) doth rather animate and embolden them to the act, than fear them from it. In so much, as I have heard some miscreants impudently say, that he is but a beast, that for such white livered punishment would abstain from such gallant pastime: but certain it is, that they who think it such sweet meat here, shall find the sauce sour and styptic[15] enough in hell.

SPUDEUS: What punishment would you have inflicted upon such as commit this horrible kind of sin?

PHILOPONUS: I would wish that the man or woman who are certainly known without all scruple or doubt to have committed the horrible fact of whoredom, adultery, incest, or fornication, either should drink a full draught of Moyses cup,[16] that is, taste of present death or else, if that be thought too severe (for in evil, men will be more merciful, than the author of mercy himself, but in goodness, farewell mercy) than would God they might be cauterized, and seared with a hot iron on the cheek, forehead, or some other part of their body that might be seen, to the end the honest and chaste Christians might be discerned from the adulterous children of Satan: But (alas) this vice (with the rest) wanteth such due punishment, as God his word doth command to be executed thereupon.

The magistrates wink at it, or else as looking through their fingers, they see it, and will not see it.

And therefore, the Lord is forced to take the sword into his own hands, and to execute punishment himself, because the magistrates will not.

For better proof whereof mark this strange and fearful judgment of God showed upon two adulterous persons there, even the last day in effect, the remembrance whereof is yet green in their heads.

There was a man whose name was W. Rasturb,[17] being certainly known to be a notorious usurer (and yet pretending always a singular zeal to religion, so that he would seldom times go without a Bible about him, but see the judgments of God upon them that will take his word in their mouths, and yet live clean contrary, making the word of God a cloak to cover their sin and naughtiness withal) who upon occasion of business visiting Lewedirb,[18] a place appointed for the correction of such that be wicked livers, saw there a famous whore, but a very proper woman, who (as is said) he knew not, but whether he did or not, certain it is that he

---

[14] condign: deserved.   [15] styptic: bitter.   [16] Moyses cup: Moses' cup, from the Passover seder; also cup used in Last Supper, Luke 22:17–39, 42.   [17] Ratsurb: Stubbes reverses the name; read backwards, it is "Brustar."   [18] Lewedirb: as above, Bridewell spelled backward.

procured her delivery from thence, bailed her,[19] and having put away his own wife before, kept her in his chamber, using her at his pleasure. Whilst these two members of the devil were playing the vile Sodomites together in his chamber, and having a little pan of coals before them wherein was a very little fire, it pleased God even in his wrath, to strike these two persons dead in a moment. The woman falling over the pan of coals was burned that all her bowels gushed out; the man was found lying by, his clothes in some parts being scorched and burned, and some parts of his body also. But which is most wonderful his arm was burned to the very bone, his shirt sleeve, and doublet not once perished, nor touched with the fire. Whereby may be thought and not without great probability of truth, that it was even the fire of God his wrath from heaven, and not any natural fire from the earth. And in this wonderful and fearful manner were these couple found: which God grant may be a document to all that hear or read the same, to avoid the like offense, and to all magistrates an example to see the same punished with more severity, to the glory of God, and their own discharge.

But so far are some from suffering condign punishment for this horrible sin, that they get good maintenance with practicing the same. For shall you not have some, yea many thousands, that live upon nothing else, and yet go clothed gentlewomenlike, both in their silks and otherwise, with their fingers clogged with rings, their wrists with bracelets, and jewels, and their purses full of gold and silver? Husbands know it not. Or if they do, some are such peasants, and such maycocks,[20] that either they will not, or (which is truer) they dare not reprove them for it. But & if the husband once reprove them for their misdemeanor, then they conspire his death by some means or other. And all this commeth to pass because the punishment thereof is no extremer, as it ought to be. And some both gentlemen and others (whereof some I know) are so nuzzled herein, that having put away their own wives, do keep whores openly, without any great punishment for it, and having been convented before the magistracy,[21] and there been deposed upon a book to put away their whores, have put them forth at one door, and taken them in at the other.

And thus they dally in their oaths with the Lord, and stop the course of the law, with *rubrum argentum*[22] whereof they have store to bestow upon such wickedness, but have not a mite to give towards any good purpose.

Wherefore, in the name of God, let all men that have put away their

---

[19] **bailed her:** paid her bail.   [20] **maycocks:** type of melon, hence thick-headed or empty-headed person.   [21] **convented before the magistracy:** summoned before the courts and magistrate. [22] *rubrum argentum:* literally red silver; from alchemy, indicating turning silver into gold.

honest wives be forced to take them again, and abandon all whores, or else to taste of the law. And let all whores be cut off with the sword of right judgment. For, as long as this immunity and impunity is permitted amongst us, let us never look to please God, but rather provoke his heavy judgments against us. And the reason is, for that there is no sin in all the world but these whores and whoremasters will willingly attempt and achieve for the enjoying of their whoredom.

And hell, destruction and death everlasting is the guerdon[23] thereof, and yet men cannot be aware of it. The Lord remove it from all his children, and present them blameless before his tribunal seat without spot or wrinkle at that great day of the Lord.

[23] guerdon: reward.

→ RICHARD LOVELACE

The Fair Beggar   *1649*

Richard Lovelace (1618–1657) was born into a privileged Kentish family and educated at Oxford University. A favorite of King Charles I, Lovelace became an important courtier, and in 1639–40 he participated in Charles's military campaign against Scotland. As a committed Royalist (a supporter of the king), he backed Charles in the crown's struggles with Parliament, and, in 1642, presented a petition that called for the restoration of the Anglican bishops who had been excluded from the Long Parliament (parliamentary sessions that lasted from 1640 to 1642 during which the Commons severely curtailed the king's royal prerogative by threatening to stop financing the government). The king's subsequent defeat, imprisonment, and ultimate execution in 1649 also spelled doom for Lovelace's fortunes. Although a member of a once wealthy and prestigious family, he died a pauper in 1657.

In addition to being a soldier and a courtier, Lovelace was also a celebrated poet of considerable skill and wit, and he is commonly grouped with other "Cavalier" poets such as Sir John Suckling and Robert Herrick. We have chosen to include Lovelace's "The Fair Beggar" because it shows us a cold aristocratic disregard for a woman who, like the prostitutes who inhabit *Measure for Measure's* Vienna, plies her trade for economic survival.

Richard Lovelace, *Lucasta: Epodes, Odes, Sonnets, Songs, &c. to Which Is Added Aramantha, a Pastoral* (London, 1649), 131–33.

Commanding asker, if it be
    Pity that you fain[1] would have,
Then I turn beggar unto thee,
    And ask the thing that thou dost crave;
I will suffice thy hungry need   5
So thou wilt but my fancy feed.

In all ill years, wa'st ever known
    On so much beauty such a dearth?
Which in that thrice-bequeathed gown
    Looks like the sun eclipsed with earth,   10
Like gold in canvas, or with dirt
Unsoiled ermines close begirt.[2]

Yet happy he that can but taste
    This whiter skin who thirsty is,
Fools dote on satin motions[3] lac'd,   15
    The gods go naked in their bliss,
At th' barrel's head there shines the vine,
There only relishes the wine.

There quench my heat, and thou shalt sup
    Worthy the lips that it must touch: 20
Nectar from out the starry cup,
    I beg thy breath not half so much;
So both our wants supplied shall be,
You'll give for love, I charity.

Cheap then are pearl embroideries   25
    That not adorn, but clouds thy waist;
Thou shalt be clothed above all price,
    If thou wilt promise me embrace't;
We'll ransack neither chest or shelf,
I'll cover[4] thee with mine own self.   30

But cruel, if thou dost deny
    This necessary alms to me;

---

[1] **fain:** gladly, or with pretended gladness. [2] **begirt:** wrapped, enclosed. [3] **motions:** puppets (used contemptuously). [4] **cover:** protect; but also to have sexual intercourse with.

What soft-soul'd man but with his eye
   And hand will hence be shut to thee?
Since all must judge you more unkind;   35
I starve your body, you my mind.

→ JOHN MARSTON

From The Dutch Courtesan   *1633*

John Marston (1576–1634), poet and satirist, gained a reputation for bitter invective against social ills; he abandoned writing in 1607 and became a clergyman. *The Dutch Courtesan* presents the adventures of Freevill and Malheureux, two young squires, and their companions as they enjoy the experiences on offer in the big city. The play generally delineates the differences (and intersections) between love and lust, using the two friends' contrasting temperaments as the vehicle for a comic change of views: Freevill, the rake whose name suggests his nature, does not resist the allure of sex, but learns in the end to love a "good" woman, while Malheureux, whose name ("unhappy") points to the result of suppressing one's natural desires, falls madly in love with a courtesan and has to learn to combine his high moral values with the reality of his passions.

ACT I, SCENE I

FREEVILL: Let me bid you good rest.

MALHEUREUX: Not so, trust me, I must bring my friend home. I dare not give you up to your own company, I fear the warmth of wine and youth will draw you to some common house of lascivious entertainment.

FREEVILL: Most necessary buildings Malheureux; ever since my intention of marriage I do pray for their continuance.

MALHEUREUX: Lov'd sir, your reason?

FREEVILL: Marry, lest my house should be made one: I would have married men love the stews, as Englishmen love the low countries,[1] wish war should be maintained there, lest it should be brought home to their own

---

[1] **the low countries**: the Netherlands; the English supported the Dutch against Spain in the Netherlands wars.

John Marston, "The Dutch Courtesan," in *The Works of Mr. John Marston Being Tragedies and Comedies, Collected into One Volume* (London, 1633), A1r–A3v.

doors: what, suffer a man to have a hole to put his head in, though he go to the pillory for it. Youth and appetite are above the club of Hercules.

MALHEUREUX: This lust is a most deadly sin sure.

FREEVILL: Nay, tis a most lively sin sure.

MALHEUREUX: Well, I am sure tis one of the head sins.

FREEVILL: Nay, I am sure it is one of the middle sins.

MALHEUREUX: Pity, tis grown a most daily vice.

FREEVILL: But a more nightly vice, I assure you.

MALHEUREUX: Well, tis a sin.

FREEVILL: I, or else few men would wish to go to heaven: and not to disguise with my friend, I am now going the way of all flesh.

MALHEUREUX: Not to a courtesan?

FREEVILL: A courteous one.

MALHEUREUX: What to a sinner?

FREEVILL: A very publican.²

MALHEUREUX: Dear my lov'd friend, let me be full with you,
Know sir, the strongest argument that speaks
Against the souls of eternity, is lust,
That wise man's folly, and the fool's wisdom:
But to grow wild in loose lasciviousness,
Given up to heat, and sensual appetite,
Nay to expose your health, and strength, and name,
Your precious time, and with that time the hope
Of due preferment, advantageous means
Of any worthy end, to the stale use,
The common bosom of a money creature,
One that sells human flesh, a mangonist.³

FREEVILL: Alas good creatures, what would you have them do? Would you have them get their living by the curse of man, the sweat of their brows? So they do, every man must follow his trade, and every woman her occupation; a poor decayed mechanical⁴ man's wife, her husband is laid up, may not she lawfully be laid down, when her husband's only rising is by his wife's falling? A captain's wife wants means, her commander lies in open field abroad, may not she lie in civil arms at home? A waiting gentlewoman, that had wont to take say⁵ to her Lady, miscarries,⁶ or so;

---

² publican: a tax collector; play on the notion of exacting fines for sins.   ³ mangonist: one who sells cheap goods.   ⁴ decayed mechanical: impoverished laborer.   ⁵ take say: also, make a trial of; serge or fine cloth.   ⁶ miscarries: the waiting-woman has had sex with ("tried" as above) her lady's male visitors, become pregnant, and lost her position.

the court misfortune throws her down, may not the city courtesy take her up? Do you know no alderman would pity such a woman's case? Why is charity grown a sin; or relieving the poor and impotent an offence? You will say beasts take no money for their fleshly entertainment, true, because they are beasts, therefore beastly; only men give to loose,[7] because they are men, therefore manly; and indeed, wherein should they bestow their money better? In land, the title may be cracked;[8] in houses, they may be burnt; in apparel, 'twill wear; in wine, alas for pity, our throat is but short; but employ your money upon women, and a thousand to nothing, some one of them will bestow that on you, which shall stick by you as long as you live.[9] They are no ungrateful persons, they will give you quit for quo;[10] do ye protest, they'll swear; do you rise, they'll fall; do you fall, they'll rise; do you give them the French crown,[11] they'll give you the French — *O justus justa justum.*[12] They sell their bodies, do not better persons sell their souls? Nay, since all things have been sold, honor, justice, faith, nay, even God himself, Ay me, what base ignobleness is it to sell the pleasure of a wanton bed?

Why do men scrape, why heap to full heaps join,
But for his Mistress, who would care for coin?
For this I hold to be denied of no man,
All things are made for man, and man for woman;
Give me my fee.[13]

MALHEUREUX: Of ill you merit well, my heart's good friend,
Leave yet at length, at length, for know this ever,
'T is no such sin to err, but to persevere.

FREEVILL: Beauty is woman's virtue, love the life's music, and woman the dainties[14] or second course of heaven's curious workmanship; since then beauty, love, and woman, are good, how can love of woman's beauty be bad and *Bonum, quo communius, eo melius,*[15] wilt then go with me?

MALHEUREUX: Whither?

FREEVILL: To a house of salvation?

MALHEUREUX: Salvation?

FREEVILL: Yes, twill make thee repent: wilt go to the family of love?[16] I will show thee my creature: a pretty nimble-eyed Dutch Tanakin,[17] an

---

[7] loose: loose behavior.   [8] cracked: broken or false.   [9] stick . . . live: i.e., they will give you a venereal disease.   [10] quit for quo: give something in exchange, here meaning the pox.   [11] French crown: the pox or syphilis, known as "the French disease."   [12] *O justus justa justum:* declension of the Latin adjective "just."   [13] Give . . . fee: reward me for my impassioned defense (as a lawyer defending his client).   [14] dainties: dessert.   [15] *Bonum, quo communius, eo melius:* A good the more held in common the better.   [16] family of love: a sect, originally Dutch, advocating free love.   [17] Tanakin: pet name for Anna.

FIGURE 24 *Detail from Crispijn de Passe's portrait of a courtesan. De Passe's book suggests that high-class prostitutes could be objects of great interest to the reading public as well as to their clients.*

honest soft-hearted impropriation,[18] a soft, plump, round-cheeked Froe,[19] that has beauty enough for her virtue, virtue enough for a woman, and woman enough for any reasonable man in my knowledge: wilt pass along with me?

MALHEUREUX: What, to a brothel, to behold an impudent prostitution? Fie on 't, I shall hate the whole sex to see her: the most odious spectacle the earth can present, is an immodest vulgar woman.

FREEVILL: Good still: my brain shall keep 't. You must go as you love me.

---

[18] **impropriation:** appropriation.   [19] **Froe:** "Frau" or woman in Dutch ("Frow" or "vrouw").

MALHEUREUX: Well. I'll go to make her loathe the shame she is.
The sight of vice augments the hate of sin.
FREEVILL: The sight of vice augments the hate of sin, very fine perdy.[20]
Exeunt.

[20] perdy: "Par Dieu" or "By God," anglicized from the French.

→ *From* Trial of a Procurer   *1489*

One Peter Manyfield, a London pimp, apparently forcibly abducted and kept
against her will as his personal sex slave a woman named Alice Burle. When
Manyfield no longer had a use for Burle, he sold her to an Easterling. It is not
completely clear if the "sale" constituted a transfer of "ownership" (which was a
legal impossibility but sometimes a practical reality), or if Manyfield sold only
Burle's sexual favors to the Easterling. In many instances, if a crime included an
act of violence such as abduction or rape it would be referred from the church
court to a secular court, which had greater powers to punish an offender. In this
case, however, despite Manyfield's admitting to the crime, the case against him
was kept in church court and the perpetrator, after failing to appear for a second
hearing, was merely banned from church services temporarily. It is interesting to
compare the treatment Manyfield receives in the church court to Pompey's fate
at the hands of Angelo and Escalus.

   The case, as it appears below, is Paul Hair's paraphrase of the original church
court entry.

Peter Manyfeld is a common procurer and has especially arranged lewdness
between Jacob Grenebarow an Easterling and various suspect women. And
Peter carried away, by stealth and violence and against her will, a certain
Alice Burle from her parents' house and kept her in his room for a long
time, committing with her the crime of fornication, and after he was tired of
her, he sold her to a certain Easterling in the Steelyard: he is cited on the
12th of January, appears and admits the crime, and should appear again but
does not and is suspended [i.e., temporarily banned from church services].

Paul Hair, ed., *Before the Bawdy Court: Selections from Church Court and other Records Relating to
the Correction of Moral Offences in England, Scotland, and New England, 1300–1800* (London:
Elek, 1972), 205.

From The Counter's Commonwealth *1617*

William Fennor was a small-time poet and pamphleteer who achieved perhaps greater fame for failing to appear in a staged contest of wits with John Taylor, the Water Poet, and for the ensuing exchange of printed insults, than for any of his other works. Fennor seems to have been briefly imprisoned in 1616 in the Wood Street Counter, or debtors prison, where he wrote this piece, portions of which are excerpted below.

CHAPTER I

[Fennor begins his account with the description of his arrest, in which he escapes one encounter with street violence only to be approached by the "bandogs" or sergeants who arrest him for debt. He describes the horrible faces of these sergeants — hence the "furies" of the paragraph that follows. They trick him into spending money entertaining them in a tavern, promising to help him get out of prison quickly.]

These furies had no sooner fastened their sharp flesh-hooks on my shoulders, but they, as their fashion is, began to exhort me to patience, telling me I ought not to be incensed against them for they were but the ministers and executioners of the law, and that the mace which they held in their clutches, was put into theirs by the hand of Justice, that they were both for the good of the commonwealth, and the discharge of their own consciences, sworn to execute their office though it were upon their own father, that I being so gracious in the Court, could not long be detained in the Counter, that after I had been resident there but one quarter of a year (if it should be my ill fate to stay there so long) I would not lose the rich experiences I should learn there for ten times so much debt I was arrested for, and, lastly, swore as they were Christians, they would do me what kindness lay in their power, either persuading my creditor to come to a reasonable composition, or provide me bail. The cormorants told me true, for they swore as they were Christians they would do me good, but being contrary to them, played the Jews, and falsified their oaths with me, for I never saw them after I was mewed up in the Counter. But before I was matriculated in one of these City universities,

---

William, Fennor, *The Counter's Commonwealth, or a Voyage Made to an Infernal Island, Long Since Discovered by Many Captains, Seafaring-men, Gentlemen, Merchants, and Other Tradesmen* (London, 1617), 3–11, 46–61, 77–80.

by persuasion they got me into a tavern not far from the prison and there milked me out of all my money to stuff their paunches with wine and good cheer. But their guts and garbage being full-gorged, they told me it was time to repair to the Counter, for if the Sheriff their master should be certified of their detaining a prisoner so long after an arrest, it would be a great prejudice to them, and small good to myself. So I, discharging the reckoning, wishing them choked and all their fellow varlets, that ever after should taste of my bounty (when I began to scent their roguery), came over with them, so bid them farewell and be hanged.

But here is one serious point not to be slipped over, for the Cerberus that turned the key of the counter-gate[1] no sooner saw those hell-guides bringing me in, but he set the door as wide open to receive me, as Westminster Hall is in the term-time to country clients,[2] which put me in mind of that odd old verse in the poet: *Noctes atque dies patet atri janua ditis.*[3]

I no sooner was entered into this Infernal Island where many men lie wind-bound[4] sometimes four or five years together but a fellow (whom at first sight I took to be a gardener, because he had somewhat a reddish beard and turned-up withal) called me to a book, no Bible or divinity, but rather of necromancy, for all the prisoners called it the Black Book. Coming to it, he demanded my name. I told him, and then he set it down as horses are in Smithfield at the toll-booth.[5] This ceremony being ended, he asked me whether I would go to the Master's side, the Knights' Ward, or any other place of a cheaper rate. I answered the best, though it were the dearest for I did hope to get my liberty before a week was expired.

Chapter 2

[Having been admitted to the prison's better lodgings, the prisoner meets his fellow inmates; they talk and drink.]

Thus, having finished our feast and waiting for no banquet we rose, every man disposing of himself as he pleased, only myself guided by the evil Fate walked in to the foreroom, where the fraternity of keepers and other servants of the house were feeding on the fragments that were reserved from

---

[1] **counter-gate:** the gate of the prison guarded by a man as hell's gate is guarded by the three-headed dog, Cerberus.   [2] **as Westminster . . . clients:** the doors were as wide as the gates of hell. An ironic reference to hopeless and costly cases welcomed at the Hall (locus of court trials).   [3] *Noctes atque dies patet atri janua ditis:* "The door to Pluto's atrium stands open day and night," a quote from Virgil's *Aeneid,* 6:127.   [4] **wind-bound:** stranded by the winds, as in sea travel.   [5] **as horses . . . toll-booth:** horses for sale had to be certified to the toll-keepers at fairs to prevent horse-thieving.

our table. I with a common salutation bade much good do them, but when they had emptied their crammed jaws, told me there was certain garnish[6] to be paid. I, now being too well acquainted with that language, told them plainly I would pay no more, to which they replied and said, that then I should have my liberty no more, for all the rest of my fellow-prisoners had paid it, and except I would be their imitators and come off roundly, I should be debarred of that privilege the rest of my associates had. I, loath to be pent up like a lion in the Tower, and have no more liberty than to look through an iron grate, demanded the sum. They told me sixpence, to send for a quart of claret wine, which was the last tester that remained in my peaceful pockets. At last, flinging it to them, I walked up to my lodging again, and there by chance espied a standish[7] and a sheet of undefiled paper, which being fit for my purpose, I made bold with, and in the midst of melancholy, wrote this character of a prison.

> It is a fabric built of the same stuff the keepers of it are made of, stone and iron. It is an unwholesome, full-stuffed, humorous body, which hath an Hole[8] in the posteriors of it, whence it vents many stinking, noisome and unsavoury smells, which is the only cause there is such a perpetual sickness and disease in it. It is a book where an honest man may learn and read a lesson of bettering himself, and where a bad man may study to be ten times worse. It is a costive[9] creature, that surfeits almost all the year long, yet very seldom doth purge itself; and when it doth, it leaveth abundance of ill humours behind. When Epimetheus opened Pandora's box, there did not more mischiefs and maladies fly out of it into the world, than there is in this cursed place, for it hath more sicknesses predominating in it, than there are in twenty French hospitals, or at the Bath, in the spring or fall of the leaf. It is a bankrupt's banqueting-house, where he sits feasting himself with dishes borrowed from other men's tables, without any honest determination to repay them again. It is a prodigal's purgatory, and a sickness that many young gentlemen and citizens' sons and heirs are incident to be troubled with, at the age of one-and-twenty or much thereabout. It is a dicing-house, where much cheating is used; for there is little square dealing to be had there, yet a man may have what bail he will for his money.

CHAPTER 3

[Fennor is called to speak with a visiting friend, who leaves him two angels (coins), which lifts his spirits; he is then waited on hand and foot by his jailors

---

[6] **garnish:** culinary pun; bribe.   [7] **standish:** inkstand.   [8] **Hole:** the lodging reserved for the poorest prisoners.   [9] **costive:** constipative.

until his money runs out. Once that happens, he moves to the next lower rank of lodgings, the Knight's ward. He meets another prisoner who promises to tell him the secrets of the prison for the "profit" of the greater commonwealth outside.]

But the Day-star no sooner began to cherish the world with his all-reviving light, but I sprung from mine hard couch, made me ready, and when the doors were open (by much entreaty) got into the yard, where having not walked half a dozen turns, but I made my repair into the cellar, more athirst to have my mind's palate quenched with his discourse, than my mouth with the best liquor in all the barrels, but having called for two cans of beer, I sent for a quart of sack[10] to whet the point of his wit, that it might wound vice the deeper. That being come, I sent for my friend who lay in the Hole, who was forthwith let out (being an old prisoner) and being come down, thus I began to salute him:

"Ingenious friend, as welcome to me as this fair day is to the world, this night hath seemed long; but the burning desire I had to confer with you concerning the discovery (you out of your love promised to reveal) made it more tedious, and if you will but disclose the main body, let me alone to unmask the face, and lay every member open to the world's eye."

"Sir," quoth he, "you seem so complete in your quality that I hope you will publish what I shall relate. If you should smother it, I rather would keep it to myself than impart it; but not doubting of your diligence in this matter, I will venture my discourse, and, good sir, give a diligent attention."

[The old prisoner reveals the many stratagems that are used to trap naïve country visitors in debt, describing a whole world of predators who live off their takings from such enterprises. He then moves on to the corruption and misdealings of the law's representatives, who often trick their targets or haul in innocent citizens for the money they are paid to deliver prisoners to the jail. Constables, however, he defends for preserving the peace, since they are unpaid and so less corrupt.]

"As the main ocean is nourished by the arms and rivers, that pay hourly tribute to him with the silver streams, and especially out of our land, by swan-blessed Thames, swift Severn, dangerous-passing Humber, and smooth-faced Trent, so is this turbulent sea the Counter by these four currents hereafter mentioned: first, unconscionable citizens; secondly, politic prodigals, *alias* engineers;[11] thirdly, catchpoles;[12] fourthly and lastly, con-

---

[10] **sack:** wine. [11] **politic . . . engineers:** gentlemen fallen on hard times who take to ensnaring other innocents in debt for kickbacks. [12] **catchpoles:** tax-gatherers.

stables and their adherents, as the beadle and his watchmen: all whose abuses I will strip naked, and jerk[13] with my tongue, till I fetch blood. The first of whom have been the only cause of my detaining in prison this four years; yet let no man think that I speak against all citizens. No! as I hope for eternal happiness, I reverence that worshipful, ancient, and fameworthy order, I mean such as maintain themselves and their families. I touch not those that care not who look and pry into their consciences, because their dealings have been so square and honest; but such as enrich themselves by fraud, deceit and sinister means, working upon the infirmity of youth, and greenwitted gallants, to increase their own store, caring not how much they decrease other men's estates. Such there are in the most flourishing and religious commonwealths in the world. In the most famous universities in Christendom there are some dunces resident that not only disgrace themselves, but also their fellow-students. It is impossible, but that in the most virtuous court there will be some parasites, so in the most goodly and glorious city under Heaven's canopy there are some asps lurking that sting the reputation of their brethren by their poisonous and corrupt dealings. Such as these I will portray and limn forth to you; and first of all I will discourse unto you to the extreme abuse of gain-greedy citizens, and in order will touch the politic prodigals, *alias* engineers, and I think soulless sergeants, and constables and beadles. But first of the first."

Chapter 6

"In ancient Rome the lictors,[14] or sergeants, went always with their staves of office in their hands, and in such apparel that the whole city knew them, and yet to this day in this form and fashion they continue, or carry about them some mark of difference. So in many other countries they are so markable that they are no sooner seen than known. But here in England (where they once went in pied coats and white rods in their hands, as a badge of infamy) they will alter their fashion of habit oftener than a whore doth her lodging, or a French count his shirts in summer-time. Proteus never changed shapes oftener than these fellows, for sometime they will go accoutred like a scholar, then like a merchant, sometime like a counselor, then a butcher, porter, or country gentleman, with their boots and spurs as dirty as if they had rid five hundred mile through the deepest sloughy way that ever was traveled; but this is (most commonly) when they go to arrest some farmer or yeoman of the country that is either but newly come into his inn, or going

---

[13] jerk: stroke with a whip.   [14] lictors: attendants to magistrates who bore official standard.

out of town. And a hundred more such stratagems have they in their head when they are well greased in the hand, or when the arrest is something dangerous. . . .

"Reason (the soul of law) and Law (the life of a commonwealth) should shine and be translucent in those that bear the office of a constable, for he being the King's deputy for the night, is the king of the night, therefore being so, he should impartially with his staff which representeth Justice, beat down disorder, and defend Equity, Peace and Innocence: but there are many constables in these days, that through their own negligence (not willfulness) do contrary to the nature of their office, for very often the beadle and watchmen in his absence, commit that which the constable himself is much blamed for, who under the pretense of seeing good order kept, as I have heard, are the first that breed disorder. But for mine own part I never was eyewitness of any of their misdemeanors, but only as I have heard it reported, therefore I dare nor will go no further than truth doth guide me. For first, I should wrong that worthy office, in relating what I have no probability for, and secondly my self, in making myself a dishonest man in print."

"Why sir," said I, "I have often heard it reported, that the beadles and watchmen are in fee with the keepers of both the Counters, and that for every man they commit they receive a groat,[15] and therefore, only for gain will (upon any light or slight fault) carry any man that comes in their way to prison, or if any man fee them, they will (if he be never so drunk, unruly, or disordered) convey him to his lodging; or otherwise, if he be unfurnished, convey him to one of the Counters. And to mine own knowledge I have known a beadle committed to the Gate House for committing a nobleman's servant (who went upon special business for the lord his master). Therefore if he had not first wronged this gentleman, and secondly the force and nature of his office, why should he being an officer be committed for his misdemeanor? Again I have seen many men come into prison (since I came hither) that have been extremely hacked and maimed with their halberds:[16] which in my opinion they cannot answer, for though they have authority to commit, they have none to kill or wound. Therefore in my judgment these abuses are insufferable, and only are upholden by their head the constable."

"Sir" (said he) "you must understand that a constable is but an island brook that pays but small tribute to the ocean the Counter, he is but *causa accidentalis*, an accidental cause, and by chance fattens the gross and vast body of it, for after his watch is sent he is bound by oath to perform his office both for the discharge of his own conscience, and the good of his prince, and country, in which duty every good subject is bound in duty to

---

[15] **groat:** a coin of small value.   [16] **halberds:** weapon combining spear and battle axe.

assist him. For a constable is the preserver of peace, the attacher of vice, and the intelligencer of injuries, and hath as strong and forcible power to commit offenders in the night as any justice of peace hath in the day; nay, if any lord, knight, or gentleman, of what degree, or fashion soever he be, coming in the night-time through the watch in an unruly fashion, is as subject to his command and authority as the poorest subject that walks the streets: and, if he should not sometimes, nay many times, clap up such personages, they would be thought very slack in their office and not worthy of that authority and power the King hath given them; for many men though they have brave outsides may commit or act as great, or more heinous mischief than those that are of a poor rank, for if the constable should not stand sentinel, how many men would be robbed in the space of one week, may of one night, which by his industry and care he preserves. . . ."

Chapter 8

[Having described how men come to be in prison, the old prisoner describes to his young acquaintance the general conditions and nature of the "commonwealth" of prisoners within.]

"In Noah's ark there were some of all sort of creature, so in the Counter some of all kind of people, for to say the right of it, it is a commonwealth though very little wealth be common there. There lies your right worshipful poor knight, your worshipful beggarly esquire, your distressed gentleman, your mechanic[17] tradesman, your prating pettifogger,[18] and juggling (liars I would say) lawyers, all these like so many beasts in a wilderness desire to prey one upon the other, for I think there are as many sins looking through the grates of a prison as there are walking through the gates of a city. For though we are all prisoners yet the causes of our restraint are divers. Some are in for debt, some for other more heinous and criminal actions, some there are that are in upon constraint, and such are they that come in for debt and can no way shun what they suffer, or have no means to give satisfaction to their creditors. Others there are that are voluntary and such are they that come in of purpose, who (if it please themselves) may keep themselves out, of which I find four kind of people that are good subjects to this commonwealth the Counter, and they are these: the first your subtle citizen; the second your riotous unthrifts; the third your politic highwayman; and the fourth and last your crafty mechanic."

---

[17] **mechanic:** manual laborer.   [18] **pettifogger:** lawyer who handles only minor cases; also, one who is a rascal.

FIGURE 25 *The Watch Outside a Prison, frontispiece illustration, from Robert Speed,*
The Counter Scuffle *(London, 1628).*

CHAPTER 9

"Sir," (said he) "you shall seldom see a butcher's dog that continually lies in the shambles[19] without a bloody mouth, and those officers that live in this place having once their finger dipped in the blood-bowl of cruelty, seldom or never can be reduced to a milder kind of usage: custom is a second nature with them, and because they daily do it, they think it is as natural with them as their meat and drink.

"But I will leave their strict dealing with old prisoners while another time, and come to their usage and behavior to new-come prisoners at their first entrance.

"The first entrance of any man into the Daedalean labyrinth,[20] after they have viewed him and know his name, then according to the fashion of this clothes (but most especially the weight of his purse) they bear themselves towards him. Flies never come to painted gallipots[21] for their gay outsides,

---

[19] **shambles:** a table or stall for selling goods. [20] **Daedalean labyrinth:** In Greek myth, Daedalus — an architect and inventor — was asked to build a labyrinth for King Minos to contain the Minotaur, a creature who was half-man and half-bull. Daedalus was later imprisoned in his own labyrinth, and built wax wings to escape; his son, Icarus, flew too close to the sun and fell to his death when his wings melted. [21] **gallipots:** glazed earthenware pots.

but their sweet insides as suckets,[22] sugars, and other preserves, so these rather respect the purse, than the person; for they had rather know he hath a silver inside than see him to have a golden outside. If they know he hath good friends that will not see him want, or that he hath means of his own correspondent to their expectation, they will fawn and flatter him in every respect more than a funeral sermon will a dead man; he shall want nothing while he wants not money, every officer will have a cap and a knee for him, every time they see him he shall command all the house, be *Dominus facto-tum,*[23] what abuse soever he offers shall be smothered suffering him to do any wrong, yet take none, when a poor man for the least offense shall be clapped into irons, and cast into the Hole, and there shall remain while such time he submits himself in all humility to Master Keeper. . . .

"I could now relate to you the villainy of the messengers, that are members of the same body, who instead of going to men's friends with letters (which concerns their liberty or relief) will sit drinking in some ale-house and neglect their business, which it may be is a perpetual undoing to the poor man. I could display the abuses of drunken tapsters that poison poor prisoners with their stinking sour beer, which they sell as dear as if it were as good as ever dyed any nose in grain: for the most we have is as you see, scarce a wine-pint for a penny, and they will not suffer us to send for it out of doors where we may have far better, and better measure, but will break such bottles our friends send in too for our relief, and will neither trust us when we have no money, nor suffer us to send for it where we may be trusted, but serve us with drinking that the worst jailer among them will scorn to taste of, but when we are all locked up into our wards will send for better out of doors, and will be drunk when many a poor soul is so dry that they are ready to choke. . . ."

[After describing the greater part of the prison and its population, the old prisoner turns to a description of the Hole, or poor section.]

"This little Hole is a little city in a commonwealth, for as in a city there are all kinds of officers, trades and vocations, so there is in this place, as we may make a pretty resemblance between them. Instead of a Lord Mayor, we have a Master Steward to oversee and correct all such misdemeanors as shall arise. He is a very upright man[24] in his dealings though he stoop in his body, but the weight of the office he bears is the cause he bends, which is a great sign of humility. And as the City hath twelve companies that exceed all the rest for authority, antiquity and riches, so hath this place twelve old prisoners

---

[22] suckets: candy.   [23] *Dominus factotum:* a head steward.   [24] upright man: play on words — an upright man was slang for a rogue or highwayman.

that help the Steward in his proceedings, who by the general voice of the house rule and bear sway over all the rest; and here as in a city is divine service said every evening, and morning; here as in a city is a commanding constable, that upon any misdemeanors offered by any man either to the steward, or the twelve shall be bravely mounted and have ten pounds with a purse, that the print of their justice shall stick upon his buttocks four-and-twenty hours after. And lastly as in a city there is all kinds of trades, so is there here, for here you shall see a cobbler sitting mending old shoes, and singing as merrily as if he were under a stall abroad; not far from him you shall see a tailor sit crosslegged (like a witch) on his cushion, threatening the ruin of our fellow-prisoners the Egyptian vermin.[25] In another place you may behold a saddler, empanelling all his wits together how to patch this Scotch pad handsomely, or mend the old gentlewoman's crupper[26] that was almost burst in pieces. You may have a physician here that for a pottle[27] of sack will undertake to give you as good a medicine for melancholy as any doctor will for five pound, and make you purge upward and downward as well as if you had taken down into your guts all the drugs in Lothbury. Besides if you desire to be removed before a judge you shall have a tinker-like attorney not far distant from you, that in stopping up one hole in a broken cause will make twenty before he hath made an end, and at last will leave you in prison as bare of money as he himself is of honesty. Here is your choleric good cook that will dress our meat when we can get any as well as any greasy scullion in Fleet Lane or Pie Corner. And twenty more than these there are, which for brevity sake I will leave out, because I would discourse unto you the majesty and state of these officers, when every Saturday at night they sit in counsel about their affairs, and thus it is."

[25] the Egyptian vermin: possibly the Egyptian rat, thought to be a carrier of insects and disease.
[26] crupper: leather strap passing under horse's tail.   [27] pottle: bottle.

✦ The Prisoners' Petition   *n.d.*

The prison in which Claudio and Barnardine are incarcerated is hardly described in the play. Lucio refers to it as a "kennel" (3.2.70), Escalus threatens Pompey with whipping (a common enough punishment inflicted in London's prisons), and Barnardine is able to secure enough alcohol to be perpetually drunk, but few other details are given. It appears, however, that Claudio is not housed with the well-to-do inmates, suggesting that he is among the poorer

---

"The Prisoners' Petition," in *A Collection of Seventy-Nine Black-Letter Ballads and Broadsides, Printed in the Reign of Queen Elizabeth, Between the Years 1559–1597* (London, 1870), 16–17.

FIGURE 26 *"Description of Charity," from* Stephen Bateman, A Crystal Glass of Christian Reformation. *"As many as intend to be partakers with Christ and his Apostles must use this work of charity, which is to feed the hungry, to clothe the naked, to harbor the harborless, and to lodge the stranger, to visit the sick, and to relieve the prisoners and poor afflicted members of Christ, this is the duties of all faithful people."*

sort. Does the lack of details about Claudio's prison mean that Shakespeare does not want his audience to think about the prevailing horrors of early modern prison life, or does it suggest that Londoners knew so well the stories of cruelty, corruption, and suffering in the prisons — some of which are detailed in the excerpt below — that there was no need to remind them?

George Whetstone's depiction of prison life in *Promos and Cassandra* (1578), a play that possibly served as a source for *Measure for Measure,* may have been inspired by Bridewell prison (Pendry 295). But, again, because Shakespeare includes so few specifics about Claudio's prison, it is difficult to draw direct parallels between it and this notorious Elizabethan workhouse and prison. It is fair to assume, however, that Elizabethan playgoers would have a vivid sense of the harsh conditions encountered in any of the city's houses of detention.

Apparently there was a historical precedent for Barnardine's refusal to be executed because, as the drunken man puts it, "I am not fitted for 't" (*Measure for Measure* 4.3.34–35). According to the *Acts of the Privy Council of England,* a man under sentence of death was remanded in 1559 "because he was not religiously prepared" to die (Pendry 136). As the Duke observes, "to transport him in the mind he is / Were damnable" (4.3.55–56).

The Prisoner's Petition

To the worshipful our good benefactor:

In all lamentable manner, most humbly beseecheth your good worship, we, the miserable multitude of very poor distressed prisoners, in the hole of the Wood-Street Counter,[1] in number fifty poor men or thereabouts, lying upon the bare boards,[2] still[3] languishing in great need, cold and misery, who, by reason of this dangerous and troublesome time, be almost famished and hunger-starved to death; others very sore sick and diseased for want of relief and sustenance, by reason of the great number, which daily increases, doth in all humbleness most humbly beseech your good worship, even for God's sake, to pity our poor lamentable and distressed cases; and now help to relieve and comfort us with your Christian and Godly charity against[4] this holy and blessed time of Easter. And we, according to our bounden[5] duties, do and will daily pray unto Almighty God for your long life and happy prosperity.

> We humbly pray your Christian and Godly charity
> to be sent unto us by some of your servants.

[1] Wood-Street Counter: a prison for debtors. [2] boards: wooden planks. [3] still: always. [4] against: near. [5] bounden: bound.

JAMES GRYFFON

The Song of a Constable   *1626*

As the title of the following ballad indicates, James Gryffon was the constable of Albury, a parish in Surrey (Rollins 379). Nothing else is known about him. The ballad reveals that some of the constable's duties made him an unloved person in

---

James Gryffon, "The Song of a Constable," in *Old English Ballads, 1553–1625,* ed. Hyder E. Rollins (Cambridge: Cambridge UP, 1920), 488–90.

English society, and we should therefore probably not be surprised by Shakespeare's satirical portrayal of Constable Elbow as an incompetent fool.

To the tune of "Jump to me, Cousin."

I, a constable, have took mine oath
    by which shall plain appear
The truth and nothing but the truth,
    whosoever my song will hear.
One great Constable in England was,   5
    another late should have been;[1]
But little ones now 'tis found will serve,
    so they be but honest men.
A Constable must be honest and just,
    have knowledge and good report,   10
And able to strain with body and brain,
    Else he is not fit for't.

Some parish puts a constable on,
    alas without understanding;
By cause they'd rule him when they have done,   15
    and have him at their commanding;
And if he commands the poor, they'll grutch[2]
    and twit[3] him with partial blindness;
Again and if he commands the rich,
    they'll threaten him with unkindness.   20
To charge or compel 'em he's busy, they'll tell 'em;
    in paying of rates they'll brawl.
Falls he but unto do that he should do,
    I'll warrant you displease them all.

He the rogues, they'll rail and they'll curse,   25
    soldiers as rude 'cause they are;
Sent to the treasurer with their pass,
    and may not bed everywhere.
If warrants do come, as often they do,
    for money, then he it demands.   30

---

[1] **One . . . been:** "The third Duke of Buckingham, executed in 1521, was the last High Constable of England who made pretensions to play a special part in public affairs. With him the hereditary character of the office perished and thereafter the Constable performed his duties only on Coronation Days" (Judges 521).   [2] **grutch:** complain.   [3] **twit:** reproach, accuse.

To ev'ryone with 's rate he does go,
    wherein they are levied by lands.
They'll say then he gathers up money of others
    to put to use for increase;[4]
Else gathers it up to run away w'it, —   35
    what terrible words be these!

Hearing a press[5] for soldiers, they'll start;[6]
    else hide themselves when we come.
Their wives then will say, "to press we ye may,
    our husbands are not at home."   40
Coin[7] for magazines,[8] sent for in haste,
    Much ado was ere they be yielded.
Yet's gather'd and paid, and I am afraid
    They will not in haste be builded.
The justices will set us by the heels[9]   45
    If we do not do as we should;
Which if we perform, the townsmen will storm, —
    Some of them hang's if they could.

The constable's warned to th' sessions[10] then,
    unwilling some goes, alas!   50
Yet there may wit and experience learn,
    if that he be not an ass.
There shall he see the justices set,
    hear three of *Oyez'es,*[11] and
Then shall he hear the commission[12] read,   55
    though little he understand.
Four free-landed[13] men are call'd for in, then,
    to be of the great inquest:[14]
The chief of our towns, with hoar on their crowns,[15]
    that what should be done knows best.   60

Choice men of every town in the shire,
    three juries there must be more,[16]

---

[4] **increase:** at interest. [5] **press:** compulsory enlistment. [6] **start:** flee suddenly. [7] **coin:** money. [8] **magazines:** storehouses (probably for corn). [9] **set . . . heels:** put in irons or the stock. [10] **sessions:** to commit (a person) to the sessions for trial. [11] *Oyez'es:* a call by the court officer: "Hear, hear ye!" [12] **commission:** a charge or warrant. [13] **free-landed:** having an estate in land. [14] **inquest:** a legal or judicial inquiry to ascertain or decide a matter of fact. [15] **hoar . . . crowns:** gray hair on their heads. [16] **choice . . . more:** "The constable evidently had his hands full with the duty of nominating men qualified to serve on these various bodies at Quarter Sessions" (Judges 521).

FIGURE 27 *A Constable, woodcut from Geoffrey Mynshul,* Essayes and Characters of a Prison *(1618).*

Call'd unto the book with "Here, sir, here,"
    the wisest of twenty before.
Then there shall he see whom has transgressed   65
    punished for his offense;

There shall he hear a number amerced,[17]
 along of their negligence.
What things are amiss, what doings there is,
 justices charge them inquire
'For Clerk of the Peace and bailies[18] at least
 a dozen, besides the crier.

Verdicts must come from these juries then,
 but howsoever they indict them,
They'll not be took till next day by ten,
 unless that their clerks do right them.
Ruff words or smooth are all but in vain,
 all courts of profit do savor;
And though the case be never so plain,
 yet kissing shall go by favor.
They'll punish the leastest and favor the greatest,
 nought may against them proceed,
And who may dare speak 'gainst one that is great —
 law what a powder[19] indeed!

Thus now my constableship's near done,
 mark hearers, sayers, and singers:
Not an officer under the sun
 but does look through his fingers.
Yet where I see one willing to mend,
 not prating nor making excuses,
Such a one if I can I'll befriend,
 and punish the gross abuses.
My counsel now use, you that are to choose,
 put able men ever in place;
For knaves and fools in authority do
 but themselves and their country disgrace.

70

75

80

85

90

95

---

[17] amerced: punished, fined. [18] bailies: bailiffs. [19] a powder: an impetuous force.

CHAPTER 4

Geography and Religion

>‹

The earliest text of *Measure for Measure*, which appears in the First Folio of 1623, contains an "extra" sheet that lists the dramatic personae and identifies the play's locale: *"The Scene Vienna."* On the face of it, there is nothing especially remarkable about a foreign setting. After all, when Shakespeare wrote *Measure for Measure*, he had already set stories in Denmark, Athens, Venice, Verona, Messina, and France, among others. The difference is that "Vienna" may have direct bearing on English local and religious politics of the day, and on James I's recent succession to the English throne. We know that *Measure for Measure* was performed before the recently crowned James I at Whitehall Palace on December 26, 1604, and a substantial body of criticism argues that Shakespeare's Duke Vincentio resembles King James. If Shakespeare's portrayal of Vienna's Duke is indeed flattering, advising, or criticizing England's new ruler, then it raises a number of fascinating and hotly debated questions concerning justice, absolutism, and the monarch's relation to the law — questions that we take up in Chapter 1, "Governance." Here we want to focus on the question of "Vienna," which becomes a vexing one when we realize that historical Vienna, as part of the Holy Roman Empire, was a staunchly Catholic city (see Fig. 28). If *Measure for Measure*'s Duke Vincentio is a portrait of the English king, then James is linked to a Catholic prince who establishes order and justice in his realm, which is

A True and Exact Defcription of the

C I T Y of V I E N N A,

Together with the Encampment of the *TURKS*, and the Relation of the moft Memorable Paffages during the late S I E G E.

FIGURE 28 *Map of Vienna. Periodically threatened or besieged by the Ottoman Empire, Vienna came to represent beleaguered Christianity fighting for its beliefs against the Islamic world.*

something that many hoped and prayed James would do after the difficult last years of Elizabeth's reign. After Henry VIII's break with Rome, England had officially become, with the exception of the years of Queen Mary's reign, a nation with a single, state-sponsored religion: the Established Protestant Church. James himself had been raised in the Protestant Scottish Kirk (with its strong Calvinist overtones), and we may well wonder what the impact of his association with Catholic Vienna could have been.

One way to approach the question is to say that the Catholic association undermines or even negates any possible link between James and the Duke. But as we argue in the Governance chapter, there are too many suggestive similarities between James and the Duke for playgoers not to wonder whether Vincentio equalled King James, even if many of them ultimately concluded that he did not. Although Catholicism was outlawed in England, there may have been as many as 35,000 Catholics in the realm in 1603 (a number that grew to 60,000 by 1640 [Smith 263]),[1] and James did not want to be on bad terms with them, partly because he prided himself on his religious tolerance, and partly because some of England's powerful noble families unofficially adhered to the Catholic faith. In 1603, a group of Catholics submitted to James a text entitled "The Catholics' Supplication" (reproduced in this section on p. 339), in which the king was asked to extend greater tolerance to adherents of the ancient faith on the grounds that Catholics were, and always had been, loyal subjects to the crown of England. Moreover, historian Roger Lockyer suggests that English Protestants were "apprehensive at what they regarded as the King's over-permissiveness" regarding Catholics. Presenting his views as typical, Lockyer quotes an early seventeenth-century letter writer to say that "it is hardly credible in what jolity [the Catholics] now live. They make no question to obtain at least a toleration if not an alteration of religion; in hope whereof many who before did dutifully frequent the [parish] Protestant church are of late become recusants"[2] (Lockyer 283). Even if this assessment is somewhat exaggerated, it is true that English Protestants had suffered greatly during the reign of "Bloody" Mary Tudor, who had reunited the English church with the church of Rome and had aggressively persecuted Protestants and burned them at the stake. Christopher Muriell the Elder tapped into Protestant anxiety when he penned and published *An Answer unto the Catholics' Supplication* (1603; excerpted in this section on p. 343), in which he reminds James of acts of treason, violence, and injustice perpetrated by Catholics when they were both in and out of power in England. And although an "alteration of religion" was of course the farthest thing from the new king's mind, James's speech to Parliament in 1604 did little to soothe the minds of apprehensive Protestants. He told the members that he would always try to balance his own faith with the "quietness" of the realm.

> I was never violent nor unreasonable in my profession [of faith]: I acknowledge the Roman Church to be our Mother Church, although defiled with some infirmities and corruptions, as the Jews were when they crucified Christ: And I am none enemy to the life of a sick man, because I would have his body purged of ill humors; no more am I an enemy to

---

[1] Lockyer places the number at 40,000 (Lockyer 281).
[2] recusants: in early modern England, Catholics who refused to attend the services of the Church of England or to recognize its authority.

their Church, because I would have them reform their errors, not wishing the downthrowing of the Temple, but that it might be purged and cleansed from corruption; otherwise how can they wish us to enter if their house be not first made clean?

(James, "A Speech . . . in the Upper House" 138–39)

To the English, who had been at war with Catholic Spain for decades and who had long lived in fear of a Spanish invasion, it was not comforting to hear their new monarch describe the Catholic Church as "our Mother Church" with merely a few "infirmities and corruptions" that might be cured as would a sick man. The Treaty of London had officially ended the war with Spain in August of 1604 (several months before the Whitehall performance of *Measure for Measure*), but English Protestants remained wary of Catholics, foreign and domestic. So what could be the implications of associating James I with the duke of a Catholic city?

Some playgoers certainly could have concluded that James's apparent tolerance of Catholics, his negotiated peace with Spain, and his efforts to marry his son Prince Henry, the heir to the English crown, to the Catholic daughter of Spain's Philip III, made him a king who might as well be a Catholic prince, as *Measure for Measure*'s Duke appears to be. This point of view would be strengthened by the Duke's secretive practices and by his spying on, and his manipulations of, his subjects, disguised in the habit of a friar — all arousing suspicion about his character and trustworthiness. In addition to being a member of a widely despised (and, in Shakespeare's England, abolished) Catholic order, the figure of the friar was a controversial one in early modern popular culture, going back even farther than Chaucer's pointed portrayal of a hypocritical and lecherous friar in the *Canterbury Tales*. We may not view Lucio as *Measure for Measure*'s leading moral authority, but he echoes Chaucer when he tells the disguised Vincentio that the Duke, despite his reputation for virtue, has "some feeling of the sport" of fornication (3.2.97). Intended to describe the Duke and not a friar, Lucio's words may nonetheless blur the distinction between the two because they are spoken to a friar who is also a duke. It is difficult to come to a definitive conclusion about the precise significance of the Duke's choice of disguise, but it could easily have raised anxiety or disapproval in the minds of playgoers who feared James's perceived pro-Catholic tendencies.

A number of critics and biographers have indicated, however, that Shakespeare himself may have been a closet Catholic or, at the very least, may have been sympathetic to the old faith (see, for instance, Schoenbaum 45–54). If this is so, then one could read James's association with the Duke as a compliment to a king who allowed Catholics to pursue their faith in peace and who finally ended the taxing war with Spain. Duke Vincentio's secret dealings in *Measure for Measure*, instead of signs of his deceit, become the tireless efforts of a prince who watches over his people to guard their welfare and preserve justice in the state. We should remember that though Catholics were in the minority in England, they were not without political influence and articulate spokesmen for their cause. William Allen's *A True, Sincere, and Modest Defense of English Catholics* (1584) eloquently refuted an earlier treatise by Queen Elizabeth's powerful minister William Cecil, who made a case that adherents to the church of Rome could be tried for treason in the secular courts. Allen's text recounts the indignities and persecutions unfairly suffered by Catholics at the hands of Protestants, and makes a simple plea that Catholics may enjoy the same liberties, especially "liberty of conscience," afforded to all English men and women.

Beyond the specific figure of the Duke, we should also consider the significance of Vienna as a place in the cultural imagination of an early seventeenth-century London audience. Some critics have reasoned that Shakespeare's Vienna indeed is the Austrian city of Vienna; others believe that for Vienna one should really read London. Most recently, Gary Taylor and John Jowett have argued that Shakespeare's original script of *Measure for Measure* in all likelihood was set not in Vienna but possibly in the Italian city of Ferrara, the locale of Middleton's *The Phoenix* (1604), which also features a disguised ruler. In the space available to us here, it is not possible to do justice to the complexity of each of these hypotheses, especially because the debate involves a controversy over whether or not a playwright other than Shakespeare may have revised *Measure for Measure* sometime between its performance at Whitehall in 1604 and its first printing in 1623 (seven years after Shakespeare's death). We will, however, describe each case briefly.

If Shakespeare's "Vienna" indeed is the historical Austrian city of the same name, we have to consider the role of that city in English and European religious politics. In England and other parts of Europe, Reformation propaganda that appeared in print and thundered from the pulpit relentlessly pronounced the Roman Catholic religion a heretical faith and officially declared the pope to be the anti-Christ. But as the sixteenth century progressed, Catholicism was not the only religion feared by the English. Printed news-sheets and English travelers who had returned from the East brought news about the Islamic religion, told exotic tales about harems and "the greater sexual freedom permitted under Islamic law," and related the Turks' stunning military exploits (Vitkus 15). Now, it is true that in some English quarters Turkish successes against Catholic strongholds in Hungary, Austria, and Bohemia were cause for celebration, but this glee was greatly tempered by an outright fear that Islam might someday spread to English shores and indeed encompass the entire globe (Vitkus 7–9). The anonymous author of *The Policy of the Turkish Empire* (1597) leaves no doubt as to what he believes the Ottomans' ultimate ambitions are:

> [A]ll their actions, councils, studies, labors, and endeavors, have been ever framed and directed, and wholly bent and intended to the enlarging and amplifying of their Empire and Religion, with the daily access[3] of new and continual conquests by the ruin and subversion of all such kingdoms, provinces, estates and professions as are any way estranged from them either in name, nation, or religion. (A4v–A4r)

In this context, Vienna is viewed as "an exposed outpost of Europe, the eastern bastion of Latin Christendom as the high tide of Turkish might twice stopped before its gates, in 1529 and again in 1683" (Spielman 1). In 1593, shortly after Matthias became Archduke of Vienna, the Turks renewed their assault on Vienna and took the nearby fortress of Raab (Spielman 25).[4] These events led Englishman George Abbot to describe Vienna in 1599 as "that noble city, which is now the principal Bulwark of all Christendom against the Turk" (A7). Abbot also recalls for English readers that it was at Vienna that Sultan Soliman the Magnificent was repelled by King Ferdinand of Hungary in 1529. Underscoring the importance of Vienna's victory, Abbot points out that the city of Buda had been less fortunate: this once "great fortress of Christendom" is now held by the Turks and "the Christians which remain there are in miserable servitude" (A7). For our purposes, it is striking that such texts are decidedly bereft of anti-Catholic polemics. In fact, in a 1595 news-sheet entitled *News from Rome, Venice, and Vienna, Touching the Present Proceedings of the Turks Against the Christians in Austria, Hungary, and Helvetia. . .* (see p. 347), the author never even identifies the citizens of Vienna as Catholics. He refers to all territories captured by the Turks as "godly nations" and refers to the Turks as the "the common enemy" of all Christians. What is more, he chastises all Christians who fail to join in the fight against the Infidel and blames Turkish successes on division within the Christian ranks:

> . . . for if mercy had had any government among Christian men, so many beauteous towns, goodly cities, glorious kingdoms had not (as they now are) either been utterly made waste, or suffered the woeful bondage of Turkish tyranny. The flourishing churches to which Christ's apostles writ, and which they and the first Fathers of the church labored, are now the receptacles of unhallowed multitudes, and only a small corner of the earth

---

[3] **access:** addition.
[4] Matthias was still in power when Shakespeare wrote *Measure for Measure*.

FIGURE 29 *St. Clare Routs the Saracens with Her Prayers, from Andraes Collaert,* Icones Sanctae Clarae *(Antwerp, 1630). The fact that St. Clare, the founder of Isabella's order, was known for resisting Saracen invaders may support the association of the play's setting with either Catholic Vienna or with a Catholic Italian city.*

professeth Christ. One Christian suffering another to be as easily consumed, as an idle or envious townsman his neighbor helplessly to be robbed or burned: else had not all Asia, some of Africa, and so much of Europe suffered so great and irrecoverable slavish bondage. (pp. 347–48)

Fynes Moryson, whose 1593 description of Vienna (included in this volume on p. 337) is probably the earliest published account of the city in English, similarly refers to Vienna as a "famous Fort against the Turks," without ever making reference to its Catholicism.[5] In *Measure for Measure*, Shakespeare does not explicitly present Vienna as a city besieged by the Turks, but brothel keeper Mistress Overdone does complain about a recent loss of customers because of the war (1.2.65), and it seems reasonable to assume that Londoners had some sense of Vienna as a heroic city that helped to safeguard parts of Europe and perhaps even England itself.

The second Vienna hypothesis is that Shakespeare meant for "Vienna" to stand in for early seventeenth-century "London." The reason for this Shakespearean subterfuge, for calling London Vienna, would be that Shakespeare did not want to arouse the ire of the Master of the Revels or London's city officials by *overtly* meddling in local or national politics. Any treatment of religious or political matters was by law off-limits to dramatists, who were also prohibited from portraying any living monarch or prince on the stage. Therefore, if *Measure for Measure*'s setting was explicitly identified as London, then it would only be a small interpretative step to conclude that the city's moral turpitude represented in the play is an indictment of the English capital, and, more momentously, that Duke Vincentio is really King James I — inferences that could have had severe legal and economic consequences for all associated with the play. It was of course common for playwrights to select foreign locations or historically distant settings for their stories, and thus to construct a buffer of deniability between their words and how others might perceive their words to bear on the English present. The presence of a Catholic nunnery in the play, and Italian sounding names such as Vincentio, Claudio, Angelo, Juliet, Isabella, Lucio, and Francisca certainly imply foreignness, but the names of Pompey the pimp, Mistress Overdone the madam, Constable Elbow, Friars Thomas and Peter, the executioner Abhorson, and Master Froth give the play a distinctly English flavor. Is it possible that Shakespeare was trying to walk a fine line between commenting on local politics and getting caught criticizing the powers that be?

Leah Marcus makes the most detailed case for viewing Vienna as London. She observes that Londoners would have recognized in *Measure for Measure*'s treatment of competing legal interests the same conflicts between "local" laws and "unlocalized" jurisdiction that also existed within the city of London and its suburbs (Marcus 165–84). Basically, London was a difficult

---

[5] Moryson's account was not published until 1617, but his reference to the *"famous* Fort" of Vienna implies that Vienna had quite a reputation.

place for King James to govern. By an earlier royal charter, the Lord Mayor and aldermen of London had been granted the right to rule that city with only limited intervention by the crown. The city fathers, however, hardly exercised absolute control over the city. Local privileges that had been granted to various districts and neighborhoods within the city walls often superceded the Lord Mayor and aldermen's jurisdiction. What is more, the city fathers had only limited jurisdiction over the so-called liberties, suburban areas that lay outside the city walls and ran along the south bank of the river Thames where most theaters were located. In *Measure for Measure*, Pompey's announcement regarding the *selective* closing of the brothels may well be an illustration of this phenomenon. He declares that "all houses [of prostitution] in the suburbs of Vienna must be plucked down," but that the brothels in the city itself "shall stand for seed" because "a wise burgher put in for them" (1.2.77, 79–80), clearly suggesting that, despite Angelo's undeniable zeal, his campaign against fornication is not universally applied, possibly in this case because certain areas of the city enjoyed protections unavailable to the suburbs. James's approach to the governance of London, according to Marcus, was to assert with increasing aggressiveness the royal prerogative, which he grounded in principles of Roman civil law[6] and which, because of Roman law's generalizing nature, crossed boundaries otherwise observed by local laws and privileges. In *Measure for Measure*, we have a Duke who cedes his authority to a deputy, just as a royal charter had granted the Lord Mayor and aldermen the right to govern London, and we see the momentary enforcement of a law against sexual incontinence that is ultimately set aside when the Duke returns to Vienna and asserts his right and power to punish all transgressors as he sees fit. Thus "local authority is overridden by royal prerogative, by the principles of Roman civil law, which fostered the idea of the monarch as the embodiment of a general, mysterious, ultimate legal authority" (Marcus 178) — something that would no doubt have pleased King James, who often argued that the monarch's power is prior, and therefore superior, to the law.

James left no doubt about his views on the royal prerogative in his speech in the Star Chamber[7] in 1616. "Incroach not upon the Prerogative of the Crown: if there fall out a question that concerns my Prerogative or Mystery of State, deal not with it, till you consult with the King or his Council, or both: for they are transcendent matters, and must not be sliberely[8] carried with over-rash wilfullness. . . . That which concerns the mystery of the

---

[6] King James hoped to use principles of Roman law "as the basis of a united Britain" (Marcus 180).   [7] **Star Chamber**: a royal court of law notorious for its harshness, secrecy, and trials without jury.   [8] **sliberely**: lightly, carelessly.

King's power is not lawful to be disputed; for that is to wade in the weakness of Princes, and to take away the mystical reverence that belongs unto them that sit in the Throne of God" (James I, "Speech in Star Chamber" 213).

A third hypothesis suggests that *Measure for Measure*'s true locale is neither "Vienna" nor "London" but that some Italian city, possibly Ferrara, was the original setting of the play. As we have it today, the play says nothing directly about any setting other than Vienna, but this does not mean the third hypothesis is invalid. Scholars have discerned a significant number of textual "traces" of an Italian setting. There is no need here to review and weigh the evidence, other than to say that it *is* possible that someone other than Shakespeare revised the play during the almost two decades following its first recorded performance. We know that *Measure for Measure* was written sometime before December 26, 1604, the date of its first recorded performance, but that it was not printed until 1623, when it appeared in the First Folio, the inaugural edition of Shakespeare's collected plays. What happened to the text between 1604 and 1623 is anybody's guess, and there is no guarantee that the play before us today is the unadulterated Shakespearean original. Scholars generally agree that the 1623 text is based not on Shakespeare's original manuscript, the so-called "foul papers," but instead derives from a handwritten copy made by the professional scribe Ralph Crane, who was associated with the King's Men (Shakespeare's acting company) in the 1620s. Again, the evidence for this attribution does not concern us, but why, we may ask, was a new copy made (at some expense to the acting company) of a play that already existed in a promptbook and had the Master of the Revels' all-important seal of approval (which was required for the play to be performed)? One possibility is that the play was significantly revised.

One passage in the play that is possibly revised was the exchange between Lucio and the two Gentlemen in act 1, scene 2.

> LUCIO: If the Duke with the other dukes come not to composition with the King of Hungary, why then all the dukes fall upon the King.
> FIRST GENTLEMAN: Heaven grant us its peace, but not the King of Hungary's!
> SECOND GENTLEMAN: Amen. (1.2.1–5)

We can be fairly certain the "the Duke" referred in the first line is Duke Vincentio, but who are the "other dukes" and who is the King of Hungary? And what peace negotiations are they talking about? And why would the First Gentleman not want peace on the King of Hungary's terms? *Measure for Measure* itself does not answer any of these questions, and we have to go outside the play — to its historical context — for answers.

It has been argued that the lines about the dukes and the King of Hungary's peace could not have been written in 1604 because there are no corresponding historical figures or events to make sense of them (see Taylor, "Mediterranean"; Jowett). Of course it is not *necessary* for Shakespeare (or anyone revising the play) to be referring to real persons. We are dealing with a work of fiction here. But another critic has suggested that the passage could make sense to an audience in 1604 because the "Duke and the dukes" and "the King of Hungary" are references to the historical Habsburg brothers — Matthias, Ernst, Albert, and Emperor Rudolf II (see Marcus 186–91) — who ruled over part or all of the Holy Roman Empire between 1576 and 1618. The younger Habsburg brothers engaged in political intrigue and military actions against Emperor Rudolf (who was also King of Hungary and who Matthias felt was a weak and ineffective ruler), and it seems possible that this is what Lucio refers to when he says that if the dukes do not come to an agreement with the King of Hungary there may be war.

What happens to our understanding of the passage if we accept the identification of Lucio's dukes and Hungarian king with the Habsburg brothers? It opens the door to the consideration of an intriguing connection between English and Hungarian Protestants. In 1604, Protestant groups in Hungary, whose religious freedom was harshly oppressed by Emperor Rudolf II, took up arms against their sovereign. Archduke Matthias, although he was a Catholic, "needed the help of the Hungarian [Protestant] estates to depose Rudolf and take over the throne" (Sugar, Hanák, and Frank 98), and pursued an alliance with the Protestant rebels. Out of a sense of loyalty, this conflict greatly concerned Protestants back in England, and "there were attempts to levy troops and money to aid the Hungarian 'brethern'" (Marcus 188). English apprehension for Hungarian Protestants may therefore rise to the surface in *Measure for Measure* in the First Gentleman's wish that "Heaven grant us its peace, but not the King of Hungary's!" Peace on Emperor Rudolf's terms would in all likelihood have spelled doom for Hungarian Protestants. If Shakespeare had Catholic sympathies, it would perhaps seem odd that the First Gentleman denounces the King of Hungary's peace.

But what if the identification of Lucio's dukes with the Habsburg brothers is incorrect? The Habsburg brothers were not dukes but *archdukes* (an important distinction), and their quarrels had not become public by 1604; nor were the Habsburg archdukes and the King of Hungary engaged in any peace negotiations in 1604 (Taylor, "Shakespeare's Mediterranean"). Does that mean that the Duke, the other dukes, and the King of Hungary are fictional creatures of Shakespeare's own imagination? Not if we seriously consider the possibility that another playwright, someone like the Calvinist Thomas Middleton, revised *Measure for Measure* around the year 1621.[9]

England was of course a staunchly Protestant nation by the early seventeenth century, but the 1620s saw an intensification of the Catholic Counter-Reformation on the European continent, and there were many in England who believed that James's ill-fated pursuit of a Spanish match for crown prince Charles (Lockyer 290–95), combined with his "conciliatory attitude toward foreign Catholic powers," spelled the end of the Protestant Reformation in England (Cressy and Ferrell 7–8). These developments worried English Protestants, and John Jowett contends that the references to the Duke, the other dukes, and the King of Hungary in act 1, scene 2 can be seen as Calvinist Middleton's attempt to construct a narrative of "Protestant resistance to the Counter-Reformation Catholic domination in Europe" (Jowett, "Audacity" 230). In 1621, Vienna was ruled by the Catholic Emperor Ferdinand II, and it was besieged by the Transylvanian prince Gábor Bethlen. Bethlen had been elected King of Hungary a year earlier by the Hungarian nobility and had joined the Protestant cause in pursuit of religious and political independence from the Holy Roman Empire. Jowett believes that Middleton changed the setting of *Measure for Measure* from Ferrara to Vienna to capitalize on these events,[10] which were described in some detail in a number of news-sheets available in London at the time. By this view, the King of Hungary referred to in 1621 is the Transylvanian Prince Bethlen, and the "duke" refers to the Emperor Ferdinand in Vienna. Furthermore, Bethlen's election would have fascinated and pleased English Protestants and a Calvinist such as Middleton because it mimics the recent elevation of James I's son-in-law, the Protestant Elector Palatine Frederick, to the Crown of Bohemia (Jowett, "Audacity" 231). Bethlen's military exploits were included in the news-sheets of 1620, as were his letter to Frederick vowing to join the Protestant cause, and the news of his impending coronation as King of Hungary. What is more, news-sheets from October 1621 directly refer to ongoing peace negotiations between Hungary and Vienna (Jowett, "Audacity" 233–34), insinuating a possible source for the First Gentleman's statement concerning the King of Hungary's peace. That the First Gentleman disparages the Protestant king's peace in a scene purportedly written by a Calvinist playwright is not a problem for Jowett, because he holds that Lucio and the two Viennese gentlemen are merely speaking as Catholics would (231).

---

[9] For these arguments, see Taylor and Jowett, *Shakespeare Reshaped,* and for a brief summary see Jowett, "Audacity" 240–43.
[10] For Taylor's argument in favor of Ferrara as *Measure for Measure*'s original setting, see "Shakespeare's Mediterranean."

It is not important that we come to a definitive conclusion here and decide who is right in this discussion. Rather, what we aim to stress is how the interpretative difficulties presented by act 1, scene 2 are symptomatic of the challenges we face in deciding how the play's topicality and the religion question can shape our understanding of *Measure for Measure* as a whole. If we go with an interpretation that favors Protestant or Calvinist issues, we end up with quite a different interpretation than if we emphasize the play's Catholic inflections. If, in 1604, Vienna might have been viewed as a Christian stronghold against the Islamic Ottoman threat, in 1621 Vienna was a Catholic city at war with the Protestant King of Hungary, and itself a potential threat against England. Our choices will shape our reading.

From an early seventeenth-century Protestant perspective, for instance, one could argue that both Isabella's desire to enter a convent and her willingness to guard her virginity at the expense of her brother's life, are a heretical throwback to days of Papism, convents, and monasteries. It makes Isabella look cold and heartless and wrong, and the Duke's proposal of marriage becomes a way to draw her back from a heretical commitment to an arcane Catholic institution that had been banned by Henry VIII in the 1530s with the Dissolution of the Monasteries Acts. If, on the other hand, we see Shakespeare as Catholic-friendly, Isabella quickly becomes a heroic bride of Christ who properly protects her immortal soul (see Fig. 29, p. 323). Her apparent hesitation in accepting Vincentio's proposal of marriage can be read as a subtle resistance to the Duke's authority and to the eradication of English monastic life. Similar binaries of course emerge when we consider other characters. The "precise" Angelo can be viewed as a Puritan or a Jesuit, Lucio as a slanderer or an astute social critic, and the Duke as a divine prince or a tyrant (see Taylor, "Shakespeare's Mediterranean," and "Power, Pathos, Character" 53–56).

Puritanism

So far we have discussed how the play's setting determines how we read its implicit commentary on religion, whether Catholic or Protestant, but Debora Kuller Shuger has recently suggested that Puritanism also affects the play and that it does so in much more profound ways than the superficial association of the "precise" Angelo with commonplace puritanical qualities such as an obsession with order and a severity that borders on cruelty. We know from the portrayal of Malvolio in *Twelfth Night* that Shakespeare did not mind making "a kind of Puritan" (2.3.139) a source of ridicule and negativity, but we have to be very careful not to associate all things puritanical in *Measure for Measure*'s Vienna solely with the tyrannical figure of Angelo.

The harsh law that condemns Claudio to death, for instance, is not Angelo's invention; he merely revives a law already on the books, as Vincentio fully expected him to when he granted Angelo the "terror" (1.1.20) of his "absolute" (1.3.13) ducal authority to "enforce or qualify the laws" at his discretion (1.1.66). The Duke therefore appears to deploy Angelo's puritanical tendencies strategically for his own political benefit. Yet the play also falls short of validating the "strict and biting" anti-fornication law that censures Claudio; when the play ends we realize that it has been conveniently forgotten. A Jacobean audience would have expected no less because it would have considered a death sentence too severe a penalty for Claudio's "crime." In fact, the Duke's apparent obsession with the sex laws of Vienna is probably just a ruse. He is less interested in regulating sexual behavior than in trying to regain sway over his subjects, who have come to disregard his authority because of his failure to enforce the city's laws. But that still does not explain why the harsh law against fornication is on the books in the first place or why it is merely ignored, and not revoked, at the play's end.

At the time Shakespeare wrote *Measure for Measure*, there were a number of Puritan sects with varying views on such issues as dogma, ritual practices, the role of ministers, and ecclesiastical garments, and it is difficult to define the movement succinctly without oversimplification. However, for our present purposes we can say that "Puritan" is a catch-all term for those English Protestants who believed that the Church of England had not gone far enough in distancing itself from the church of Rome and its liturgical practices as described in the 1559 Elizabethan settlement. Although Puritans did not come to dominate the social and political scene until the 1640s, they were hardly without influence at the time of James I's succession. On his way to London from Scotland in 1603, the king designate was presented with the Millenary Petition (so called because it was apparently signed by 1,000 English ministers) in which Puritans championed further simplification of the ceremonies in the Church of England and called for stricter moral discipline. James's decision to include Puritans in the discussions of religious ceremonies and doctrines at the Hampton Court conference the following year indicates that the Puritan movement, though routinely vilified, was a legitimate force in English religious politics.

In the public arena, Puritans opposed gaming, dancing, drunkenness, swearing, showy dress, and any kind of illicit or improper sexual behavior. They were especially zealous about controlling sexual activity, and several bills endeavoring to criminalize adultery were introduced in Parliament, including one in 1604 (Shuger 30). Puritans also strongly disapproved of the theater on grounds that it was an inherently sinful institution. Not only was it considered a sin to participate in putting on a theatrical spectacle, it was thought that the theater also defiled "those who merely see or hear it" (Barish 80). The argument that a spectator did not participate in a stage murder or sexual indecency was discounted because "by attending, and enjoying, and applauding, the spectator approves, in effect, what [he or she] sees and so shares in the sins [he or she] beholds" (Barish 80). Needless to say, the Puritan city fathers in London, who often tried to interfere with the day-to-day operations of the playhouses, and who therefore directly affected Shakespeare's livelihood, could hardly expect to be portrayed with sympathy on the stage.

And yet, the law that condemns Claudio, but which itself is *not* condemned by Claudio or Isabella or the Duke (or anyone else who does not directly benefit financially or hedonistically from the sex trade), is Puritan in nature. The influential Puritan writer Martin Bucer, citing Ephesians (5.3), sternly warned his readers to "Let not fornication be named among you." "For," he continued,

> God has judged it necessary that those guilty of these crimes and misdeeds should pay the commonwealth the penalty of death in order to spread the fear of offending, since by their sins they have done damage by suggesting a license for delinquency. And so whoever decides that these misdeeds of impiety and wickedness are to be kept out or driven from the commonwealth of Christians by more mitigated punishment than death necessarily makes himself wiser and more loving than God as regards the salvation of men. (Bucer 381)

As harsh as Bucer's claim may sound, Claudio and Isabella not only neglect to blame the law, they appear to credit it. Isabella pleads for her brother's life but simultaneously refers to the law from which she begs mercy a "just but severe law" (2.2.45). Likewise, Claudio rails against "the demigod Authority" that can make him pay for his offense, yet says of the law that "still 'tis just" (1.2.100). What is more, he justifies the existence of the law because it protects us from "too much liberty" (102). To our ears it may sound odd that someone would wish to be protected from too much freedom, but Claudio's conception of human nature requires that he be restrained. "Our natures," he says, "do pursue, / Like rats that ravin down their proper bane, / A thirsty evil, and when we drink we die" (105–07). The "thirsty evil" here is sexual pleasure, and Claudio believes (as many Jacobean Londoners would have) that unless we are restrained by law we will, like rats who greedily consume poison, pursue pleasure to our own destruction.

Debora Shuger views this nexus between sexual pleasure and self-destruction as central both to *Measure for Measure* and to the theologian Martin Bucer's quest to make God's law the law of England. In his *Kingdom of Christ (De regno Christi)*, which Shuger contends articulates what "would become the Puritan social program for the next 75 years" (11), Bucer addresses Edward VI and describes how England may under the king's rule become a good society if God's law becomes the law of the land. In this work, which takes some of its intellectual inspiration from Plato's *Laws*, Cicero's *De re publica* and *De legibus*, and Josephus's *Against Apion*, Bucer espouses the view that God's universal law can only come to fruition in human society if individualism is largely, if not entirely, erased. God's word, as revealed in Scripture, must be followed to the letter, otherwise "how can it be 'right for us wretched little men, on our own part completely ignorant of what is good, to modify the laws of the Son of God'" (Bucer qtd. in Shuger 21). Our first task is to recognize what God's law is, what the institutions "of Christ our King are," and then "to spend ourselves and all we have observing these things . . . however burdensome this seems to our flesh" (quoted in Shuger 21). What is required is complete conformity to God's law, and Bucer advocates the appointment of "overseer[s] of piety and virtue" to create "a system of moral and religious surveillance" that regulates people's "unlimited desire for power and honor and pleasure" (quoted in Shuger 23). Sexual sin and pleasure receive special attention in Bucer's account because, as Shuger attests, they create a sphere of privacy within the commonwealth. Such a sphere, Bucer learned from Plato, is diametrically opposed to the idea of community insofar as it inhibits the "laws' ability to order both individual souls and the social body" (Shuger 14). The only way to confront those who pursue sexual pleasure anyway is with harsh penalties, including death.[11] In other words, Bucer's motivation is not primarily a "Puritanical" revulsion of sexual sin itself but an abhorrence of what such sin signifies: sexual pleasure is by nature a private pleasure that withdraws individuals from the community governed by God's law.

Returning now to *Measure for Measure*, we can see how Jonathan Dollimore's political argument unexpectedly dovetails with a Puritan obsession with strict adherence to God's law (see Dollimore 73ff). It seems that the Machiavellian Duke of Vienna and Martin Bucer have essentially the same objective: they want all citizens of the state to live within the confines of the law. The Duke confesses that he "let slip" law enforcement in general for fourteen years (1.3.21), yet appoints as his replacement a man whom he fully anticipates will foremost prosecute sexual vices. When Lucio defends lechery, the Duke retorts that it is "too general a vice, and severity must cure it" (3.2.82). Yet his decision to forget about Claudio's death sentence at the end of the play suggests that sexual sin in and of itself is not what concerns him.

---

[11] As Shuger points out, English common law was not very aggressive in its regulation of sexual behavior (30–31).

Rather, like Bucer (and Cicero before him), the Duke understands that illicit sexual behavior is private (and therefore withdraws the participants from the well-governed community) but also that it is not private *enough* (because sexual misdeeds often become public) and therefore all too often openly flouts the law's — or, in this case, the Duke's — authority. The only crucial difference between the positions of the Duke and Bucer is that the former may cynically appropriate the "pow'r divine" (that Angelo attributes to him in the final scene) for purely political purposes, whereas Bucer may sincerely wish to bring the kingdom of Christ to England.

✦ *From* The Geneva Bible   *1557–1560*

In its title and in many passages, *Measure for Measure* makes direct reference to biblical passages, excerpted below. The Geneva Bible (1557–60) is one of a number of authorized Bibles based on the original Hebrew and Greek published during the Reformation, and would have been in current use at the time of the play's composition. It was largely replaced by The King James Bible (begun in 1607, first printed 1611), also known as The Authorized Version, created by a commission appointed by King James I.

MATTHEW 5:14–16

[Duke Vincentio applies these verses in his praise of Angelo in act 1, scene 1.]

Ye are the light of the world. A city that is set on a hill can not be hid.

Neither do men light a candle and put it under a bushel, but on a candlestick, and it giveth light unto all that are in the house.

Let your light so shine before men, that they may see your good works, and glorify your Father which is in heaven.

LUKE 11:33–36

[Although it begins with the same image as the verse above from Matthew, these lines from Luke suggest the problem with entrusting Angelo with great power — that his "eye is evil" and he does not guard well enough against temptation.]

No man lighteth a candle and putteth it in a privie place, neither under a bushel: but on a candlestick, that they which come in may see the light.

The Bible and Holy Scriptures Contained in the Old and New Testament (Geneva, 1560).

The light of the body is the eye: therefore when thine eye is single,[1] then is thy whole body light: but if thine eye be evil, then thy body is dark.

Take heed therefore, that the light which is in thee be not darkness.

If therefore thy whole body shall be light, having no part dark, thee shall all be light even as when a candle do light thee with the brightness.

MATTHEW 6:1–4

[The concerns of these verses resonate with both Angelo's and the Duke's behavior, with their emphasis on hypocrisy vs. the secret wisdom and observance of God.]

Take heed that ye give not your alms before men, to be seen of them, or else ye shall have no reward of your Father which is in heaven.

Therefore when thou givest thine alms, thou shalt not make a trumpet to be blown before thee, as the hypocrites do in the Synagogues and in the streets, to be praised of men. Verily, I say unto you, they have their reward.

But when thou dost thine alms, let not thy left hand know what thy right hand doeth.

That thine alms may be in secret, and thy Father that seeth in secret, he will reward thee openly.

And when thou prayest, be not as the hypocrites: for they love to stand and pray in the Synagogues, and in the corners of the streets, because they would be seen of men. Verily I say unto you they have their reward.

But when thou prayest, enter into thy chamber: and when thou hast shut thy door, pray unto thy Father which is in secret, and thy Father which seeth in secret, shall reward thee openly.

MATTHEW 7:1–5

[In the following verses, we hear the balanced cadences and the language from which the play's title is borrowed, as well as the message that judgment and justice must be tempered with a sense of one's own sin and unworthiness.]

Judge not that ye be not judged.

For with what judgment ye judge, ye shall be judged, and with what measure ye meet, it shall be measured to you again.

And why seest thou the mote that is in thy brother's eye, and perceivest not the beam that is in thine own eye?

---

[1] **single:** that is, of one piece, or without blemish or fault.

Or how sayest thou to thy brother, Suffer me to cast out the mote out of thine eye, and behold a beam is in thine own eye?

Hypocrite, first cast out the beam out of thine own eye, and then shalt thou see clearly to cast out the mote out of thy brother's eye.

Mark 4:21–24

[Mark gives another version of the image of the light under the bushel, the idea of secrecy, and the balance of measuring.]

Also he said unto them, Is the candle light to be put under a bushel, or under the table, and not to be put on a candlestick?

For there is nothing hid, that shall not be opened: neither is there a secret but that it shall come to light.

If any man have ears to hear, let him hear.

And he said unto them, Take heed what you hear. With what measure ye meet, it shall be measured unto you: and unto you that hear, shall more be given.

➜ FYNES MORYSON

From An Itinerary   *1617*

Fynes Moryson (1566–1630) was born in Lincolnshire, the son of a member of Parliament for Great Grimsby. Moryson was educated at Cambridge University, where he was chosen fellow at Peterhouse College in 1587. He traveled widely in Europe and wrote a survey of his travels that documents in some detail the places and the peoples he encountered on those travels. Although it is the earliest known description of Vienna printed in English, Moryson's *Itinerary* was not published until after Shakespeare wrote *Measure for Measure*. As such, *An Itinerary* cannot have exerted any direct influence on Shakespeare, but Moryson's text does give us an impression of what Vienna looked like when Shakespeare composed his play (bits and pieces of which Shakespeare may have learned about from other English travelers to the city). Certainly, the description of Vienna as a bulwark against Islamic invaders reflects a view widely held

---

Fynes Moryson, *An Itinerary written by Fynes Moryson . . . Containing His Ten Years' Travel Through the Twelve Dominions of Germany, Bohmerland, Switzerland, the Netherlands, Denmark, Poland, Italy, Turkey, France, England, Scotland, and Ireland* (London, 1617), 66–67.

by the English in the 1590s. Finally, Moryson's text would of course have been available to Thomas Middleton, who may have revised *Measure for Measure* in 1620 or 1621.

PART 1: VIENNA

After dinner we rode two miles and a half through a very large plain, fruitful of corn and pasture, with many pleasant woods, and compassed round above with mountains, and came to Vienna, vulgarly called *Wien*. Near the city on the north side the river Danube runneth by, from the east to the west, three arms whereof close together (with some ground between, which many times is overflowed), we passed by three bridges, whereof one hath twenty-nine arches, the other fifty-seven, and the third fifteen, each of those arches being some eighteen walking paces long. Between the second bridge and the third, next to the city, is a pleasant grove, and good part of the ground under the bridges is many times dry; but when the river riseth, it doth not only fill all the beds but overfloweth the fields on both sides. At the gate of *Wien*, each man paid for his horse two pochanels;[1] and when we came to the inn, the host sent our names written to the magistrate. *Wien*, the metropolitan city of Austria, is a famous fort against the Turks, upon the confines of Austria, which if they should once gain, their horsemen might suddenly spoil[2] the open countries of Bohemia, and Moravia,[3] and good part of Silesia.[4] The city is of a round form, and upon the north side there is an ascent to it upon a hill, otherwise without[5] the walls on all sides the ground is plain, except the west side, where mountains lie a good distance from the city; and upon that side the Sultan of the Turks[6] encamped, upon the hills near the gallows, when, in the time of the Emperor Rudolphus,[7] he besieged the city, or rather came to view it with purpose to besiege it the next summer. The streets are narrow, but the building is stately, of freestone.[8] Two towers of the church are curiously engraven, the like whereof is not in Germany, except the tower or steeple of Strasburg. The common report is that two chief workmen had great emulation in building them; and

---

[1] **pochanels:** presumably a Viennese coin.   [2] **spoil:** mar or destroy.   [3] **Moravia:** English name for a part of the Austro-Hungarian empire.   [4] **Silesia:** a province in the east of Germany (Ger. *Schlesien*).   [5] **without:** outside.   [6] **Sultan of the Turks:** Suleiman I (the Magnificent; 1494?–1566), sultan of Turkey.   [7] **Rudolphus:** Rudolf I (1552–1612).   [8] **free-stone:** a fine-grained limestone or sandstone that can be cut or sawn easily.

that one, having finished his tower, found means to break the neck of the other, lest his workmanship should excel that he had done. One of the towers some three years past was shaken with an earthquake, and indeed the houses of this city are many times shaken therewith, and they have a prophecy of old that this city shall be destroyed with an earthquake. It is dangerous to walk the streets in the night, for the great number of disordered people, which are easily found upon any confines, especially where such an army lieth near, as that of Hungary, governed by no strict discipline. Ernestas and Mathias,[9] archdukes of Austria, and brothers to the Emperor Rudolphus, did this time lie there, both in one house, and did eat at one table, and in the time of their meals it was free for strangers and others to come to the room. I stayed there three days at *Wien* to ease my weary horse, and I paid each meal twenty-four creitzers,[10] for oats the day and night eighteen, and in like sort for hay six creitzers.

[9] **Ernestas and Mathias:** Archduke Ernst III (1553–1595) and Emperor Matthias (1557–1619).
[10] **creitzers:** obsolete form of kreuzer, a coin (originally silver, then copper) in use in Germany and Austria.

↬ The Catholics' Supplication   *1603*

As we noted already, there was a significant Catholic presence in England when James I ascended to its throne, even though the religion had been outlawed in favor of the Protestant Church of England. One of the most biting accusations against English Catholics was that they owed their first allegiance to the pope, and that they were therefore necessarily traitors to England and its monarch. The charge is credible insofar as Henry VIII had set himself and his successors up as rival "popes" when he broke with Rome over the divorce issue and declared himself head of the English Church. Clearly, it was very difficult for anyone to be loyal to the pope *and* to the head of the Church of England, given that the two were at extreme variance. Acutely aware of the predicament, the author of *The Catholics' Supplication* tries to convince King James I that English Catholics can and always will be the crown's loyal subjects. His passionate plea for tolerance toward Catholics may shed light on how at least some audience members viewed Shakespeare's Catholic Vienna.

The Catholics' Supplication, printed together with Christopher Muriell, *An Answer unto the Catholics' Supplication Presented unto the King's Majesty for a toleration of Popish Religion in England* (London, 1603).

Most puissant Prince and Orient[1] Monarch,

Such are the rare perfections and admirable gifts of wisdom, prudence, valor and justice, wherewith the bountiful hand of God's divine majesty hath endued[2] your Majesty, as in the depth of your provident judgment, we doubt not but you foresee what concerneth both the spiritual and temporal government of all your kingdoms and dominions.

Notwithstanding your Grace's most afflicted subjects and devoted servants, the Catholics of England, partly to prevent sinister informations which happily may possess your sacred ears before answer be heard; partly almost as men overwhelmed with persecutions for our consciences, we are enforced to have speedy recourse in hope of present redress from your Highness, and to present these humble lines unto your royal person to plead for us some commiseration and favor.

What allegiance or duty can any temporal prince desire or expect at his vassals' hands which we are not addressed to perform? How many noblemen and worthy gentlemen, most zealous in the Catholic religion, have endured some loss of lands and livings, some exile, other imprisonments, some the effusion of blood and life for the advancement of your blessed mother's[3] right unto the scepter of Albion?[4] Nay, whose finger did ever ache but Catholics', for your Majesty's present title and dominion? How many fled to your court offering themselves as hostages for their friends to live and die in your Grace's quarrel, if ever adversary had opposed himself against the equity of your cause? If this they attempted with their prince's disgrace[5] to obtain your Majesty's grace, what will they do, nay, what will they not do to live without disgrace in your Grace's favor?

The main of this realm, if we respect religion (setting petty sects aside), consisteth upon four parts: Protestants, who have domineered all the former queen's days; Puritans, who have crept up apace among them; atheists or politicians, who were bred upon their brawls and contentions in matters of faith; and Catholics, who as they are opposite to all, so are they detested of[6]

---

[1] Orient: rising (as the sun rises); possibly a reference to James's assumption of the English throne. [2] endued: instructed, educated; also inducted, as to be inducted into a lordship; also dressed (figuratively). [3] your blessed mother's: Mary Stuart, Queen of Scots (1542–67; executed 1587), a Catholic and mother of James I of England. As a descendent of Margaret Tudor (daughter of Henry VII), Mary claimed the English crown and attempted with aid of foreign Catholic powers to supplant Elizabeth I. [4] Albion: England. [5] their prince's disgrace: to earn the disfavor of Elizabeth I. The author asks rhetorically, if we Catholics so willingly incurred the wrath of Elizabeth to aid you in your pursuit of the English crown, then what will we not do to earn your favor now that you are king? [6] of: by.

all because Error was ever an enemy to Truth. Hardly all, or any of the first, two, three can be suppressed, and therefore we beseech your Majesty to yield us as much favor as others of contrary religion (to that which shall be publicly professed in England) shall obtain at your hands. For if our fault be like, or less, or none at all, in equity our punishment ought to be like, or less, or none at all. The gates, arches, and pyramids of France proclaimed the present king *Pater patriae et pacis restitutor,*[7] because that kingdom being well nigh torn in pieces with civil wars and made a prey to foreign foes, was by his provident wisdom and valor acquitted in itself, and hostile strangers expelled; the which he principally effected by condescending to tolerate them of an adverse religion to that was openly professed. Questionless, dread Sovereign, the kingdom of England, by cruel persecution of Catholics, hath been almost odious to all Christian nations; trade and traffic is decayed, wars and blood hath seldom ceased, subsidies and taxes never so many, discontented minds innumerable; all which your Majesty's princely connivancy[8] to your humble suppliants, the afflicted Catholics, will easily redress, especially at your Highness's ingress.[9] *Si loqueris ad eos verba lenia, erunt tibi servi cunctis diebus,*[10] said the sage counselors of Solomon[11] to Rehoboam.[12] For enlargement after affliction resembleth a pleasant gale after a vehement tempest, and a benefit in distress doubles the value thereof.

How grateful will it be to all Catholic princes abroad, and honorable to your Majesty, to understand how Queen Elizabeth's severity is changed into your royal clemency; and that the lenity of a man reedified[13] that which the misinformed anger of a woman destroyed; that the lion rampant[14] is passant[15] whereas the passant had been rampant? How acceptable shall all your subjects be to all Catholic countries, who are now almost abhorred of all, when they shall perceive your Highness prepareth not pikes and prisons for the professors of their faith, but permitteth them temples and altars for the use of their religion? Then shall we see with our eyes, and touch with our fingers, that happy benediction of Esau[16] in this land, that swords are

---

[7] *Pater patriae et pacis restitutor:* father of the country and restorer of the peace (Henri IV, the first Bourbon king of France [1589–1610]).   [8] connivancy: tacit permission or sanction.   [9] ingress: entrance (into his new English kingdom).   [10] *Si loqueris ad eos verba lenia, erunt tibi servi cunctis diebus:* If you were to speak soothing words to them, you will have servants for all days (or "forever").   [11] Solomon: king of Israel, builder of the First Temple, noted for his wisdom.   [12] Rehoboam: the first king of Judah (2 Chronicles 9:31–12:16), son of King Solomon.   [13] reedified: rebuilt, restored.   [14] rampant: rearing or standing with the forepaws in the air (suggesting fierceness).   [15] passant: walking and looking toward the right side, with three paws on the ground and the right forepaw raised.   [16] Esau: Son of Isaac and Rebecca who sold his birthright to his younger twin brother, Jacob, for food. As a result, Jacob, and not Esau, received his father's blessing and God's favor (Genesis 25:24–34).

changed into plows, and lances into scythes.[17] And all nations admiring us will say, *Hic sunt semen cui benedixit dominus.*[18] We request no more favor at your Grace's hands than that we may securely profess that Catholic religion, which all your happy predecessors professed, from Donaldus[19] the first converted unto your Majesty's peerless mother[20] last martyred.

A religion venerable for antiquity, majestical for amplitude,[21] constant for continuance, irreprehensible[22] for doctrine, inducing to all kind of virtue and piety, dissuading from all sin and wickedness. A religion beloved by all primitive pastors, established by all ecumenical councils, upheld by all ancient doctors,[23] maintained by the first and most Christian emperors, recorded almost alone in all ecclesiastical histories, sealed with the blood of millions of martyrs, adorned with the virtues of so many councilors, beautified with the purity of thousands of virgins, so conformable to natural sense and reason, and finally so agreeable to the sacred text of God's word and gospel. The free use of this religion we request, if not in public churches, at least in private houses; if not with approbation, yet with toleration, without molestation.

Assure your Grace that howsoever some Protestants or Puritans, incited by moral honesty of life, or innate instinct of nature, or for fear of some temporal punishment, pretend obedience unto your Highness's laws; yet certainly the only Catholics for conscience's sake observe them. For they, defending that prince's precepts and statutes, oblige no subject under penalty of sin, with little care in conscience to transgress them, which principally are tormented with the guilt of sin. But Catholics confessing merit in obeying, and demerit in transgressing, cannot but in soul be grievously tortured at the least prevarication thereof. Wherefore, most merciful Sovereign, we your long afflicted subjects, in all dutiful submission, protest before the majesty of God and all his holy angels, as loyal obedience, and as immaculate allegiance unto your Grace as ever did faithful subjects in

---

[17] **swords . . . scythes:** the source of this phrase seems to be Isaiah 2.4, and it is not clear why it is here associated with Esau. Esau's father, Isaac, said to him, "By your sword you shall live" (Genesis 28:39), but the connection appears to go no further, unless we read the passage in which swords are turned into plows and lances into scythes as a metaphor for the Esau-Jacob relationship. As a result of losing his birthright (and the deception by Jacob to receive his father's blessing [Genesis 27:1–29]), Esau vowed to kill his brother. But Jacob fled, and the brothers lived in enmity for years. Some twenty or thirty years later, Jacob sought peace with Esau and offered him many gifts. The feuding brothers were then reconciled (Genesis 33:4–11).
[18] *Hic sunt semen cui benedixit dominus:* these men are the seed which the Lord blessed.
[19] **Donaldus:** first Christian king of Alba (the territories of present day Scotland), ninth century.   [20] **mother:** Mary, Queen of Scots (1542–67), executed by England's Elizabeth I in 1587.
[21] **amplitude:** excellence, dignity, grandeur.   [22] **irreprehensible:** not reprehensible, irreproachable.   [23] **doctors:** the doctors of the church, certain early church "fathers" distinguished by their eminent learning (*Oxford English Dictionary*).

England or Scotland unto your Highness's progenitors; and intend as sincerely with our goods and lives to serve you as ever did the loyalest Israelites King David,[24] or the trusty legions the Roman emperors. And thus expecting your Majesty's customary favor and gracious bounty, we rest your devoted suppliants to him whose hands do manage the hearts of kings, and with reciprocate mercy will requite the merciful.

Let them all, o Lord, if it be thy will be done, be converted, and agree with us in one truth. Amen.

Your sacred and Majesty's most devoted servants,
The Catholics of England.

[24] **David:** the second king of Israel and Judah.

→ CHRISTOPHER MURIELL

From An Answer unto the Catholics' Supplication *1603*

Christopher Muriell's response to *The Catholics' Supplication* is a point by point refutation of the arguments raised by the Catholics in favor of a greater toleration of their faith. We have not reproduced his entire text because the particulars of Muriell's argument are less important for our purposes than is his tone, which is full of venom, long-standing resentment, sarcasm, and a deep suspicion toward English Catholics.

To the Most Gracious Renowned Christian King, James, by the grace of God, of England, Scotland, France, and Ireland, King, defender of the true Catholic and Apostolic faith . . .

Most gracious and renowned Christian King, whereas the papists[1] (who usurp the name of Catholics) having posted unto your Majesty to exhibit unto your royal person a "Supplication" full of untruths, I, one of the meanest[2] of your Majesty's most humble and loyal subjects, moved with zeal of the holy and undoubted true religion, now professed in England, have thought it not inconvenient (with your Grace's favor, which I humbly crave)

[1] **papists:** those who believe in papal supremacy.   [2] **meanest:** humblest.

Christopher Muriell, *An Answer unto the Catholics' Supplication Presented unto the King's Majesty for a Toleration of Popish Religion in England* (London, 1603), A3r–B1v, B2v–B3v, B4v–B4r.

to answer the chief and most material points of the said "Supplication" because it tendeth to the grievous slander of our late deceased sovereign Queen Elizabeth, and also of the noble and worshipful personages of this your Grace's realm of England; and the rather because I hear that some favorites of the Roman religion do so highly extol and advance the learned and eloquent penning of the same, and the imaginary validity and force thereof, that they vaunt that it cannot be contradicted, yet doubt I not but that the plain verity of this short answer will be of sufficient force to daunt their expectations, and to bewray[3] their untruths, to their deserved discredit. The said "Supplication" consisteth of seven several parts, as by perusal thereof may appear.

1. The first part is their *exordium*,[4] wherein they pretend faith and dutiful obedience and loyalty unto your Majesty, the which protestation I pray God they may affect in verity, in as effectual and ample manner as they have in flourishing and glosing show[5] of words professed the same. But I commit that to God who searcheth in the hearts and reins,[6] time tries all things: *nil fictum diuturnam esse potest.*[7]

2. In the second part they do complain that they were overwhelmed with grievous persecutions by the severity of our late deceased queen.[8] We do not a little marvel that they blushed not to inform your Grace with so manifest untruths, if they supposed (as they in words pretend) that God hath blessed you with a wise and understanding heart, rightly to discern between truth and falsehood; for I dare boldly affirm that they cannot prove that any one received sentence of death only for professing the Romish religion, except treason were thereunto also annexed. And if it may please your most gracious Majesty to weigh in equal balance the persecutions (to use their own words) they suffered either by imprisonment or fining by the purse (wherewith very few in comparison were touched) your Highness shall understand that their own willful obstinacy, and not the Queen Majesty's severity urged the same; for whensoever it pleased them to resort to their parish churches unto divine prayers, they had present releasement[9] both of their imprisonment and also of their fines and fees. But seeing that their unjust exclamations enforce me to call to fresh remembrance the most savage and brutish dealings of the papists in Queen Mary's days, how they then domineered, your Highness cannot be ignorant [of], how unmerciful they did torment unto death the faithful servants and saints of God for professing the glori-

---

[3] bewray: expose. [4] *exordium:* the opening part of a speech or treatise. [5] glosing show: to give a fair appearance to; to veil in specious language (*OED*). [6] reins: kidneys (the seat of feelings or affections). [7] *nil . . . potest:* nothing that is false can be long lasting. [8] queen: Elizabeth I (reigned from 1558 to 1603). [9] releasement: release.

ous gospel of our redeemer Christ Jesus. Some they tormented with most sharp and long imprisonments, some they whipped with rods, some they secretly murdered in prison, but the greatest and general number were sacrificed in the fire, in which kind of torment they spared none, no not any degrees of persons, not so much as women great with child, but tormented them to death, even when the children did fall out of the mothers' wombs into the fire, in the view of the papists, who, being past shame and grace, nothing regarded it. Yea, such was their raging madness that they digged up the dead bones of those two godly and learned fathers, Martin Bucer and Paulus Phagius,[10] and burned them in Cambridge. . . . But to return to our late deceased queen, whether as the papists do unjustly charge her that she was a grievous persecutor of them, their assertion consisteth of contrarities,[11] for after the death of her brother King Edward[12] they undelayedly[13] persecuted her Grace. In the days of Queen Mary,[14] they tossed her from prison to prison, threatening her with continual death, so that she daily expected the axe to sever her sacred head from her princely shoulders. And once a precept was given for the executing thereof to the Lieutenant of the Tower by the treacherous dealing of one of the Pope's minions (then bearing great sway in England), in so much that if the Lieutenant of the Tower had not himself presently posted unto the court unto the queen her sister to understand certainly her pleasure therein, she had died before the queen had been acquainted therewith. . . .

[The section continues with a description of Catholic attempts to overthrow Elizabeth I, and concludes by stating that God has protected the queen from her Catholic assailants.]

3. In the third part, this generation of vipers relate unto the world their own wicked and treacherous endeavors to induce some, to some now living, to aspire unto the royal dignity of this kingdom. O cursed parasites and false-hearted papists, cannot you be solicitors of mischief but you must needs brag thereof? It argues that discord and rebellion are the chiefest virtues (if I may so say) of your new and false Catholic Romish religion. But most gracious King, let us praise and glorify God who hath so directed your

---

[10] **Bucer . . . Phagius:** Martin Bucer (1491–1551), an influential and reform-oriented theologian of German birth, and contributor to the English *Book of Common Prayer;* his grave was restored on orders of Elizabeth I in 1560. Paulus Phagius (1504–1549), German theologian and professor of Hebrew at Cambridge University.   [11] **contrarities:** contradictions.   [12] **King Edward:** Edward VI (1537–1553), son of Henry VIII, reigned from 1547 until 1553, and instituted several Protestant reforms in the church.   [13] **undelayedly:** without delay.   [14] **Queen Mary:** Mary I reigned from 1553 until 1558, and, having been raised in the Catholic faith, changed England's official religion back to Catholicism.

godly proceedings by his holy spirit, and hath also given you wisdom and fortitude to rely upon his divine providence, who worketh all things for the best, to them that serve and love him. And that it hath now pleased God to crown your royal head with the crowns of these kingdoms of England, France, and Ireland, it cannot be anywise[15] imputed unto the papists, for they were (like traitors) wholly bent another way, until they perceived that their designs were in vain, and their hopes frustrated. . . . The Lord bless and preserve you from the practices and conspiracies of the wicked Romanists (for surely they hate you in their hearts because you profess the gospel of Christ as your predecessor Queen Elizabeth did) who if (notwithstanding their flourishing show of words) their wicked and desired expectations had been effected, when the general invasion of this land was intended (your Majesty knoweth by whom) never had your Grace enjoyed the scepter of these kingdoms of England and Ireland, yea hardly (if they could have effected the contrary) should you have retained the kingdom of Scotland, which then (and now also God be thanked) you possess quietly.[16] . . .

5. In the fifth part they make their humble suit unto your Grace that they may obtain freedom to use the Romish religion freely without molestation, though not openly, yet secretly, alleging two reasons: the first is, that because they be restrained of that liberty, your kingdom is abhorred of[17] all kingdoms that profess the Romish religion. The second reason is that it would be a joyful thing to all the said kingdoms to grant them[18] their said suites. And to the end to induce your Majesty to grant their requests, they allege two arguments. The first is that the now French king yielding to the papists to secure the use of the Romish religion, they honored him with these venerable titles, *pater patriae, et pacis restitutor.*[19] If it be true that he now deserveth these honorable titles, why then since that time hath not that honorable king been freed from the dangerous conspiracy of the papists, who have diverse times since sought to murder him? If it please your renowned Majesty to peruse the treacheries of the papists, you shall find that they have greater murdering hearts than cursed Cain, who murdered his own brother. For to omit the many and continual treasons and conspiracies of the papists against our deceased queen, did not a graceless monk poison King John,[20] did not a cursed friar of France murder with a poisoned pen knife the last deceased French king?[21] Did not the bishops, monks, fri-

---

[15] anywise: in any way.   [16] quietly: in peace.   [17] of: by.   [18] them: i.e., the English Catholics.
[19] *pater patriae, et pacis restitutor:* father of the country and restorer of the peace.   [20] King John: King John of England (1166–1216), who reigned from 1199 until 1216, when he was poisoned by a monk at Swinstead Abbey.   [21] friar . . . king: on August 1, 1589, Henri III (1551–1589) was mortally wounded by a fanatical monk named Jacques Clément, who plunged a knife in his stomach. Henri died the next day.

ars, and Jesuits[22] of Spain cause the king's eldest son of Spain to be murdered, in letting him blood? Did not the papists of France urge the King of France to commit a tragical butcherly massacre at Paris,[23] in poisoning the Queen of Navarre,[24] and in a brutish butcherly order to murder the most part of the peerless nobility in France, their wives and children, with a great number of the common people in diverse parts of the realm . . . ?

The second argument is drawn from the grave and wise council of Solomon's councilors unto Rehoboam[25] (*si loqueris eos bona verba*, etc.[26]). This text is as rightly alleged as the devil alleged the scripture unto our savior Jesus Christ when he tempted him, for their was no request made unto Rehoboam as concerning religion but only for a mitigation of grievous exactions. And the counsel of Solomon's councilors in that behalf was both wise, right, and good. . . .

[22] Jesuits: members of the Society of Jesus, a Catholic order founded by Ignatius Loyola in 1534; often used pejoratively to mean a crafty schemer. [23] massacre at Paris: the Bartholomew Day Massacre in 1572, during which thousands of French Huguenots (Protestants) were killed by the Catholics. [24] Navarre: the former kingdom of Navarre is today a region in northeast Spain and southwest France. [25] Rehoboam: the first king of Judah (2 Chronicles 9:31–12:16), son of King Solomon. [26] si . . . etc.: The entire Latin quotation from *The Catholics' Supplication* reads: "*Si loqueris ad eos verba lenia, erunt tibi servi cunctis diebus*" (If you were to speak soothing words to them, you will have servants for all days (or "forever").

From News from Rome, Venice, and Vienna *1595*

News from Rome, Venice, and Vienna is one of a number of news pamphlets that informed Londoners about the religious and political struggles on the European continent. Some of these pamphlets are primarily sensational in character in that they focus on the heroics and devastation of war, but others contain detailed information about the religious and political subtleties that drive the military conflicts. *News from Rome, Venice, and Vienna* contains both.

Men's unbelieving hearts hasten to late repentance, and the unwillingness of Christians either to assist other[s] gives way for Infidels to insult all over.

Christ's prophecy is now performed, the days ware[1] worse and worse, charity is grown cold: for if mercy had had any government among Christian

[1] ware: are spent, squandered.

News from Rome, Venice, and Vienna, Touching the Present Proceedings of the Turks Against the Christians in Austria, Hungary, and Helvetia [present-day Switzerland], *otherwise called Sevenbergh* (London, 1595), A3–B1v, B1v–B3v, B3r.

men, so many beauteous towns, goodly cities, glorious kingdoms had not (as they now are) either been utterly made waste, or suffered the woeful bondage of Turkish tyranny. The flourishing churches to which Christ's apostles writ,[2] and in which they and the first Fathers of the church labored, are now the receptacles of unhallowed multitudes, and only a small corner of the earth professeth Christ. One Christian suffering another to be as easily consumed[3] as an idle or envious townsman his neighbor helplessly to be robbed or burned: else[4] had not all Asia, some of Africa, and so much of Europe suffered so great and irrecoverable slavish bondage. How many goodly nations the unbelieving offspring of Ottoman[5] have subjected, sufficiently [our[6]] late experience expresseth, and the purpose of the common enemy to subject the rest, immediate proof explaineth.

Amurath,[7] now Emperor of Turkey, glorying in the usurped seat of the Greek Empire, not long since subjected to Mahomet,[8] the son of Amurath his predecessor, ambitiously by his tyrannous Bassaes[9] incited, hath attempted the affliction of Austria, the unconquered part of Hungary, Poland, Helvetia, and other kingdoms neighboring Greece, whose proceedings since the 25th of December last, till the middle of January, this small pamphlet handleth.

Raab is a town near [the] Danube in Hungary, which in the end of the last harvest, the Turks violently after long siege entered, sparing neither age nor sex, but making the infants' days equal with the aged elders, both young and old by their cruelty at once perished. The winning of which place hath not smally[10] weakened the other forts of Hungary in the Christian's power.[11] After they had tyrannously insulted over[12] Raab, they immediately bent their forces against Comar,[13] the people of which city, assisted by the hand of God, and resolved rather to die than subject themselves to the slavery of infidels, valiantly defended themselves, and violently compelled the huge multitude of the Turks to raise their siege and retire to Raab, which they had lately taken. From sundry parts of Christendom since the 25th of December

---

[2] writ: wrote.   [3] consumed: to be burned up, reduced to ashes.   [4] else: otherwise.   [5] Ottoman: the Ottoman Empire (c. 1300–1918) of the Turks which, at one time, comprised much of southeast Europe, northeast Africa, and southwest Asia.   [6] our: the text is unreadable here. [7] Amurath: Sultan Murad III, who ruled the Ottoman Empire from 1574 to 1595. His reign marked the beginning of the decay of the empire.   [8] Mahomet: Sultan Muhammed III, who reigned from 1595 to 1603.   [9] Bassaes: probably a plural form of Bassa, an obsolete form of Bashaw (Pasha), meaning "head," "leader."   [10] smally: a little.   [11] in the Christian power: under control of Christian forces.   [12] insulted over: "insult" generally means "attack" or "assault" in a military context such as this, but in combination with "over" it may also mean "leap," thus suggesting that the Turkish forces leapt over Raab and attacked Comar. [13] Comar: a city on the river Danube.

these certain and unreprovable[14] intelligences have been sent: *videlicet*,[15] it is certified from Rome the last of January.

The emperor[16] majesty's legates had audience before the Pope, who desired a subsidy should be levied on the clergy, for the cutting off of an arm of the river of Danube that falls in by Comar, thereby not only to defend the said town and the parts thereabouts but also to hinder the Turks from having intercourse[17] to Ooven; and besides it would be a means to spare many soldiers that must be employed in these parts. To this the pope condescended, with promise to aid the emperor with all he might. Justiniano[18] is appointed the collector.[19]

The same time also it was certified that the great matter of Malta was reconciled, being authorized from the pope to be accountable to no state.

It is also concluded that the Prince of Sevenbergh, otherwise called Helvetia, upon whose burden the first war between the Turks and Christians must need lie, shall have 20,000 crowns monthly to maintain the war, and if (which God forbid) he be expulsed [from] Helvetia, he shall have some dominion allotted him in the empire and 200,000 crowns yearly.

Moreover at Rome, the same day arrived this news that Archbishop of Toledo in Spain, being ninety-four years of age, deceased, and left behind him a million of ready money, half a million in debts, and five hundred thousand crowns in plate,[20] robes, and costly apparel and other jewels; making five executors, of which the King of Spain is principal, who hath obtained that his money should be employed to the church's use, seeing the said archbishop hath bequeathed nothing to his kindred, whom belike he provided for in his lifetime.

Alberto the cardinal, succeeding in the bishopric and possessing these goods, hath granted half of them to be employed against the Turk.

FROM VIENNA THE 11TH OF JANUARY

At five of the clock that day in the morning came these ill news: that eight hundred Turks, some on foot but most part horse, came from Raab to Saint Georgen, and that the fifth date of this said month the Turks has taken Prûg near Leyten, and burned the cities and country of the Lord Herryth, making excursions within eight miles of Vienna, murdering the people, or

---

[14] **unreprovable:** that which cannot be rejected or proved invalid. [15] *videlicet:* namely.
[16] **emperor:** Emperor Ferdinand II. [17] **intercourse:** entrance. [18] **Justiniano:** We have been unable to identify this Justiniano. [19] **collector:** i.e., of the subsidy levied on the clergy by the pope. [20] **plate:** precious metal, usually silver. The term is derived from the Spanish coin *real de plata.*

making them slaves, robbing, spoiling, and burning the whole country, and threatening within few days to gather head against Vienna.

Likewise, the said 11th of January a governor of horsemen (being in a hold[21] hard by[22]) required to have aid, and the magistrates of Vienna have taken order that every citizen (according to his ability) should keep a proportion of horse and footmen till other preparation may be made.

The Grave[23] Hardigh being taken prisoner by the Turks fought to break prison, his brother having provided a ladder of ropes for his escape, and forty horses for his rescue. But it was discovered, and they all slain or taken.

Three sudden fires have been lately in Vienna, yet by God's great mercy but one house at a time burned; nevertheless the fearful multitude construe it to be an ominous presage of sad misfortune.

FROM PRAGUE THE 10TH OF JANUARY

This day the emperor's ambassadors returned to Prague from the King of Poland with this answer: that the Polonians[24] would willingly assist the emperor upon condition the emperor would do as much for him if the Turks should move war upon Polonia, of which to be resolved he requireth the princes electors[25] to send their ambassadors to his parliament holden[26] in Poland.

Maximillian Archduke of Austria intends to be general against the Turks. Charles of Mansfield will come with 3,000 horsemen, one thousand of them being hard,[27] and two regiments of foot of 6,000 are promised out of the lower Germany to be sent into Hungary with all speed.

This tenth of January a legate came to the emperor at Prague, with four demands from Charles the Duke: first for necessaries concerning his marriage, and relief for three years till the wars were somewhat quieted in Hungary. Secondly, that he be taken as a sessor[28] or prince in the empire, incorporated in the kingdom of Hungary, conditioning that if he died without issue male, his lands being Moldau, Walachia,[29] and Bulgaria, shall come to the succeeding kings of Hungary. Thirdly, that the emperor would send him four thousand horsemen at his proper charge. Fourthly, that the emperor should not enter into peace with the Turk without his knowledge. But what the emperor resolves to answer is not yet known.

---

[21] hold: a fortified place of defense. [22] hard by: nearby. [23] Grave: Count. [24] Polonians: Poles. [25] princes electors: a number of European princes who among them elected the emperor of the Holy Roman Empire. [26] holden: held. [27] hard: armored. [28] sessor: assessor (one who sits beside, and hence is an equal in rank). [29] Moldau: a region north of Vienna and east of the River Moldau; Walachia: region in eastern Europe, south of the Transylvanian Alps (combined with Moldavia in 1861 to become Romania; now a separate republic).

From Vienna the 6th of January

The last night in the evening Syfrid van Colneyt sent his servant to Vienna, certifying the state that the Turks and Tartars in great numbers were come over the passage at Altenbergh[30] and fired[31] a town called Saint Peters, and remained that night at Saint Johns. But the day before they were at St. Nicholas, Sturne, Cabastain, Somerain, Zuidenbergh, and other neighboring places between Altenbergh and Prague, and he feared they had taken some of those places, spoiled the people, and hazarded Altenbergh by reason there was but two hundred men at arms therein, the enemy being twenty thousand strong, and very well furnished with all munition.[32]

Presently, the same day, came another messenger, certifying that the enemy is come to Prague and Meneshoffen, firing many towns, killing multitudes of people, and taking divers prisoners so that Altenbergh is in great danger to be taken away, as Raab.

More from Vienna the 8th of January

The second of this month came the ambassadors from Sevenbergh, the chief man's name being Bapteri Istuan, accompanied with them of Moldau, and were lodged at the Lord of Westenahers. Next day they had audience before Maximillian, the emperor's brother.

About four o'clock in the afternoon they came to John de Medices, and the fourth day journeyed to Prague, to the emperor.

Two days after came tidings that fifteen thousand Turks were come to Raab with intention to take Altenbergh, which they may easily do by reason the rivers are so extremely frozen and the help so small.

Presently after came worse news that four and twenty thousand Turks were entered Austria, wherefore that evening every thirtieth man was chosen in that city beside the quarter of Vienna Wald,[33] who were mustered the seventh of this month at Brûg under Leyther.

By the last parliament, all things stand as before but the enemy grows very strong; our soldiers for want of pay being unwilling to serve; certain of the General of Seenebergh's soldiers mutinying for want of pay are gone upward into the empire and will make us have a very ill name. The money which they received, they left word, should pay for their horses.

One of my lord the duke's servants that was sent to the Lord Haunce Wererne, general for the Margrave[34] of Bourgan toward Nysadell, brought

---

[30] **Altenbergh:** probably Altenburg, a town north of Vienna.   [31] **fired:** burned.   [32] **munition:** ammunition.   [33] **Wald:** forest.   [34] **Margrave:** hereditary title of certain princes of the Holy Roman Empire (originally a German title given to military governors of border provinces).

tidings that the Turks and Tartars did great harm thereabout, none resisting them, the people only determining of flight.

FROM CASSAU, DECEMBER THE 28TH

The Turks and Tartars gather daily in great multitudes about Inla, led by the Bassa[35] of Tamusweer and the Bassa of Selnick, desirous to do some service (while the Teysca and other waters are frozen) against Tartasail of Teyny. Against whom the Christians on our side make head, looking for certain knowledge which way they intend to take, and being assured of their march, we will with them of Sevenbergh, meet them, committing ourselves to God in whose quarrel we willingly lay down our lives, hoping he will defend his distressed and afflicted flock.

[35] **Bassa:** obsolete form of Bashaw or Pasha, meaning "head" (*bash*) or "leader."

→ GÁBOR BETHLEN

Letter to the King of Bohemia   *August 28, 1620*

The letters collected in *The Present State of Affairs Betwixt the Emperor and King of Bohemia, and their Confederates* (1620) would have been of great interest to Londoners not only because they contained a wealth of information about the religious wars that raged on the European continent but also because the King of Bohemia mentioned in the title was none other than Frederick V (1596–1632), the Elector Palatine, who had married Elizabeth Stuart, daughter of James I, in 1613. The coronation (and brief rule) of Frederick as King of Bohemia cast him as the defender of the Protestant faith and main opponent of Ferdinand II, the Holy Roman Emperor, at the beginning of the Thirty Years' War. Although King James I had resisted repeated efforts by European Protestants to draw him into the conflict, it is clear that the English sympathized deeply with their fellow Protestants and hungered for news about their fate.

The anonymous letters written from the Vienna area are possibly written by a member (or members) of the entourage of Prince Christian von Anhalt-Bernburg (1568–1630), a Protestant prince referred to only as "our general the Prince of Anhalt" in the letter written from Prague and dated September 1, 1620 (*Present State of Affairs* 8). What distinguishes these letters chronicling the fighting and politicking in 1620 from *News from Rome, Venice, and Vienna* (1595)

The Present State of the Affairs Betwixt the Emperor and King of Bohemia, and Their Confederates, trans. from French and Dutch originals (London, 1620), 1–2.

(see p. 347 in this volume) is that the latter treatise is largely silent about faction-alism and religious divisions within the Christian community and instead pres-ents the conflict as Christianity vs. Islam, or Christian vs. Turk, while the letters of 1620 focus almost exclusively on the bitter confrontation between papists and Protestants. As a group, the letters collected in *The Present State of Affairs* are remarkably detailed and sophisticated in their reporting on the clash between Ferdinand II and his Protestant opponents. They convey the fear among the Protestant armies in 1620 when, despite military success that had led them to the gates of Vienna, it became clear that Ferdinand had forged an alliance with the king of Spain and the mighty Duke Maximilian of Bavaria, which turned the military tide in favor of the Catholics and eventually led to the loss of Bohemia and the banishment of King Frederick and Queen Elizabeth (the "Winter Queen") to The Hague.

Gábor Bethlen (1580–1629), the author of the first letter included here, was a Calvinist nobleman and prince of Transylvania (a part of present day Romania) who invaded Hungary in 1619 and was elected its titular king by Protestant nobles in 1620. In late 1619, Bethlen combined his forces with those of Moravia and Bohemia (to whose leader, the Elector Palatine Frederick, the first letter below is addressed), and marched on Vienna, where the Holy Roman Emperor, Ferdinand II, was ensconced. The first letter tells English readers of the strong bond between two powerful Protestant princes and of their commitment to the "true religion." This letter as well as the second letter, which speaks of Bethlen's coronation as king of Hungary, were available in print to English readers and may have been on the mind of Thomas Middleton (or another playwright) involved in a possible revision of *Measure for Measure* circa 1619–20. Gábor Bethlen could well be the king of Hungary referred to by Lucio in his exchange with the two Gentlemen (*Measure for Measure* 1.2.2). It would certainly make sense that as Viennese Catholics, Lucio and the two Gentlemen would not desire peace on Bethlen's terms. In England, however, peace on Bethlen's terms would of course have been viewed as a positive development.

To the most excellent and illustrious Prince and Lord Frederick,[1] by the grace of God, King of Bohemia . . .

Great King: the hopes and desires of your Majesty's friends and our confed-erates have met at last with peace and contentment, whilst all the faithful and well affected people, states, and nobility, joining hearts and voices, have now in the end with one consent delivered up the government of this king-dom into our hands, not doubting of our care and endeavor to protect and

---

[1] **Frederick:** the Protestant Elector Palatine who married the daughter of James I and was crowned King of Bohemia in 1619.

defend the same; a work whom none but men deprived of reason will acknowledge unto other than the immediate power of God; whither for our own good or prejudice, he that disputeth it boldly inquires after the unsearchable councils of God. But it is enough that no times from the foundation of the world have given examples or testimony of a more hearty and unanimous consent in the defense of true religion, the love of God and the maintaining of Christian liberty, than are these that hath thus brought forth two such kings. Wherefore, since we are thus designed and called forth, let us with care and wisdom boldly enter into the defense of the common cause, and in the name thereof we salute your Majesty. Nothing, no not our own blood binding us to more love and service than we profess to your Majesty, desiring but so much honor as to have time and place to agree of a meeting where sincerely and as brothers we may confer of the affairs of religion and the public weal[2] of our countries, whereof shortly and with speed I shall write more at large to your Majesty.

Your brother gossip[3] and confederate,

Gabriel [Gábor Bethlen]

[2] weal: well-being.   [3] gossip: a familiar acquaintance, a friend.

✦ Letter from Vienna   *September 5, 1620*

This letter announces the coronation of Gábor Bethlen as King of Hungary.

As his imperial majesty [Emperor Ferdinand II] heard the propositions and demands of the estates of Hungary, he was mightily enraged, and would not grant them any requests, which caused them proceed suddenly to the coronation of [Gábor] Bethlen, who was elected the 25th of August, and the 9th of this month to be crowned,[1] which sudden and unlooked for change hath not a little stirred his majesty, who presently hath sent word to Spain, [the] Pope, Bavaria, and Saxony, so that Dampier his going for Hungary goes slowly forwards, the Lord Breuner, Governor of Raab, is made general

---

[1] 25th . . . crowned: on this date, the Hungarians deposed the House of Habsburg and elected Bethlen their king.

The Present State of the Affairs Betwixt the Emperor and King of Bohemia, trans. from French and Dutch originals (London, 1620), 11–12.

for his imperial Majesty in Hungary, and Esterhasie[2] and Palfie[3] with other Hungarians to the number of 10,000, who yet holds for the emperor. These will go to Hungary if they can; there is here great terror and fear for Bethlen [and] his great army, who with 20,000 horsemen is fallen in Styria[4] and Bavaria. All passages are beset in the best fashion that may be.

Bethlen with his wife is arrived at Pressburgh[5] in most great pomp and triumph, who after his coronation goes presently to meet with the Bohemian, who hath also a mighty army, and not likely to go out of Austria this year. They have all necessaries plenty, where to the contrary our men dies, and in three months hath not received any pay — God help us.

[2] Esterhasie: Miklós Esterházy (1582–1645), leading Hungarian politician who supported military and governmental reform but who nonetheless favored Habsburg rule over Hungary.
[3] Palfie: Count Pál Pálffy, a Hungarian nobleman and supporter of the Habsburg emperor.
[4] Styria: province in southeast Austria.   [5] Pressburgh: Bratislava, situated on the easternmost border of Slovakia with Austria.

Bibliography

❊

Primary Sources

Abbot, George. *A Brief Description of the Whole World.* London, 1599.
Augustine. *The City of God.* Trans. Gerald Walsh, Demetrius Zema, and Grace Monahan. New York: Doubleday, 1958.
———. *De Sermone Domini in Monte Secundum Matthaeum.* Trans. John J. Jepson. *St. Augustine, The Lord's Sermon on the Mount.* Westminster: Newman P, 1948. Excerpted in *Narrative and Dramatic Sources of Shakespeare.* Vol. 2: *The Comedies, 1597–1603.* Ed. Geoffrey Bullough. New York: Columbia UP, 1958.
Becon, Thomas. *Works.* London, 1564.
The Bible and Holy Scriptures Conteyned in the Olde and Newe testament. Geneva, 1560.
The Book of Common Prayer, and Administration of the Sacraments and Other Rites and Ceremonies of the Church of England. 1559. London, 1603.
Buchanan, George. *De Jure Regni apud Scotos, or A Dialogue Concerning the Due Privilege of Government in the Kingdom of Scotland.* 1579. Trans. Philalethes. 1680.
Calendar of State Papers Venetian, XVII.
The Catholics' Supplication. London, 1603.
Certain Sermons or Homilies Appointed to Be Read in Churches in the Time of Queen Elizabeth I (1547–1571). Gainesville: Scholars', 1968.

Cinthio, G. B. Giraldi. "The Story of Epitia." In *Gli Hecatommithi.* 1565. *Narrative and Dramatic Sources of Shakespeare.* Vol. 2: *The Comedies, 1597–1603.* Ed. Geoffrey Bullough. New York: Columbia UP, 1958. 420–30.

A Collection of Seventy-Nine Black-Letter Ballads and Broadsides, Printed in the Reign of Queen Elizabeth, Between the Years 1559–1597. London, 1870.

Crooke, Helkiah. *Microcosmographia.* London, 1618.

Culpeper, Nicholas. *A Directory for Midwives, or a Guide for Women in Their Conception, Bearing and Suckling Their Children.* London, 1651.

Day, Richard. *A Book of Christian Prayers, Collected out of the Ancient Writers, and Best Learned in Our Time; Worthy to Be Read with an Earnest Mind of All Christians in These Dangerous and Troublesome Days, That God for Christ's Sake Will Yet Still Be Merciful unto Us.* London, 1608.

De Pisan, Christine. *The Book of the City of Ladies.* Trans. Brian Anslay. London, 1521.

Dekker, Thomas. *The Honest Whore* (part 1). London, 1604.

———. *Lantern and Candlelight. Or the Bellman's Second Night Walk in Which He Brings to Light a Book of More Strange Villanies, Than Ever Were Till This Year Discovered.* London, 1608.

———. *A Rod for Runaways.* London, 1625.

Dupuis, Francis. *La vie et la legende de madame saincte Claire.* 1563. Trans. Charlotte Balfour. London: Longman, 1910.

Fennor, William. *The Counter's Commonwealth, or a Voyage Made to an Infernal Island, Long Since Discovered by Many Captains, Seafaring-men, Gentlemen, Merchants, and Other Tradesmen.* London, 1617.

Goodman, Nicholas. *Hollands Leaguer.* 1602. Ed. Dean Stanton Barnard, Jr. The Hague: Mouton, 1970.

Gryffon, James. "The Song of a Constable." *Old English Ballads, 1553–1625.* Ed. Hyder E. Rollins. Cambridge: Cambridge UP, 1920.

Hair, Paul, ed. *Before the Bawdy Court: Selections from Church, Court, and Other Records Relating to the Correction of Moral Offences in England, Scotland, and New England, 1300–1800.* London: Elek, 1972.

Harman, Thomas. *A Caveat or Warning for Common Cursitors Vulgarly Called Vagabones, Set Forth by Thomas Harman, Esquire, for the Utility and Profit of His Natural Country.* 1567. London, 1573.

Harrison, William. *The Description of England.* 1577. Ed. Georges Edelen. Ithaca: Cornell UP, 1968.

Hayward, John. *Annals of the First Four Years of the Reign of Queen Elizabeth.* Ed. John Bruce. London: Camden, 1840.

James I. *Basilikon Doron.* 1599. *King James VI and I: Political Writings.* Ed. J. P. Sommerville. Cambridge: Cambridge UP, 1994. 1–61.

———. *Letters of King James VI & I.* Ed. G. P. V. Akrigg. Berkeley: U of California P, 1984.

———. "A Speech, As It Was Delivered in the Upper House of the Parliament . . ." 1603. *King James VI and I: Political Writings.* Ed. J. P. Sommerville. Cambridge: Cambridge UP, 1994. 132–46.

———. "A Speech in the Star Chamber, 20 June, 1616." *King James VI and I: Political Writings.* Ed. J. P. Sommerville. Cambridge: Cambridge UP, 1994.

———. "A Speech to the Lords and Commons." 1609. *King James VI and I: Political Writings.* Ed. J. P. Sommerville. Cambridge: Cambridge UP, 1994. 179–203.

———. *The True Law of Free Monarchies.* 1598. *King James VI and I: Political Writings.* Ed. J. P. Sommerville. Cambridge: Cambridge UP, 1994. 62–84.

Jonson, Ben. *The Works of Benjamin Jonson.* London, 1616.

L. S. *Prothylantinon, or, Some Considerations of a Notable Expedient to Root out the French Pox from the English Nation with Excellent Defensive Remedies to Preserve Mankind from the Infection of Pocky Women.* London, 1673.

Languet, Hubert. *Vindiciae contra tyrannos, a defence of liberty against tyrants, or, Of the lawful power of the prince over the people, and of the people over the prince being a treatise written in Latin and French by Junius Brutus [pseud.] and translated out of both into English. . . .* 1579. London, 1648.

Latimer, Hugh. *Fruitful Sermons Preached by the Right Reverend Father and Constant Martyr of Jesus Christ, M. Hugh Latimer.* London, 1578.

Lovelace, Richard. *Lucasta: Epodes, Odes, Sonnets, Songs, &c., to Which Is Added Aramantha, a Pastoral.* London, 1649.

Machiavelli, Niccolò. *The Prince.* 1532. Trans. Russell Price. Ed. Quentin Skinner and Russell Price. Cambridge: Cambridge UP, 1995.

———. *The Prince, Also the Life of Castruccio Castracani of Lucca and the Means Duke Valentine Us'd to Put to Death Vitellozzo Vitelli . . .* 1532. Trans. E. D. London, 1640.

Marlowe, Christopher. *The Jew of Malta.* c. 1590. *The Complete Plays of Christopher Marlowe.* Ed. Irving Ribner. New York: Odyssey P, 1969. 177–239.

Marston, John. *The Works of Mr. John Marston Being Tragedies and Comedies, Collected into One Volume.* London, 1633.

Martin, Richard. "A Speech Delivered to the King's Most Excellent Majesty, in the Name of the Sheriffs of London and Middlesex." 1603. *The Progresses, Processions, and Magnificent Festivities of King James the First, His Royal Consort, Family, and Court.* Vol. 1. Ed. John Nickols. London, 1828. 130–31.

Middleton, Thomas. *The Phoenix.* 1603–1604. Ed. Lawrence Danson and Ivo Kamps. *The Complete Works of Thomas Middleton.* Ed. Gary Taylor. Oxford: Oxford UP, forthcoming.

Moryson, Fynes. *An Itinerary Written by Fynes Moryson Gent. . . . Containing His Ten Years' Travel Through the Twelve Dominions of Germany, Bohmerland, Switzerland, the Netherlands, Denmark, Poland, Italy, Turkey, France, England, Scotland, and Ireland.* London, 1617.

Muriell, Christopher. *An Answer unto the Catholics' Supplication Presented unto the King's Majesty for a Toleration of Popish Religion in England.* London, 1603.

Mynshul, Geoffrey. *Essays and Characters of a Prison and Prisoners. Written by G. M. of Grayes-Inne, Gent.* London, 1618.

News from Rome, Venice, and Vienna, Touching the Present Proceedings of the Turks against the Christians in Austria, Hungary, and Helvetia Otherwise Called Sevenbergh. London, 1595.

The Night-Walker: or, Evening Rambles in Search after Lewd Women, with the Conferences Held with Them &c. Ed. G. Stevens Cox. St. Peter's Port: Toucan P, 1970.

The Nun's Rule or the Ancrene Riwle. New York: Cooper, 1966.

The Present State of Affairs Betwixt the Emperor and King of Bohemia. London, 1620.

Overbury, Thomas. "Characters." *Sir Thomas Overbury His Wife. With Additions of New Characters, and Many Other Witty Conceits Never Before Printed.* London, 1622.

Perkins, William. *Christian Economy, or, A Short Survey of the Right Manner of Erecting and Ordering a Family According to the Scriptures.* London, 1609.

The Policy of the Turkish Empire. London, 1597.

Raleigh, Walter. *The Prince, or Maxims of State Written by Sir Walter Raleigh, and Presented to Prince Henry.* London, 1650.

Riche, Barnaby. *The Adventures of Brusanus, Prince of Hungary, Pleasant for All to Read, and Profitable for Some to Follow.* London, 1592.

Shakespeare, William. *The Complete Works of William Shakespeare.* 5th. ed. Ed. David Bevington. Boston, MA: Addison-Wesley, 2004.

Smith, Henry. "A Preparative to Marriage." *The Sermons of Master Henry Smith Gathered into One Volume.* London, 1594.

Stow, John. *Survey of London.* London, 1603.

Stuart Royal Proclamations. Vol. 1: King James I, 1603–1625. Ed. James F. Larkin and Paul L. Hughes. Oxford: Clarendon, 1973.

Stubbes, John. *The Discovery of a Gaping Gulf Whereinto England Is Like to Be Swallowed by Another French Marriage, If the Lord Forbid Not the Banes, by Letting Her Majesty See the Sin and Punishment Thereof.* London, 1579.

Stubbes, Philip. *Anatomy of Abuses.* London, 1583.

Swetnam, Joseph. *The Arraignment of Lewd, Idle, Froward and Unconstant Women.* London, 1615.

Swinburne, Henry. *A Treatise of Spousals, or Matrimonial Contracts: Wherein All the Questions Relating to That Subject Are Ingeniously Debated and Resolved.* London, 1686.

T. E. *The Law's Resolutions of Women's Rights: Or, The Law's Provision for Women.* London, 1632.

Tyndale, William. *The Obedience of a Christian Man.* Antwerp, 1528.

Vives, Juan Luis. *A Very Fruitful and Pleasant Book Called Instruction of a Christian Woman, Made First in Latin, by the Right Famous Clerk M. Luis Vives, and Translated out of Latin into English, by Richard Hyrde.* London, 1592.

Webster, John. *The Duchess of Malfi.* c. 1612, published 1623. Ed. Elizabeth M. Brennan. New York; Norton, 1983.

West, Richard. *The Court of Conscience, or Dick Whippers Sessions with the Order of His Arraigning and Punishing of Many Notorious, Dissembling, Wicked, and Vicious Livers in This Age.* London, 1607.

Willymat, William. *A Loyal Subject's Looking-Glass.* London, 1604.

Secondary Sources

Adair, Richard. *Courtship, Illegitimacy and Marriage in Early Modern England.* New York: Manchester UP, 1996.

Andrews, John F., ed. *Shakespeare's World and Work.* Vol. 3. New York: Scribner, 2001.

Archer, Ian W. *The Pursuit of Stability: Social Relations in Elizabethan London.* Cambridge: Cambridge UP, 1991.

Barish, Jonas. *The Antitheatrical Prejudice.* 1981. Berkeley: U of California P, 1985.

Black, James. "The Unfolding of *Measure for Measure*." *Aspects of Shakespeare's "Problem Plays."* Ed. Kenneth Muir and Stanley Wells. Cambridge: Cambridge UP, 1982. 77–86.

Bradshaw, Graham. *Shakespeare's Scepticism.* Ithaca, NY: Cornell UP, 1987.

Brinkworth, E. R. C. *Shakespeare and the Bawdy Court of Stratford.* London: Phillimore, 1972.

Bucer, Martin. *De Regno Christi.* 1557. Trans. Wilhelm Pauck and Paul Larkin. In *Melanchthon and Bucer,* ed. Wilhelm Pauck. The Library of Christian Classics, vol. 19. Philadelphia: Westminster P, 1969. 174–394.

Bullough, Geoffrey, ed. *Narrative and Dramatic Sources of Shakespeare. Volume II: The Comedies, 1597–1603.* New York: Columbia UP, 1958.

Burford, E. J. *The Orrible Synne: A Look at London Lechery from Roman to Cromwellian Times.* London: Calder, 1973.

Chambers, E. K. *The Elizabethan Stage.* Oxford: Clarendon P, 1923.

Coleridge, Samuel T. *Coleridge's Writings on Shakespeare.* Ed. Terence Hawkes. New York: Capricorn, 1959.

Cressy, David, and Lori Anne Ferrell, eds. *Religion and Society in Early Modern England.* New York: Routledge, 1996.

Dekker, Thomas. *The Honest Whore* (part 1). London, 1604.

Dollimore, Jonathan. "Transgression and Surveillance in *Measure for Measure.*" *Political Shakespeare: New Essays in Cultural Materialism.* Ed. Jonathan Dollimore and Alan Sinfield. Ithaca: Cornell UP, 1985. 72–87.

Dowden, Edward. *Shakespeare: A Critical Study of His Mind and Art.* New York: Harper, 1881.

Dutton, Richard. *Mastering the Revels: The Regulation and Censorship of English Renaissance Drama.* London: Macmillan, 1991.

Eccles, Mark, ed. *Measure for Measure.* A New Variorum Edition of Shakespeare. New York: MLA, 1980.

Elton, G. R. *The Tudor Constitution.* 2nd ed. Cambridge: Cambridge UP, 1982.

Greenblatt, Stephen. *Shakespearean Negotiations: The Circulation of Social Energy in Renaissance England.* Berkeley: U of California P, 1988.

Haigh, Christopher. *Elizabeth I.* 2nd ed. New York: Longman, 1998.

Hawkins, Harriett. "'The Devil's Party': Virtues and Vices in *Measure for Measure.*" *Aspects of Shakespeare's "Problem Plays."* Ed. Kenneth Muir and Stanley Wells. Cambridge UP, 1982. 87–95.

Heinemann, Margot. *Puritanism and Theater: Thomas Middleton and Opposition Drama under the Early Suarts.* Cambridge: Cambridge UP, 1980.

Houston, S. J. *James I.* New York: Longman, 1995.

Hughes, Paul L., and James F. Larkin, eds. *Tudor Royal Proclamations. Vol. 3. The Later Tudors.* New Haven: Yale UP, 1969.

Ingram, Martin. *Church Courts, Sex and Marriage in England 1570–1640.* Cambridge: Cambridge UP, 1987.

Jowett, John. "The Audacity of *Measure for Measure* in 1621." *The Ben Jonson Journal.* 8 (2001): 229–47.

———. "Introduction" to *Measure for Measure. The Complete Works of Thomas Middleton.* Gen. eds. Gary Taylor, et. al. Oxford: Oxford UP, forthcoming.

Judges, A. V. *The Elizabethan Underworld.* London: Routledge, 1930.

Kamps, Ivo. "Ruling Fantasies and Fantasies of Rule: Middleton's *The Phoenix* and Shakespeare's *Measure for Measure.*" *Studies in Philology* 92.2 (1995): 248–73.

Kenyon, J. P. *The Stuart Constitution, 1603–1688.* 2nd ed. Cambridge: Cambridge UP, 1986.

Kernan, Alvin. *Shakespeare, The King's Playwright: Theater in the Stuart Court, 1603–1613.* New Haven: Yale UP, 1995.

Kirsch, Arthur. "The Integrity of *Measure for Measure.*" *Shakespeare's Christian Dimension: An Anthology of Commentary.* Ed. Roy Battenhouse. Bloomington, IN: Indiana UP, 1994. 181–87.

Knight, G. Wilson. *The Wheel of Fire: Interpretations of Shakespearean Tragedy with Three New Essays.* 1930. London: Methuen, 1949.

Lever, J. W., ed. *Measure for Measure.* By William Shakespeare. The Arden Edition. Cambridge: Harvard UP, 1966.

Levin, Richard. *New Readings vs. Old Plays: Recent Trends in the Reinterpretation of English Renaissance Drama.* Chicago: U of Chicago P, 1979.

Lockyer, Roger. *The Early Stuarts: A Political History of England, 1603–1643.* New York: Longman, 1989.

Marcus, Leah S. *Puzzling Shakespeare: Local Reading and Its Discontents.* Berkeley: U of California P, 1988.

McDonald, Russ. *The Bedford Companion to Shakespeare: An Introduction with Documents.* 2nd ed. Boston: Bedford, 2001.

McMullan, John L. *The Canting Crew: London's Criminal Underworld, 1550–1700.* New Brunswick: Rutgers UP, 1984.

Molnár, Miklós. *A Concise History of Hungary.* 1996. Cambridge: Cambridge UP, 2001.

Mullaney, Steven. *The Place of the Stage: License, Play, and Power in Renaissance England.* Chicago: U of Chicago P, 1988.

Nichols, John. *The Progresses, Processions, and Magnificent Festivities of James the First.* Vol. 1. London, 1828.

Patterson, Annabel. *Censorship and Interpretation: The Conditions of Writing and Reading in Early Modern England.* Madison: U of Wisconsin P, 1984.

Pendry. "The Prisoners' Petition." *A Collection of Seventy-Nine Black-Letter Ballads and Broadsides, Printed in the Reign of Queen Elizabeth, Between the Years 1559–1597.* London, 1870.

Powers, Alan W. *"Measure for Measure* and Law Reform in 1604." *The Upstart Crow* 15 (1995): 35–47.

Ridley, Jasper. *Henry VIII: The Politics of Tyranny.* New York: Fromm, 1986.

Salgado, Gamini. *The Elizabethan Underworld.* New York: St. Martin's, 1992.

Schoenbaum, Samuel. *William Shakespeare: A Compact Documentary Life.* New York: Oxford UP, 1978.

Sharpe, J. A. *Crime in Early Modern England.* New York: Longman, 1984.

Shuger, Deborah Kuller. *Political Theologies in Shakespeare's England: The Sacred and the State in* Measure for Measure. New York: Palgrave, 2001.

Skinner, Quentin, and Russell Price, eds. Nicolò Machiavelli, *The Prince.* Trans. Russell Price. Cambridge: Cambridge UP, 1995.

Smith, Alan G. R. *The Emergence of the Nation State: The Commonwealth of England, 1529–1660.* New York: Longman, 1984.

Sommerville, J. P. *Politics and Ideology in England, 1603–1640.* New York: Longman, 1986.

——, ed. *King James VI and I: Political Writings.* Cambridge: Cambridge UP, 1994.

Spielman, John P. *The City and the Crown: Vienna and the Imperial Court, 1600–1740.* West Lafayette, IN: Purdue UP, 1993.

Stephenson, Carl, and Frederick George Marcham, eds. *Sources of Constitutional History: A Selection of Documents from A.D. 600 to the Interregnum.* Vol. 1. New York: Harper and Row, 1972.

Stevenson, David. *The Achievement of Shakespeare's* Measure for Measure. Ithaca, NY: Cornell UP, 1966.

Stone, Lawrence. *The Family, Sex and Marriage in England, 1500–1800.* Abridged ed. New York: Harper, 1979.

Sugar, Peter F., Peter Hanák, and Tibor Frank, eds. *A History of Hungary.* Bloomington, IN: Indiana UP, 1990.

Taylor, Gary. "Power, Pathos, Character." *Harold Bloom's Shakespeare.* Ed. Christy Desmet and Robert Sawyer. New York: Palgrave, 2001. 43–63.

——. "Shakespeare's Mediterranean *Measure for Measure."* *Shakespeare and the Mediterranean: The Selected Proceedings of the International Shakespeare Association World Congress, Valencia, 2001.* Ed. Thomas Clayton, Susan Brock, and Vincent Forés. Newark: U of Delaware P, 2004. 243–69.

Taylor, Gary, and John Jowett. *Shakespeare Reshaped, 1606–1623.* Oxford: Oxford UP, 1993.

Tillyard, E. M. W. *Shakespeare's Problem Plays.* 1950. London: U of Toronto P, 1968.

Vickers, Brian. Introduction. *Shakespeare: The Critical Heritage. 1623–1692.* Ed. Vickers. London: Routledge, 1974.

——, ed. *Shakespeare: The Critical Heritage. 1623–1692.* Vol. 1. London: Routledge, 1974.

Virgil. *The Aeneid of Virgil.* Trans. Allen Mandelbaum. New York: Bantam, 1981.
Vitkus, Daniel J. Introduction. *Three Turk Plays from Early Modern England.* Ed.
    Vitkus. New York: Columbia UP, 2000. 1–52.
———. "Trafficking with the Turk: English Travelers in the Ottoman Empire
    during the Early Seventeenth Century." *Travel Knowledge: European "Dis-
    coveries" in the Early Modern Period.* Ed. Ivo Kamps and Jyotsna G. Singh.
    New York: Palgrave, 2001. 35–52.

Acknowledgments

INTRODUCTION

Figure 1. Scene of an Execution, from Raphael Holinshed, *The First Volume of the Chronicles of England, The History of Scotland* (1577), STC 13568, scene of an execution from page 598. By permission of the Folger Shakespeare Library.

Figure 2. Panorama/View of London, by C. L. Visscher, (1616). By permission of the Folger Shakespeare Library.

Figure 3. Illustration of Vienna, from Georg Braun, *Civitates Orbis Terrarum*. By permission of the Folger Shakespeare Library.

Measure for Measure from *The Complete Works of Shakespeare*, 5e. Ed. David Bevington. Copyright © 2004 by Addison-Wesley Educational Publishers, Inc. Reprinted by permission of Pearson Education, Inc.

CHAPTER 1

Figure 4. Portrait of King James attributed to John de Critz the elder. By permission of the Trustees of Dulwich Picture Gallery.

Figure 5. Frontispiece, James I, *Workes* (1616). By permission of the Folger Shakespeare Library.

Figure 6. The Wicked Man Is Moved to Mercy by No Entreaty, from Claude Paradin, *The Heroicall Devises of M. Claudius Paradin, Whereunto Are Added the Lord Gabriel Symeons and Others* (1562). By permission of the Folger Shakespeare Library.

Figure 7. Description of Justice, from Stephen Bateman, *A Christall Glasse of Christian Reformation* (1585), STC 1585. By permission of the Folger Shakespeare Library.

Figure 8. A Man Praying as he Confronts his Death, from Isaac Ambrose, *Prima and Ultima: First and Last Things or Regeneration* (1640). By permission of the Folger Shakespeare Library.

Figure 9. A Man in the Stocks for Seditious Libel, from *Roxburgh Ballads*, Vol. 5 Parts 1–2, (1883), page 174. By permission of the Folger Shakespeare Library.

Figure 10. "Maledicentia" (Slander), from Andrea Alciati, *Emblematum Libellus*. By permission of the Folger Shakespeare Library.

CHAPTER 2

Figure 11. Frontispiece, Samuel Rowlands, *'Tis Merrie When Gossips Meet* (London 1602). By permission of the Folger Shakespeare Library.

Figure 12. Constable Elbow Accuses Pompey before Angelo, by Henry Singleton, *Measure for Measure*, Act 2, Scene 1 (1798). By permission of the Folger Library.

Figure 13. Dice Game, from "The Female Ramblers," from *Roxburgh Ballads*, Vol. 8, parts 1–2 (1895). By permission of the Folger Shakespeare Library.

Figure 14. Isabella Kneels to the Duke, by Henry Singleton, *Measure for Measure*, Act 5, Scene 1 (1798). By permission of the Folger Library.

Before the Bawdy Court: Selections from Church Court and other Records Relating to the Correction of Moral Offenses in England, Scotland, and New England, 1300–1800, ed. Paul Hair, (London: Elek, 1972). p. 53, 55–56, 93–94, 105–106, 111, 119, 120. Reprinted by permission of Elek Books.

Figure 15. Great Grief Assails the Lecherous Mind, from Stephen Bateman, *A Christall Glasse of Christian Reformation* (1585), STC 1585. By permission of the Folger Shakespeare Library.

St. Augustine, *The Lord's Sermon on the Mount* (394), trans. John J. Jepsom (Westminster: The Newman Press, 1948), p. 59–61. Reprinted by permission of The Paulist Press.

Cinthio, G. B. Giraldi, "The Story of Epitia" from *Gli Hecatommithi*, in *Narrative and Dramatic Sources of Shakespeare*, ed. Geoffrey Bullough, Vol. 2, *The Comedies*, 1597–1603, (New York: Columbia UP, 1958), p. 420–430. Reprinted by permission of Columbia University Press.

Figure 16. St. Clare on her Deathbed, from Andraes Collaert, *Icones Sanctae Clarae* (Antwerp 1630). Reprinted by permission of the Universiteitsbibliotheek of the University of Maastricht, Netherlands.

CHAPTER 3

Figure 17. Title page illustration of Holland House, from Nicholas Goodman, *Hollands Leaguer* (1632), STC 12027. By permission of the Folger Shakespeare Library.

Figure 18. Gallants Choosing Whores at a Brothel, from Crispijn de Passe, *Le Miroir des Plus Belles Dames* (1641). By permission of the Folger Shakespeare Library.

Figure 19. A Whore Is a Deepe Grave: and an Harlot, from Stephen Bateman, *A Christall Glasse of Christian Reformation* (1585), STC 1585. Reprinted by permission of the Folger Shakespeare Library.

Figure 20. Frontispiece from Thomas Dekker, *A Rod for Run-aways* (London 1625). Reprinted by permission of the Huntington Library.

James I, *Stuart Royal Proclamations of James I, 1603–1625*, ed. James F. Larkin and Paul L. Hughes (Oxford: Clarendon Press, 1973), p. 47–48. Reprinted by permission of Clarendon Press.

Figure 21. A Man Being Led to the Gallows, from Thomas Harmon, *A Caveat for Common Cursitors* (1567), STC 12787. By permission of the Folger Shakespeare Library.

Figure 22. Barnardine, by Robert Smirke, *Measure for Measure*, Act 4, Scene 3 (1800). By permission of the Folger Shakespeare Library.

Figure 23. Taverngoers from "The Bachelors' Banquet," from *Roxburgh Ballads*, Vol. 2, parts 2–3 (1874). By permission of the Folger Shakespeare Library.

Figure 24. "La belle zavonnare cour," from Crispijn de Passe, *Le Mirroir des Plus Belles Dames* (Paris, 1641). By permission of the Folger Shakespeare Library.

Figure 25. Frontispiece, The Watch Outside a Prison, from Robert Speed, *The Counter Scuffle* (1628), page 628. By permission of the Folger Shakespeare Library.

Figure 26. Description of Charitie, from Stephen Bateman, *A Christall Glasse of Christian Reformation* (1585), STC 1585. By permission of the Folger Shakespeare Library.

Figure 27. Woodcut of a Constable, from Geoffrey Mynshul, *Essayes and Characters of a Prison* (1618), STC 18319. By permission of the Folger Shakespeare Library.

CHAPTER 4

Figure 28. A True and Exact Description of the City of Vienna (1683). Reprinted by permission of the Huntington Library.

Figure 29. St. Clare Routs the Saracens with Her Prayers, from Andraes Collaert, *Icones Sanctae Clarae* (Antwerp 1630). Reprinted by permission of the Universiteitsbibliotheek of the University of Maastricht, Netherlands.

Index

><